T0302270

Crowdfunding and Entrepreneurship

This accessible text provides an insight into the growing global trend of crowdfunding as a source of entrepreneurial finance.

Grounded in academic literature, this book looks at the micro and macro issues within crowdfunding, from the entrepreneur's access to finance at the business level, to the role of government in regulating the market. It helps the reader develop a sound understanding of crowdfunding as a source of finance, the crowdfunding process and potential options when faced with start-up funding issues.

A range of international case studies of successful and unsuccessful crowdfunding campaigns help readers to apply theory to real-life scenarios. Readers are also supported throughout the book with chapter objectives and summaries, key terms, discussion questions and further reading guidance. Instructor materials such as slides and test questions are available as digital supplements.

Crowdfunding and Entrepreneurship will be a valuable resource for students of new venture creation and entrepreneurial finance, as well as entrepreneurs exploring crowdfunding as an option for business development.

Ignatius Ekanem is Senior Lecturer in Business and Management at Middlesex University Business School, London. He is the author of *Writing a Business Plan: A Practical Guide*, also from Routledge.

Steve Ideh is a chartered accountant and certified management consultant with over 25 years' experience in finance. He is an adjunct faculty member at several business schools and a regular speaker at entrepreneurship events.

Crowdfunding and Entrepreneurship

Ignatius Ekanem and Steve Ideh

Routledge
Taylor & Francis Group

LONDON AND NEW YORK

Designed cover image: Getty

First published 2024
by Routledge
4 Park Square, Milton Park, Abingdon, Oxon OX14 4RN

and by Routledge
605 Third Avenue, New York, NY 10158

Routledge is an imprint of the Taylor & Francis Group, an informa business

British Library Cataloguing-in-Publication Data
A catalogue record for this book is available from the British Library

Library of Congress Cataloging-in-Publication Data
Names: Ekanem, Ignatius, author. | Ideh, Steve, author.
Title: Crowdfunding and entrepreneurship / Ignatius Ekanem
    and Steve Ideh.
Description: Abingdon, Oxon ; New York, NY : Routledge, 2024. | Includes
    bibliographical references and index.
Identifiers: LCCN 2023027487 (print) | LCCN 2023027488 (ebook) |
    ISBN 9781032046310 (hardback) | ISBN 9781032046280 (paperback) |
    ISBN 9781003193975 (ebook)
Subjects: LCSH: Crowd funding. | Entrepreneurship.
Classification: LCC HG4751 .E528 2024 (print) | LCC HG4751 (ebook) |
    DDC 658.15/224—dc23/eng/20230725
LC record available at https://lccn.loc.gov/2023027487
LC ebook record available at https://lccn.loc.gov/2023027488

ISBN: 978-1-032-04631-0 (hbk)
ISBN: 978-1-032-04628-0 (pbk)
ISBN: 978-1-003-19397-5 (ebk)

DOI: 10.4324/9781003193975

Typeset in Times New Roman
by Apex CoVantage, LLC

Access the Support Material: www.routledge.com/ 9781032046310

Contents

Preface

Entrepreneurship development forms the bedrock of business evolution of many nations without which there can be no real economic development. The most pervasive challenge facing entrepreneurship in any economy is the lack of funding and the difficulty in securing finance for start-ups and small businesses. The inability of an entrepreneur to provide collateral security for loans and the stiff competition for other available sources of funding necessitates the search for other veritable means of financing entrepreneurship.

This book is based on a collection of research materials carried out in different global economic contexts and settings. The ideas come from a variety of experiences and academic disciplines. The particular theme drawn from the book is the understanding of the features of a "good" crowdfunding campaign and the case studies of the positives and the negatives of a crowdfunding campaign. In this respect the book offers the reader an opportunity, through a combination of chapters, to acquire knowledge of crowdfunding, the crowdfunding process and the awareness of actions to take when faced with start-up funding issues.

The book considers the problems facing entrepreneurs in raising start-up funds and the prospect for other source(s) of financing. It considers crowdfunding as a veritable additional option to financing small businesses in any economy and makes recommendations based on findings.

Therefore, the aim of this book is to provide a clear understanding of the crowdfunding process by examining issues and challenges faced by entrepreneurs and would-be entrepreneurs. Presently, apart from a few unreliable internet documents with scanty information about crowdfunding, there are insufficient academic books based on empirical findings that are written specifically to guide business owners and would-be entrepreneurs on how to source crowdfunding. However, there are a few texts books on business and financial management which include just a chapter on crowdfunding written in a way that is unsuitable for non-financial managers. This book is written to fill this gap.

The structure of the book

Chapter 1, which is the introductory chapter, explores the definition of a small business, the characteristics of entrepreneurs, capital structure of a business and sources of entrepreneurial finance. The small business definition is based on the EU and US definitions. For the characteristics of entrepreneurs, the chapter examines, among others, high need for achievement, self-confidence, risk-taking propensity, need for independence, ambiguity tolerance, creativity and innovativeness. It then examines the factors which make small firms' capital structure different from that of large firms. This chapter also explores the traditional sources of financing available to small firms, including hybrid entrepreneurship; family, friends, and fans; debt; equity and, of course, crowdfunding which is a new category of financing that can serve as a source to launch and grow new ventures.

Chapter 2 provides a definition of crowdfunding. It discusses the various types of crowdfunding, including donations-based crowdfunding, equity-based crowdfunding; peer-to-peer (P2P) lending, product pre-sale crowdfunding, rewards-based crowdfunding. In this chapter, the characteristics required of a crowdfunding entrepreneur are discussed and also the requirements of crowdfunding platforms and best hints to increase the odds of funding such as dedicated project pages, analytics, project monitoring, and tutorials. The chapter also discusses how platform intermediaries or funding portals connect contributors with entrepreneurs.

Chapter 3 discusses the financial behaviour of entrepreneurs in relation to crowdfunding. In this chapter, the relationship between the pecking order hypothesis and crowdfunding is examined together with the use of pecking order theory to determine the financing options of entrepreneurs. The chapter features an in-depth discussion of the pecking order theory to show how entrepreneurs tend to choose the form of financing that enables them to retain control. This chapter explores how small business owners use different categories of financing in various development stages. The chapter also discusses how entrepreneurs could choose investors according to their immediate needs while increasing their chances of survival. In this chapter, the need to understand the different types of entrepreneurship including social entrepreneurs and mission led enterprises and their financial needs is also explored.

Chapter 4 provides an exploration of the resource-based theory in crowdfunding by exploring the role of crowdfunding in developing entrepreneurship and how this may be achieved. It does so by examining the link between resource-based theory and crowdfunding and how entrepreneurs leverage crowdfunding to get entrepreneurial efforts off the ground. This chapter explores the resource-based theory in great depth to demonstrate how resources which are available to a firm and which are valuable, rare, difficult to imitate and non-substitutable are able to position a firm for long-term success, superior performance and competitive advantage.

Chapter 5 addresses the reduction of the risk of information asymmetry through crowdfunding. The chapter starts with the discussion of the concept of information asymmetry and how it constitutes a major obstacle for small businesses seeking finance. The chapter then goes on to discuss how crowdfunding reduces the risk associated with information asymmetry which is often claimed to be one of the main reasons that financiers shy away from early stage financing. The chapter explains how reducing information asymmetry may result in lower transaction costs for obtaining debt, opportunity to finance multiple investment, economies of scale, and better firm performance. It also examines how the lack of transparency on business models and cash projections increases the risk for lenders and limits the number and amount of funds available to the entire small business pool within defined markets.

Chapter 6 examines the trends in the market of digital finance. This chapter examines business trends, small ventures and start-ups without collateral security for large investors which are successful in using crowdfunding for development. It discusses how financial services are rapidly digitizing, moving formerly confidential and exclusive programmes from in-person to online in an effort to create convenience and more touchpoints with consumers, thus enhancing financial inclusion. The chapter explores how this trend represents a massive change in financial services marketing. It examines the implications of these shifts for crowdfunding, especially during the Covid-19 pandemic.

Chapter 7 provides an assessment of the features of a good crowdfunding campaign including its positives and negatives. It discusses the right strategies that should be put in place, the composition of the pitch about the new idea and the creation of awareness. In discussing the composition of the pitch, the chapter stresses how it must be attractive to the audience to enable investment; how it needs to present achievable goals and include true facts and data which supports the product as well as emphasizing the desirable characteristics of the product. It also includes in the discussion of the pitch the vital part played by effective communication and keeping the audience well informed with the up-to-date progress and news to make it a success.

In Chapter 8, the major problems and threats encountered by entrepreneurs in sourcing crowdfunding are identified. The chapter begins by stressing that every source of entrepreneurial finance has its challenges and drawbacks and crowdfunding is no exception. It discusses, among other problems, the difficulties of getting on crowdfunding platforms as compared to the traditional ways of raising finance; the difficulties of building up interest before the project launch; the possibility of stealing the concept of a project on a crowdfunding site, and having to return finance pledged if the funding target is not reached. More importantly, the chapter discusses how to avoid the crowdfunding minefield such as the damaged reputation of a business if the project fails, stealing of business ideas on a crowdfunding site, and giving away too much of the business to investors.

Chapter 9 examines how entrepreneurs leverage social network including family and friends and the information they provide to access crowdfunding. However, this chapter also examines how mobilizing funders outside this close network positively contributes to the success of a crowdfunding success. It explores how to attract funding from more distant/potential resources (latent ties) in addition to existing networks (strong and weak ties), by examining usage of social media (Facebook and Twitter) and the crowdfunding platform.

Chapter 10 discusses the dynamic state of crowdfunding as a new market niche. It discusses the popularity of crowdfunding as an alternative source of finance for new ventures and its impact on start-ups despite its challenges. The chapter concludes by examining the prospects of crowdfunding bridging the entrepreneurial funding gap.

Chapter 11 examines the possible areas for government assistance and the current regulatory framework, as well as the development of blockchain technology and how it can solve the problems of regulatory compliance and security. It examines the efforts governments can make towards the development of crowd-funding since the primary challenge for every entrepreneur or would-be entre-preneur remains that of funding their entrepreneurial endeavours. This includes support, information, advice and training. The chapter also examines how the government can invest into local businesses, social enterprises, and charities through peer-to-peer (P2P) lending platforms.

The last chapter (Chapter 12) presents four case studies with three successful and one unsuccessful crowdfunding campaign. These case studies are intended to help the student to put theory into practice, and to learn the strategies adopted by these companies which made them successful or unsuccessful. The case studies are selected to ensure international diversity.

Ignatius Ekanem and Steve Ideh
March 2023

Acknowledgements

The authors and publishers would like to thank all the research authors whom we have properly referenced in this book. We would like to thank the publishing staff at Routledge. In particular, we would like thank Natalie Tomlinson, Editor – Economics, Finance, Accounting and Entrepreneurship Textbooks who was very supportive through the proposal which later became a project; and Andrew Harrison, Editor – Business Textbooks, who kept us on track throughout the production process.

Every effort has been made to trace and acknowledge ownership of copyright and to clear permission for material reproduced in this book. The publishers will be pleased to make the necessary arrangements at the earliest opportunity to clear permission with any copyright holders whom it has not been possible to contact. In this regard, we would like to thank Dr. Robyn Owen of Middlesex University for permission to reproduce the Craft Beer Micro Brewery Case: Wildcraft Brewery (Norfolk) as Case Study 1 in Chapter 12.

Finally, we would like to thank our respective families for their help, support and encouragement while this work was in progress. We claim any errors and omissions as our own.

About the authors

Dr Ignatius Ekanem, PhD, MBA, SFHEA is Senior Lecturer at Middlesex University Business School, London. He specializes in financial management of small and medium-sized enterprises (SMEs), small business development and economic regeneration. He has published in reputable journals, including *The British Accounting Review, International Small Business Journal, Journal of Small Business and Enterprise Development, International Journal of Entrepreneurial Behaviour Research* and *International Journal of Consumer Studies and Social Science and Medicine*. He has written two books and seven book chapters and is a co-author of over 20 official reports. His most recent books include, *Understanding Bankruptcy: Global Issues, Perspectives and Challenges*, Nova Science Publishers, New York; and *Writing a Business Plan: A Practical Guide*, Routledge, London. He has also written and presented many conference papers both in the UK and internationally. He has received Best Paper Awards from Barclays Bank for "Best Paper on General Under-represented Groups" – ISBE 2003 Conference; and from the *International Small Business Journal* for "Best Paper for Academic Rigour "– ISBE 2004 Conference. He holds an MBA from London South Bank University, London and a PhD in financial management and PGCHE, both from Middlesex University, London. He is a Senior Fellow of the Higher Education Academy (SFHEA).

Steve Ideh, MBA, FCA, FIMC is a chartered accountant and certified management consultant with over 25 years' cognate experience covering professional practice, banking, financial services regulation, entrepreneurship and financial management consulting, governance and risk management. Steve has led/managed projects in financial due diligence, turn-around management, mergers & acquisitions, forensics, process development and regulatory compliance and has served at various times as part of executive management at Stanbicibtc Bank, Nestoil and Chrome Groups of companies. Currently a doctoral candidate at the Swiss Business School, Steve is a member of faculty of a number of business schools and a regular speaker at entrepreneurship and leadership development events. He is the author of *Quick Win Tips for Entrepreneurs*.

1 Crowdfunding and entrepreneurship

Setting the stage

Learning objectives

- Explore the definition of a small business
- Review the characteristics of entrepreneurs
- Understand capital structure of business and sources of entrepreneurial finance
- Explore the traditional sources of financing available to small firms
- Introduce crowdfunding as an alternate source of entrepreneurial finance

Introduction

Entrepreneurship forms the mainstay of developed economies and is a vital contributor to employment, economic and export growth. The role of entrepreneurship in economic development as articulated by Kumar (2019) includes "promoting capital formation, creating large-scale employment opportunities, promoting balanced regional development, reducing concentration of economic power, wealth creation and distribution". According to the World Bank (2020), small and medium enterprises (SMEs) account for about 90% of businesses and over 50% of employment world-wide. The report also posits that SMEs are responsible for seven out of every ten jobs in emerging markets.

This clearly illustrates the significance of entrepreneurship and small-scale industries in the economic development of nations. Despite the growth and importance of entrepreneurship in the nation's economies, the most difficult task confronting entrepreneurs is raising adequate seed capital. Lavinsky (2010) explains that a large number of entrepreneurs have been having difficulties in raising venture capital. Entrepreneurial finance has hitherto concentrated on traditional sources of funding, such as family, friends, angel investors, banks and venture capital (Metelka 2014). However, with the advent of technology, the financing sources for entrepreneurs have taken a new and additional dimension.

Definition of small and medium enterprises (SMEs)

There is no one definition of a small or medium-sized enterprise that is universally recognized by everyone. Initial definitions of "small" enterprises focused primarily on qualitative characteristics. Small and Medium-sized Enterprises (SMEs) are

DOI: 10.4324/9781003193975-1

Table 1.1 EU categorization of SMEs

Company type	Micro	Small	Medium
No. of employees	<10	<50	<250
Turnover (EURO)	<2M	<10M	<50M
Balance sheet size	<2M	<10M	<43M

primarily non-subsidiary businesses that operate independently and have a number of employees that is lower than the threshold number which differs from country to country. As it is in the European Union, the customary upper limit for designating a firm as a small or medium-sized enterprise (SME) is 250 employees. However, the maximum number of employees that is considered to be an SME in the United States is 500, whereas in other countries the maximum number of employees is considered to be 200. Micro-businesses can have as few as five employees and as many as ten, but small businesses typically have fewer than 50 workers.

One way to categorize small and medium-sized enterprises is by the amount of financial assets. However, a new definition went into effect throughout the European Union on January 1, 2005. This definition applies to all community legislation and financial programming, as well as state aid, which mandates that SMEs are eligible for higher levels of national and regional aid than large corporations. Medium-sized businesses (those with 50–249 employees) now have a higher financial ceiling of 50 million euros, small businesses (10–49 employees) have a higher ceiling of 10 million euros and micro firms (those with less than ten employees) have a higher ceiling of 2 million euros, all thanks to the new definition.

Alternately, the maximum size of the balance sheets of medium, small, and micro enterprises is 43 million euros, 10 million euros and 2 million euros, respectively.

An independent status is necessary for a small or medium-sized business, in addition to meeting the requirements for the minimum number of employees and either of the two financial thresholds. The new definition distinguishes between free enterprises, partner enterprises, and linked enterprises (European Union 2020). The distinction is as follows:

1 Free enterprises/autonomous: if the enterprise is either completely independent or has one or more minority partnerships (each less than 25%) with other enterprises.
2 Partner enterprises: if holdings with other enterprises rise to at least 25% but no more than 50%, the relationship is deemed to be between partner enterprises.
3 Linked enterprises: if holdings with other enterprises exceed the 50% threshold, these are considered linked enterprise.

Characteristics of successful entrepreneurs

Generally, if you come from a lineage of people who could not work for someone else, you are a lousy employee, value your freedom or you see more than one definition of job security, then you are likely to step out as an entrepreneur. While entrepreneurs exhibit certain traits, they also share some common characteristics. Knörr *et al.* (2013) argue that creativity, willingness to take risks, and independence raise the likelihood of becoming an entrepreneur and lower the likelihood of becoming an employee.

Entrepreneurial people are primarily ambitious and innovative. According to Beugelsdijk and Noorderhaven (2005), entrepreneurs differ from the general public and salaried workers in numerous ways. They are more focused; they have higher individual responsibility and exertion. In this context, Omerzel and Kušce (2013) assert that the propensity to take risks, self-efficacy and the urge for independence are the most influential elements in becoming an entrepreneur. The need for independence has been singled out as a factor for business creation by authors such as Birley and Westhead (1994), Shane *et al.* (2000) and others.

The following are some of the important personal qualities that an entrepreneur should possess: passion, self-belief/confidence, creative thinking, perseverance, discipline, risk-taking propensity and a high need for achievement. Entrepreneurs typically have a propensity to choose for themselves a line of business that is congruent with their own personal values. In addition to this, they typically run their company by relying on the powerful and unique qualities that they possess. These characteristics can be discussed as follows:

(i) Passion

Without passion, no one achieves much. Successful entrepreneurs are enthusiastic about their work. Their passion consumes their very being, and they are willing to do anything to satisfy it. Successful entrepreneurs live and breathe their passion, and no one can convince them otherwise.

Passion is the fuel that propels an entrepreneur to keep going. Research shows that passion is the major factor which determines an entrepreneur's creativity, persistence and venture performance. In other words, the more passionate the entrepreneur, the more likely they will succeed. An entrepreneurial passion is a motivational attitude which is characterized by positive emotional stimulants, internal drive and engagement with meaningful work that is significant to an entrepreneur's self-identity. Passion is essential for success of entrepreneurial ventures and makes the difference between the success and failure of an entrepreneur.

Passion is the drive, ambition and love of what someone does, and it provides an entrepreneur with a unique view of the world that other people often do not see. Passion is the innate ability of an entrepreneur which cannot be learned or acquired. It fires their hard work, determination, and creativity to reach their goals and attain significant heights. Passion is important in entrepreneurship because it defines a person's desire and ability to overcome all odds to achieve desired outcomes. It helps the entrepreneur to overcome the fear of failure. It is an entrepreneur's passion that draws the right people including investors to him/her and helps them to succeed in their enterprise.

(ii) Creativity

The business climate is determined by the personality traits and motivations of individual entrepreneurs. Business processes and situations are frequently distinctive in their complexities, and fluctuating requirements. Entrepreneurs must be able to wear different caps and exhibit the ability to operate as creators or innovators, marketing and sales specialists, investors and accountants, all at the same time. Therefore, the more knowledgeable and skilled an entrepreneur is, the better (Frese and Gielnik 2014). "Successful entrepreneurs think creatively and are willing to think outside the box. It really does not matter if the business idea has already been tried; they just find better ways to do things" (Ideh 2017, p. 19).

A successful entrepreneur must be creative. Creativity means the ability to think in a practical way. It is the ability to bring something new into being. Creative entrepreneurs tend to have more originality than others and are able to produce solutions that fly in the face of established knowledge. Creative entrepreneurs are also inclined to be more adaptable and prepared to consider a range of alternative approaches. They challenge the status quo by providing alternative ideas for ways the organization operates, noticing a challenge that needs a solution and detecting an opportunity the organization could take to improve its processes.

Through understanding the situation and reflecting on the issues, new linkages are contemplated and possible new combinations of components are made. From this emerge viable solutions or possibilities that are subjected to evaluation.

(iii) Innovativeness

A successful entrepreneur is an innovator. He is one who brings about a change through the introduction of new technological processes or products. He changes technological possibilities and alters convention through innovative activities. He does something in a new way or through a new method.

Innovation does not necessarily mean a new or an earth-shattering invention. Innovation includes products and services that are novel or add value to existing products and services, or differ in some way from products and services offered elsewhere in the market. A successful entrepreneur is a problem solver. He finds solution to problems.

Innovative entrepreneurs develop business models which help them to meet the needs of an organization and improve their competitiveness in the market (McKenna 2023). Entrepreneurs use innovative ideas to create business models or make improvements to existing ones. It is innovativeness which enables an entrepreneur to identify new trends and market demand. It helps a business to produce new goods or services that appeal to its target audience or exploit existing products or services.

(iv) Self-confidence

Success requires a strong code of ethics, a burning drive and a firm trust in oneself. A successful entrepreneur is adept at having faith in his intuition and ideas.

Self-confidence or self-efficacy is an important concept for a successful entrepreneur. It translates into self-belief in the capability to mobilize resources, motivate others and produce a change (Deakins and Freel 2012). Self-confidence is a belief in oneself that they can do whatever they set out to do. It is an indispensable quality of a successful entrepreneur.

Entrepreneurs who are self-confident tend to deal immediately and decisively with problems and conflicts. They have high self-esteem and have no problem in empowering others and encouraging them to be their best. On the other hand, an entrepreneur with low self-esteem can be controlling and a micro-manager and does not encourage growth and opportunity for others.

(v) High desire for success/achievement

A high need for achievement is a desire to excel and to achieve a goal in relation to a set of standards. High achievers are those that accept responsibility for decisions and for achieving solutions to problems. It is important to note that for a successful entrepreneur satisfaction is gained from finding the solution to a problem rather than with monetary reward.

A high achieving entrepreneur is not galvanized into activity by the prospect of profit only. He works hard anyway, provided there is an opportunity of achieving something. He may regard money as a measure of achievement, but money is not an end in itself. However, he does need feedback of evidence of his achievement, and money can provide such feedback.

(vi) Visionary

Entrepreneurs are visionaries and dream about success. They build and conceive vivid images of success and fulfilment in their imaginations, which motivate and drive them considerably more than their contemporaries.

A visionary entrepreneur is someone with strong foresight or deep insight. A successful entrepreneur needs to have a clear vision of what he/she wants to achieve. The visionary quality is part of the fabric of an entrepreneur's motivation. Nothing noble or noteworthy is ever done on earth without vision. A successful entrepreneur with vision will be at the right place at the right time because for them, timing is everything.

Ahmetoglu (2018) argues that a visionary entrepreneur has some key ingredients which differentiates them from the rest. Firstly, a visionary entrepreneur is able to envisage the future. They are different because they are obsessed with the future and think far ahead of others. Secondly, they are not only preoccupied with the future, they also want to do something about that future; they want to change things for the better. They are the type of people that are always looking at where things can be improved and consequently make big improvements. Visionary entrepreneurs have that constant desire to change things for the better, but those who are really visionary think big in terms of the change they wish to make. Finally, visionary entrepreneurs have the unique ability to make others believe in their vision as much as they do themselves, convincing others that the better future described is one they want to live in (Ahmetoglu 2018). Steve Jobs is a classic example of this visionary entrepreneur. He had to convince people that what they need is an affordable home computer, when no one had a clue as to why they needed it. This requires the ability to influence people but also a tendency to do so consistently.

Other examples of entrepreneurs with vision can include Richard Branson, Oprah Winfrey and Mark Zuckerberg. Tango and Ferragamo (2023) opine that Sir Richard Branson saw the potential for a global brand delivering everything from music festivals to space travel, Oprah Winfrey built her media empire around self-help and inspiring women in a way no one else ever had before or has since, while Mark Zuckerberg's Facebook continues to set the standard for social media through its evolution and customer-centric innovations.

(vii) Natural leadership

Most successful entrepreneurs are born leaders. They possess the potential to inspire others since they are hard-working and charismatic. Because they are certain of their destination, they are able to convince others to follow them. Followership is naturally attracted to leadership.

Natural leadership is a transformational leadership. It allows leaders to not only achieve success, but to transform the thoughts and actions of individuals, groups and even organizations. Bennett (2019) argues that there are some characteristics of a transformational leader. The first is charisma which is defined as a compelling attractiveness or charm. Charisma is what compels people to follow a leader. A transformational leader must also have vision as discussed earlier. Successful transformational leaders are able to articulate a vision of change that their followers can identify with. The vision becomes the common goal. A transformational leader also has the ability to inspire others to do their best, challenge themselves and achieve.

Bennett (2019) also suggests that a transformational leader would not ask a follower to do something that he himself would not do. The energy and enthusiasm of a transformational leader are often described as "contagious". Transformational leaders are good at delegating tasks to their followers in order to expand skills and develop their individual leadership potential.

(viii) Discipline

An entrepreneur must be disciplined, determined and persistent. Successful entrepreneurs resist the urge to do what is unimportant or to take the easy way out, and instead are able to determine the most important and optimal course of action. Campbell (2020) opines that the most successful people in life are disciplined; that disciplined entrepreneurs have the resourcefulness to solve their problem in one way or another, and that without discipline no one can solve anything.

Entrepreneurship is about facing challenges and each challenge offers the opportunity to grow, to improve upon our skillset, to test our edges and to learn new ways to solve problems (Campbell 2020). When entrepreneurs are challenged and they remain disciplined, their problem-solving skills are called to the forefront and they remain focused. Entrepreneurs are people who are willing to work harder than anyone else and are not satisfied to live an average life. Disciplined entrepreneurs crave testing the edges of who they are and what they can become. They do not mind working extra hours or going the extra mile if it means they learn something valuable that gets them more quickly and efficiently to the result of their desired outcome (Campbell 2020).

Disciplined entrepreneurs know that success does not always come easily. Therefore, they welcome surprises and view failures as opportunities which guide them towards a successful direction. Disciplined entrepreneurs understand patience as a virtue, which does not mean waiting and doing nothing. Rather, it means working hard while they wait and trusting that there will be a positive outcome in the end. But in the meantime, they continue to work hard to develop new opportunities.

Disciplined entrepreneurs are willing to seek guidance and to change their minds. Disciplined entrepreneurs are not afraid to ask for guidance when necessary or to go out of their comfort zone to establish new patterns of behaviour that will help them move forward. They are extremely resourceful. If they do not have what they need, they are determined to figure out how to secure the resources they need or to "make do" with what is available. These types of people refuse to take no for an answer because they have the resourcefulness to solve their problem in one way or another (Campbell 2020).

(ix) Perseverance

Successful entrepreneurs do not use the word quit in their vocabularies. They recognize that quitters do not succeed and that, like life, business is full of ups and downs, so they resolve not to quit during the difficult times. When the going gets difficult, it is their resilience and ability to persevere that differentiates the successful entrepreneurs from the others.

Perseverance means persistence. Entrepreneurs accept setbacks and are even prepared to start from scratch in order to achieve their goals. They know they are likely to encounter some failures on the path to success, and this is why persistence is one of the key characteristics of a successful entrepreneur.

Entrepreneurs accept perseverance and persistence as a learning process. According to Tango and Ferragamo (2023), there is an 18% chance that a first-time entrepreneur will succeed. After failing once and learning the lessons from this failure, the entrepreneur's chance of succeeding increases to 20%, and with each successive attempt, the probability of success rises to 30% (Tango and Ferragamo 2023).

(x) Risk-taking propensity

The decision to assume business risk is indicative of a certain personality type. According to Hvide and Panos (2014), risk-tolerant individuals are more likely to launch businesses. A major portion of the drive to take risks in business is derived from the motivation to achieve success. Entrepreneurs are motivated by the conviction that their personal destinies are the product of their own actions. Another attribute of entrepreneurs is the capacity to make decisions under unclear conditions. This is the willingness of entrepreneurs to accept measured risk and uncertainty (Burns 2022). It is the willingness to risk their money, reputation and personal standing if the business fails. As already mentioned, entrepreneurs are motivated by achievement itself rather than by money. For such individuals, money is merely a measure of achievement and success.

A successful entrepreneur is a risk-taker. He/she breaks new grounds. Risk-taking means the capacity to tolerate risks. A successful entrepreneur has the psychological make-up to cope with any failure. He/she learns from failure as some successes are accidental successes. Risk tolerance does not in any way mean that they are reckless risk-takers.

On the contrary, successful entrepreneurs are moderate or calculated risk-takers. Successful entrepreneurs tend to be cautious and are opportunity-focused, as opposed to risk-focused. They assess situations thoroughly and do not pursue options which they consider to have a small probability of success. A moderate or a calculated risk involves the principle of *affordable loss*.

The principle of affordable loss advocates that entrepreneurs only makes investments that they can afford to lose, thereby recognizing that new ventures often fail. It focusses on the business's downside to protect or minimize risk (Sarasvathy 2008). The principle speaks of the expert entrepreneurs limiting risk by understanding what they can afford to lose at each step, instead of seeking large all or nothing opportunities. They choose goals and actions where there is an upside even if the downside ends up happening.

Under the principle of affordable loss, the entrepreneur makes small experimental investments and sees what happens (e.g. Richard Branson explains that when he established Virgin Atlantic he negotiated a deal with Boeing so that he could use one of their planes and give it back to them if the venture failed). This is an example of "affordable loss".

(xi) Independence

Entrepreneurs are independent, autonomous and reliant on themselves to achieve predetermined goals, for which they are willing to take risks and make appropriate sacrifices (Sidik 2012). This can also be referred to as the need to "be to your own boss". It is the most often cited entrepreneurial trait. However, independence can mean different things to different people: doing things differently, being in a situation where you can fulfil your potential or controlling your own destiny (Burns 2022).

For most business owners, independence is an extension of their personality and defines their core thinking (GlobalLinker 2021). Workplace autonomy is a powerful motivator for entrepreneurs. According to Waltower (2023), having the independence to make your own decisions is considered the key benefit of being an entrepreneur. The main reason most people want to become their own boss is the freedom, satisfaction and flexibility it offers them (Waltower 2023). Freedom nurtures creativity and business owners thrive on pursuing their passion and coming up with innovative solutions to real problems.

GlobalLinker (2021) suggests that *flexibility is freedom and that* entrepreneurship ensures that the person at the helm enjoys a certain amount of flexibility in terms of managing their work-life balance. The ability to do what one wants, when one wants and where one wants can be a big motivator to start one's own business (GlobalLinker 2021). Independence allows the entrepreneur to be in control of their schedule, and to do what they really enjoy doing is important to entrepreneurs.

(xii) High internal locus of control

Locus of control speaks of where the control of events resides. Locus of control is often regarded as a crucial indicator of entrepreneurship potential. There are two types of locus of control – internal locus of control and external locus of control. The internal locus of control is a strong indicator of a successful entrepreneur.

An entrepreneur with a high internal locus of control likes to be in charge of their environment and their own destiny (Burns (2022). They believe that the buck stops with them. If nothing is going right they blame themselves rather than other people. Their outlook is epitomized by the statement "*What happens to me is my own doing*". Successful entrepreneurs have higher internal locus of control than unsuccessful leaders.

On the other hand, entrepreneurs with external locus of control are those who believe that their lives are dominated by chance events outside their own control. They believe that powerful people or "fate" controls their destiny. They are more likely to blame other people for their own misfortune instead of themselves.

Capital structure

Capital structure refers to the amount of debt and/or equity employed by a company to fund its operations and finance its assets (CFI 2022). A company's capital structure is typically expressed as a debt-to-equity ratio.

A company uses debt and equity capital to fund its business's operations, capital expenditures and other investments. There are trade-offs firms have to make when a company decides whether to use debt or equity to finance its operations, and managers will balance the two to find the optimal capital structure (CFI 2022).

Optimal capital structure

CFI (2022) defines the optimal capital structure of a firm as the proportion of debt and equity that results in the lowest weighted average cost of capital (WACC) for the firm. In practice, this technical definition is not always used as companies often have a philosophical view of what should be the ideal structure (CFI 2022). In order to optimize the structure, a company can issue either more debt or equity. The new capital acquired may be used to invest in new assets or may be used to repurchase debt/equity which is currently outstanding, as a form of recapitalization.

Companies that use more debt than equity to finance their assets and fund operating activities have a high gearing ratio and an aggressive capital structure (Tuovila 2022). A company that pays for assets with more equity than debt has a low gearing ratio and a conservative capital structure. However, Tuovila (2022) argues that a high gearing ratio and an aggressive capital structure can also lead to higher growth rates, whereas a conservative capital structure can lead to lower growth rates. It is therefore crucial for the company management to find the ideal mix of debt and equity, which is referred to as the optimal capital structure, to finance operations.

However, Modigliani and Miller (1958) posit that companies have only three ways to raise money to finance their operations and fuel their growth and expansion. They can borrow money by issuing bonds or obtaining loans; they can re-invest their profits in their operations, or they can issue new stock shares to investors. Modigliani and Miller (1958) further argue that with certain assumptions in place, it is irrelevant whether a company finances its growth by borrowing, by issuing stock shares, or by reinvesting its profits. Nevertheless, it is important to recognize that due to the lack of access to the stock exchange by most small firms and market imperfections, there is a finance gap in small firms.

Determinants of capital structure

Cost, profitability, tangibility, tax and size affect capital structure, according to both theoretical and empirical research. Other factors impacting capital structure include non-debt tax shields, growth potential and volatility. On the basis of a large number of empirical studies conducted on US companies, Harris and Raviv (1990) conclude that "leverage increases with fixed assets, non-debt tax shields, investment opportunities, and firm size, and decreases with volatility, advertising expenditure, the likelihood of bankruptcy, profitability, and product uniqueness". However, recent research has enhanced our knowledge of the factors that determine capital structure. For example, Wald (1999) demonstrates that non-debt tax shields reduce leverage as opposed to increasing it.

The differences between small firms' and large firms' capital structure

The organization of their capital and the processes by which they make decisions regarding their funding are handled very differently by small and large companies respectively (Serrasqueiro *et al.* 2011). The information gap, the level of risk, the growth potential, the moral hazards and the resources already available within the company are some of the primary aspects that go into how small businesses choose to finance their enterprises (López-Gracia and Sogorb-Mira 2008; Schwienbacher and Larralde 2010).

It is interesting to examine small firms since, in contrast to large firms, they do not have access to finance channels that are very well developed. This makes the topic of small businesses all the more exciting. Because of informational imbalances and agency issues, there is a restriction placed on the availability of external finance; as a result, banks have emerged as the dominant source of capital for small enterprises. This is due to the fact that banks are better suited to assess the quality of small firms as well as address agency and information issues (Berger and Udell 1998). One more distinction that can be made between small businesses and large businesses is the fact that smaller businesses frequently lack the expertise and resources necessary to determine which market segment best suits their requirements. This is an important factor to take into consideration when comparing small businesses and large businesses.

When they are just starting out and going through their developmental stages, small enterprises face significant dangers. Due to a lack of antecedences and credit history, a lack of business focus and track record, a lack of tangible assets to secure debt, as well as information asymmetry, small enterprises and younger firms face the danger of risk diversification (Harrison 2013; López-Gracia and Sogorb-Mira 2008; Serrasqueiro and Nunes 2012).

A further distinction can be made between small and large businesses in terms of the available financing options. Small businesses are distinguished from large businesses by a number of characteristics, including high transaction costs, the concentration of control on a small number of people, and financial restraints imposed by creditors. In addition to their sensitivity to market changes, small companies typically have significant transaction costs, which prevent them from being listed on a stock exchange (López-Gracia and Sogorb-Mira 2008; Sannajust *et al.* 2014).

One of the most essential things that owners of small and nascent firms can do to mitigate or lessen the effects of these barriers is to persuade lenders that the business idea will be successful. Because of these identical features, the available options for funding are restricted, as is the ability to gain access to the cash (Serrasqueiro and Nunes 2012). As a result of these circumstances, small businesses have to think about their potential sources of finance in a fundamentally different way than do large firms.

Small businesses would be able to secure more favourable financing terms if they can provide more information about their operations. The lack of transparency or full disclosure on financial and business operations increases the perception of risk for lenders. It reduces the pool of available funds in the market for small businesses. Information asymmetry issues may be reduced by establishing trust and long-term relationships between firms and their creditors (Serrasqueiro *et al.* 2011). This, in turn, could reduce transaction costs and enhance firm performance while also providing multiple investment opportunities and economy of scale, (Serrasqueiro *et al.* 2011).

While reviewing the financing decisions of small and medium-sized businesses through the lens of the business life cycle, La Rocca *et al.* (2011, p. 1) argue that "the controversy in the empirical literature regarding the determinants of capital structure decisions is based on a failure to take into account the different degrees of information opacity, and, consequently, firms' characteristics and needs at specific stages of their life cycles". The findings indicate that as a company progresses through the various phases of its life cycle in a nation that is bank-oriented, the company tends to adopt specific financing techniques and a different hierarchy of financial decision-making. Debt, contrary to the common belief, is shown to be essential to the activities of a firm in its early phases, representing the first choice. In contrast, as a company reaches the maturity stage, it re-balances its capital structure by gradually exchanging internal capital for external debt. Additionally, the pecking-order theory (discussed in Chapter 3) is shown to be highly applicable to companies that have successfully integrated their business.

Sources of entrepreneurial finance

Entrepreneurial finance is a sub-set of traditional corporate finance (Wright and Robbie 1998). Corporate finance has traditionally focused on larger publicly traded companies, whereas entrepreneurial finance has traditionally focused on smaller, privately held businesses (Cumming *et al.* 2019). Entrepreneurial finance, according to Cosh *et al.* (2009), includes a variety of finance types and providers, such as venture capital, private equity, private debt, trade credit, IPOs, business angel finance and crowdfunding, among other forms of finance, such as grants, funding from incubators or accelerators, and support from family and friends.

Industry experience, prior experience in starting a business, financing knowledge, education, individual risk profile and goals are some characteristics that could make accessing financing easier for the entrepreneur or improve risk acceptance to investors (Gartner *et al.* 2012). The lack of knowledge of opportunities and alternatives and courses of action designated for small businesses is a significant drawback to obtaining financing. This drawback may mean that entrepreneurs are unable to source enough capital and hence are unable to optimize company value (Seghers *et al.* 2012). Limited or inadequate knowledge can result in the small business owner not being able to explore available financing opportunities and hence reduce the cost of financing transactions. Inability to take advantage of financing options means small businesses may resort to more traditional options thereby losing or diluting ownership and control. Increase in entrepreneurial experience would usually reduce these biases (Fraser *et al.* 2015).

Increasing ties with the financial community have a way of increasing knowledge of financing options. It has been established that some entrepreneurs start businesses for social reasons and benefits rather than to maximize wealth as traditional finance research assumes (Seghers *et al.* 2012; Bruton *et al.* 2015). However, some others decide based on some other preferences such as maintaining control and refraining from indebtedness, or perhaps for want of understanding of available alternatives. Despite the differences in goals, entrepreneurs make a vital contribution to society and the economy through their ventures (Metelka 2014). The various sources of small business finance are discussed in the following sections.

(i) Personal savings

The first source of funding for small businesses is the personal savings of the business owner. Personal savings can be categorized as internal equity (Barkham *et al.* 1996). In most cases, this is the only way an owner of a small firm provides finance for his or her business; thus, they are able to retain all the shares of the company (Keasey and Watson 1993). The reasons for this are: firstly, it is generally difficult for owner-managers to sell shares to members of the public due to the riskiness of the small firm (Barkham *et al* 1996). It is not, generally, possible to reduce these risks by careful scrutiny of the firm because the costs of this process are high relative to the level of funds required (Keasey and Watson 1993). Secondly, small firms retain all the shares of the company because owner-managers are, generally, not willing to part with ownership or share control of their companies (Bank of England 1998).

Therefore, personal finance from the founder remains the most common source of finance especially for small businesses. This is because of the essential conservatism of many entrepreneurs towards both debt and external equity. Secondly, it is because of the difficulty which some entrepreneurs face in raising external finance. Research has shown that 60% of start-ups are estimated to rely on personal funds (Fraser *et al*. 2015).

In a research conducted by the author on clothing and printing industries, personal savings were an important source of investment finance in the clothing industry and for plant and machinery of low technology. They were also used for the purchase of computers for administrative purposes (Ekanem 2002). The main advantage of using personal finance is that it saves money on interest payments on bank loans (particularly if these are in the form of overdrafts, rather than term loans, negotiated against a planned investment programme), and from the entrepreneur's standpoint it involves lower risk. The major disadvantage is loss of personal savings.

(ii) Friends, family and fans financing

This is finance which is usually in the form of a loan that an entrepreneur obtains from either family members or friends in order to help finance their start-up or growing business. External equity in small firms is rare and can only be undertaken by investors with special knowledge or interest such as the entrepreneur's family and friends since the need for information is reduced due to the personal knowledge of the capabilities of the entrepreneur.

Just as personal funding discussed earlier, friends/family financing is the most common source of debt finance for start-ups. These are people with whom the entrepreneur has close relationships and who know that he/she is reliable and competent. Therefore, on the face of it there should be no problem in asking for such a loan. However, while borrowing money from friends and family may seem an easy alternative to dealing with bankers, it can actually be a much more delicate situation than dealing with a financial institution.

Before 2008, funding for the early stages of start-up and development were all from founders, their families, friend and fans and also from state grants (Harrison 2013). Funding from these sources dropped following the 2008 recession as a result of dwindling household budgets. Subsequently, entrepreneurs used personal funds and turned to short-term borrowing according to the pecking order theory (Serrasqueiro and Nunes 2012).

**Advantages and disadvantages of raising finance
from friends and family**

Advantages:

- Friends or family will be flexible. On a practical level, they may offer loans without security or accept less security than banks.
- They may lend funds interest-free or at a low rate.
- They may agree to a longer repayment period or lower return on their investment than formal lenders.
- They may also seek a lower rate of initial return than commercial backers.
- They already know your character and circumstances and so are less likely to need a detailed business plan.

Disadvantages:

- Transactions of this nature can be complex.
- Any misunderstandings about the arrangement can damage relationships.
- There is a risk your investors may offer more than they can afford to lose.
- They may demand their money back when it suits them but not your business.
- They may also want to get more involved in the business, which may not be appropriate.

Source: NIBusinessInfo, 2023

Tips on approaching friends or family for finance

It is a good idea to approach friends and family in the same way the entrepreneur would a formal lender:

- The entrepreneur should be crystal clear about their own expectations. They should specify how long they need the money for.
- The entrepreneur should detail the repayment level they can afford.
- They should spell out how many shares or what profit the investor will receive – and when any returns will be paid.
- The entrepreneur should clarify whether an investor will have any financial liabilities for the business activity.
- The entrepreneur should draw up a formal written agreement.
- They should think twice about approaching a friend or family member if other sources of finance have turned them down. They should analyze the reasons for this and review their business proposition. They should remember that if the business fails, lenders and investors may lose their money.
- They should pass on the reasons that others gave for turning them down.

Source: NIBusinessInfo, 2023

(iii) Retained profits

Another type of internal equity comes from retained profits of the company. The most important source of finance in small firms is retained profits (Poutziouris *et al.* 1999). Generally, retained profits provide a good source of investment finance but profits in small firms take time to accumulate and may not be available in sufficient amount at the right time for investment decisions to take advantage of market opportunity (Barkham *et al.* 1996). The majority of small businesses still rely on internal funds as their primary source of finance, with 79% of small firms using retained profits and 72% using cash flow to fund their activities (Bank of England 1998). Keasey and Watson (1994) find internal equity to be as important as bank finance in the sense that it contributes around 31% to firms financing structure. However, its availability depends on the profitability of the business (Binks and Ennew 1996). Therefore, small firms faced with a shortfall of funding from internal resources to meet investment plans will place reliance on debt such as bank finance.

In Ekanem (2002), clothing firms were using retained profits to finance their investment and were regarded as a good source of investment finance for small firms. However, as Barkham *et al.* (1996) argue, profits take time to accumulate in small firms and may not be available in sufficient amounts at the point of making the investment.

(iv) Trade credit

Trade credit is a type of finance in which a customer is allowed to purchase goods or services and pay the supplier at a later scheduled date without paying cash up-front. It is often a business-to-business (B2B) arrangement or agreement. Normally, the business that provides trade credits gives the buyer 30, 60, or 90 days to pay, with the transaction recorded through an invoice. In some cases, entrepreneurs may be able to negotiate longer trade credit repayment terms, which provides an even greater advantage.

Trade credit is a major source of short-term finance. It is a good way for businesses to free up cash and finance short-term growth. It is a form of credit with no interest. Trade credit provides flexibility in paying creditors. It is relatively more stable than a short-term loan such as bank overdraft in which the bank manager can withdraw the facility within a short notice. With trade credit there is no demand for collateral security by the creditor.

Although trade credit is apparently a free source of finance, its true costs are the cost of not taking discounts associated with the sale for early payment, the higher unit costs charged by the supplier, and loss of goodwill for any late payment.

(v) Bank finance

The most widely available external source of investment finance for small firms is debt finance from high street and merchant banks. A number of studies have indicated that the vast majority of small businesses in the UK depend on banks for short-term loans and overdrafts to finance their investment requirements (e.g. Keasey and Watson 1993; Binks and Ennew 1996). Thus, banks represent the main external source of entrepreneurial finance. According to Keasey and Watson (1993) bank debt represents 31% of business liabilities. The Bank of England (1998) confirms that the main external source of entrepreneurial finance is still banks, in the form of overdrafts and term loans although its importance has declined in recent years as small businesses increasingly diversify their sources of finance (Bank of England 2000, 2001).

The Bank of England (2001) reports that bank lending has moved away from overdrafts towards more term loans as a form of finance. This reflects the realization that the banks need to diversify sources of finance for small firms. For quite a long time now, the relationship between banks and small businesses has been criticized regarding their approach to lending, the short-term nature of the financial products, and the customer perceptions of service quality (Binks and Ennew 1996). The criticism regarding the approach to lending concerns the excessive demand for collateral security (Binks *et al.* 1993). Edwards (1987) criticizes the short-termism in the UK bank practice as constituting a major constraint on economic development, whilst Binks (1987) provides evidence of the demand for longer-term, more flexible debt products. The service quality criticism is that the banks are lacking sympathy and understanding of the financial needs of small businesses and use their monopoly position to impose onerous terms on small firms (Keasey and Watson 1993).

The main reason why small firms depend so much upon bank finance for external funding is that banks are probably best able to monitor cheaply, through the bank account, the ability of firms to service their debts (Cosh and Hughes 1994). Thus, banks are in the best position to overcome the acute information asymmetries of small firms through their ability to monitor and enforce lending contracts at low cost. They argue that banks are also able to discourage entrepreneurs from undertaking too risky projects through the short-term nature of their loans which are secured on the business and/or personal assets of the entrepreneur and which are frequently reviewed.

However, Deakins and Freel (2012) argue that the information required by the bank to assess perfectly and to monitor risky projects is not costless to obtain because when conditions of uncertainty combine with asymmetric information, two problems arise for the banks, namely, adverse selection and moral hazard. Adverse selection occurs "when either the bank provides finance for a venture that subsequently fails or refuses finance for a venture that would have been successful" (Deakins and Freel 2012, p. 148); whereas, moral hazard arises because "once an entrepreneur has raised the bank loan, there is no guarantee that they will act in the best interest of the bank" (Deakins and Freel 2012, p. 148). Deakins and Freel (2012) argue that moral hazard is more difficult to control for the bank because it is a monitoring problem and for relatively small amounts of finance it is not economic for the bank to monitor performance closely.

Although the banks argue that they have moved emphasis away from collateral towards lending decisions based on business plans and cash flow projections, research such as that by Deakins and Hussain (1994) has revealed that banks are still concerned primarily with the personal financial position of the entrepreneur and gearing in assessing business propositions. Almost two-thirds of entrepreneurs still consider collateral as an issue (North *et al.* 2010) thus giving rise to a finance gap.

Deakins and Freel (2012) argue that a finance gap arises because of miss-matches between supply and demand, i.e. the demand from small firms is greater than the willingness of financial institutions to supply the finance at current market conditions. However, other researchers (e.g. Cowling *et al.* 1991) argue that it is the small firms' owners themselves who seem to be most opposed to a type of financing that requires greater involvement in the business by outside investors.

(vi) Leasing/hire purchase

Leasing is a contract under which the legal ownership of the asset remains with the lessor (Bank of England 1998). There are essentially two types of lease, a finance lease and an operating lease (Bank of England 2000). The Bank of England (2000) defines a finance lease as a long-term non-cancellable lease, generally requiring the lessee to pay all maintenance costs. An operating lease is one in which the period of contract is less than the life of the asset and the lessor pays all maintenance and servicing costs (Bank of England 2000). The report points out that small firms tend to make more use of operating leases, because of the increased flexibility regarding maintenance of the asset and future upgrades.

Hire purchase contracts, on the other hand, result in the purchaser building up ownership of the asset over a pre-determined period (Bank of England 2000). Both leasing and hire purchase agreements provide the business with access to 100% finance without reducing capital reserves or increasing gearing levels (Bank of England 1999). They also allow businesses to spread out payments over the life of the asset with payments structured to accommodate the asset's expected pattern of income generation (Bank of England 2000). The flexibility to upgrade equipment in line with the growth of the business is also viewed as advantageous (Bank of England 2001).

The Bank of England (1998) argues that operating leases and hire purchase continue to be the forms of asset-based finance most frequently used by small businesses, accounting for 31% of all external finance. The report also indicates that leasing is size dependent, with smaller companies more likely to depend on leasing than their larger counterparts. It also states that businesses of different sizes had different reasons for making use of leasing. Smaller businesses tended to use leasing to finance their survival and growth, whereas larger companies used leasing for tax advantages (Bank of England 2000).

The type of assets which should be financed in these ways are those which are highly durable with good second-hand value such as machinery, vehicles and office equipment since the second-hand value of the assets forms the main security to the providers of finance (Cooper 1987). Cooper (1987) suggests that assets which require regular maintenance or updating due to technological advancement are best financed by a lease rather than hire purchase.

Hire purchase was also found to be a popular source of investment finance mainly in the printing firms in Ekanem (2002) for two reasons. Firstly, it was used because of the amount of money involved (sometimes up to £0.75 million for a single piece of equipment), which is difficult to fund from retained profits, personal savings or from bank loans. Secondly, and more importantly, it was used because of its medium-term nature.

(vii) Factoring/invoice discounting

Factoring is a scheme where a factor advances up to 80% of the invoice value immediately, with the remainder (minus the service charge and interest) being paid when the transaction is completed (Bank of England 2000). The main attraction of the scheme is that it allows small businesses to concentrate on their business rather than chasing debts since a factor can dedicate more resources to credit management than the small firms (Ekanem 2002). Factoring has become increasingly important to small firms as a source of finance (Bank of England 2001). A survey by the British Chambers of Commerce shows that there was a discernible move towards the use of factoring/invoice discounting with 11% of respondents using receivables finance (BCC 1997).

Invoice discounting is the purchase by the discounter and sale by a company of book debts on a continuing basis (occasionally selectively) for immediate cash (Bank of England 2001). The Bank of England (2000) indicates that factoring and invoice discounting are particularly appropriate for small firms unable to draw on further overdraft facilities because they enhance access to cash flow and remove the problems incurred from late payments. However, the Bank of England (2001) points out that the majority of small firms prefer factoring to invoice discounting because it enables them to outsource their financial management controls, although some fear that this might reduce their contact with clients. The report also points out that invoice discounting is in any case typically available only to businesses with a turnover in excess of £1 million, because it is not generally possible to provide it on a small scale at a price that would be attractive.

(viii) Government-assisted finance

The final and potentially very useful source of investment finance for small firms is a government grant (Deakins and Freel 2012). Grants are not necessarily "free" money because they are often tied to specific objectives such as the purchase of capital equipment but they do represent finance for expansion at below market interest rates (Barkham *et al.* 1996). The problem with grants as a source of small firms' investment finance is twofold: First, there is still some lack of awareness among businesses of the grants available and how to access them (Bank of England 1998). Second, there has been something of a shift in emphasis away from direct financial assistance towards "softer" forms of aids such as information, advice and training (Austin *et al.* 1995).

(ix) Venture capital (VC)

VC is a widely used form of financial intermediation that is particularly well suited to stimulate the development of innovative fast-growing businesses that can make an impact on the local/national economy (Ekanem *et al*. 2019). It is a niche form of financing which is most established in the US and UK, but even in these countries it is only around 2% of SMEs with potential high growth (PHG) that use VC (North *et al*. 2013).

Mason and Owen (2016) recognize that successful nurturing of VC markets requires a holistic overarching policy approach which builds on Gilson's (2003) simultaneity of VC engineering theory – developing entrepreneurship and finance in tandem within an entrepreneurial finance ecosystem. This requires pipeline development of businesses (Mason and Brown 2013), evaluation of changes in the entrepreneurial finance escalator in terms of the availability and complementarity of different types of finance – such as between business angels and VCs, public co-finance of VC schemes to encourage private investment into finance escalator gaps, finance networking and intermediaries, and investment exit market opportunities to enable optimal portfolio company exit value and recycling of returns into new investments.

In terms of what venture capitalists look for before investing, the evidence in Ekanem *et al*. (2019) suggests that they would prefer to invest in a venture where the management team is sufficiently high quality and professional, with a proper understanding of their business valuation as well as good understanding of the industry as a whole. Payne *et al*. (2009) suggest a better understanding of the decision-making process can enable more prudent decisions regarding investments and stages of funding. Without this understanding, small business owners would prefer to be on friendly terms with the investor so that they would bend the rules and not be so stringent when conducting their due diligence. Due diligence is also what would be expected of a responsible investor, especially in the aftermath of the global financial crisis (North *et al*. 2013).

However, most of the times, the small business environment is so uncertain that a fully developed legal and regulatory environment based on common law can help in the understanding of the industry and reduction of the cost of due diligence (Scheela and Van Dihn 2004). Ekanem *et al*. (2019) argue that both formal and informal institutions can provide the proper incentives and help reduce transaction problems; the more developed these institutions, the more they are likely to reduce transaction problems and encourage VC funding (Li and Zahra 2012).

Properly functioning institutions, especially financial institutions as well as political stability (Lingelbach 2015) would also help in the provision of adequate and sufficient information to reduce the risk of moral hazard and adverse selection caused by information asymmetry (Carpenter and Peterson 2002). The correction of the institutional deficit may also require stable markets, regulations, taxes, export facilities and assistance. Extant literature only reported favourable perceptions of the regulatory institutional environment with positive association with feasibility (Urban 2013). However, Ekanem *et al*. (2019) indicate that the regulatory environment has a real and significant impact on VC development since inappropriate institutional development and corruption lead to a negative impact on VC development in emerging economies.

With regards to proximity, the finding supports Lutz *et al.* (2013) who suggest that even in economies with a dense infrastructure such as Germany, spatial proximity between investor and investee impacts the likelihood of an investment. Although there is a counter-argument that VCs will source the best deals irrespective of location, many commentators consider spatial proximity between investor and investee to play an important role in VC (Amini 2013; SQW 2015). However, as discussed earlier, well-developed institutions with adequate infrastructure and good quality of public services (Lingelbach 2015) as well as sector syndication with trusted and established local investment partners can overcome this problem (Abell and Nisar 2007).

Lastly, exit strategy was important to VCs in emerging economies. Jiang *et al.* (2014) argue that although the role of VCs in initial public offerings (IPOs) is well rehearsed in developed markets, limited attention has been paid to the role of VCs in IPOs by SMEs in emerging markets. This is probably because VCs are prepared to sell their investment via trade sales, syndication, or sale to larger later stage VCs. Again, a fully developed institution provides improved macroeconomic factors that directly improve exit strategies by developing a stock market and alternative private equity options (Scheela and van Dihn 2004). It is a key argument that exit strategies are crucial to the development of VC markets, enabling recycling of funds and encouraging more investors into the market and an IPO feeder market is integral to this (Baldock 2016; Mason and Owen 2016).

(x) Business angel

A business angel investor is someone who invests their own money in a small business in exchange for a minority stake (usually between 10% and 25%). Business angels tend to be entrepreneurs or people with extensive experience in the business world. They are private investors rather than institutions.

However, angel investment is about more than just money. Business angels offer mentoring and support, and businesses that receive investment will generally benefit from the investor's time, skills, contacts and business knowledge. They take a hands-on approach as they will spend lots of time with the entrepreneur and help to push the business forward. It is, therefore, important for a business angel and the entrepreneur to have a strong relationship, as they are likely to spend a considerable amount of time working closely together.

The benefits of angel investors include:

1 **Expert mentoring** – An angel investor offers strategic, financial and sector-related advice to help achieve growth in the business.
2 **Retain control** – Angel investors typically take a 10% to 25% share of your business, which leaves the business owner firmly in control.
3 **Validation** – Business angels can give the business credibility for later rounds of investment (for example, from venture capitalists).

(xi) Initial public offering

An initial public offering (IPO) is the process of offering shares of a private company to the public in a new stock issuance for the first time. An IPO allows a company to raise equity capital from public investors.

Fernando (2021) indicates that the transition from a private to a public company can be an important time for private investors to fully realize gains from their investment as it typically includes a share premium for current private investors. It also allows public investors to participate in the offering.

An IPO is an important step for a company as it provides the company with access to raising a lot of money (Fernando 2022) which allows the company to grow and expand. Fernando (2022) argues that the increased transparency and share listing credibility can also be a factor in helping it obtain better terms when seeking borrowed funds as well.

When a company reaches a stage in its growth process where it believes it is mature enough for the rigours of SEC regulations along with the benefits and responsibilities to public shareholders, it starts to advertise its interest in going public. IPOs can now be auctioned on the internet, which is an innovation that has further reduced the cost of small businesses going public (Hurt 2015).

(xii) Crowdfunding

The landscape of corporate financing has been significantly altered as a result of the development of technology. According to Belleflamme *et al.* (2014), in this day and age of information technology, business owners now have the ability to make use of a different strategy referred to as crowdfunding as an alternative way to raise money for their companies. Corroborating this, Belleflamme *et al.* (2014) suggest that the past decade has seen the expansion of information technologies, which has had a significant impact on the financing practice known as "crowdfunding".

The term "crowdfunding" originated from the concept of "crowdsourcing", which is about using the "crowd" to acquire ideas, feedback, thoughts and solutions to create corporate activities. Crowdfunding refers to the practice of raising money from a large number of individuals through the use of the internet. In addition, Riedl (2013) and Khan *et al.* (2017) state that crowdfunding gives veritable assistance for entrepreneurs who are adopting and exploiting new sources of finance for their businesses.

Crowdfunding (CF) has the capacity to change the capital structure of ventures, which can then affect the future funding requirements for entrepreneurs. One of the main reasons for the growth of CF is the challenges entrepreneurs faced in obtaining financing through traditional means. CF enables the entrepreneur to appeal to a pool of potential investors (funders) who may then provide small amounts of money in support of the venture. Empirical literature suggests that motives vary between crowdfunders and traditional fundraising. For instance, while the crowd investors may lack the expertise to assess the viability and/or profitability of projects and are not able to assess the risks and uncertainties of the subject ventures, they may be willing to support projects with small donations if they identify with the projects, thereby providing social proof of the concept (De Buysere *et al*. 2012; Yu *et al*. 2017).

Crowdfunding derives from crowdsourcing and micro-finance, but it is a unique class of fundraising, made possible by social media and dedicated internet sites (Morduch 1999; Poetz and Schreier 2012). Crowdfunding explores the availability of vast networks of people (the crowd) and the convenience of the internet to bring funders and project owners together. This combination thus increases the pool of investors beyond the traditional circles and has created the opportunity for project owners to raise money from anyone with funds to invest. Crowdfunding provides opportunities to innovators and entrepreneurs to pitch to a crowd of investors wherever they might be around the globe. Chapter 2 deals with the subject of crowdfunding in greater details.

Summary

Before now the main sources of entrepreneurial finance had been the traditional sources of funding. However, with the advancement of technology, the financing sources for entrepreneurship have taken a new dimension all together. In recent years, crowdfunding has emerged as a veritable source of funding for start-ups, particularly in developed nations such as the United States, the United Kingdom, Canada and Germany, where public policies and regulatory frameworks have also been largely established. In recent years, crowdfunding has developed into a competitive alternative to more conventional sources of early-stage capital, and this trend is expected to continue. A recent global industry report on crowdfunding places the volume of crowdfunding in 2015 at an estimated \$34.4 billion, which is an increase from \$16.2 billion in 2014 and \$6.1 billion in 2013 (Massolution 2015). Over 218,000 businesses across the United States raised capital through various online alternative finance platforms in 2016, contributing to the industry's total market volume in the United States reaching \$35.2 billion in that same year (Ziegler *et al*. 2017).

This book is part of a larger effort to promote the three-pillars architecture for crowdfunding (Aderemi *et al*. 2021), and like the subject matter itself, it is a collaborative endeavour. The more individuals participate in relevant research, the faster and better the industry will grow. Whether you are a novice in this sector, a seasoned explorer, or just a curious cat, this is an open invitation to collaborate in investigation and knowledge sharing. In addition to enlightening and introducing readers to the topic of crowdfunding, this book intends to elevate the level of discourse in academic circles and beyond. It seeks to stimulate thought and debate on this intriguing topic. It is also intended to provide tools to those who recognize promise in the phenomenon of crowdfunding. Moreover, it is a call to investors, entrepreneurs, researchers, academics, government organizations, and all stakeholders to join the debate and enrich it by contributing their perspectives and thus help cultivate, develop and grow the crowdfunding industry.

Discussion questions

1 "In addition to meeting the requirements for the number of employees and one of the two financial thresholds, a small and medium-sized enterprise (SME) is required to be independent." What are the basic requirements for the definition of the SME according to the European Union?
2 "While entrepreneurs exhibit certain traits, they also share some common characteristics." What are the key characteristics of successful entrepreneurs?
3 "Small and large firms differ both in the way they structure their capital and in the way they arrive at their financing decisions." Discuss the key considerations for small firms as regards capital structure.
4 Enumerate and discuss the key sources of entrepreneurial finance.

Test questions

1 To what extent do you see yourself as enterprising and/or entrepreneurial?
2 Students should break into two groups to debate the following:

(a) Entrepreneurs are special and have to be born.
(b) Entrepreneurial skills can be acquired and the environment that fosters entrepreneurship is important.
(c) In arguing statements (a) and (b), the groups should debate which of the two statements is the most credible and persuasive case.

3 What personality traits would you associate with successful entrepreneurs?

Glossary of key terminologies

Capital generation   The conscious efforts of the enterprise owners to increase its capital for use.
Community legislation   Regulations, directives and decisions of general application, binding on all member states.
Entrepreneurship   The way by which new products and services are created through the acquisition of knowledge.
Financial asset   A liquid asset that gets its value from a contractual right or ownership claim.
Financial ceiling   The maximum permitted level in a financial transaction.
Information asymmetry   An imbalance between two negotiating parties in their knowledge of relevant factors and details.
Innovation   The practice of developing and introducing new things.
SME   Small and medium-sized enterprises.

Recommended reading

1 Kozubíková, L., Belás, J., Bilan, Y., and Bartoš, P., 2015. Personal characteristics of entrepreneurs in the context of perception and management of business risk in the SME segment. *Economics and Sociology*, 8 (1), 41–54.

2 Nair, K.R.G., and Pandey, A., 2006. Characteristics of entrepreneurs: An empirical analysis. *The Journal of Entrepreneurship*, 15 (1), 47–61. Available from: https://doi.org/10.1177/097135570501500104
3 Serrasqueiro, Z.S., Armada, M.R., and Nunes, P.M., 2011. Pecking Order Theory versus Trade-Off Theory: are service SMEs' capital structure decisions different? *Service Business*, 5 (4), 381–409.

References

Abell, P., and Nisar, T.M., 2007. Performance effects of venture capital firm networks. *Management Decision*, 45 (5), 923–936.
Aderemi, A.M., Maulida, S., and Maikabara, A.A., 2021. Prospects and challenges of crowdfunding as an alternative funding option in Nigeria. *Muqtasid: Jurnal Ekonomi dan Perbankan Syariah*, 12 (1), 17–31.
Ahmetoglu, G., 2018. *Every entrepreneur has a vision, but few are visionary!* Available from: www.linkedin.com/pulse/every-entrepreneur-has-vision-few-visionary-dr-gorkan-ahmetoglu [Accessed 14 March 2023].
Amini, S., 2013. The amount of raised capital by small IPOs: Spatial effect on the UK alternative investment market. *International Journal of Entrepreneurial Behavior & Research*, 19 (3), 344–358.
Austin, S., Berry, A., Faulkner, S., Johnson, J., and Hughes, M., 1995. Finance, new technology and SMEs: A comparative study of the UK and France. *In*: F. Chittenden, M. Robertson and I. Marshall, eds. *Small firms – Partnerships for growth*. Orange: Chapman.
Baldock, R., 2016. An assessment of the business impact of the UK's Enterprise Capital Funds. *Environment and Planning C: Government Policy*, 34 (8), 1556–1581.
Bank of England, 1998. *Finance for small firms, A fifth report*, January. Bank of England: Bank of England Quarterly Bulletin.
Bank of England, 1999. *Finance for small firms, A sixth report*, January. Bank of England: Bank of England Quarterly Bulletin.
Bank of England, 2000. *Finance for small firms, A seventh report*, January. Bank of England: Bank of England Quarterly Bulletin.
Bank of England, 2001. *Finance for small firms, An eighth report*, March. Bank of England: Bank of England Quarterly Bulletin.
Barkham, R., Gudgin, G., Hart, M., and Hanvey, E., 1996. *The determinants of small firm growth: An inter-regional study in the United Kingdom*. London: Jessica Kingsley Publishers, 1986–1990.
Belleflamme, P., Lambert, T., and Schwienbacher, A., 2014. Individual crowdfunding practices. *Venture Capital*, 15 (4), 313–333.
Bennett, K., 2019. *What is meant by transformational leadership?*. Available from: https://smallbusiness.chron.com/characteristics-visionary-leadership-31332.html [Accessed 15 March 2023].
Berger, A.N., and Udell, G.F., 1998. The economics of small business finance: The roles of private equity and debt markets in the financial growth cycle. *Journal of Banking & Finance*, 22 (6–8), 613–673.
Beugelsdijk, S., and Noorderhaven, N., 2005. Personality characteristics of self-employed; an empirical study. *Small Business Economics*, 24 (2), 159–167.
Binks, M., and Ennew, C., 1996. Financing small firms. *In*: P. Burns and J. Dewhurst, eds. *Small business and entrepreneurship*. London: Macmillan Press.

Binks, M., Ennew, C., and Reed, G., 1993. *Small Businesses and their Banks 1992*. Knutsford: Forum of Private Business.

Binks, M.R., 1987. *Long term debt and the financing of investment in the UK*. New York: Employment Department, Springer.

Birley, S., Westhead, P., 1994. A taxonomy of business start-up reasons and their impact on firm growth and size. *The Journal of Business Venturing*, 9, 7–31.

British Chamber of Commerce, 1997. Small firms survey no. 24: finance. *BCC*, July. Available from: https://www.britishchambers.org.uk/page/policy-and-media-centre/policy-reports-publications/tax [Accessed 24 May 2021].

Bruton, G., Khavul, S., Siegel, D., and Wright, M., 2015. New financial alternatives in seeding entrepreneurship: Microfinance, crowdfunding, and peer – to – peer innovations. *Entrepreneurship Theory and Practice*, 39 (1), 9–26.

Burns, P., 2022. *Entrepreneurship and Small business: Start-up, growth and maturity*. 5th ed. London: Macmillan Education Limited.

Campbell, S., 2020. *Discipline is what leads to success*. Available from: www.entrepreneur.com/leadership/discipline-is-what-leads-to-success/321379 [Accessed 15 March 2023].

Carpenter, R.E., and Peterson, B.C., 2002. Capital market imperfections, high-tech investment, and new equity financing. *The Economic Journal*, 112, 54–72.

CFI, 2022. *Capital structure*. Available from: https://corporatefinanceinstitute.com/resources/accounting/capital-structure-overview/ [Accessed 27 January 2023].

Cooper, S., 1987. *Financial management, EW FACT professional studies series (ACCA)*. London: Emile Woolf and Associates.

Cosh, A., Cumming, D., and Hughes, A., 2009. Outside enterpreneurial capital. *The Economic Journal*, 119 (540), 1494–1533.

Cosh, A., and Hughes, A., 1994. Size, financial structure and profitability: UK companies in the 1980s'. *In*: A. Hughes and D. Storey, eds. *Finance and the small firm*. London: Routledge.

Cowing, M., Samuels, J., Sugden, R., and Love, J., 1991. Small firms and scottish clearing banks. *Quarterly Economic Commentary*, 17 (2), 64–69.

Cumming, D., Deloof, M., Manigart, S., and Wright, M., 2019. New directions in entrepreneurial finance. *Journal of Banking & Finance*, 100, 252–260.

De Buysere, K., Gajda, O., Kleverlaan, R., Marom, D., and Klaes, M., 2012. *A framework for European crowdfunding*. Available from: https://www.fundraisingschool.it/wp-content/uploads/2013/02/European-Crowdfunding-Framework-Oct-2012.pdf

Deakins, D., and Freel, M., 2012. *Entrepreneurship and small firms*. 6th ed. London: McGraw-Hill.

Deakins, D., and Hussain, G., 1994. Risk assessment with asymmetric information. *International Journal of Bank Marketing*, 12 (1), 24–31.

Edwards, G.T., 1987. *The role of banks in economic development*. 1st ed. London: Palgrave Macmillan.

Ekanem, I., 2002. *The investment decision-making process in small manufacturing Enterprises: with particular reference to printing and clothing industries*. Thesis (PhD). Middlesex University.

Ekanem, I., Owen, R., and Cardoso, A., 2019. The influence of institutional environment on venture capital development in emerging economies: The example of Nigeria. *Strategic Change*, 28, 95–107.

European Union, 2020. *User guide to the SME definition*. Luxembourg: Publications Office of the European Union.

Fernando, J., 2021. *Initial Public Offering (IPO)*. Available from: https://www.investopedia.com/terms/i/ipo.asp [Accessed 01 May 2022].

Fraser, S., Bhaumik, S.K., and Wright, M., 2015. What do we know about entrepreneurial finance and its relationship with growth? *International Small Business Journal*, 33 (1), 70–88.

Frese, M., and Gielnik, M.M., 2014. The psychology of entrepreneurship. *Annual Review of Organizational Psychology and Organizational Behavior*, 1 (1), 413–438.

Gartner, W.B., Frid, C.J., and Alexander, J.C., 2012. Financing the emerging firm. *Small Business Economics*, 39 (3), 745–761.

Gilson, R.J., 2003. Engineering a venture capital market: Lessons from the American experience. *Stanford Law Review*, 55, 1067–1068.

Global Linker, 2021. *What does 'independence' mean to entrepreneurs?* Available from: www.globallinker.com/bizforum/article/what-does-lsquoindependence-mean-to-entrepreneurs/1245#/overlay/signup/articleview/1245 [Accessed 16 March 2023].

Harris, M., and Raviv, A., 1990. Capital structure and the informational role of debt. *The Journal of Finance*, 45 (2), 321–349.

Harrison, R., 2013. Crowdfunding and the revitalisation of the early stage risk capital market: Catalyst or Chimera? *Venture Capital*, 15 (4), 283–287.

Hurt, C., 2015. Pricing disintermediation: Crowdfunding and online auction IPOs. *University of Illinois Law Review*, 2015 (1), 2015.

Hvide, H.K., and Panos, G.A., 2014. Risk tolerance and entrepreneurship. *Journal of Financial Economics*, 111 (1), 200–223.

Ideh, S., 2017. *Quick win tips for entrepreneurs (Entrepreneurial Development Series)*. Basildon, UK: Nukan Publications.

Jiang, P., Cai, C., Keasey, C., Wright, M., and Zhang, Q., 2014. The role of venture capitalist in small and medium-sized enterprise initial public offerings: Evidence from China. *International Small Business Journal*, 32 (6), 619–643.

Keasey, K., and Watson, R., 1993. *Small firm management: Ownership, finance and performance*. Oxford: Blackwell.

Keasey, K., and Watson, R., 1994. The bank financing of small firms in UK: Issues and evidence. *Small Business Economics*, 6, 349–362.

Khan, M.K., Zhao, X., Akram, U., Hashim, M., and Kaleem, A., 2017. Crowdfunding: An innovative approach to start up with entrepreneurship. *In*: *Proceedings of the tenth international conference on management science and engineering management*. Singapore: Springer, 1293–1304.

Knörr, H., Alvarez, C., and Urbano, D., 2013. Entrepreneurs or employees: A cross-cultural cognitive analysis. *International Entrepreneurship and Management Journal*, 9 (2), 273–294.

Kumar, C., 2019. *What is the role of an entrepreneur in economic development?* Available from: www.preservearticles.com/business/role-of-an-entrepreneur-in-economic-development/1770 [Accessed 14 March 2023].

La Rocca, M., La Rocca, T., and Cariola, A., 2011. Capital structure decisions during a firm's life cycle. *Small Business Economics*, 37, 107–130.

Lavinsky, D., 2010. Funding fathers. *Smart Business Online*. Available from: https://www.archives.gov/publications/prologue/2010/winter/founders.html founders [Accessed 12 March 2023].

Li, Y., and Zahra, S.A., 2012. Formal institutions, culture and venture capital activity: A cross-country analysis. *Journal of Business Venturing*, 27, 95–111.

Lingelbach, D., 2015. Developing venture capital when institutions change. *Venture Capital: An International Journal of Entrepreneurial Finance*, 17 (4), 327–363.

López-Gracia, J., and Sogorb-Mira, F., 2008. Testing trade-off and pecking order theories financing SMEs. *Small Business Economics*, *31*(2), 117–136.

Lutz, E., Bender, M., Achleitner, A., and Kaserer, C., 2013. Importance of spatial proximity between venture capital investors and investees in Germany. *Journal of Business Research*, 66 (11), 2346–2354.

Mason, C., and Brown, R., 2013. Creating good public policy to support high growth firms. *Small Business Economics*, 40 (2), 211–225.

Mason, C., and Owen, R., 2016. Developing a globalisation of venture capital thesis: How are small, peripheral economies seeking to establish sustainable venture capital ecosystems? *In: Paper to entfin conference*, 8–9 July. Lyon: University of Lyon.

Massolution, C.L., 2015. *Crowdfunding industry report*. Available from: http://reports. crowdsourcing. org/index. php.

McKenna, P., 2023. *Innovative Entrepreneurship: Definition, Tips and FAQs*. Available from: www.indeed.com/career-advice/career-development/innovative-entrepreneurship [Accessed 15 March 2023].

Metelka, A., 2014. *Crowdfunding-startups' alternative funding source beyond banks, business angels and venture capitalists*. Master Thesis Entrepreneurship. Blekinge Institute of Technology, School of Management. Available from: https://www.diva-portal.org/smash/get/diva2:831531/FULLTEXT01.pdf [Accessed 15 March 2023].

Modigliani, F., and Miller, M.H., 1958. The cost of capital, corporation finance and the theory of finance. *American Economic Review*, 261–297.

Morduch, J., 1999. The microfinance promise, *Journal of Economic Literature*, 37 (4), 1569–1614.

North, D., Baldock, R., and Ekanem, I., 2010. Is there a debt finance gap relating to Scottish SMEs? A demand-side perspective, *Venture Capital: An International Journal of Entrepreneurial Finance*, 12 (3), 173–192.

North, D., Baldock, R., and Ullah, F., 2013. Funding the growth of UK technology-based small firms since the financial crash: Are there breakages in the finance escalators? *Venture Capital*, 15 (3), 237–260.

Omerzel, G.D., and Kušce, I., 2013. The influence of personal and environmental factors on entrepreneurs' performance. *Kybernetes*, 42 (6), 906–927. Available from: http://dx.doi. org/10.1108/K-08-2012-0024.

Owen, R., 2015. *The future of early stage and growth finance in Northern Ireland*. Report to the Department for Enterprise, Trade and Investment (DETI).

Payne, G., Davis, J., Moore, C., and Bell, R., 2009. The deal structuring stage of the venture capitalist decision-making process: Exploring confidence and control. *Journal of Small Business Management*, 47 (2), 154–179.

Poetz, M.K., and Schreier, M., 2012. The value of crowdsourcing: Can users really compete with professionals in generating new product ideas? *Journal of Product Innovation Management*, 29 (2), 245–256.

Poutziouris, P., Chittenden, F., and Michaelas, N., 1999. *The financial affairs of private companies: Research*. Manchester, UK: MBS, University of Manchester.

Riedl, J., 2013. Crowdfunding technology innovation. *Computer*, 46 (3), 100–103.

Sannajust, A., Roux, F., and Chaibi, A., 2014. Crowdfunding in France: A new revolution? *Journal of Applied Business Research (JABR)*, 30 (6), 1919–1928.

Sarasvathy, S., 2008. *Effectuation: Elements of entrepreneurial expertise*. Cheltenham: Edward Elgar.

Scheela, W., and Van Dihn, N., 2004. Venture capital in a transition economy: The case of Vietnam. *Venture Capital*, 6 (4), 333–350.

Schwienbacher, A., and Larralde, B., 2010. Crowdfunding of small entrepreneurial ventures. *In*: *Handbook of entrepreneurial finance*. Oxford: Oxford University Press.

Seghers, A., Manigart, S., and Vanacker, T., 2012. The impact of human and social capital on entrepreneurs' knowledge of finance alternatives. *Journal of Small Business Management*, 50 (1), 63–86.

Serrasqueiro, Z., and Nunes, P.M., 2012. Is age a determinant of SMEs' financing decisions? Empirical evidence using panel data models. *Entrepreneurship Theory and Practice*, 36 (4), 627–654.

Serrasqueiro, Z.S., Armada, M.R., and Nunes, P.M., 2011. Pecking order theory versus trade-off theory: Are service SMEs' capital structure decisions different? *Service Business*, 5 (4), 381–409.

Shane, S., and Venkataraman, S., 2000. The promise of entrepreneurship as a field of research, *Academic Management Review*, 25 (1).

Sidik, I.G., 2012. Conceptual framework of factors affecting SME development: Mediating factors on the relationship of entrepreneur traits and SME performance. *Procedia Economics and Finance*, 4, 373–383.

SQW (2015). The future of early stage and growth finance in Northern Ireland. Synthesis Report, https://www.economy-ni.gov.uk/sites/default/files/publications/deti/future-of-early-stage-and-growth-finance-in-ni-synthesis-report-final.pdf [Accessed 15 January 2023].

Tango, J., and Ferragamo, A., 2023. *The traits of entrepreneurs*, Boston, MA: Harvard Business School Technical Note 823–099.

Tuovila, A., 2022. *Capital structure definition, types, importance, and examples*. Available from: www.investopedia.com/terms/c/capitalstructure.asp [Accessed 27 January 2023].

Urban, B., 2013. Social entrepreneurship in an emerging economy: A focus on the institutional environment and SESE. *Managing Global Transitions: An International Research Journal*, 11 (4), 3–25.

Wald, J.K., 1999. How firm characteristics affect capital structure: An international comparison. *Journal of Financial Research*, 22 (2), 161–187.

Waltower, S., 2023. The top reason most entrepreneurs start businesses. *Business News Daily*. Available from: www.businessnewsdaily.com/4652-entrepreneur-motivation-benefits.html [Accessed 15 March 2023].

World Bank, 2020. *Global economic prospects, June 2020*. The World Bank.

Wright Robbie, M.K., 1998. Venture capital and private equity: A review and synthesis. *Journal of Business Finance & Accounting*, 25 (5–6), 521–570.

Yu, S., Johnson, S., Lai, C., Cricelli, A., and Fleming, L., 2017. Crowdfunding and regional entrepreneurial investment: an application of the CrowdBerkeley database. *Research Policy*, 46 (10), 1723–1737.

Ziegler, T., Suresh, K., Garvey, K., *et al.*, 2017. *The annual middle east & Africa alternative finance industry report*. Cambridge: Cambridge Center for Alternative Finance.

2 What is crowdfunding?

Learning objectives

- Define and explain crowdfunding and its types
- Discuss the evolution and benefits of crowdfunding
- Explore the characteristics of crowdfunding entrepreneurs
- Explore how platform intermediaries or funding portals connect investors with entrepreneurs

Introduction

Entrepreneurship forms the mainstay of developed economies and is a vital contributor to employment, economic and export growth. According to the World Bank (2019), globally, small and medium-sized enterprises (SMEs) account for approximately 90% of businesses and over 50% of employment. The report also posits that SMEs are responsible for seven out of every ten jobs in emerging markets.

This clearly illustrates the significance of entrepreneurship and small-scale industries in the economic development of a nation. As a field of research, entrepreneurship is a very well researched phenomenon in the area of entrepreneurial finance. However, entrepreneurial finance has, up to recently, concentrated on conventional sources of funding such as banks, angel investors and venture capital (Metelka 2014).

Despite the growth and importance of entrepreneurship in a nation's economy, the most difficult tasks confronting entrepreneurs are raising adequate seed capital. Lavinsky (2010) explains that a large number of entrepreneurs have difficulties in raising venture capital. But with the advent of technology, the financing sources for entrepreneurs have taken another dimension. The emergence of technology has changed the business financing landscape. Belleflamme *et al.* (2014) state that in the era of information technology, entrepreneurs now have the opportunity to tap into an alternative method of capital generation known as crowdfunding (CF). Corroborating Belleflamme *et al.* (2014), Ma and Liu (2017) assert that the last decade has witnessed the growth of information technologies which has greatly impacted on the financing practice known as "crowdfunding". This means that crowdfunding provides alternative financial resources.

DOI: 10.4324/9781003193975-2

Belleflamme *et al.* (2014) posit that since its inception, "crowdfunding" stems from the concept of "crowdsourcing", which is the practice of soliciting input from a large group of people in order to generate new corporate initiatives. Crowdfunding describes an original model of financing for innovative ventures through the use of new media with a global appeal (Belleflamme *et al.* 2014; Lehner and Nicholls 2014). Khan *et al.* (2017) express that in adopting and utilizing new sources of funds for entrepreneurs, the capital structure of ventures can be altered by crowdfunding, which in turn can have an effect on the funding needs of entrepreneurs in the future (Stocker and Sucharow 2012).

Crowdfunding markets all over the world have seen substantial expansion in recent years. With about €48.5 billion raised globally between 2010 and 2017 (Chervyakov and Rocholl 2019), crowdfunding has drawn increased economic, political and regulatory interest on an international scale. However, numerous problems about the right design, implementation and practicality of these markets remain unresolved.

The majority of crowdfunding transactions take place in North America and the United Kingdom. The European Union's market share (excluding the United Kingdom) remains modest, with little cross-border activity (Zhao 2019). One major factor holding these markets back is Europe's inconsistent and unclear regulatory environment. This is seen even more so in developing economies of Asia-Pacific and Africa where regulation is weak or almost non-existent. This chapter delves into crowdfunding, discussing its merits and pitfalls, analyzing the traits of successful crowdfunding entrepreneurs, the needs of crowdfunding platforms, and providing best tips to increase the likelihood of funding. It also investigates the roles played by platform intermediaries or funding portals in connecting contributors with project owners.

Definition of crowdfunding

Crowdfunding is a process that enables small businesses to raise small units of funds from a large number of individuals for the financing of projects through the use of online technology (Mollick 2014). The financial crises of 2008, in conjunction with the growth of technology related to social media, gave birth to crowdfunding (Bruton *et al.* 2015). Incorporating additional instances of the phenomenon, such as internet-based peer-to-peer (P2P) lending, Mollick (2014) offers a broader definition of "crowdfunding" as "the efforts by entrepreneurial individuals and groups – cultural, social, and for-profit – to fund their ventures by drawing on relatively small contributions from a relatively large number of individuals using the internet, without standard financial intermediaries" (Mollick (2014, p. 1).

Crowdfunding is also defined as "an open call, typically made over the internet, for the availability of financial resources in the form of donations (without rewards) or in exchange for some sort of reward and/or voting rights in order to support initiatives for specific purposes" (Lambert and Schwienbacher 2010, p. 6).

Crowdfunding serves a form of online capital market which bridges barriers and enables small businesses and start-ups to access financing through their social network (Harrison 2013; Valanciene and Jegeleviciute 2013; Colgren 2014). It grew out of earlier forms of fundraising that also relied on a large number of individuals making small contributions (Ordanini *et al.* 2011). Crowdfunding has its roots in the operating involvement of the "crowd" via social media, as hinted by its etymology, which is a composite of "crowd" and "funding" (Kim 2017; Oh and Kim 2017). In comparison to traditional fundraising approaches, crowdfunding is a more effective way to raise awareness and finances for non-profit projects by utilizing social media (Saxton and Wang 2014; Katherine and Daniel 2016).

During the United States' financial crisis of 1990, small business lending dropped by as much as 38%. The 2008 credit crisis worsened a decline in lending, which had already lowered available funds for innovative initiatives by US$14 billion to US$88 billion (Sannajust *et al.* 2014; Comeig *et al.* 2014). According to Bruton *et al.* (2015), the low savings interest regime after the crises encouraged peer-to-peer lending.

The JOBS Act of 2012 was passed in the United States as a response to the rising popularity of crowdfunding campaigns. This law allows small enterprises to raise money on the stock market, which boosts economic growth, employment and innovation (Gobble 2012; Kitchens and Torrence 2012; Kitchens and Torrence 2012; Stemler 2013; Valanciene and Jegeleviciute 2013; Mollick 2014). It also increases investor safety and better capital market conditions for entrepreneurs: that's the result of this piece of regulation.

Crowdfunding, like any emerging topic, is an evolving concept, making full definitions excessively restricting (Mollick 2013). A rare published overview of the subject by Schwienbacher and Larralde (2010) defined the concept as an open invitation, primarily over the internet, for financial support in the form of small contributions in exchange for some type of incentive. Still, this all-encompassing definition leaves out cases that have been labelled "crowdfunding" by academics in other fields, such as social media-based peer-to-peer solicitations (Lin and Viswanathan 2013) and other concerted efforts by fans or friends of project initiators (Burkett 2011). Crowdfunding has numerous current (and likely future) applications; as a result, it is challenging to come across a broad description of the concept. Mollick (2014, p. 2) provides an entrepreneurial context for the phenomenon by defining crowdfunding as "the efforts of entrepreneurial individuals and groups; cultural, social, and for-profit to raise funds for their projects by soliciting modest contributions from a large number of people via the internet, by-passing traditional financial middlemen".

Crowdfunding is different from microfinance, which is a bank-based lending process in which the bank is the only contributor, risk-taker and provider of funds (Adhikary 2015). On the other hand, in a crowdfunding process, small contributors are the suppliers and take on the risk, while the funds come from the crowdfunding platforms (CFPs). Most importantly, companies that want to grow need a lot more money than they can get from microfinance institutions. Crowdfunding uses the power of social networks to help business owners get money. Therefore, crowdfunding fills the gap between microfinancing and big investors (Adhikary 2015).

Crowdfunding generally is a process whereby small businesses or start-ups solicit funding from the public through the facilitation of a crowdfunding platform (CFP). These funds are raised by an aggregate number of investors each contributing a small amount (Ley and Weaven 2011). Crowdfunding is a process which allows people of common interest to support a cause or project through contribution of small amounts (Valanciene and Jegeleviciute 2013).

Crowdfunding, therefore, is a merger of crowdsourcing and microfinance which allows individuals to invest in small businesses or start-ups seamlessly through an online social platform (Fink 2012). The Statue of Liberty is an early example of funding through crowdsourcing (Harrison 2013). Generally, then, crowdfunding is a blend of sociology, finance, management, economics and information systems which allow users to exchange products and ideas effortlessly (Golić 2014; Gerber and Hui 2013). Crowdfunding is a stimulant of the financial systems in that it transfers moneys from small unit backers to socially laudable projects thereby resolving economic challenges as well as rapid urbanization and employment (Golić 2014).

Crowdfunding refers to actions in which the public donates or invests in a diversity of initiatives, from the creation of cultural or creative material to the founding of start-ups, through platforms such as social networks (Mollick 2014). Crowdfunding, unlike conventional fundraising practices such as off-line contributions or the use of automatic response systems (ARS), is not limited by geographical locations.

Other benefits include the ability to use a variety of interpersonal networks through a social networking service (SNS). In addition, the funding mechanism brings efficiency in that it necessitates lower intermediary expenditures such as promotion costs and wages. As a result of these advantages, crowdfunding has become a viable source of financing for non-profit organizations, cultural, creative endeavors, experimental technologies, as well as enterprises that cannot secure conventional financing, such as bank credits or stock offerings (Kim and Lee 2014).

Despite general improvements in credit availability since 2012, small businesses continue to experience difficulty in securing bank finance thus paving the way for the rise of crowdfunding (England *et al*. 2015). Crowdfunding opens the door into a new billion-dollar funds market, bridges the funding gap and enables entrepreneurs to birth their ideas and sustain their business (Stemler 2013; Belleflamme *et al*. 2014). Enterprises can now mitigate their risks by resorting to crowdfunding in place of family and friends or bank loans (Sannajust *et al*. 2014). The crowd-sourced fund, therefore, serves as veritable bridging capital pending when business angels and venture capitalists are interested in the business (Tomczak and Brem 2013). Crowdfunding, therefore, becomes a new source of financing which can plug the financing gaps for entrepreneurs and entrepreneurship.

Advancement in internet technology has brought about the rise of crowdfunding as it enables people to connect, share ideas and create content. It has enabled people to access money regardless of where they live. It also gives users the ability to choose by making information readily available and thus reducing information asymmetries, resulting in a better and more sophisticated market place. Technology also allows for the processing of more information and increased consumption

(Labrecque *et al*. 2013; Valanciene and Jegeleviciute 2013). Furthermore, the shift in market interaction and lower communication costs brought about by the internet has created economic value between sellers and social networks, improving information quality and accessibility while easing project monitoring (Labrecque *et al*. 2013). Technological advancement has brought about increased information access and ease of interaction, thus creating favourable conditions for crowdfunding to thrive (Labrecque *et al*. 2013).

Features of crowdfunding

There is no uniform definition of crowdfunding as of yet. As a result of reviewing a variety of definitions, the following is a summary and main feature of crowdfunding:

1 Crowdfunders – also known as backers, are people who may be well-informed investors. They provide market information and ideas as well as support the projects in other ways but most of all, provide the finance for the business.
2 The financial contribution from each crowdfunder is negligible in contrast to the total amount raised. The more individuals that donate to a project, the more money the project owner will raise, and the better the chance that the crowdfunding campaign will be successful.
3 Crowdfunders may receive rewards, specified privileges, or a specific sum of money as a reward for their contribution. However, donation-based crowdfunders do not expect anything for their support for a project.
4 Every crowdfunding campaign is run on the internet via crowdfunding platforms. Donors can therefore use the internet to gather information about the project and the project owner before making a decision. Because it removes distance barriers between investors and the project, this is another way that crowdfunding differs from conventional forms of funding.

Evolution and development of crowdfunding

While the idea of private individuals lending money without the aid of middlemen is not novel or inventive, the use of online platforms to carry out such transactions makes crowdfunding a novel phenomenon (Bachmann *et al*. 2011). Though crowdfunding has been generally bandied as an innovative approach to project funding, crowdfunding's core concept is not new (Aladejebi 2020). The origin of crowdfunding according to researchers, is the broader concept of crowdsourcing with history dating as far back as the 1700s (Belleflamme *et al*. 2014; Bretschneider *et al*. 2014; Kuppuswamy and Bayus 2015).

The platform for the Statue of Liberty is an example that has been referenced on crowdfunding from time to time. In 1885, the publisher of the *World* newspaper in New York, Joseph Pulitzer, asked the public to donate financially to the installation of a statue and generated $102,000 in five months, with 80% of donors contributing less than $1 each (Harris 1986). British rock band Marillion conducted one of the most well-known and successful crowdfunding initiatives. In 1997, this band's supporters gave $60,000 to assist their North American tour (Vassallo 2014). More recently, in 2008, the Obama campaign organization used crowdfunding to generate almost US$750 million for President Barack Obama's presidential campaign in the United States. People who contributed less than $200 made up about a half of the total number of contributors (Kappel 2009).

Crowdfunding, a long-standing form of microfinance, has seen an increase in popularity since the advent of the internet (Helmer 2011). A growing number of websites on the internet that provide the service known as crowdfunding platforms make crowdfunding possible (Gedda *et al.*, 2016 cited in Aladejebi 2020). Theoretically and practically, crowdfunding has been gaining attention since 2007, but it became more prominent during the 2008 financial crisis in response to the challenges faced by early-stage businesses in obtaining financing (Freedman and Nutting 2015; Mendes-Da-Silva *et al.* 2016; Hussain and Haque 2017). Crowdfunding has become more and more popular in rich nations, and it is now catching on in underdeveloped nations all over the world. The financial crises of 2007–2008 and the quickening development of the internet are responsible for the exponential expansion of crowdfunding. The significance of the financial crisis cannot be overstated. Since the financial crisis in 2008, it is well-known that there has been a significant reduction in bank credit, especially in Europe and North America (and, more crucially, after the bankruptcy of the Lehman Brothers in 2008). As a result, funding for people and small and medium-sized enterprises (SMEs) decreased dramatically during the financial crisis, leaving a need that crowdfunding may fill as a different way to raise money (Dapp 2013; Hagedorn and Pinkwart 2013).

The total volume of funding raised as of 2015 was completely skewed in favour of the three regions of North America, Asia and Europe accounting for 49.94, 30.6 and 18.81% respectively. The three regions together account for nearly all global crowdfunding activity. South America raised 0.25%, while Oceania and Africa raised 0.19 and 0.07% respectively (Leon and Mora 2017). The average yearly growth rate of sums raised between 2011 and 2017 is the strongest indicator of the quick ascent of the market. This growth rate averaged approximately 80% in the United States, 85% in Europe, and 557% in Asia throughout that time period. When compared to the trends that existed prior to 2015, the rate of growth of crowdfunding in Europe in 2017 remained very low at only 34% (Chervyakov and Rocholl 2019). A historical timeline of crowdfunding is shown in Table 2.1.

The development of crowdfunding resulted in the adoption of pertinent legislation to regulate its activities in many nations. The United States of America became the first country in the world to establish and carry out legislation for equity crowdfunding when the Jumpstart Our Business Start-ups (JOBS) Act of 2012 was passed into law in 2012. By 2016, the US Securities and Exchange Commission had put these regulations into effect (Catalini *et al.* 2016). Soon after, other nations including Italy, France, Germany, Belgium, the United Kingdom, Austria and Nigeria followed suit (Egene 2016; Hornuf and Schwienbacher 2017). Although they may take a different approach, these policies all essentially aim to reduce the risks faced by investors. A bare minimum of information must often be disclosed to comply with regulations, both concerning the issuer of the security and the operations of the company.

Table 2.1 Timeline of crowdfunding

1886	The pedestal on which the Statue of Liberty stands gets crowdfunded by New York citizens.
2000	ArtistShare, the first reward based crowdfunding website for music, launches the dedicated crowdfunding platform to help artists obtain funds.
2000	Internet-enabled giving goes mainstream with the emergence of sites such as JustGiving, which is the first major microloan platform for entrepreneurs in underprivileged countries.
2005	Michael Sullivan, founder of FundaVlog, is credited with coining the term "crowdfunding".
2006	First peer-to-peer lending platform is released with Prosper with the launch of ZOPA.
2008	The Economic crisis occurs, big banks begin to cut back small business lending.
2008	Indiegogo launches reward-based crowdfunding platform.
2009	Kickstarter launches reward-based crowdfunding platform.
2010	AngelList unveils equity-based angel investing. Gofundme launches charity-based crowdfunding.
2011	Crowdfunder and CircleUp launch equity-based platforms; Obama Administration reveals the Start-up America Initiative focused on rebooting small business.
2011	Obama Administration passes the Jumpstart Our Business Start-up Act a.k.a. JOBS Act.
2014	Kickfurther launches first inventory-based crowdfunding platform.
2015	Title III of the JOBS Act passes allowing non-accredited investors to invest in equity of companies.

Sources: Adapted from Nesta, 2013; Freedman & Nutting, 2015; Chen, 2016; Fundable, 2017

In addition, there are limits placed on the total amount that an individual crowd investor is permitted to contribute, which may be determined by the total amount of investable wealth the individual possesses, as well as caps placed on the total sum that an individual issuer is permitted to bring in during a given calendar year (Hervé and Schwienbacher 2018). It is now possible for small businesses to obtain funding through the capital market, which will contribute to the expansion of the economy, the creation of new jobs, and the stimulation of innovative thinking. These rules have improved the conditions of the capital markets for business owners while ensuring the safety of investors (Gobble 2012; Kitchens and Torrence 2012; Mollick 2013; Valanciene and Jegeleviciute 2013; Kitchens and Torrence 2012; Mollick 2014; Stemler 2013).

Types of crowdfunding

Based on investor and consumer outcomes, five crowdfunding categories have been identified: reward-based, product pre-sales, donations, equities and securities and peer-to-peer lending. This categorization is based on investor and consumer benefits and outcomes (Mollick 2014; Belleflamme *et al.* 2014). Although each venture is unique and limited to specific online social platforms, they all employ the concept of large numbers of investors supporting with small amounts of money. Crowdfunding categories also vary in terms of complexity, return on investment, decision power, originality and contracts (Meric *et al.* 2015). Additionally, crowd-funding offers benefits for public relations, market research and the legitimacy of projects (Meric *et al.* 2015). Mollick (2014) and Massolution (2015) categorize crowdfunding into four models: donation, reward, lending and equity-based. Ark-rot *et al.* (2017) and Leon and Mora (2017) categorize crowdfunding into dona-tion-based, reward-based, equity-based, and royalty-based lending, based on the scopes, motives and outcomes.

The non-financial return models and the financial return models, each having two types, make up the framework of crowdfunding models. These kinds of crowd-funding are equity-based, lending-based, donation-based, and reward-based, de-pending on the type of return provided to potential funders (De Buysere *et al.* 2012; Bretschneider *et al.* 2014).

Financial crowdfunding involves the assumption that the investor would receive a financial return on his investment; as a result, the incentives and desire to invest are typically centred on money. This term encompasses equity, loan and royalty crowdfunding mechanisms (Andersen and Mauritzen 2015). The converse is true for non-financial crowdfunding, as there is no direct way for the crowdfunder to re-ceive a financial return on their contribution. Non-financial crowdfunding models include reward and donation campaigns, while the goals of the crowdfunders may vary (Andersen and Mauritzen 2015).

(i) Donation-based crowdfunding

Donation-based crowdfunding (DBC), which is non-financial return-based, is mostly used by non-profit organizations and civic groups to generate money (Mol-lick 2014). To help a given initiative reach its bigger financing goal, people make tiny donations (mostly charitable in type). Investors contribute to projects through "donation-based" crowdfunding with no expectation of receiving anything in re-turn (Dushnitsky and Marom 2013; Fink 2012).

With DBC, fundraisers can submit an online request for funding, notably from social and cultural organizations, creative businesses and community-based or-ganizations. By connecting contributors with fundraisers and recipients of modest, regional philanthropy and public good projects, DBC seeks to eliminate the mid-dleman in the traditional charitable giving industry.

(ii) Rewards-based crowdfunding

This is a non-financial return-based crowdfunding where individuals contrib-ute small amounts to finance specific projects. Investors are given a small gift for their contributions with the rewards-based crowdfunding model. This gift which cannot be company equity can be such items as signed mementos, opportunity to meet with celebrities, and are usually tiered according to the size of donation made or some other intrinsic value (Valanciene and Jegeleviciute 2013; Colombo *et al.* 2015). This type of funding is thus popular because of the social reputation and the intrinsic value of participating (Cholakova and Clarysse 2015).

In spite of the popularity of rewards-based crowdfunding (RBC), project initiators must take proper care in budgeting for the projects as well as the gifts as the cost of gifts including shipping has been estimated to be about 50% of needed fund (Buff and Alhadeff 2013). Kickstarter (2015) estimates $25 as the most common level of rewards, and average contribution as $70. Appropriate budgeting is needful to avoid underfunding and financial loss.

(iii) Product pre-sale crowdfunding

Supporters of the product pre-sales model (also known as prepayment) anticipate receiving "a physical but non-monetary incentive or product" in exchange for their contributions at a later date. In an RBC project, backers would make monetary contributions and receive incentives at varying levels (Burtch *et al.* 2013; Lin and Viswanathan 2016; Thürridl and Kamleitner 2016; Zhang *et al.* 2020). Prepayment enables project initiators to raise money to fund the initial cost of production and inventory. This model allows the entrepreneur to discriminate in pricing, allowing early purchasers to pay less than the market price (Belleflamme *et al.* 2014). Investors get prototypes. The corporation undertakes market research in addition to finance because the crowdfunding campaign's success indicates investor interest in the product. Innovative enterprises and small goods suit this type (Rossi 2014). The risk with this method is that the final product may be delivered late or never delivered as promised.

(iv) Peer-to-peer lending crowdfunding

Investors have more control over the projects they fund, the amounts they lend, and the rates of return they receive when using peer-to-peer lending. The majority of businesses that are run for profit make use of peer-to-peer lending. Because these loans are unsecured, there is a greater possibility of defaulting on them (Bruton *et al.* 2015). Kiva.org is currently the most widely used venue for online peer-to-peer lending (Meyskens and Bird 2015; Burtch *et al.* 2014). Both Puddle and Prosper are well-known names in the world of peer-to-peer lending platforms (Meyskens and Bird 2015).

Peer-to-peer loans are the most common type of fundraising activity for debt-based crowdfunding platforms. Between the years 2010 and 2017, approximately €37.4 billion was raised through peer-to-peer lending across the globe, of which €11.8 billion was raised in the EU alone (Chervyakov and Rocholl 2019). According to a study that was conducted by Baeck *et al.* (2014), peer-to-peer (P2P) business lending experienced an astounding growth of 288% in 2014, going from £193 million in 2013 to £749 million in 2014. As a result, it has emerged as a significant player in the consumer credit scene in the UK. It is more difficult to do market research with this model in comparison to earlier versions, and there are legal ambiguities with regard to the insurance of both individuals and businesses. These are both disadvantages of this model.

(v) Equity and securities crowdfunding

Consumers can take part in new or existing businesses, either directly or indirectly, through equity and security crowdfunding, also known as investment-based crowdfunding. This type of crowdfunding involves the purchase of investments such as shares or debentures by consumers. Fundraisers come from diverse areas, including high technology, health care and consumer goods. Under the JOBS Act, a company can offer stakes to the public through this sort of crowdfunding (2012). The Act permits the Securities Exchange Commission (SEC) to oversee the process by loosening some of its stringent restrictions involving financial burden, accounting and disclosure requirements, and the maximum amount that can be raised over a 12-month period (Williamson 2013; Stemler 2013; Gelfond and Foti 2012; Aronson 2013; Levine and Feigin 2014). Websites such as Crowdfunder, Early Shares, In Crowd Capital, and Start-up offer equity-funding (Stemler 2013). Due to the absence of a secondary market for these assets, the only way for investors to generate a return on their investments is to purchase shares either directly from the management of the company or from other corporations during the takeover (Čondić-Jurkić 2015). Compared to peer-to-peer lending, the average amount funded is more (Zhao 2019).

(vi) Royalty crowdfunding

In royalty crowdfunding, the entrepreneur obtains funds in exchange for a royalty fee or a part of future sales or profits based on the amount invested (Outlaw 2013; Massolution 2015). This means that with royalty crowdfunding, backers invest in a project or company and once the project and/or company generates revenue, all backers get a percentage of that revenue. For example, if royalty crowdfunding is used to develop and launch a new software product, the money would be used to build and release the software. Once the software brings in revenue, a percentage of that revenue would be given back to the investors who backed the product.

Royalty crowdfunding is excellent if cash is needed to fund a project in its early stages provided there are people to believe in the product, service, or business being developed (and, more specifically, its potential for profit). However, it can be harder to get backers since there is no guarantee on their investment (if the product does not generate revenue, investors will not see their royalties). FreshBooks (2022) argues that if rewards-based crowdfunding is the best-known form of crowdfunding, then royalty crowdfunding is arguably the least.

(vii) Hybrid crowdfunding

Multiple methods of crowdfunding are combined to create hybrid crowdfunding. This funding technique may be advantageous for corporations and crowdfunders alike (De Buysere *et al.* 2012). If an entrepreneur employs a combination of incentive and loan crowdfunding, for instance, the crowdfunder will receive both monetary and non-monetary rewards.

A fictional case study of rewards-based crowdfunding

Carla's designer lights

Setting the stage

Carla is a designer based in Prague. She has recently finished building a prototype of her designer lighting system. It is an ultra-modern concept using recycled industrial materials and the system received praise at last year's Milan's Design expo. She has lined up a manufacturer that will develop the main parts as well as a small team to put the lights together, arrange deliveries and installations. In total this means that in order for Carla to start her business she needs to find €41k to cover her costs during the first six months. Given that she wants to sell each of the lights at €200 a piece this means that she needs to sell 205 pieces to cover her costs for the first six months. She considered approaching the bank for a loan but given her lack of collateral, outstanding student loan and short time in business, she realized she would not meet the basic qualifications. She decided to try crowdfunding.

Preparation

Carla spent the first week researching crowdfunding websites. She collected and read blogs and articles about rewards crowdfunding, and she identified and investigated interesting examples that were similar to hers and that were successful. By the end of that week she felt she understood what it was and what she needed to do. Carla had her product accredited and ready to go and had already thought through her business concept and financials, so she turned her attention to understanding the crowd, her customers. Via social media, she identified influencers in her field, respected individuals with a solidly engaged following that could help share her message. She spent time talking to these people, joining conversations and making friends and connections, so that when she was ready to launch her campaign she had a strong online crowd to support her. She chose a platform which she knew to be reputable, with the right kind of audience, but on which she could still have high visibility.

Creating the pitch

Carla knew the pitch was crucial to her success so she took great care to carefully hone her story. She spent time considering her story and key messages, and the rewards (one of them being the designer light itself, a €200 pledge). Carla knew from her research of other crowdfunding projects that a short video would be essential to help tell her story, demonstrate the quality of her design, and help backers get to know her, her team, and the company ethos. She made a film showing her constructing a light and created a webpage for her business, so she could add her products and describe them further. Carla also arranged a videoconference with the platform's advisor to ask her to review her campaign and suggest improvements, as well as checking for any technical or legal issues applicable in Prague. Carla spent three weeks meeting and speaking to a lot of people, doing her research and creating a crowd around her project. When Carla thought that the buzz was large enough, she launched the campaign.

Fundraising

As soon as the campaign launched, Carla started to work on the next phase of the crowdfunding process. Carla spent time on her campaign every day, talking to her crowd, letting them know that the campaign was live, encouraging them to participate and to share it with their friends. She talked to journalists and found a lot of interest in her crowdfunding quest as well as her innovative products as a result. Carla received messages from interested people asking questions, and also comments suggesting features she had not thought of and other improvements. She took these on board, and thanked each one of those making suggestions, as part of her efforts to nurture her crowd.

Post-campaign

Carla's campaign worked and she was able to exceed her target, with 145 lights sold! It was a great success, since not only did she have enough to start production, build stock and cover her costs for three months, but she was also able to sell half of her stock of lights before they even arrived from the factory. The first thing Carla did was to put the production process in motion and thanked all the people involved. She then created a production timetable and informed her crowd when they could expect their lights to be delivered, and began all the admin involved in starting to operate as a business. But Carla did not stop interacting with her crowd. She gave them regular updates on progress and tapped into their expertise when questions arose. Because they became enthusiastic users of her products they also became her best advocates, acting as a marketing and PR platform to spread the word further, helping sell even more of her lights.

Source: Adapted from https://ec.europa.eu/docsroom/documents/8984/attachments/1/translations/en/renditions/native

Crowdfunding platforms

Entrepreneurs and investors use crowdfunding platforms as an active intermediary. To begin with, platforms enforce crowdfunding regulations to monitor transactions between funders and founders. Second, they institute and implement procedures and rules to mitigate the risks associated with crowdfunding. In addition, they offer project-specific value-added services. The majority of crowdfunding campaigns currently take place on dedicated platforms, but this was not the case initially. Although the platform functions as an intermediary, its function is distinct from that of conventional intermediaries like banks (Allen and Santomero 2001; Boot and Thakor 2000). The latter chooses initiatives independently, whereas a crowdfunding platform defers to the crowd.

Prior to the advent of Indiegogo in 2008 and Kickstarter in 2009, few fundraisers put up their own website to launch a crowdfunding campaign (Belleflamme *et al.* 2013). The British software business Trampoline Systems, for example, attempted to raise $1 million without using any platform to support its development. They eventually limited their securities sales to accredited investors.

There is a plethora of platforms available nowadays; some specialize in specific project areas, while others are generalists. Some follow an all-or-nothing funding strategy, requiring that a fundraising threshold be met first, while others follow a keep-it-all funding model, enabling all funds to be maintained; still others allow entrepreneurs to choose between the two (Cumming *et al.* 2021).

In recent times, several sites have made it possible to choose between different types of crowdfunding. Indiegogo, for example, now allows users to run equity crowdfunding campaigns in addition to reward-based campaigns (https://equity. indiegogo.com/; Hornuf and Schwienbacher 2017).

An entrepreneur has the option of choosing the form of crowdfunding that is best suited to his or her company in the event that the entrepreneur is unable to secure the required amount of funding from more traditional sources. The objective of the platform, which is to connect entrepreneurs (or projects) with funders (or contributors) in a less expensive manner than would be possible without the platform, is to accomplish this in a manner that is analogous to a two-sided market (Evans 2011). Examples of these expenditures include fees related with acquiring information about the project and its owner and negotiating a contract between the many parties involved.

A typical platform serves a specific purpose and has its business focus. A platform should, at the very least, provide a dedicated project page for project initiation, tutorials, analytics and project monitoring (Gerber and Hui 2013). But generally, crowdfunding platforms conduct due diligence on the fundraiser and the information provided mitigates investors' risks including the information asymmetry between project owners and investors. This process is one way of weeding low-quality projects. The level of due diligence however varies depending on the platform. Due to fierce competition among platforms, unsecured fundraisers may be permitted entry into the market (Yoon *et al.* 2019). Several regulators such as the Financial Conduct Authority in the United Kingdom have yet to establish particular information disclosure standards, enabling individual crowdfunding platforms to set their standards. Furthermore, certain platforms do not evaluate the qualifications of investors in order to attract more funding. According to Wang *et al.* (2018), the rising failure rates of Chinese P2P lending projects are due in part to platforms' illegal pooling of funds from investors. Furthermore, UK platforms must inform investors about the dangers associated with financial crowdfunding. Investor education tends to differ, with some platforms requiring investors to complete a test as part of the registration process while others only indicate potential risks for investors.

Considering the foregoing, an entrepreneur should review the platform-specific requirements and tips to improve his chances of running a successful campaign. Entrepreneurs usually should list projects with sufficient details to persuade contributors or investors; give out rewards or benefits (if any) and include any other information necessary, including target amount, deadline; an audio-visual is also advised (Voelker and McGlashan 2013). Both the Securities Exchange Commission (SEC) and the JOBS Act provide guidelines to be followed by funding platforms to protect investors and prevent fraud and abuse (Stemler 2013). In addition to these, crowdfunding platforms are required to hold funds until project campaigns are ended, and the platform has conducted due diligence on initiators and intended use and provide required disclosures (Gelfond and Foti 2012; Rechtman and O'Callaghan 2014).

Platform intermediaries

Although the platform functions as an intermediary, as already discussed earlier, its role differs from that of traditional intermediaries such as banks which choose initiatives on their own, while a crowdfunding site defers to the investing contributors (Boot and Thakor 2000; Allen and Santomero 2001). The sole responsibility of the platform in its capacity as a middleman is to facilitate communication between the two market participants. In addition, in contrast to banks, platforms do not typically play a role in the collection of data; rather, they serve merely as a location where the information that is provided by the parties is collected in order to lower the costs for everyone involved (Hornuf and Schwienbacher 2016).

Crowdfunding utilizes internet-based social platforms to connect funders or investors with projects (Stemler 2013). Sites such as Kickstarter, Indiegogo as well as CrowdCube, and others based in the United Kingdom are listed as top crowdfunding sites (Marlett 2015). Connecting capital with businesses is the primary goal of intermediaries. This is particularly so as small businesses cannot drive sufficient traffic to their websites to raise finance (Tomczak and Brem 2013).

Since its inception in April 2009, through to September 2015, Kickstarter, the world's largest crowdfunding platform, has successfully raised funds for over 92,600 projects totalling $1.9 billion (Kickstarter 2015). Kickstarter is a crowdfunding platform that raises funds for projects of arts, technology and food industries (Voelker and McGlashan 2013). It charges a fee equivalent to 5% of the amount raised if the project is successfully funded within 30 days (Tomczak and Brem 2013; Kuppuswamy and Bayus 2018; Voelker and McGlashan 2013). With this model, the chances of successful crowdfunding are significantly enhanced (Frydrych *et al*. 2014). Indiegogo creates fixed, flexible funding and "not funded" campaigns at a 5% cost to project owners whether or not the flexible projects meet their goals (Bradley and Luong 2014). For fixed funding, a 5% fee is payable only if the campaign achieves its funding objective (Copeland 2015). Funds are returned to donors where campaigns failed to meet their targets (Bradley and Luong 2014).

Since inception, the largest peer-to-peer platform Kiva has facilitated loans for over one million borrowers (Bruton *et al*. 2015; Burtch *et al*. 2014). A portfolio of 288 microfinance institutions help vet and select entrepreneurs for funding; only the principal sum is paid back to the lenders (Burtch *et al*. 2014; Meyskens and Bird 2015). Most of Kiva investors are from the United States, while the majority of projects funded are from developing countries (Burtch *et al*. 2014). Other major crowdfunding platforms include Fundable, MegaTotal, and Puddle.

Puddle majorly serves business or project owners who are unable to access traditional sources. Puddle members put money into the pool, then have the ability to borrow up to five times that amount with little difficulty, and the interest on those loans is predetermined (Meyskens and Bird. 2015). Fundable, on the other hand, is a platform that not only accepts monetary, in-kind, and skill-set donations, but also provides financing based on rewards or equity (Bradley and Luong 2014). The Poland-based equity and royalty-based platform, MegaTotal, specializes in music. Investors make contributions and then select projects of interest to invest in, with a promise of returns based on a rank order of contribution, if projects are successful (Galuszka and Brzozowska 2021).

Characteristics of crowdfunding entrepreneurs

Research has identified risk-taking, competitive aggressiveness, trustworthiness, self-efficacy and certain preferences as characteristics shared by entrepreneurs who use crowdfunding. Harburg *et al*. (2015) while interviewing 53 founders from different platforms, half of whom have met their project goals, found that crowdfunding either increased or decreased self-efficacy in entrepreneurs. Public validation of the project tends to build self-efficacy while a lack of validation decreased self-efficacy. Yeoh (2014) found that entrepreneurs would instead seek donations from friends and family (FF) and community members online rather than ask in person, mostly when the project was for social purposes. Meanwhile, Davidson and Poor (2015) found that dependence on FF and acquaintances is a pointer to project failure.

Social entrepreneurs were more to be trusted than non-social firms (Lehner 2013); while projects signalling empathy, warmth, conscientiousness were likely to attract sufficient interest; such loans, if obtained were more likely to be unpaid (Moss *et al*. 2015). Furthermore, ventures received funding when they displayed autonomy and were competitively aggressive and those that were proactive in their approach were more likely to default in loan payments (Moss *et al*. 2015). Users of

Kiva are advised to be deliberate in their choice of words in order to enhance their chances of success. Belleflamme *et al.* (2014) observed that founders with small initial funding needs preferred the pre-sales model while founders of the profit-sharing model had preferences for more noteworthy capital requirements.

Forty per cent of all project initiators tested products in their social network using the pre-purchase model but would rather not use it again because they lacked knowledge on crowdfunding and also because of the time and effort spent in the process (Song and van Boeschoten 2015). Entrepreneurs must appraise all these characteristics before using crowdfunding and more research is also required to expand these traits.

Benefits of crowdfunding

Crowdfunding portends multiple benefits for small businesses. Benefits such as idea validation, proof of concept and marketing are at the centre while solving business problems and building community and making a social impact are also recognized and observed to be in the mix (Lehner and Nicholls 2014; Mancuso and Stuth 2014). The small venture owner also importantly wants to retain control. One major problem small business owners face when seeking traditional funding is information asymmetry. With crowdfunding, less information is required to be provided on the business, and no detailed contracts are required (Macht and Weatherston 2014). Crowdfunding employs collective reasoning and decision making to evaluate and raise funds, according to Bruton *et al.* (2015). Benefits include business growth while the funding gap problem is addressed, products and services are advertised, and market feedback is gathered (Sigar 2012). Other benefits include:

(i) Elimination of geographical barriers

The success of traditionally funded entrepreneurial ventures is often highly constrained by geography (Mollick 2014). The elimination of geographical barriers and the necessity for a personal connection with stakeholders makes crowdfunding appeal to start-ups. However, Agrawal *et al.* (2010) argue that although the online platform seems to eliminate most distance-related economic frictions such as monitoring progress, providing input and gathering information, it does not eliminate social-related frictions. Local investors also invest relatively early in a single round of financing, and are less responsive to decisions by other investors (Agrawal *et al.* 2010).

(ii) Appealing to the young and tech-savvy

The process is also appealing to young, "tech-savvy" investors (Gelfond and Foti 2012). Sherman (2023) argue that the millennials are the most tech-savvy and socially conscious of the generations, and are a largely untapped demographic for non-profits and non-governmental organizations (NGOs) but that many current crowdfunding platforms are not engaging millennial and younger potential donors as much as they could. Sherman (2023) cites an example of Givebutter as a crowdfunding platform that presents donors with a personal touch that is currently not offered in the crowdfunding industry. She argues that Givebutter is created by millennials for millennials, while existing crowdfunding platforms present a transactional experience.

(iii) Proof of demand

Ingram *et al.* (2014), in a study, observed that an entrepreneur used crowdfunding to prove demand for his product and was after that, able to obtain a bank loan. Entrepreneurs need to know that consumers want the product and more importantly whether they are willing to pay for it (Key 2016). Key (2016) concludes that there is no better way of confirming that there is a demand for the goods or services than running a successful crowdfunding campaign.

The more the entrepreneur knows about the target market for his product, the more they will reduce their financial risk, and crowdfunding can be an excellent tool for conducting market research (Odjick 2021). Odjick (2021) argues that manufacturing a product without any indication of how it will sell could cost a significant amount of time and money especially if it turns out that the demand for it is not strong. The knowledge the entrepreneur has that there is a demand for the product allows him/her to plan and scale their business with confidence.

(iv) Retention of control

Crowdfunding allows the small business owner to build capital without conceding ownership and rights thus maintaining control of the firm. This is another benefit of crowdfunding over traditional sources of funding ventures (Gerber and Hui 2013; Sigar 2012). Business control and rights are given up when entrepreneurs work with VCs on the other hand (Valanciene and Jegeleviciute 2013).

Loss of control is to be expected, as venture capitalists and angel investor are after all betting their capital against the success of the business. Therefore, it is reasonable they should have some say about the direction of the business. On the other hand, crowdfunding is different since entrepreneurs are not required to surrender such rights. While business owners might want to listen to supporters, they remain firmly in control of the business.

(v) Means of feedback

Crowdfunding can also be used to provide feedback for solving the firm's challenges at no cost to the firm. The collective intelligence of the crowd can also be used to resolve company challenges more than individuals can resolve efficiently (Ordanini *et al.* 2011; Sannajust *et al.* 2014). In addition to funds, the crowd offers value in the form of feedback, suggestions on product or service design and improvement, production and cost efficiency as well as publicity (Schwienbacher and Larralde 2010; Mancuso and Stuth 2014|). The business thus obtains better customer perception and acceptance (Schwienbacher and Larralde 2010). Sanna-just *et al.* (2014) validate these signals in a French study in which they determine the benefits of crowdfunding as an alternative means of venture financing.

(vi) Empowerment of the crowd

The consumer influences the founder's decision; hence crowdfunding provides empowerment to the fans, but a critical finding was that the crowd provided free labour to the founder. It was, therefore, a mutually visible and beneficial relation-ship (Galuszka and Brzozowska 2015). In the examination of journalism projects in Spain, Cohen (2017) observed that while the partnership between the public and journalists resulted in contents being what contributors' want, journalists lost their freedom even though they had financial independence.

(vii) Increased market reach

Crowdfunding plays a crucial role in promoting the firm to potential investors and customers. Marketing reduces product development time as well as the costs associated with it (Sannajust *et al.* 2014; Mollick 2014). Entrepreneurs can in-crease market share by using crowdfunding to reach a hitherto unreached market, and to test product prices, and other product potentials (Gerber and Hui 2013; Mancuso and Stuth 2014).

(viii) Risk diversification

Crowdfunding diversifies project risks among its diverse donors (Colgren 2014; Profatilov *et al.* 2015). Crowdfunding enables high-risk firms access to funding while diversifying risk amongst multiplied contributors, thus minimizing risk, (Turan 2012). This is one of the valuable advantages of crowdfunding. It is more convenient and carries much less financial risk because if for some reason the crowdfunding campaign fails, there is no fee to pay except to return what has been contributed. Therefore, it is free in essence.

Summary

The economic advantages crowdfunding offers small businesses over other tradi-tional means of financing are immense. Small businesses can receive and deploy funds faster than other financing options (Meric *et al.* 2015). Venture owners can obtain funding for purchase of equipment which they can thereafter retain (Profa-tilov *et al.* 2015) and can attract funds from across the world without any barriers and therefore not be tied down to any local investors (Mashburn 2013).

The adaptation of crowdfunding has the potential of disrupting conventional business models while stimulating new and potential investments in entrepre-neurial ventures, and also changing the structure of existing investments (Kshetri 2015). According to Macht and Weatherston (2014), two-thirds of entrepreneurs in the United Kingdom who encounter funding challenges are unaware of crowdfunding. Crowdfunding may become more popular if countries and governments create enabling environments, according to Kshetri (2015).

Discussion questions

1　What do you understand by the term crowdfunding; what are the key features and stakeholders of crowdfunding?
2　Crowdfunding categories vary in terms of complexity, return on investment decision power and contracts. Discus the categories of crowdfunding.
3　What is the role of platform intermediaries in crowdfunding campaigns?
4　Enumerate and discuss the benefits of crowdfunding.

Test questions

1　What is the difference between product crowdfunding and equity crowdfunding?
2　Can you run a campaign simultaneously on more than one crowdfunding platform?
3　Should you opt for an equity-based crowdfunding or one that is based on a system of reward? Critically evaluate your answer.
4　Financial crowdfunding involves an expectation of financial returns on investment. Discuss the three financial crowdfunding models.

Glossary of key terminologies

Collective intelligence　The sharing of knowledge, data and skills by a group of individuals for the purpose of solving societal issues.

Crowdfunders　People who provide market information and ideas as well as support the projects through financial contributions.

Entrepreneur　A person who establishes a business or firms with the expectation of profiting from the financial risk.

Financial system　A collection of institutional units and markets that interact in a typically complex manner to mobilize capital for investment and provide facilities, including payment systems, for financing commercial activities.

Funding gap　The gap between the demand for finance and the willingness of financial institutions to supply it at current market conditions.

Information asymmetry　One party in a contract has more or better information than the other.

JOBS Act　A statute aimed to stimulate funding of small firms in the United States by relaxing a number of existing regulations and enhancing access to public capital markets for developing growth companies.

Platforms　An intermediary in the crowdfunding process that connects project owners with investors.

Project initiators　Individuals who introduce projects to platforms for the purpose of raising capital for the implementation of the projects.

Regulatory framework   A legal provision that provides defined responsibilities and strategies to assure businesses and the community that the process used to establish and maintain regulation will yield the greatest possible results and protection.

Technological advancement   A change to the method of producing or delivering a product or service that decreases the amount of resources required.

Recommended reading

Cumming, D., and Hornuf, L., 2018. *The economics of crowdfunding*. London: Palgrave Macmillan.

De Buysere, K., Gajda, O., Kleverlaan, R., Marom, D., and Klaes, M., 2012. *A framework for European crowdfunding*. Available from: http://www.crowdfundingframework.eu/

Dresner, S., 2014. *Crowdfunding: A guide to raising capital on the internet*. New York: Bloomberg Financial.

Mitra, D., 2012. The role of crowdfunding in entrepreneurial finance. *Delhi Business Review*, 13 (2), 67–72.

Moritz, A., and Block, J.H., 2016. Crowdfunding: A literature review and research directions. *Crowdfunding in Europe*, 25–53.

References

Adhikary, B.K., 2015. Small business finance in Bangladesh: Can "crowdfunding" be an alternative? *Review of Integrative Business and Economics Research*, 4 (4), 1–21.

Agrawal, A., Catalini, C., and Goldfard, A., 2010. The geography of crowdfunding. *SSRN Electronic Journal*. Available from: https://doi.org/10.2139/ssrn.1692661

Aladejebi, O., 2020. Crowdfunding: An emerging source of raising funds in Nigeria. *Archives of Business Review*, 8 (7), 381–404.

Allen, F., and Santomero, A.M., 2001. What do financial intermediaries do? *Journal of Banking & Finance*, 25 (2), 271–294.

Andersen, L.M.K., and Mauritzen, L.J., 2015. *Crowdfunding as a tool for start-ups to raise capital* (Doctoral dissertation). Master Thesis within the profile of Business Analysis and Performance Management Norwegian School of Economics

Arkrot, W., Unger, A., and Åhlström, E., 2017. *Crowdfunding from a marketing perspective* (International Business School). Jönköping: Jönköping University.

Aronson, D.H., 2013. SEC rule changes signal new regulatory environment for private securities offerings. *Corporate Finance Review*, 18 (2), 13–24.

Bachmann, A., Becker, A., Buerckner, D., Hilker, M., Kock, F., Lehmann, M., and Funk, B., 2011. Online peer-to-peer lending-A literature review. *Journal of Internet Banking and Commerce*, 16 (2), 1–18.

Baeck, P., Collins, L., and Zhang, B., 2014. Understanding alternative finance. *The UK alternative finance industry report, 2014*. Cambridge: Cambridge Centre for Alternative Finance.

Belleflamme, P., Lambert, T., and Schwienbacher, A., 2013. Individual crowdfunding practices. *Venture Capital*, 15 (4), 313–333.

Belleflamme, P., Lambert, T., and Schwienbacher, A., 2014. Crowdfunding: Tapping the right crowd. *Journal of Business Venturing*, 29 (5), 585–609.

Boot, A.W., and Thakor, A.V., 2000. Can relationship banking survive competition? *The Journal of Finance*, 55 (2), 679–713.

Bradley III, D.B., and Luong, C., 2014. Crowdfunding: A new opportunity for small business and entrepreneurship. *The Entrepreneurial Executive*, 19, 95.

Bretschneider, U., Knaub, K., and Wieck, E., 2014. Motivations for crowdfunding: What drives the crowd to invest in start-ups? *In: Proceedings of the European Conference on Information Systems (ECIS) 2014*, 9–11 June. Tel Aviv, Israel. ISBN 978-0-9915567-0-0. Available from: http://aisel.aisnet.org/ecis2014/proceedings/track05/6

Bruton, G., Khavul, S., Siegel, D., and Wright, M., 2015. New financial alternatives in seeding entrepreneurship: Microfinance, crowdfunding, and peer – to – peer innovations. *Entrepreneurship Theory and Practice*, 39 (1), 9–26.

Buff, L.A., and Alhadeff, P., 2013. Budgeting for crowdfunding rewards. *MEIEA Journal*, 13 (1), 27–44.

Burkett, E., 2011. A crowdfunding Exemption? Online investment crowdfunding and US securities regulation. *Transactions: The Tennessee Journal of Business Law*, 13 (1/4), 63.

Burtch, G., Ghose, A., and Wattal, S., 2014. An empirical examination of peer referrals in online crowdfunding. *In: 35th international conference on information systems: Building a better world through information systems, Information Systems Research, ICIS 2014*.

Catalini, C., Fazio, C., and Murray, F., 2016. *Can equity crowdfunding democratize access to capital and investment opportunities?* Massachusetts Institute of Technology.

Chervyakov, D., and Rocholl, J., 2019. How to make crowdfunding work in Europe (No. 2019/6). *Bruegel Policy Contribution n° 6| March 2019*. Available from: https://euagenda. eu/upload/publications/untitled-208945-ea.pdf [Accessed 12 January 2023].

Cholakova, M., and Clarysse, B., 2015. Does the possibility to make equity investments in crowdfunding projects crowd out reward–based investments? *Entrepreneurship Theory and Practice*, 39 (1), 145–172.

Cohen, M., 2017. *Crowdfunding as a financing resource for small businesses* (Walden dissertations and Doctoral Studies Collection). Available from: https://scholarworks.waldenu.edu/dissanddoc?utm_source=scholarworks.waldenu.edu%2Fdissertations%2F3757&utm_medium=PDF&utm_campaign=PDFCoverPages.

Colgren, D., 2014. Tech practices: The rise of crowdfunding social media, big data, cloud technologies. *Strategic Finance*, 95 (10), 56–58.

Colombo, M.G., Franzoni, C., and Rossi–Lamastra, C., 2015. Internal social capital and the attraction of early contributions in crowdfunding. *Entrepreneurship Theory and Practice*, 39 (1), 75–100.

Comeig, I., Del Brio, E.B., and Fernandez-Blanco, M.O., 2014. Financing successful small business projects. *Management Decision*, 52 (3), 365–377.

Čondić-Jurkić, I., 2015. Crowdfunding – What do we know about this alternative source of financing? *Notitia-časopis za održivi razvoj*, 1 (1), 71–83.

Copeland, A.J., 2015. Crowdfunding a new church: A multimodal analysis of faith-related giving rhetoric on Indiegogo. *Online-Heidelberg Journal of Religions on the Internet*, 9.

Cumming, D., Hornuf, L., Karami, M., and Schweizer, D., 2021. Disentangling crowdfunding from fraudfunding. *Journal of Business Ethics*, 182 (2), 1–26.

Davidson, R., and Poor, N., 2015. The barriers facing artists' use of crowdfunding platforms: Personality, emotional labor, and going to the well one too many times. *New Media & Society*, 17 (2), 289–307.

Dapp, T., 2013. *Crowdfunding, An alternative source of funding with potential*. Deuthsche Bank Research, Frankfurt am Main Germany.

De Buysere, K., Gajda, O., Kleverlaan, R., Marom, D., and Klaes, M., 2012. *A framework for European crowdfunding*. Available from: https://www.fundraisingschool.it/wp-content/uploads/2013/02/European-Crowdfunding-Framework-Oct-2012.pdf [Accessed 12 January 2023].

Dushnitsky, G., and Marom, D., 2013. Crowd monogamy. *Business Strategy Review*, 24 (4), 24–26.

Egene, G., 2016. SEC rules out crowdfunding in Nigeria for now. *Thisday[online]*. Available from: http://www. thisdaylive. com/index. php/2016/08/15/secrules-out-crowdfunding-in-nigeria-for-now [Accessed 15 June 2022].

England, D., Hebden, A., Henderson, T., and Pattie, T., 2015. The agencies and 'one bank'. *Bank of England Quarterly Bulletin*, Q1.

Evans, D.S., 2011. Platform economics: Essays on multi-sided businesses. *Competition Policy International*. Available from: www.competitionpolicyinternational.com [Accessed 12 January 2023].

Fresh Books, 2022. *The 5 types of crowdfunding: Which is right for your business?* Available from: www.freshbooks.com/blog/crowdfunding-crowdinvesting-crowdlending [Accessed 14 December 2022].

Fink, A.C., 2012. Protecting the crowd and raising capital through the crowdfund act. *The University of Detroit Mercy Law Review*, 90, 1.

Freedman, D.M., and Nutting, M.R., 2015. The growth of equity crowdfunding. *Value Examiner*, 6–10.

Frydrych, D., Bock, A.J., Kinder, T., and Koeck, B., 2014. Exploring entrepreneurial legitimacy in reward-based crowdfunding. *Venture Capital*, 16 (3), 247–269.

Galuszka, P., and Brzozowska, B., 2015. Crowdfunding: Towards a redefinition of the artist's role – the case of MegaTotal. *International Journal of Cultural Studies*, 20, 1–17.

Galuszka, P., and Brzozowska, B., 2017. Crowdfunding and the democratization of the music market. *Media, Culture & Society*, 39 (6), 833–849.

Gedda, D., Nilsson, B., Athen, Z., and Soilen, K.S., 2016. Crowdfunding: Finding the optimal platform for funders and entrepreneurs. *Technology Innovation Management Review*, 6 (3), 31–40. Available from: www.timreview.ca

Gelfond, S.H., and Foti, A.D., 2012. US $500 and a click: Investing the "crowdfunding" way. *Journal of Investment Compliance*, 13 (4), 9–13.

Gerber, E.M., and Hui, J., 2013. Crowdfunding: Motivations and deterrents for participation. *ACM Transactions on Computer-Human Interaction*, 20 (6), 1–32. Available from: https://doi.org/10.1145/2530540

Gobble, M.M., ed., 2012. Everyone is a venture capitalist: The new age of crowdfunding. *Research Technology Management*, 55 (4), 4–7.

Golić, Z., 2014. Advantages of crowdfunding as an alternative source of financing of small and medium-sized enterprises. *Zbornik radova Ekonomskog fakulteta u Istočnom Sarajevu*, 8, 39–48.

Hagedorn, A., and Pinkwart, A., 2013. *Crowdinvesting as a financing instrument for startups in Germany: A critical platform analysis*. Leipzig: HHL Leipzig Graduate School of Management.

Harburg, E., Hui, J., Greenberg, M., and Gerber, E.M., 2015. Understanding the effects of crowdfunding on entrepreneurial self-efficacy. *In: Proceedings of the 18th ACM conference on computer supported cooperative work & social computing*, Evanston, IL: Northwestern University, 3–16.

Harris, J., 1986. *A statue for America: The first 100 years of the statue of liberty*. New York: Simon & Schuster.

Harrison, R., 2013. Crowdfunding and the revitalisation of the early stage risk capital market: Catalyst or chimera? *Venture Capital*, 15 (4), 283–287.

Helmer, J., 2011. A snapshot on crowdfunding. *In: Working papers firms and regions (R2/2011)*. Karlsruhe: Fraunhofer Institute for Systems and Innovation Research ISI.

Hervé, F., and Schwienbacher, A., 2018. Crowdfunding and innovation. *Journal of Economic Surveys*, 32 (5), 1514–1530.

Hornuf, L., and Schwienbacher, A., 2016. Crowdinvesting: Angel investing for the masses? In Landström, H. & Mason, C. (eds.), *Handbook of research on business angels*. Cheltenham: Edward Elgar Publishing.

Hornuf, L., and Schwienbacher, A., 2017. Should securities regulation promote equity crowdfunding? *Small Business Economics*, 49 (3), 579–593.

Hussain, M.E., and Haque, M., 2017. Empirical analysis of the relationship between money supply and per capita GDP growth rate in Bangladesh. *Journal of Advances in Economics and Finance*, 2 (1), 54–66.

Ingram, C., Teigland, R., and Vaast, E., 2014. Solving the puzzle of crowdfunding: Where technology affordances and institutional entrepreneurship collide. *In: 2014 47th Hawaii international conference on system sciences*. Hawaii: IEEE, 4556–4567.

Islam, M.T., and Khan, M.T.A., 2021. Factors influencing the adoption of crowdfunding in Bangladesh: A study of start-up entrepreneurs. *Information Development*, 37 (1), 72–89.

Katherine, C., and Daniel, S., 2016. Crowdsourcing for a better world: On the relation between IT affordances and donor motivations in charitable crowdfunding. *Information Technology & People*, 29, 221–247.

Kappel, T., 2009. Ex ante crowdfunding and the recording industry: A model for the US. *Loy. LA Entertainment. Law Review*, 29 (3/3), 375.

Key, S., 2016. *The hidden benefit of crowdfunding: Proof of demand.* Available from: https://inventright.com/the-hidden-benefit-of-crowdfunding-proof-of-demand/ [Accessed 19 March 2023].

Khan, M.K., Zhao, X., Akram, U., Hashim, M., and Kaleem, A., 2017. Crowdfunding: An innovative approach to start up with entrepreneurship. *In: Proceedings of the tenth international conference on management science and engineering management*. Singapore: Springer, 1293–1304.

Kickstarter, P.B.C., 2015. *Kickstarter.* Available from: https://medium.com/kickstarter/kickstarter-is-a-pbc-heres-what-that-means-and-why-it-matters-d90b2389ea6c [Accessed 1 September 2022].

Kim, J., 2017. *Analysis of reward-based crowdfunding participation intention – Perceived risk perspective*. Seoul: Graduate School of Seoul National University.

Kim, S.G., and Lee, S.G., 2014. Can crowd funding be the economic basis for the independence of small-scale culture & arts? A study on funding experiences of indie Musicians. *Media Gender Culture*, 29, 5–42.

Kitchens, R., and Torrence, P.D., 2012. The JOBS Act-crowdfunding and beyond. *Economic Development Journal*, 11 (4), 42.

Kshetri, N., 2015. Success of crowd-based online technology in fundraising: An institutional perspective. *Journal of International Management*, 21 (2), 100–116.

Kuppuswamy, V. and Bayus, B. 2015 Crowdfunding Creative Ideas: The Dynamics of Project Backers in Kickstarter, Available at SSRN: http://dx.doi.org/10.2139/ssrn.2234765.

Kuppuswamy, V., and Bayus, B.L., 2018. A review of crowdfunding research and findings. *In*: P.N. Golder and D. Mitra, eds. *Handbook of research on new product development*. Cheltenham: Edward Elgar Publishing, 361–373.

Labrecque, L.I., vor dem Esche, J., Mathwick, C., Novak, T.P., and Hofacker, C.F., 2013. Consumer power: Evolution in the digital age. *Journal of Interactive Marketing*, 27 (4), 257–269.

Lambert T., and Schwienbacher, A., 2010. *An empirical analysis of crowdfunding*. Available from: http://ssrn.com/abstract=1578175

Lavinsky, D., 2010. Funding fathers. *Smart Business Online.* Available from: https://www.archives.gov/publications/prologue/2010/winter/founders.html [Accessed 12 March 2023].

Lehner, O.M., 2013. Crowdfunding social ventures: A model and research agenda. *Venture Capital*, 15 (4), 289–311.

Lehner, O.M., and Nicholls, A., 2014. Social finance and crowdfunding for social enterprises: A public – private case study providing legitimacy and leverage. *Venture Capital*, 16 (3), 271–286.

Leon, I., and Mora, J., 2017. The role of awareness in crowdfunding campaigns. The Empirical evidence for the Caribbean. Inter-American Development Bank.

Levine, M.L., and Feigin, P.A., 2014. Crowdfunding provisions under the new rule 506 (c). *The CPA Journal*, 84 (6), 46–51.

Ley, A., and Weaven, S., 2011. Exploring agency dynamics of crowdfunding in start-up capital financing. *Academy of Entrepreneurship Journal*, 17 (1), 85.

Lin, M., Prabhala, N.R., and Viswanathan, S., 2013. Judging borrowers by the company they keep: Friendship networks and information asymmetry in online peer-to-peer lending. *Management Science*, 59 (1), 17–35.

Lin, M., and Viswanathan, S., 2013. *Home bias in online investments: An empirical study of an online crowd funding market*. Available from: https://funginstitute.berkeley.edu/wp-content/uploads/2013/11/Home_Bias_Online_Investments.pdf [Accessed 12 January 2023].

Lin, M., and Viswanathan, S., 2016. Home bias in online investments: An empirical study of an online crowdfunding market. *Management Science*, 62 (5), 1393–1414.

Ma, Y., and Liu, D., 2017. Introduction to the special issue on Crowdfunding and FinTech. *Financial Innovation*, 3, 1–4.

Macht, S.A., and Weatherston, J., 2014. The benefits of online crowdfunding for fund-seeking business ventures. *Strategic Change*, 23 (1–2), 1–14.

Mancuso, J., and Stuth, K., 2014. Seven Deadly Mistakes to Avoid on social media. *Successful Marketing*, 11.

Marlett, D., 2015. Crowdfunding art, science and technology: A quick survey of the burgeoning new landscape. *Leonardo*, 48 (1), 104–105.

Mashburn, D., 2013. The anti-crowd pleaser: Fixing the crowdfund act's hidden risks and inadequate remedies. *Emory Law Journal*, 63, 127.

Massolution, C.L., 2015. *Crowdfunding industry report*. Available from: http://reports.crowdsourcing.org/index.php?route=product/product&product_id=54 [Accessed 15 January 2022].

Mendes-Da-Silva, W., Rossoni, L., Conte, B.S., Gattaz, C.C., and Francisco, E.R., 2016. The impacts of fundraising periods and geographic distance on financing music production via crowdfunding in Brazil. *Journal of Cultural Economics*, 40 (1), 75–99.

Meric, J., Bouiass, K., and Maque, I., 2015. More than three's a crowd . . . in the best interest of companies: Crowdfunding as zeitgeist or ideology. *Society and Business review*, 10 (1), 23–39.

Metelka, A., 2014. *Crowdfunding: Start-ups' alternative funding source beyond banks, business angels and venture capitalists*. Sweden: Blekinge Institute of Technology School of Management.

Meyskens, M., and Bird, L., 2015. Crowdfunding and value creation. *Entrepreneurship Research Journal*, 5 (2), 155–166.

Mollick, E., 2014. The dynamics of crowdfunding: An exploratory study. *Journal of Business Venturing*, 29, 1–16.

Mollick, E.R., 2013. *Swept away by the crowd? Crowdfunding, venture capital, and the selection of entrepreneurs*, 25 March 2013. Available at SSRN: http://dx.doi.org/10.2139/ssrn.2239204

Moss, T.W., Neubaum, D.O., and Meyskens, M., 2015. The effect of virtuous and entrepreneurial orientations on microfinance lending and repayment: A signaling theory perspective. *Entrepreneurship Theory and Practice*, 39 (1), 27–52.

Odjick, D., 2021. *How to do crowdfunding in 2022: With expert tips and examples from successful campaigns*. Available from: www.shopify.com/uk/blog/crowdfunding#4 [Accessed 19 March 2023].

Oh, S., and Kim, H., 2017. Crowdfunding performance: The effect of social capital and the mediating role of electronic word-of-mouth. *Journal of Internet Electronic Commerce Research*, 17, 155–169.

Ordanini, A., Miceli, L., Pizzetti, M., and Parasuraman, A., 2011. Crowd-funding: Transforming customers into investors through innovative service platforms. *The Journal of Service Management*, 22, 443–470 [CrossRef].

Outlaw, S., 2013. *Cash from the Crowd: How to crowdfund your ideas and gain fans for your success*. California: Entrepreneur Press.

Profatilov, D.A., Bykova, O.N., and Olkhovskaya, M.O., 2015. Crowdfunding: Online charity or a modern tool for innovative projects implementation? *Asian Social Science*, 11 (3), 146.

Rechtman, Y., and O'Callaghan, S., 2014. Understanding the basics of crowdfunding. *The CPA Journal*, 84 (11), 30–33.

Riedl, J., 2013. Crowdfunding technology innovation. *Computer*, 46 (03), 100–103.

Rossi, M., 2014. The new ways to raise capital: An exploratory study of crowdfunding. *International Journal of Financial Research*, 5 (2), 8–18. Available from: https://doi.org/10.5430/ijfr.v5n2p8

Sannajust, A., Roux, F., and Chaibi, A., 2014. Crowdfunding in France: A new revolution? *Journal of Applied Business Research (JABR)*, 30 (6), 1919–1928.

Saxton, G.D., and Wang, L., 2014. The social network effect: The determinants of giving through social media. *Nonprofit and Voluntary Sector Quarterly*, 43 (5), 850–868.

Schwienbacher, A., and Larralde, B., 2010. Crowdfunding of small entrepreneurial ventures. *In: Handbook of entrepreneurial finance*. Oxford, UK: Oxford University Press.

Sherman, L., 2023. *How a new crowdfunding platform garnered overnight success by appealing to the millennial sensibility*. Available from: https://techdayhq.com/community/articles/how-a-new-crowdfunding-platform-garnered-overnight-success-by-appealing-to-the-millennial-sensibility [Accessed 19 March 2023].

Sigar, K., 2012. Fret no more: Inapplicability of crowdfunding concerns in the internet age and the JOBS Act's safeguards. *Administrative Law Review*, 473–506.

Song, Y., and van Boeschoten, R., 2015. Success factors for Crowdfunding founders and funders. *arXiv preprint arXiv:1503.00288*. Available from: https://arxiv.org/ftp/arxiv/papers/1503/1503.00288.pdf

Stemler, A.R., 2013. The JOBS Act and crowdfunding: Harnessing the power – And money – Of the masses. *Business Horizons*, 56 (3), 271–275.

Stocker, M.W., and Sucharow, L., 2012. Startups, raising money by crowdfunding may scare off other investors. *Business Insider*.

Thürridl, C., and Kamleitner, B., 2016. What goes around comes around? Rewards as strategic assets in crowdfunding. *California Management Review*, 58 (2), 88–110.

Tomczak, A., and Brem, A., 2013. A conceptualized investment model of crowdfunding. *Venture Capital*, 15 (4), 335–359.

Turan, A.H., 2012. Internet shopping behavior of turkish customers: Comparison of two competing models. *Journal of Theoretical and Applied Electronic Commerce Research*, 7 (1), 77–93.

Valanciene, L., and Jegeleviciute, S., 2013. Valuation of crowdfunding: Benefits and drawbacks. *Economics and Management*, 18 (1), 39–48.

Vassallo, W., 2014. *Crowdfunding in the age of knowledge. Anyone can make a project. The future is today*. Milano: Franco Angeli.

Voelker, T.A., and McGlashan, R., 2013. What is crowdfunding? Bringing the power of Kickstarter to your entrepreneurship research and teaching activities. *Small Business Institute Journal*, 9 (2), 11–22.

Wang, T., Liu, X., Kang, M., and Zheng, H., 2018. Exploring the determinants of fundraisers' voluntary information disclosure on crowdfunding platforms: A risk-perception perspective. *Online Information Review*, 42 (3), 324–342.

Williamson, J.J., 2013. The JOBS act and middle-income investors: Why it doesn't go far enough. *Yale Law Journal*, 122, 2069–2080.

World Bank., 2019. *Small and medium enterprises (SMEs) finance*. Available from: https://www.worldbank.org/en/topic/smefinance [Accessed 12 March 2023].

Yeoh, P.L., 2014. Internationalization and performance outcomes of entrepreneurial family SMEs: The role of outside CEOs, technology sourcing, and innovation. *Thunderbird International Business Review*, 56 (1), 77–96.

Yoon, Y., Li, Y., and Feng, Y., 2019. Factors affecting platform default risk in online peer-to-peer (P2P) lending business: An empirical study using Chinese online P2P platform data. *Electronic Commerce Research*, 19, 131–158.

Zhang, Y., Tan, C.D., Sun, J., and Yang, Z., 2020. Why do people patronize donation-based crowdfunding platforms? An activity perspective of critical success factors. *Computers in Human Behavior*, 112, 106470.

Zhao, Y., 2019. *Understanding UK rewards-based crowdfunding as an alternative source of entrepreneurial finance*. Available from: http://hdl.handle.net/10034/623133.

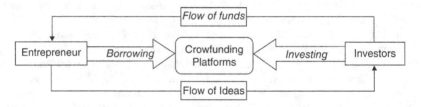

Figure 2.1 Crowdfunding model
Source: Islam and Khan (2021)

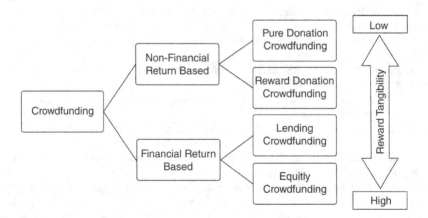

Figure 2.2 Categories of crowdfunding
Source: Islam and Khan (2021)

3 The financial behaviour of entrepreneurs in relation to crowdfunding

Learning objectives

- Review the pecking order theory
- Understand the motives underlying financing options
- Understand the various stages of entrepreneurial development
- Explore the financing options for entrepreneurs' development stages

Introduction

This chapter features an in-depth discussion of the pecking order theory and how pecking order theory is used to determine the financing options that enable business owners to retain control. In this chapter, the relationship between the pecking order hypothesis and crowdfunding is explored alongside how small business owners use different categories of crowdfunding in various development stages. We discuss how entrepreneurs could choose investors according to their immediate needs while increasing their chances of survival. We also explore the different types of SMEs including social entrepreneurs and mission led enterprises and their financial needs.

Penrose (1952) is credited with being the first person to build the life cycle theory. The theory's primary objective is to describe the progression of a company as it moves through the stages of its lifetime. A company's life cycle can be broken down into several stages, each of which is the product of a unique combination of internal and external influences (Dickinson 2011). Although a company does not evolve in the same way as the product that it manufactures and sells, all growing businesses go through certain stages of growth that can be linked to the progression of a product's design that the company is responsible for creating and selling. A firm goes through many crises as it develops, which necessitates changes and makes it harder for the owner and manager to plan for future growth (Scott and Bruce 1987).

Despite the many theoretical and empirical research on the enterprise life cycle, there is no consensus on the number of phases, the number of variables that influence it, or the organization of those components. Most organizations generate multiple products, each of which may be in a different stage of growth, which may explain why there isn't universal consensus on anything (Dickinson 2011).

DOI: 10.4324/9781003193975-3

Although multiple components of a firm can be investigated and analyzed at various stages of its life cycle, this chapter focuses on the capital structure and its aspects. Two basic theories influence capital structure decisions, namely the trade-off theory and the pecking order theory. The ideal capital structure, according to the static trade-off theory, is achieved when the tax advantage of borrowing is marginally balanced by the costs of financial distress. In accordance with the pecking order theory, firms favour internal funds over external funds and debt over equity if external funds are required. Thus, the debt ratio indicates the total external financing requirement. The pecking order of behaviour on the other hand, is a natural consequence of asymmetric information models. What is the viability of crowdfunding as a potential new source of funding for the commercial endeavours of businesses within the confines of these frameworks?

Pecking order and trade-off theories

There is a vast body of literature in corporate finance that analyzes the capital structure as a reflection of firm financing behaviour. Capital structure in various regions has been explained using two models, the static trade-off theory and the pecking order theory (Swinnen *et al.* 2005; Serrasqueiro *et al.* 2011). Capital structure is a topic that has attracted a lot of attention from academics in the field of finance since the publication of the fundamental article by Modigliani and Miller in 1958.

(i) Static trade-off theory

According to the static trade-off theory, there is a ratio of financial debt that should be optimum in order to maximize company value. The optimal level of debt issuance is achieved when the marginal value of the benefits of issuing more debt is equal to the rise in the present value of the expenses of doing so. In other words, the marginal value of the benefits of issuing more debt must be equal to the rise in the present value of the expenses (Myers 2001). There is a possibility that you will be able to deduct from your taxes the interest that you pay on your debt. Due to the fact that interest payments can be deducted from a company's taxable income, the likelihood of the company taking on debt has increased. This apparently easy result could be made more complicated by factors such as personal taxes (Miller 1977) and non-debt tax shelters (DeAngelo and Masulis 1980). Debt also helps reduce tensions between managers and shareholders, which is a win-win. Managers are motivated to squander free cash flow on luxuries and wasteful investments. Debt financing restricts managers' access to free cash flow, hence aiding in the management of agency issues (Jensen and Meckling 1976). The expenses of financial hardship (Modigliani and Miller 1963) and agency costs caused by disagreements between owners and borrowers are related with issuing additional debt (Jensen and Meckling 1976). When a company incurs significant debt and is unable to meet its interest and principal payments, financial hardship is likely to ensue.

There is a one-of-a-kind capital structure that is beneficial to investors and works well with static trade-off models. It is generally accepted that a corporation will determine the degree of debt it wants to carry and then makes efforts in that direction over time. The optimal capital structure for the company will require making trade-offs between the consequences of corporate and personal taxes, costs associated with bankruptcy and agency charges, among other factors. Examples of static trade-off models include those developed by Modigliani and Miller (1958, 1963), Miller (1977) and Diamond (1989). These models can be classified as either tax-based or agency-cost-based.

(ii) Pecking order theory

There is no well-defined goal debt ratio, as stated by the pecking order idea, which was initially established by Myers and Majluf (1984). The prevalent school of thought maintains that companies should prioritize retained earnings (also known as accessible liquid assets) as their principal source of investment money. Next on the list of priorities is debt that has a lower level of risk, then dangerous stock financing from the outside.

This is because of the problem of asymmetric knowledge that exists between insider investors and other types of investors. Debt ratios shift when there is a mismatch between a company's internal cash flow (after accounting for dividends) and the opportunities available for real investment, despite the fact that the elements investigated by the trade-off model are deemed to be of second-order. The original Myers-Majluf notion has been built upon in a variety of works, some of which are Krasker (1986), Brennan and Kraus (1987), Narayanan (1988), Noe (1988), Constantinides and Grundy (1989) and Heinkel and Zechner (1990), amongst others.

Myers' (1984) notion of pecking order is an alternative capital structure theory. According to the pecking order theory, a firm's capital structure is determined by its preference for internally generated money over external borrowing. If external finance is necessary, debt is preferable to equity. Asymmetric information and the existence of transaction costs can be used to explain the pecking order theory. A firm incurs asymmetric information costs when it chooses not to employ external funding and consequently foregoes an investment with a positive NPV. Managers (insiders of the company) have access to more accurate information than outside investors. Because of this, managers are more likely to take advantage of opportunities. When the market price of the firm's securities is higher than the firm's actual value, managers will issue securities. The difference between the market price of a firm's securities and its true worth arises because investors can misprice equities when they have inadequate knowledge about the value of the firm's assets (Myers and Majluf 1984). When the market overvalues existing shares, corporations have an incentive to issue additional shares, since sophisticated investors are aware. Consequently, investors will rationally modify the price they are willing to pay, causing the market for new assets to be under-priced. If corporations must issue equity to finance new projects, under-pricing may be so severe that new investors obtain a greater proportion of the NPV of the new project, resulting in a loss for existing shareholders. If this is the case, then the project will be rejected even if it has a positive NPV, since managers will prioritize the interests of existing owners.

This underinvestment can be prevented if the new project is financed using securities that are not so drastically discounted (Myers 1984; Myers and Majluf 1984).

There is a possibility that the pecking order hypothesis can also be explained by the presence of transaction costs. The transaction expenses associated with external borrowing have a significant impact on the choice of funding sources that are pursued. In the beginning, companies will finance themselves through their own internal equity, then move on to external loan financing, and then turn to external equity financing. Because debt financing is associated with lower transaction costs, it comes first in the financing order, followed by equity issuance (Baskin 1989). According to the findings of Baskin (1989), the cost of raising debt in the markets of the United States can be as low as 1% of the amount of cash that is raised, whereas the cost of raising stock can range anywhere from 4 to 15%. When all other sources of finance have been used up, the remaining alternative is to issue new shares, which comes with significant transaction expenses.

The reliance on internal finance may also be the result of management's desire to avoid external financing due to the fact that it would subject them to the discipline of the market (Myers 1984). The possibility of the company's owner and manager losing control of the business is particularly painful to them (Holmes and Kent 1991; Hamilton and Fox 1998). As a result, managers are very hesitant to take on new shareholders, and they will make every effort to finance as much of their business with money from within the company as is practically possible. If there is not enough money in retained earnings, management will select the source of funding that places the fewest restrictions on them. Because there is no demand for collateral and no covenants are enforced, management will pick short-term financing because of this. The next item on the list will be an offering of stocks, which will be followed by the sale of long-term debt. Asymmetric knowledge and transaction costs are the forces that predominate in defining optimal leverage in trade-of models, according to the idea that was proposed by Myers (1984). In the beginning, most companies choose to finance investment projects using their own internal cash flows rather than incurring the associated borrowing fees. If there is still a need for funding, they will use external capital in the following order: first with safe debt, then with risky debt, and last with equity offerings. If there is still a need for funding, they will do this since there is still a need for it.

Therefore, the pecking order theory predicts that there is no long-term goal capital structure. This is in contrast to the trade-off hypothesis, which states that there is such a structure. Because there are two different kinds of equity, there is no such thing as an ideal debt-to-equity ratio. In terms of importance, retained earnings rank highest, and the issuing of new shares ranks lowest (Myers 1984).

The vast majority of empirical studies on capital structure, such as Bradley *et al.* (1984), Titman and Wessels (1988), Rajan and Zingales (1995) and Wald (1999), use data from industrialized nations, primarily the United States, to study the drivers of capital structure. This is true for the vast majority of empirical studies on capital structure. Studies on emerging markets have become more prevalent in recent years, with notable examples including Booth *et al.* (2001) and Wiwattanakantang (2001).

While the goal of trade-off theory is for businesses to achieve a target debt ratio at which marginal benefits equal marginal costs of debt, the pecking order theory is a preferred order for choosing funding sources that minimize the cost of capital. The trade-off theory's objective is for businesses to achieve a target debt ratio at which marginal benefits equal marginal costs of debt (Serrasqueiro *et al.* 2011). It was found by Serrasqueiro *et al.* (2011) that small businesses in Portugal's service sector choose loan over equity, which confirms the pecking order theory over the trade-off theory. Although it appears that the static trade-off model, rather than the pecking order hypothesis, is more effective in describing the peculiarities of the capital structure for Chinese listed companies (Swinnen *et al.* 2005).

Static trade-off versus pecking order in small firms

Capital structure theories assume rational economic decision-making. They believe reasonable managers maximize shareholder wealth. Numerous empirical researches have examined capital structure determinants as predicted by the static trade-off theory. Asset structure, firm size, growth potential, profitability and others determine the ideal goal capital structure (Rajan and Zingales 1995; Chittenden *et al.* 1996; Jordan *et al.* 1998; Titman and Wessels 1988). Instead of this time-consuming approach, organizations may adopt the industry average as their ideal aim. Companies in the same industry have a similar optimal point.

Lev (1969) found that financial ratios, such as the equity-to-debt ratio, tend to converge to industry averages over time. Adjustment occurs more quickly for short-term items (such as current ratios) and variables that are managed by an organization than for long-term items and variables that are not managed by an organization (Lev 1969). Bowen *et al.* (1982) discovered that over the course of five and ten years, businesses have a statistically significant propensity to modify their debt to equity ratios towards the norm for their industry.

According to the research of Martin and Scott (1974), companies choose to issue debt rather than equity when their financial leverage is modest in comparison to the norms of their industry. As the quantity of debt increases, the company will issue a decreasing amount of debt due to the risk of bankruptcy. The use of industry averages as desirable financial values provides evidence for the theory that industrial class influences the financial architecture of corporations (Scott and Martin 1975; Ferri and Jones 1979). It is no longer appropriate for managers to make decisions when they have limited knowledge, time, cognitive capacities, and subjectivity (March 1978). Alternative decision-making models are superior due to the challenging, volatile and unpredictable nature of the environment in which managers work (Sadler-Smith 2004).

The bounded rationality model is a better fit for the decision-making process in corporations. Within the framework of constrained rationality, March (1978) presented the concept of restricted rationality. It appears that smaller companies utilize less logic. Because people have difficulty considering all of their options and gathering all of the pertinent information, limited rationality implies that they simplify their decision-making processes (March 1978). Therefore, many owner-managers of small businesses lack the knowledge and skills necessary to search for potential sources of funding (Hutchinson 1999). They lack both the managerial experience and the management team necessary to make decisions that are well-informed and optimal (Ang 1991). As a result, business owners might not have enough money to choose the optimal target. They require direction and a list of references. Companies that are comparable may provide direction. Because SMEs lack capital structure knowledge, the behaviour principle suggests they utilize industry averages as financial targets (Emery *et al.* 2004).

Instead of estimating their optimal debt level or ratio by balancing the costs of borrowing money with the benefits of doing so, small and medium-sized businesses may, out of ignorance, rely on the industry average. This is contrary to the predictions of the trade-off theory. The static trade-off hypothesis postulates that companies would modify their debt ratios in order to achieve a target that has already been decided upon. When the intended financial value is set to the average debt ratio for the industry, companies that already have a debt ratio that is lower than the average will choose to take on more debt, while companies that already have a debt ratio that is higher than the average will choose to take on less debt. It makes no difference whether a company adopts the industry average for illogical or sensible reasons; the goal is the same.

Because the variables used to describe one model can also be applied to the other model, empirically distinguishing between the two models has proven to be difficult (Booth *et al.* 2001). As a consequence of this, numerous recent empirical investigations have included cross-sectional testing of a number of variables that can be supported by either of these two theories (Swinnen *et al.* 2015); this in and of itself stresses the need for more research to be conducted. According to La Rocca *et al.* (2011), the dispute that exists in the empirical literature about the drivers of capital structure decisions is caused by a failure to account for information opacity as well as the characteristics and requirements of the firm at its various life cycle stages.

Crowdfunding and the firm's life cycle

There have only been a few studies that have demonstrated that small business owners turn to crowdfunding when they have no other finance choices left to pursue. For example, Corrado Accardi attempted to create a new pizza firm in the United Kingdom but was unable to secure funding from business angels, venture capitalists, or any other source. As a result, Accardi went to crowdfunding to raise money and was able to do so to the tune of 440 thousand British pounds (Coomber 2015).

Schwienbacher and Larralde (2010) conducted a case study investigation of a European company. They discovered that the owners of the company turned to crowdfunding after depleting their bank accounts, local incubators and personal resources and being unable to acquire capital from business angels and private individuals. When a bank reduced its credit line for a shoe manufacturer during the 2008 financial crisis, the researcher Stoeckl (2014) utilized a case study approach to explain how the manufacturer turned to crowdfunding as a means of obtaining money. O'Toole *et al.* (2015) found that due to the lack of access to bank financing, only a small fraction of Irish companies employed crowdfunding. These examples demonstrate why and how small business owners use crowdfunding in comparison to other possibilities for obtaining money. Entrepreneurs have a duty to conduct a cost-benefit analysis comparing the various forms of crowdfunding to more conventional means of obtaining financing (Belleflamme *et al.* 2014).

It is crucial to make note of the similarities between crowdfunding and other conventional forms of financing before moving on to an analysis of the potential role that crowdfunding could play in the life cycle of the company. Motylska-Kuzma (2015) performed an analysis on the connection between the cost of capital and the level of firm control. She concluded that the peer-to-peer crowdfunding model had parallels with commercial papers and bank loans, and that the equity crowdfunding model had parallels with the issuing of shares. Both of these models were considered to be forms of crowdfunding.

There is evidence in the existing body of literature to imply that enterprises in various stages of development, that is, from the point of establishment all the way up until the maturity stage, use crowdfunding. Both Collins and Pierrakis (2012) and Motylska-Kuzma (2015) arrive at the same conclusion when they state that firms use crowdfunding after they have exhausted resources from friends and families and particularly in the period of development when the firm is not attractive enough for venture capitalist funds and after business angels stop being active.

Despite the fact that there are multiple varieties of crowdfunding that, due to their distinct characteristics, would fit at various stages of growth, crowdfunding is not dimensioned in the research cited here. The research conducted by Paschen (2017) resulted in the development of a model that considers the many different types of crowdfunding and how they relate to the life cycle of start-ups. Paschen adopted a three-stage model of the life cycle that was proposed by Lewis and Churchill (1983), and the donation model is linked with the reward model, as in Lewis and Churchill (1983) and Motylska-Kuzma (2015). This was done in order to better understand the relationship between the two models. Instead of concentrating on the organization as a whole, this strategy places primary emphasis on the various stages of a product's life cycle. In spite of the fact that the donation model, due to the traits it possesses, fits in the process of generating business concepts, it is unknown how many businesses are actually capable of utilizing this model. To be more specific, the donation model is most commonly utilized for investment projects that offer specific social advantages; however, it is not sufficient to expect investors to invest and be less dissatisfied by the failure of the project just because they contributed a small amount. This is because it is unrealistic to believe that investors will invest and be less dissatisfied by the failure of the project (Paschen 2017). In addition to this, Paschen (2017) does not take into consideration the pre-purchase model, which is responsible for a sizeable portion of the total funds received through crowdfunding projects (Rossi 2014).

In their study, Belleflamme *et al.* (2014) construct the theoretical framework and carry out an assessment of the factors that play a role in selecting one model over another, specifically the pre-purchase model and the equity model. In this scenario, the company has the ability to implement a price discrimination strategy, wherein it will use the pre-purchase model for projects that require a lower amount of capital and the equity model for initiatives that require a higher amount of capital. In their study, they stress the difficulties of merging traditional forms of finance as well as crowdfunding into a life cycle framework. This is due to the complexity and multi-dimensionality of the platform that crowdfunding utilizes. The reasons companies choose to use crowdfunding are distinct from the reasons they choose to use traditional channels. Crowdfunding campaigns not only provide finances, but also more information and comments about products (Agrawal *et al.* 2015).

Individuals who invest through crowdfunding platforms, on the other hand, are driven by reasons that are distinct from those that inspire financial organizations that specialize in providing company financing. People become involved in crowdfunding campaigns because they are interested in making monetary gains, they place a high value on innovation, they have a desire to communicate with other investors, and they feel a connection to the business or product in which they invest (Ordanini *et al.* 2011). In addition, the returns on investments are contingent upon a number of different assumptions. For example, business angels make significant investments and benefit from non-standard contracts. However, in equity crowdfunding, similar arrangements would incur enormous transaction costs. As a result, standard contracts are most usually employed instead of non-standard ones (Hornuf and Schwienbacher 2015).

Because the demand and supply sides of crowdfunding do not meet the assumptions of these models, it is difficult to incorporate crowdfunding into any theory of financing firms through their life cycle. This is because the assumptions for these models are not met for crowdfunding on the demand and supply sides. In addition, the weaknesses that are inherent in various models of finance may be highlighted even further by crowdfunding efforts. As a result, the issue of information asymmetry in the pecking order theory may be made worse by equity crowdfunding, because individual investors typically lack the knowledge and/or experience necessary to evaluate investment ideas and/or the firm. Therefore, businesses would try to indicate their quality in equity crowdfunding much more than they would with business angels, and there is a theoretical danger that they will not be successful in crowdfunding campaigns despite the fact that they could be profitable businesses (Ahlers *et al.* 2015).

Types of entrepreneurship

According to the findings of Barot's (2015) study, there are two distinct types of entrepreneurial activity.

(i) Opportunity-based entrepreneurship

The first type of entrepreneurship is one that is driven by opportunities. An entrepreneur is someone who spots a potential profit-making opportunity and then makes the decision to pursue that opportunity as a career. Opportunities-based entrepreneurship, according to Baptista *et al.* (2014), is defined as initiating venture activities because of a new idea and personal amplifications. However, opportunities-based entrepreneurship, according to Jinjian *et al.* (2020), is defined as beginning a business because of an opportunity. This type of entrepreneurship has to do with business opportunities that arise from unmet needs.

(ii) Necessity entrepreneurship

A second type of entrepreneurship is the necessity entrepreneurship. According to Barot (2015), a necessity entrepreneur has no other choice but to start their own company in order to make a living. In this particular scenario, going into business for yourself is not a choice but a necessity. People at this point in their lives do not place a high value on entrepreneurial endeavours because they are in a position where they have no other viable options in the labour market (Gries and Naudé 2011).

A study that was carried out by Aulet and Murray (2013) distinguished between other types of entrepreneurships, namely innovation-driven entrepreneurship, and small and medium-sized enterprises.

(iii) Innovation-driven entrepreneurship

This is entrepreneurship formed by innovation-driven factors. This type of innovation-driven entrepreneurship (IDE) is similar to other types of entrepreneurship in that it promotes the concept of innovation in business with the intention of pursuing global opportunities by bringing new innovations to customers that have a distinct advantage over existing alternatives and a significant capacity for expansion. Innovation refers to the introduction of novel concepts in the areas of technology, the marketplace, or business models. The idea that an entrepreneur should be innovation-driven is extremely important because it places an emphasis on the entrepreneur's awareness of the need to build a competitive advantage. This is something that an entrepreneur can only accomplish by taking the resources that are available today and doing something unique with them.

(iv) Small and medium-sized entrepreneurship

Another type of entrepreneurship is known as small and medium-sized enterprises (SMEs), and these are distinguished from IDEs by their restricted access to global markets, their focus on serving local markets in traditional ways and their lack of a competitive advantage. SMEs cater to regional markets using tried-and-tested, well-understood business concepts and have a limited advantage over their competitors. SMEs' success depends on the business acumen of the entrepreneur, their ability to execute their project, and the prevailing local demand; however, the entrepreneur does not face the complex set of technical, market and business risks that are faced by IDEs.

IDEs and SMEs are distinct from one another due to the fact that innovation necessitates the collaboration of skilled individuals in teams that are centred on the business model, process and technology challenges that are faced by business organizations. In contrast, the realm of SMEs is concerned with issues of revenue, cash flow and job creation over time (Aulet *et al.* 2013).

Financial needs of small and medium-sized firms

The financial theory and market efficiency implications of the capital structure theories derived from the examination of public corporations can be completely applied to small and medium-sized businesses. In this scenario, the size of the business is irrelevant. There are significant contrasts in terms of financial management and prospective investors between real-world small businesses and miniature versions of large corporations (Orsag and Dedi 2011).

(v) Hybrid entrepreneurship

Hybrid entrepreneurs are individuals who start a business while in a permanent wage paying job. Hybrid entrepreneurship is a low-risk way to gain experience as an entrepreneur and can be a good strategy for testing business concepts in the market (Kritskaya *et al.* 2017). The risk of business failure and the constraint faced in sourcing finance could be reduced through hybrid entrepreneurship which allows the individual to work full time on a job while starting and developing an entrepreneurial venture. This approach allows the entrepreneur to learn the ropes, increasing the chances for success (Raffiee and Feng 2013; Geho and Frakes 2013). Hybrid entrepreneurship provides an option in the financing of new ventures.

The concept of hybrid entrepreneurship is different from part-time entrepreneurship since it excludes entrepreneurs who are unemployed or unemployable because they are too young, too old, or not able to work (e.g. due to physical or mental disabilities), and part-time workers, i.e. individuals who work less than 30 hours per week in their job (Schulz *et al.* 2016). Kritskaya *et al.* (2017) suggest the following differences between hybrid entrepreneurs and full-time entrepreneurs with regard to business gestation, performance and survival:

- Hybrids are less likely to reach central milestones in business gestation process
- Hybrids report significant lower accumulated sales, accumulated labour costs and accumulated earnings than full-time entrepreneurs
- Firms started by hybrids have higher chances of survival than firms started by full-time entrepreneurs

(vi) Social entrepreneurship

Included in the realm of social entrepreneurship is the concept of social enterprise, which can be defined as the application of business strategies to not-for-profit organizations. In recent years, non-profit organizations have increasingly turned to social enterprise in an effort to fund their social goals. However, very little research has been done to determine how the use of social enterprises affects overall investment or the circumstances under which social firms are significantly more effective. According to research conducted by Smith *et al.* (2012), the launch of a social enterprise has a detrimental impact on the amount of money contributed by individuals. On the other hand, some of these unfavourable consequences may be lessened if people have the impression that the social enterprise is both mission-oriented and capable. The data also suggest that the perspectives of donors about social enterprises can have an effect on the outcomes that are seen in a given situation.

A social enterprise is a business with primarily social objectives, whose surpluses are principally reinvested for that purpose in the business or in the community, rather than being driven by the need to maximize profits for shareholders (DTI 2002). A social enterprise can also be defined by using examples which include development trusts, community enterprises, housing associations, football supporters' trusts, social firms, leisure trusts and co-operatives. It is often referred to as a third sector organization (Deakins and Freel 2012).

In the rapidly expanding field of social entrepreneurship, organizations seek novel solutions to intractable social problems such as hunger, poverty and education. These organizations frequently leverage business knowledge, strategies and tactics to achieve their social goals. Social entrepreneurship is an example of a field that is undergoing rapid development (Dees 1998; Skloot 1988; Bloom 2009; Nicholls 2006; Bloom and Smith 2010; Smith and Stevens 2010). In the field of social entrepreneurship, social enterprise is one of the most common types of social entrepreneurship.

In this form of social entrepreneurship, organizations that are not-for-profit start businesses with the intention of making a profit and generating money (Dees 1998; Skloot 1988). Although engaging in commercial activities by non-profit organizations is not a new practice, the size and scope of these social enterprises are expanding due to a number of factors. These factors include an increasingly competitive environment for economic resources, the promotion of successful commercial activities through the media or trade associations and the potential for unrestricted income (Skloot 1988; Foster and Bradach 2005). There are a variety of reasons why charitable organizations participate in social enterprise (Dees 1998). To start with, social enterprises have the potential to develop more sustainable sources of funding through the creation of a business, as opposed to relying on charitable philanthropy, which can be negatively impacted by economic downturns and donor fatigue.

Second, social enterprises have the potential to improve the quality of life for those who live in underserved communities (Weisbrod 1998). Non-profit organizations that partner with social enterprises may not only see an increase in funding but also receive assistance in achieving their social missions. This is especially true in situations where the social enterprise is mission-driven and the social mission is carried out through the enterprise itself. The ability of non-profit organizations to expand their sources of funding to include earned income, in addition to grants and contributions, may be made possible via social businesses (Lazarevski *et al.* 2008).

Advantages of social enterprises

Social enterprises usually operate with a purpose of creating value for the society while at the same time generating income as well as wealth. The solutions offered by social enterprises can be innovative, unique, people and environment friendly and cost effective. These attributes are also challenging to the sustainability of social enterprises, but the ones that are able to meet the challenges are the ones that create impact in the society. These are the enterprises that are advantageous to the society, people and the environment.

Social enterprises typically deal with people who live at the bottom of the pyramid; therefore they are beneficial to the poor by providing them with means of livelihood. Since social enterprises do not operate as conventional businesses, they offer flexible working conditions and environment which are conducive to many categories of people. The employment they offer may be both short term and long term in nature or it may be specially targeted to a specific group of people or a geographic community or to people with disabilities.

There are advantages of a social enterprise which are entrepreneur specific such as:

(i) There are many incentives and schemes from the government for this purpose. Therefore, for this reason, it could be said it is easier for social entrepreneurs to raise capital at below market rates (MariaDB 2023).

(ii) Marketing and promotion for social enterprises are also easy. Since a social problem is being tackled with a solution, it is easier to attract attention of the people and media. The degree of publicity often depends on the degree of uniqueness of the solution.

(iii) It is easier to garner support from likeminded individuals since there is a social side to the enterprise. It is also easier to get people onboard at lower salaries compared to conventional businesses.

There are also advantages that are specific to the environment and the society which include:

(i) Services offered can be customized better to suit the needs of the individual or the problem.

(ii) The solutions offered by social enterprises either in the form of products or services are reasonable and cost effective compared to those offered by a for-profit organization. Such products and services include basic amenities such as health care, education and micro finance which are affordable to people all over the world including the poorest.

Although lots of organizations have also made corporate social responsibility an integral part of their business functioning but not many actually mean to create a difference. It is just a means to achieve more profits; but social enterprises actually aim to add value.

Challenges faced by social enterprises

Social enterprises face a number of challenges. The most common challenges can be (Hossain 2020):

(i) Lack of funding

The greatest challenge for social enterprises is funding as most social enterprises are unable to obtain start-up capital. Since most of the social entrepreneurs are single individuals, it is extremely difficult for them to assemble sufficient start-up funds. Although some social enterprises do well over time, but some of them struggle to survive and become sustainable due to lack of funding. The attitude of traditional financial institutions such as banks (or indeed other financial institutions) is unhelpful to social enterprises. The attitude of financial institutions is due to the misconception that social enterprises are not profitable and therefore not able to pay back any finance provided to them. Other reasons for the lack of funding include lack of collateral by most social enterprises. Most social enterprises lack quality proposals and business plans to justify funding. Social enterprises are also unwilling to take on external finance because of the risks.

(ii) Balancing social purpose while securing income

Social entrepreneurs have multiple missions of social purpose and income generation. This means duality of mission of sorting out social issues and at the same time being able to generate sufficient income to earn profit. This duality of purpose has constituted a big problem for social enterprises.

(iii) Inability to scale-up operation

Principally, social enterprises are often set up as a result of market failure when the government is unable to meet societal needs. Most of the time social enterprises begin with eagerness to address the problem, but they lack the ability to scale up the operation to another level. This is partly due to lack of sufficient support in funding and other resources which affect their sustainability. It is also partly due the inability to prove legitimacy. The inability to scale up operation could also be because the social issue for which the social enterprise was set up may no longer be relevant or have been fulfilled.

(iv) Lack of management skills and business strategy

The lack of management skills and business strategy is another major challenge facing the majority of social enterprises. These lead to the inability to come up with non-competitive products. The focus on social needs tends to limit the ability to develop products or services that can be competitive in the market. The lack of management skills is more likely to impede on their ability to adequately engage in business planning, which involves financial forecasts, sales and marketing. Integral to this is the fact that most of the workforce are predominately volunteers who prioritize activities that secure their personal income.

Grameen Bank: an example of social entrepreneurship

Muhammad Yunus was inspired during the Bangladesh famine of 1974 to make a small loan of US$27 to a group of 42 families as start-up money for small ventures, without the burdens of paying high interests to moneylenders and loan sharks. Yunus believed that making such loans available to a larger population could stimulate businesses and reduce the widespread rural poverty in Bangladesh.

Yunus developed the principles of the Grameen Bank from his research and experience (*Grameen Bank* is Bengali for "Rural" or "Village" Bank). He began a research project, together with a national commercial bank and the University of Chittagong, extending microcredit to test his method for providing credit and banking services to the poor in the rural area. In 1976, the village of Jobra became the first to be served by the project. Over the next two years, the project expanded to other villages in the area. The project, with support from the Bangladesh Bank, was extended in 1979 to the Tangail District. The project's services expanded to other districts of Bangladesh over the next few years.

By an ordinance of the Bangladesh government dated 2 October 1983, the project was converted into the Grameen Bank. Bankers Ron Grzywinski and Mary Houghton of ShoreBank, a community development bank in Chicago, helped Yunus with the official incorporation of the bank under a grant from the Ford Foundation. The bank's repayment rate suffered from the economic disruption following the 1998 flood in Bangladesh, but it recovered in the subsequent years. By the beginning of 2005, the bank had loaned over US$4.7 billion and by the end of 2008, US$7.6 billion to the poor.

As of 2017, the Bank had about 2,600 branches and nine million borrowers, with a repayment rate of 99.6%. Ninety-seven per cent of the borrowers were women. The Bank has been active in 97% of the villages of Bangladesh. Its success has inspired similar projects in more than 64 countries around the world, including a World Bank initiative to finance Grameen-type schemes.

Grameen Bank is now expanding into wealthy countries as well. As of 2017, Grameen America had 19 branches in 11 US cities. Nearly 100,000 of its borrowers being all women.

Funding

The bank has gained its funding from different sources, and the main contributors have shifted over time. In the initial years, donor agencies used to provide the bulk of capital at low rates. By the mid-1990s, the bank started to get most of its funding from the central bank of Bangladesh. More recently, Grameen has started bond sales as a source of finance. The bonds are implicitly subsidized, as they are guaranteed by the Government of Bangladesh, and still they are sold above the bank rate. In 2013, Bangladesh parliament passed the "Grameen Bank Act" which replaces the Grameen Bank Ordinance, 1983, authorizing the government to make rules for any aspect of the running of the bank.

Source: Adapted from https://en.wikipedia.org/wiki/Grameen_Bank

Summary

The significance of crowdfunding can be understood in two ways. On the one hand, it has a minor impact in contrast to small business funding in general. On the other hand, this is one of the few efforts accessible to assist creative ventures, and it is also quite unique in comparison to microfinancing, where it is now possible to know exactly what type of project is being funded.

In recent years, the worldwide use of crowdfunding has increased significantly. In 2012, a total of $2.7 billion was raised through crowdfunding; by 2015, that figure had increased to $34.4 billion (Massolution 2016). With the growing importance of crowdfunding, the quantity of scholarly studies on the subject has also increased. One of the subjects was the contrast between crowdfunding and conventional ways of finance.

Even though the theoretical frameworks that comprise crowdfunding are still in the process of developing, it is not impossible to incorporate crowdfunding into the context of financing businesses throughout all stages of their life cycle. On the other hand, there are obstacles, such as the fact that there are significant gaps between the demand and supply sides of the market. When opposed to more conventional ways of finance, crowdfunding presents businesses with a number of advantages that encourage their adoption of the practice. When it comes to the supply side, investors have diverse amounts of information, different reasons for investing, and different philosophies for maximizing profits and spreading risk. Additional research is necessary in order to include crowdfunding into models of financing businesses throughout all stages of an enterprise's life cycle.

Discussion questions

1 Discuss the various motives underlying financing options.
2 Discuss the two basic theories that influence capital structure decisions.
3 "When it comes to financing their projects, entrepreneurs have varied incentives and, as a result, exhibit diverse behaviors." Discuss.
4 Discus the pecking order theory and why business owners use it to determine their financing options.
5 What role can crowdfunding play in the various stages of entrepreneurial development?

Test questions

1 Drawing on the pecking order theory, do you consider equity crowdfunding as a "first" or a "last" resort?
2 "Entrepreneurial firms with more internally generated funds are less likely to seek equity crowdfunding". Justify this statement.
3 What are the challenges usually faced by social entrepreneurs and mission led enterprises?

Glossary of key terminologies

Information asymmetry   An imbalance between two parties in their knowledge of relevant facts.

Business angels   A private individual, often with a high net-worth, and usually with business experience, who directly invests part of their assets in new and growing private businesses.

Capital structure   The specific mix of debt and equity used to finance a company's assets and operations.

Collateral   An asset that a lender accepts as security for a loan.

Determinants   A factor which decisively affects the nature or outcome of something.

Diversity   The condition of having or being composed of differing elements.

Donor fatigue   A lessening of public willingness to respond generously to charitable appeals, resulting from the frequency of such appeals.

Economic downturn   A reverse growth in the economy.

Empirical studies   A way of gaining knowledge by means of direct and indirect observation or experience.

Life cycle   The series of stages that a company undergoes as it passes from its formation and through to maturity and decline.

Marginal benefit   The additional satisfaction that a consumer receives when the additional good or service is purchased. The marginal benefit generally decreases as consumption increases.

SMEs   Small and medium-size enterprises.

Recommended reading

Frank, M.Z., and Goyal, V.K., 2008. Trade-off and pecking order theories of debt. *In: Handbook of empirical corporate finance*, 135–202.

Horvatinović, T., and Orsag, S., 2018. Crowdfunding in a context of financing firms through their life cycle. *Zagreb International Review of Economics & Business*, 21 (1), 105–118.

Huang, G., 2006. The determinants of capital structure: Evidence from China. *China Economic Review*, 17 (1), 14–36.

La Rocca, M., La Rocca, T., and Cariola, A., 2011. Capital structure decisions during a firm's life cycle. *Small Business Economics*, 37 (1), 107–130.

Shneor, R., Zhao, L., and Flåten, B.T., 2020. *Advances in crowdfunding: Research and practice*. New York: Springer Nature, 531.

Swinnen, S., Voordeckers, W., and Vandemaele, S., 2005. Capital structure in SMEs: Pecking order versus static trade-off, bounded rationality and the behavioural principle. *European Financial Management Association*, 7 (1), 1–40.

Troise, C., and Tani, M., 2020. Exploring entrepreneurial characteristics, motivations and behaviours in equity crowdfunding: Some evidence from Italy. *Management Decision*, 59 (5), 995–1024.

Xiang, D., and Worthington, A., 2015. Finance-seeking behaviour and outcomes for small- and medium-sized enterprises. *International Journal of Managerial Finance*, 11 (4), 513–530.

References

Agrawal, A., Catalini, C., and Goldfarb, A., 2015. Crowdfunding: Geography, social networks, and the timing of investment decisions. *Journal of Economics & Management Strategy*, 24 (2), 253–274.

Ahlers, G.K., Cumming, D., Günther, C., and Schweizer, D., 2015. Signaling in equity crowdfunding. *Entrepreneurship Theory and Practice*, 39 (4), 955–980.

Ang, J.S., 1991. Small business uniqueness and the theory of financial management. *Journal of Small Business Finance*, 1 (1), 1–13.

Aulet, W., and Murray, F., 2013. *A tale of two entrepreneurs: Understanding differences in the types of entrepreneurships in the economy.* Available from SSRN 2259740.

Baptista, R., Karaöz, M., and Mendonça, J., 2014. The impact of human capital on the early success of necessity versus opportunity-based entrepreneurs. *Small Business Economics*, 42, 831–847.

Barot, H., 2015. Entrepreneurship-A key to success. *The International Journal of Business and Management*, 3 (1), 163–165.

Baskin, J., 1989. An empirical investigation of the pecking order hypothesis. *Financial Management*, 26–35.

Belleflamme, P., Lambert, T., and Schwienbacher, A., 2014. Crowdfunding: Tapping the right crowd. *Journal of Business Venturing*, 29 (5), 585–609 (Agrawal *et al.* 2014).

Bloom, P., 2009. Overcoming consumption constraints through social entrepreneurship. *Journal of Public Policy & Marketing*, 28, 128–134.

Bloom, P., and Smith, B.R., 2010. Identifying the drivers of social entrepreneurial impact: theoretical development and an exploratory empirical test of Scalers. *Journal of Social Entrepreneurship*, 1 (1), 126–145.

Booth, L., Aivazian, V., Demirguc-Kunt, A., and Maksimovic, V., 2001. Capital structures in developing countries. *The Journal of Finance*, 56 (1), 87–130.

Bowen, R.M., Daley, L.A., and Huber Jr, C.C., 1982. Evidence on the existence and determinants of inter-industry differences in leverage. *Financial Management*, 10–20.

Bradley, M., Jarrell, G.A., and Kim, E.H., 1984. On the existence of an optimal capital structure: Theory and evidence. *The Journal of Finance*, 39 (3), 857–878.

Brennan, M., and Kraus, A., 1987. Efficient financing under asymmetric information. *The Journal of Finance*, 42 (5), 1225–1243 (Narayanan (1988)).

Chittenden, F., Hall, G., and Hutchinson, P., 1996. Small firm growth, access to capital markets and financial structure: Review of issues and an empirical investigation. *Small Business Economics*, 8, 59–67.

Collins, L., and Pierrakis, Y., 2012. The venture crowd crowdfunding Equity Investment into Business. *Nesta*. Available from: www.nesta.org.uk/sites/default/files/the_venture_crowd.pdf [Accessed 1 March 2017].

Constantinides, G.M., and Grundy, B.D., 1989. Optimal investment with stock repurchase and financing as signals. *The Review of Financial Studies*, 2 (4), 445–465.

Coomber, S., 2015. Small data. *London Business School Review*, 26 (2), 4–5.

Deakins, D., and Freel, M., 2012. *Entrepreneurship and small firms*. 6th ed. London: McGraw-Hill.

DeAngelo, H., and Masulis, R.W., 1980. Optimal capital structure under corporate and personal taxation. *Journal of Financial Economics*, 8 (1), 3–29.

Dees, J.G., 1998. Enterprising nonprofits: What do you do when traditional sources of funding fall short. *Harvard Business Review*, 76 (1), 55–67.

Diamond, D., 1989. Reputation acquisition in debt markets. *Journal of Political Economy*, 97 (4), 828–862.

Dickinson, V., 2011. Cash flow patterns as a proxy for firm life cycle. *The Accounting Review*, 86 (6), 1969–1994 (Ucbasaran, Shepherd, Lockett, & Lyon, 2013).

DTI, 2002. *Social enterprise: A strategy for success*. Available from: www.readkong.com/page/social-enterprise-a-strategy-for-success-4601561 (Accessed 21 March 2023].

Emery, D.R., Finnerty, J.D., and Stowe, J.D., 2004. *Corporate financial management*. 2nd ed. Upper Saddle River: Prentice Hall.

Ferri, M.G., and Jones, W.H., 1979. Determinants of financial structure: A new methodological approach. *The Journal of Finance*, 34 (3), 631–644.

Foster, W., and Jeffrey, B., 2005. Should nonprofits seek profits? *Harvard Business Review*, 83, 92–100.

Geho, P.R., and Frakes, J., 2013. Financing for small business in a sluggish economy versus conflicting impulses of the entrepreneur. *The Entrepreneurial Executive*, 18, 89.

Gries, T., and Naudé, W., 2011. Entrepreneurship and human development: A capability approach. *Journal of Public Economics*, 95 (3–4), 216–224.

Hamilton, R.T., and Fox, M.A., 1998. The financing preferences of small firm owners. *International Journal of Entrepreneurial Behavior & Research*, 4 (3), 239–248.

Heinkel, R., and Zechner, J., 1990. The role of debt and preferred stock as a solution to adverse investment incentives. *Journal of Financial and Quantitative Analysis*, 25 (1), 1–24.

Holmes, S., and Kent, P., 1991. An empirical analysis of the financial structure of small and large Australian manufacturing enterprises. *Journal of Small Business Finance*, 1 (2), 141–154.

Hornuf, L., and Schwienbacher, A., 2015. Funding dynamics in crowdinvesting, theorie und politik – Session. *Financial Economics*, II (B10-V3), ZBW.

Hossain, S., 2020. *What are the challenges faced by social enterprises? HotCubator*. Available from: https://hotcubator.com.au/social-entrepreneurship/what-are-the-challenges-faced-by-social-enterprises/ [Accessed 21 March 2023].

Hutchinson P., 1999. Small enterprise: Finance, ownership and control. *International Journal of Management Reviews*, 1 (3), 343–365.

Jensen, M., and Meckling, W., 1976. Theory of the firm: Managerial behaviour, agency costs and ownership structure. *Journal of Financial Economics*, 3 (4), 305–360.

Jinjiang, H., Nazari, M., Yingqian, Z., and Ning, C., 2020. Opportunity-based entrepreneurship and environmental quality of sustainable development: A resource and institutional perspective. *Journal of Cleaner Production*, 256 (20), 120390.

Jordan, J., Lowe, J., and Taylor, P., 1998. Strategy and financial policy in UK small firms. *Journal of Business Finance & Accounting*, 25, 1–27.

Krasker, W.S., 1986. Stock price movements in response to stock issues under asymmetric information. *The Journal of Finance*, 41 (1), 93–105.

Kritskaya, L., Kolvereid, L., and Isaksen, E., 2017. Hybrid entrepreneurs: Characteristics and achievements. *Entreprendre & Innover*, 3 (34), 7–19.

La Rocca, M., La Rocca, T., and Cariola, A., 2011. Capital structure decisions during a firm's life cycle. *Small Business Economics*, 37, 107–130.

Lazarevski, K., Irvine, H., and Dolnicar, S., 2008., The effect of funding changes on public sector nonprofit organizations: The case of bushcare NSW. *Journal of Nonprofit and Public Sector Marketing*, 20 (2), 213–227.

Lev, B., 1969. Industry averages as targets for financial ratios. *Journal of Accounting Research*, 290–299.

Lewis, V.L., and Churchill, N.C., 1983. The five stages of small business growth. *University of Illinois at Urbana-Champaign's Academy for Entrepreneurial Leadership Historical Research Reference in Entrepreneurship*, 3 (3), 1–12.

March, J.G., 1978. Bounded rationality, ambiguity, and the engineering of choice. *The Bell Journal of Economics*, 9 (2), 587–608.

Maria, D.B., 2023. *Advantages of social enterprises, management study guide.* Available from: www.managementstudyguide.com/social-enterprises-advantages.htm [Accessed 21 March 2023].

Martin, J.D., and Scott Jr, D.F., 1974. A discriminant analysis of the corporate debt-equity decision. *Financial Management*, 71–79.

Massolution, 2016. *Crowdfunding industry 2015 Report.* Available from: http://reports. crowdsourcing.org/index.php?route=product/productandpath=20andproduct_id=54.

Miller, M.H., 1977. Debt and taxes. *Journal of Finance*, 23, 261–275.

Modigliani, F., and Miller, M., 1958. The cost of capital, corporation finance, and the theory of investment. *American Economic Review*, 48, 261–297.

Modigliani, F., and Miller, M., 1963. Corporate income taxes and cost of capital: A correction. *American Economic Review*, 53, 433–443.

Motylska-Kuzma, A., 2015. Cost of crowdfunding as a source of capital for the small company. *In: Proceedings of international academic conferences, September 2015.* London: International Institute of Social and Economic Sciences, 462–474.

Myers, S.C., 1984. The capital structure puzzle. *Journal of Finance*, 39, 575–592 (Miller, 1977).

Myers, S.C., 2001. Capital structure. *Journal of Economic Perspectives*, 15 (2), 81–102.

Myers, S.C., and Majluf, N.S., 1984. Corporate financing and investment decisions when firms have information that investors do not have. *Journal of Financial Economics*, 13 (2), 187–221.

Narayanan, M.P., 1988. Debt versus equity under asymmetric information. *Journal of Financial and Quantitative Analysis*, 23 (1), 39–51.

Nicholls, A., 2006. *Social entrepreneurship: New models of sustainable social change.* New York: Oxford University Press.

Noe, T.H., 1988. Capital structure and signaling game equilibria. *The Review of Financial Studies*, 1 (4), 331–355.

Ordanini, A., Miceli, L., Pizzetti, M., and Parasuraman, A., 2011. Crowd-funding: Transforming customers into investors through innovative service platforms. *Journal of Service Management*, 22 (4), 443–470.

Orsag, S., Dedi, L., and Mihalina, E., 2011. Banks in transition countries as one of most attractive investments. *UTMS Journal of Economics*, 2 (1), 1–20.

O'Toole, C.M., Lawless, M., and Lambert, D., 2015. Non-bank financing in Ireland: A comparative perspective. *The Economic and Social Review*, 46(1), 133–161.

Paschen, J., 2017. Choose wisely: Crowdfunding through the stages of the start-up life cycle. *Business Horizons*, 60 (2), 179–188. Available from: https://doi.org/10.1016/j. bushor.2016.11.003

Penrose, E.T., 1952. Biological analogies in the theory of the firm. *American Economic Review*, 42 (5), 804–819.

Raffiee, J., and Coff, R.W., 2013. *Perceptions of firm-specific human capital: An empirical exploration.* Available from: SSRN 2253472.

Rajan, R.G., and Zingales, L., 1995. What do we know about capital structure? Some evidence from international data. *The Journal of Finance*, 50 (5), 1421–1460.

Rossi, M., 2014. The new ways to raise capital: An exploratory study of crowdfunding. *International Journal of Financial Research*, 5 (2), 8–18. Available from: https://doi.org/10.5430/ijfr.v5n2p8

Sadler-Smith, E., 2004. Cognitive style and the management of small and medium-sized enterprises. *Organization Studies*, 25 (2), 155–181.

Schulz, M., Urbig, D., and Procher, V., 2016. Hybrid entrepreneurship and public policy: The case of firm entry deregulation. *Journal of Business Venturing*, 31, 272–286.

Schwienbacher, A., and Larralde, B., 2010. *Crowdfunding of small entrepreneurial ventures. Handbook of entrepreneurial finance.* Oxford: Oxford University Press.

Scott, D.F., Jr., and Martin, J.D., 1975. Industry influence on financial structure. *Financial Management*, 4 (1975), 67–73.

Scott, M., and Bruce, R., 1987. Five stages of growth in small business. *Long Range Planning*, 20 (3), 45–52. Available from: https://doi.org/10.1016/0024–6301(87)90071–9.

Serrasqueiro, Z.S., Armada, M.R., and Nunes, P.M., 2011. Pecking order theory versus trade-off theory: Are service SMEs' capital structure decisions different? *Service Business*, 5 (4), 381–409 (Silver *et al.* 2016).

Smith, B.R., Cronley, M.L., and Barr, T.F., 2012. Funding implications of social enterprise: The role of mission consistency, entrepreneurial competence, and attitude toward social enterprise on donor behavior. *Journal of Public Policy & Marketing*, 31 (1), 142–157.

Smith, B.R., and Stevens, C., 2010. Different types of social entrepreneurship: The role of geography and structural embeddedness on measurement and scaling of social value. *Entrepreneurship & Regional Development*, 22 (6), 575–598.

Stoeckl, V.E., 2014. Lonely rebel or pioneer of the future? Towards an understanding of moral stakeholder framing of activist brands. *Advances in Consumer Research*, 42, 371–376.

Swinnen, J., Deconinck, K., and Vandemoortele, T., Vandeplas, A., eds., 2015. *Quality standards, value chains and international development. Economic and political theory.* Cambridge, England: Cambridge University Press.

Swinnen, S., Voordeckers, W., and Vandemaele, S., 2005. Capital structure in SMEs: Pecking order versus static trade-off, bounded rationality and the behavioural principle. *European Financial Management Association*, 7 (1), 1–40.

Titman, S., and Wessels, R., 1988. The determinants of capital structure choice. *The Journal of Finance*, 43 (1), 1–19.

Wald, J.K., 1999. How firm characteristics affect capital structure: An international comparison. *Journal of Financial Research*, 22 (2), 161–187.

Weisbrod, Burton A., 1998. The nonprofit mission and its financing: Growing links between nonprofits and the rest of the economy. *In*: B. Weisbrod, ed. *To profit or not to profit: the commercial transformation of the nonprofit sector.* Cambridge, MA: Cambridge University Press, 1–24.

Wiwattanakantang, Y., 2001. *The equity ownership structure of Thai firms* [Working Paper, 2001–2008]. Tokyo: Hitotsubashi University, Center of Economic Institutions.

4 Exploring Resource-Based Theory in crowdfunding

Learning objectives

- Discuss the resource-based theory in relation to crowdfunding
- Discuss the resource exchange theory in relation to crowdfunding
- Define the characteristics of resources that lead to sustained competitive advantage as illustrated by the resource-based theory and the resource exchange theory
- Understand the difference between resources and capabilities
- Be able to explain the difference between tangible and intangible resources

Introduction

Crowdfunding generally overlooks exchange of other resources on crowdfunding platforms. This chapter discusses The Resource-Based Theory (RBT) and explores the perspective of how humans interact with technology and how resources are exchanged. It also explores the roles that users adopt on crowdfunding platforms and the mechanisms used to broker the exchange of resources for venture creation.

Therefore, this chapter provides an understanding of resources exchanged and the support mechanisms in crowdfunding. Resource exchange theories deals with how people leverage different types of resources to get entrepreneurial ventures off the ground (Barney 1991). Access to capital is crucial in starting a new business venture, but entrepreneurs often start new businesses with little available capital (Newbert 2007).

Entrepreneurs also leverage social networks and the information these networks bring to the table. The role of social networks in sourcing crowdfunding is explored in the next chapter. They also leverage human resources and their attributes such as level of education and training. Similarly, entrepreneurs add intangible elements of leadership to the mix of resources which cannot be replaced by businesses (Newbert 2007). Therefore, it is pertinent to state that some resources in venture creation may be limited or restricted such as start-up capital, including other intrinsic resources such as skills and experience. These resources may also be in short supply in new ventures which may put small businesses in a difficult position.

DOI: 10.4324/9781003193975-4

Origin and background of Resource-Based Theory

The RBT originated from an article written by Jay Barney in 1991 titled, "Firm Resources and Sustained Competitive Advantage". As a result of this article the RBT became the dominant paradigm in strategic planning as a reaction against the 1980s' school of thought which focused managerial attention on external factors such as the structure of the industry. In contrast, the resource-based theory argued that sustainable competitive advantage derives from developing superior capabilities and resources available to the firm.

Many academics have argued that the resource-based perspective had existed since the 1930s. They argue that Barney was influenced by Wernerfelt's work in 1984 (Wernerfelt 1984). However, other academics argue that the RBT is a new paradigm although it has its roots in economic theories, notably Penrose's work, *The Theory of the Growth of the Firm* in 1959.

The Resource-Based Theory

The Resource-Based Theory (RBT) suggests that firms are heterogeneous because they possess different kinds of resources. This means that firms can have different strategies because they have a different mix of resource. The theory focuses attention on the firm's internal resources which it identifies as assets, capabilities and competencies with the potential to deliver superior competitive advantages (Barney 1991; Penrose 1959; Peteraf 1993; Prahalad and Hamel 1990; Teece *et al.* 1997; Wernerfelt 1984).

Therefore, RBT is a managerial framework which is used to determine the strategic resources a firm can exploit to achieve sustainable competitive advantage. The central tenet of the theory is that instead of an organization looking at the competitive business environment to get a niche in the market or to have an edge over competition and threats, it should instead look into itself for the potentials and resources it already has available.

What this means essentially is that it is easier for a firm to exploit new opportunities using resources and competencies that are already available to the firm, rather than having to acquire new skills, traits or functions for different opportunities. Supporters of the RBT argue that these resources and competencies should be prioritized within organizational strategy development.

The Resource-Based Theory is interdisciplinary in nature in that it was developed within the disciplines of economics, ethics, law, management, marketing, supply chain management and general business (Hunt 2013). Using accounting and finance concepts, the RBT distinguishes between two types of resource (assets): tangible and intangible assets.

Types of resources

Grigoriou *et al.* (2016) classify organizational resources into two main types: tangible and intangible. The distinction between the two arises from the fact that tangible resources are physical in nature such as land, capital and vehicles whereas intangible resources exist only in concept, for instance, intellectual property and trademarks.

i) Tangible assets

Tangible assets are physical items with a clear purchase value used by a business to produce goods and services. They are also known as hard assets. Machinery, land and property are examples of fixed assets, which are essential in the running of the business. These resources can be generally and easily bought on the market and thus offer little competitive advantage since other organizations can also buy similar items easily if they want to.

ii) Intangible assets

Intangible assets in accounting are resources with long-term financial value to a business. They are not material objects and cannot be touched or physically seen. Intangible resources do not exist physically, but they have value. Examples of intangible assets include a business's reputation, copyrights, trademarks and brand recognition. These are items which other competitors or comparable organizations cannot buy on the market. Intangible assets improve a small business's long-term worth as opposed to tangible (physical) assets and their main source of competitive advantage.

The distinction between types of resources is important as they can be confusing because the term "resource" can be used in different ways within everyday common language. For example, cash is an important resource as well as tangible goods such as vehicles and property. Therefore, it is important not to consider tangible assets such as machinery and vehicles as strategic although they are valuable in their own right, but they cannot convey sustainable competitive advantage since they can be easily acquired by competitors.

Assumptions of Resource-Based Theory

Studies such as Kamasak (2015), Holdford (2018), Suardhika *et al.* (2018), Cho and Linderman (2020) suggest that the core idea of the RBT is that for an organization to develop an innovation, there is need to focus on its potential and resources as opposed to evaluating the business environment in order to identify market gaps that can generate competitive advantage. In the context of this book, the findings suggest that crowdfunding ought to be influenced by the inherent resources and capabilities within individual firms that can generate competitive advantage and improve financial performance as opposed to identifying market niches to be addressed.

In addition to identifying the core idea of the theory, there is also further need to identify the assumptions that it is based upon. Cho and Linderman (2020) summarize the assumptions into two, whereby it is argued that the resources under the RBT must be both heterogeneous and immobile. Heterogeneity is discussed as the variability of skills and resources between organizations. As a result, organizations can employ strategies that differ from other rivals in the same market. The second assumption is that the resources ought to be immobile, in that, they are unable to move freely between organizations within the short-term period in such a way that rivals are challenged in replicating them (Kim *et al.* 2014).

The assumptions on which the resource-based theory is based can be explained and summarized as below:

a) Heterogeneous

The first main assumption is that the resources are different from one organization to the other. If resources are the same in all organizations, they would not be able to compete with each other by employing different strategies. Therefore, there would not be a competitive advantage as there would be perfect competition, which of course does not exist in the real world.

b) Immobile

The second assumption is that resources cannot move, at least in the short term, from one organization to another. Consequently, organizations cannot replicate the resources of another organization or implement the same strategies.

The characteristics of strategic resources

Kamasak (2015) postulates that for an organization to create competitive advantage from its resources, they ought to have four main attributes; valuable, rare, imperfectly imitable and non-substitutable (VRIN). The VRIN acronym was developed by Barney (1991) in a framework that outlined the features of resources that generate competitive advantage as discussed later. However, later in 1997, Barney advanced the acronym to VRIO – valuable, rare, imitable and organized (Barney 1997).

Based on the VRIO framework, it is suggested that resources that create competitive advantage in an organization should not only be valuable, rare and imitable, but also, organized in a way to help the firm capture value (Cardeal and António 2012). The argument advanced is that, an organization would be unable to create competitive advantage if its systems and processes are not designed to help it fully exploit the resources. In the context of crowdfunding, it is therefore suggested that innovation in entrepreneurship would arise from the exploitation of inherent capabilities and utilization of resources that are valuable, rare, imitable and organized in a way that enables individual organizations to capture value.

Therefore, the Resource-Based Theory suggests that organizations must develop unique, firm-specific core competencies that will allow them to outperform competitors by doing things differently (Cardeal and António 2012). Barney (1991) states that for resources to hold potential as sources of sustainable competitive advantage, they must be valuable, rare, imperfectly imitable and not substitutable (VRIN). The acronym VRIN, as further revised as VRIO, can be explained as follows:

- *Valuable*

Resources can only be valuable if they help to increase the value of the service or product supplied to customers or consumers. If resources do not meet this condition then they are not valuable and cannot lead to a competitive advantage.

- *Rare*

Resources are rare if they cannot be easily acquired by any organization. In other words, they are unusual or uncommon and can only be acquired by one of very few organizations.

- *Inimitable*

This means that the resources must not be capable of being imitated or must be costly to imitate or substitute. They must be perfectly inimitable. If they can be imitated or substituted, then there cannot be a competitive edge over organizations which do not have these resources.

- *Organized to add value*

The resources must be organized in such a way as to add value since resources on their own do not automatically gain a competitive advantage. If the organization, its systems and its processes are not designed to exploit the resource to its fullest, then it cannot hope to gain a competitive advantage. For example, if a firm does not properly utilize its talent or knowledge in staff members or correctly utilize the organization's positive reputation, such resources cannot convey a competitive advantage.

Barney (1991) suggests that it is only when all of these factors are fulfilled can one gain a sustained competitive advantage, and can innovate and get ahead in the market. BusinessBalls (2019) indicates that the process for maximizing an advantage using the RBT should be as follows:

a) Identify the organization's potential key resources
b) Evaluate whether the resources fulfil the VRIO criteria
c) Develop and nurture the resources that pass these criteria

Southwest Airlines: a case study of resources that create competitive advantage

In 1971, an upstart firm named Southwest Airlines opened for business by offering flights between Houston, San Antonio, and its headquarters at Love Field in Dallas. From its initial fleet of three airplanes and three destinations, Southwest has grown to operate hundreds of airplanes in scores of cities. Despite competing in an industry that is infamous for bankruptcies and massive financial losses, Southwest marked its 38th profitable year in a row in 2010.

Why has Southwest succeeded while many other airlines have failed?

Historically, the firm has differed from its competitors in a variety of important ways. Most large airlines use a "hub and spoke" system. This type of system routes travellers through a large hub airport on their way from one city to another. Many Delta passengers, for example, end a flight in Atlanta and then take a connecting flight to their actual destination. The inability to travel directly between most pairs of cities adds hours to a traveller's itinerary and increases the chances of luggage being lost. In contrast, Southwest does not have a hub airport; preferring instead to connect cities directly. This helps make flying on Southwest attractive to many travellers.

Apart from direct flights, Southwest has also been more efficient than its rivals. While most airlines use a variety of different airplanes, Southwest operates only one type of jet – the Boeing 737. This means that Southwest can service its fleet much more efficiently than can other airlines. Southwest mechanics need only the know-how to fix one type of airplane, for example, while their counterparts with other firms need a working knowledge of multiple planes. Southwest also gains efficiency by not offering seat assignments in advance, unlike its competitors. This makes the boarding process move more quickly, meaning that Southwest's jets spend more time in the air transporting customers (and making money) and less time at the gate relative to its rivals' planes.

Organizational culture is the dimension along which Southwest perhaps has differed most from its rivals. The airline industry as a whole suffers from a reputation for mediocre service and indifferent employees. In contrast, Southwest enjoys strong loyalty and a sense of teamwork among its employees.

One tangible indicator of this culture is Southwest's stock ticker symbol. Most companies choose stock ticker symbols that evoke their names. Ford's ticker symbol is F, for example, and Walmart's symbol is WMT. When Southwest became a publicly traded company in 1977, executives chose LUV as its ticker symbol. LUV pays a bit of homage to the firm's humble beginnings at Love Field. More important, however, LUV represents the love that executives have created among employees, between employees and the company, and between customers and the company. This "LUV affair" has long been and remains a huge success. As recently as March 2011, for example, Southwest was ranked fourth on *Fortune* magazine's World's Most Admired Company list.

Source: Adapted from Schlangenstein and Hughes (2010).

Evaluation of resources

Gaining a sustainable competitive advantage is central to strategic management. Therefore, the resource-based theory provides the strategy to evaluate potential factors that can be harnessed and deployed to achieve a competitive advantage. The central tenet of the resourced-based theory is that all resources are not of equal importance nor possess the same potential that can convey a sustainable competitive advantage. The theory posits that the sustainability of a competitive advantage depends on whether or not the resources can be easily imitated or substituted. Barney (1991) argues that understanding the causal relationship between the sources of a competitive advantage and strategies that can lead to success is difficult in practice. Therefore, managers must invest a great deal of effort in identifying, understanding and classifying such resources.

Adegbile (2018) suggests that the RBT model separates resource evaluation process into three complementary yet interdependent components, namely, resource inventory (evaluating, adding and shedding), bundling and leveraging. First, resource inventory highlights the need for entrepreneurs to constantly evaluate and modify resources accordingly. This involves the continuous evaluation, shedding and acquisition/development of resources for an entrepreneurial opportunity. Second, resource bundling involves the reconfiguration of resources into bundles that constitutes a strategy for exploiting opportunities and creating a competitive advantage. Lastly, leveraging involves the development and implementation of an effective business model.

Many empirical studies have further employed the resource-based theory in leading innovation in organizations. For instance, Suardhika *et al.* (2018) had revealed that SMEs depend on the mastery of social capital as a basis of their innovation strategies and to enhance their competitive advantages by improving business performance. Cho and Linderman (2020) also suggested the use of the resource-based theory as an alternative approach to innovation to the existent market-based Product Life Cycle (PLC). Findings from the research showed that companies which tended to rely mainly on knowledge-based resources (KBR) and property-based resources (PBR) focused on both product and process innovation simultaneously. However, where organizations adopted only knowledge-based resources (KBR) in their innovation processes, they shifted their focus towards process as opposed to product innovation. Kamasak (2015) had also reported that the innovation performance of organizations was significantly influenced by the innovation strategies adopted and the technological capabilities of firms. As such, it was suggested that firms could enhance their innovation strategies through the reconfiguration of their resource bases associated with technological investments.

The resource-based theory relies on the premise that for a firm to own and sustain a competitive advantage, it must own and control resources and capabilities that are distinctive, peculiar and highly sought after (Kraaijenbrink *et al*. 2010). While vital resource ownership and control is the main proponent of success in the resource-based theory, it may also be argued that resource constraint may hinder crowdfunding as the entrepreneur is forced to solve problems using what is available to him (Soni and Krishnan 2014). Hence, the concept of resource-based theory of innovation may be worth exploring as a theory which could be adapted to explain the concept of crowdfunding.

Drummond *et al*. (2018) describe the resource evaluation process as a process of interaction through the actions of various actors in relationships and networks. They conceptualize the process as obtaining access to resources and co-creating value in the market place. Using the business to business (B2B) context, Drummond *et al*. (2018) explain the interaction process as taking place when business ventures establish and cultivate relationships over a period of time and multiple interactions. As a result, the interaction process increases interdependence between the organizations which leads to significant increase in resource mobilization which are important in providing inter-firm linkages that enhance competitive advantage.

Drummond *et al*. (2018) categorize the interaction process into four perspectives. The first is prospecting and engaging with the actors and implementing with the organization's activities designed to develop and manage the business relationships for the benefit of the company. Secondly, information could be searched and shared among the firms which enables them to develop and maintain their relationships. Thirdly, the process involves different collaborative activities such as co-creation of new products, services, joint ideas, etc. between the firms and their networks. Finally, the process involves operational co-ordination and reconfiguration involving product adaptation, processes and exchanges between collaborating firms which are important for success and achieving competitive advantage.

Assembling resources through Resource-Based Theory

New ventures are typically resource deficient entities which have certain characteristics that prevent efficient resource transaction processes with external resource providers (Ciabuschi *et al*. 2011; Frydrych and Bock 2013). The liability of newness creates a problem for entrepreneurs to realize early-stage resource assembly (Schoonhoven and Romanelli 2001). However, the aim of nascent ventures is to overcome this problem through specific strategies (Alvarez and Busenitz 2001). The RBT posits that firm legitimacy is critical in the entrepreneurial resource assembly process. Therefore, the lack of legitimacy prevents access to strategic resource providers and affects the enterprise development (Ahlstrom and Bruton 2002).

In new venture formation, the initial entrepreneurial actions are primarily to create legitimacy which will subsequently help in more efficient resource assembly (Lounsbury and Glynn 2001). There are, however, different factors that affect the creation of new ventures, namely, the level of education, experience and heterogeneity of the entrepreneurial team (Dalziel *et al.* 2011), the institutionalization of the entrepreneurial story in a business plan (Delmar and Shane 2004) and the utilization of existing certificates and authorizations to create reputation (Sorescu *et al.* 2007).

Frydrych and Bock (2013) argue that legitimacy creation and resource assembly through crowdfunding can be understood through the RBT perspective. Furthermore, Mollick (2012) provides initial understanding on some factors that positively influence the funding outcome in crowdfunding. These are in accordance with previous legitimacy studies which highlight the importance of (i) social capital (Shane and Cable 2002), measured in number of Facebook friends, and (ii) the project quality by applying Chen *et al.*'s (2009) approach of preparedness as a signal of quality (Pollack *et al.* 2012).

Critiques of Resource-Based Theory

The proponents of RBT argue that competitive advantage is obtained when internal resources are properly harnessed and managed. However, critics of the theory argue that it fails to place more emphasis on strategic planning and ignores regulatory policy and market competition. The reality is that both internal factors and strategic planning are important for an organization's performance, although internal resources are more important when considering a firm's competitive edge over competitors.

Other critics argue that the RBT frameworks only suggest that potential internal resources should be identified and developed by managers of an organization, but do not suggest the means of doing it. However, it can be argued that managers have the capability to improve the processes and systems that create higher-value resources, which could over the longer term have a more significant impact on the performance of the organization (Kraaijenbrink *et al.* 2010; Wernerfelt 1984).

It has also been critiqued that RBT frameworks do not take technological advancement into consideration. Critics argue that RBT ignores innovations and inventions which can have a dramatic effect on the value of resources. Others have also argued that RBT can only be applicable in the short term as it ignores organizational learning which is crucial to the success of an organization in the long term (Eisenhardt and Martin 2000).

Other criticisms include the extreme rarity of resources that match the VRIO criteria, the limits of the VRIO criteria itself in determining value, the unclear and indeterminate nature of VRIO itself, and the ambiguous nature of the term *resources*. The general concluding thought is that RBT can be useful for developing competitive advantage, particularly in the short term, but should be considered in partnership with other frameworks and theories when performing long-term strategic planning (Eisenhardt and Martin 2000).

Linking resources with capabilities

Capabilities are another key concept within resource-based view. While resources are what an organization owns, capabilities are what the organization does. Capabilities arise over time as the firm builds on its strategic resources. For example, a firm can develop the capability of providing excellent customer service by building on its strong organizational culture. Therefore, capability is how an organization captures its potential value that is offered by its resources. In this sense, capability is an important part of the equation since they are needed to organize and manage the resources so that they can be exploited in such a way that adds value to customers and gives the organization the competitive edge over competitors. It is by so doing that customers are attracted to the organization, but not because it owns strategic resources.

Capabilities can be developed by firms to enable them to keep pace with the changing environment. For example, a firm can buy and sell firms in order to maintain its market leadership. Others can keep building on new brands in order to capture the market or maintain its leadership. Eisenhardt and Martin (2000) argue that dynamic capabilities are a set of specific and identifiable processes such as product development, strategic decision making and alliancing. They are neither vague nor tautological, although they are idiosyncratic in their details and path dependent in their emergence. Teece (2007) links dynamic capabilities to entrepreneurial behaviour, giving rise to potential path dependency based on previous experience of external financing and the influences of those financiers (Baldock 2015).

Barney (1991) argues that a firm cannot preserve sustained competitive advantage by engaging in strategic planning since their competitors can imitate this action, but can do so by having a good reputation, for example, which is valuable, rare, difficult to imitate and non-substitutable. Barney (1991) also argues that a firm's reputation is a socially complex resource, and because of the complexity it enhances the firm's chances of achieving a sustained competitive advantage.

Dynamic capabilities draw from the evolutionary theory of a firm and is an extension of the RBT (Bakker-Rakowska 2014). Teece *et al.* (1997) define dynamic capabilities as a firm's ability to integrate, build and reconfigure internal and external competences to address rapidly changing environments. These capabilities are regarded as antecedent organizational and strategic routines by which managers acquire resources, modify, integrate and recombine them to generate new value-creating strategies (Bakker-Rakowska 2014). Thus, dynamic capabilities represent an organization's ability to obtain a new form of competitive advantage, given the distinctive managerial and organizational processes (Eisenhardt and Martin 2000).

Relationships, such as the one with stakeholders, are also valuable resources, defined by the notion of social capital (Bakker-Rakowska 2014). Social capital can be defined as "the sum of the actual and potential resources embedded within, available through and derived from the network of relationships possessed by an individual or social unit" (Nahapiet and Ghoshal, 1998, p. 243). In their study, Svendsen *et al.* (2001) use this terminology to measure the quality of a firm's relationships with its stakeholders and place importance on mutual trust and reciprocity as well as shared understanding of goals. They argue that when social capital is understood in those terms, it creates value for the organization.

In order to capture the concept of "stakeholder capital", entrepreneurs have to leverage knowledge, networking and learning as the main components in creating dynamic capabilities (Bakker-Rakowska 2014). The importance of relationships and interactions in knowledge transfer cannot be overemphasized both within and across the boundaries of an entrepreneurship. Tsai and Ghoshal (1998) argue that these relationships and interactions constitute exchange of knowledge between a firm and stakeholders. Thus, increased stakeholder engagement can be seen as a source of knowledge which generates VRIO-resources, needed for the achievement of sustained competitive advantage, while it also bears the risk of disclosing important information towards the third party (Bakker-Rakowska 2014).

Bakker-Rakowska (2014) argues that an effective strategy is stakeholder management which enables access to knowledge and developing increased learning capability, resulting in better reputation and trust (Rodriguez *et al.* 2002), all being VRINO-resources, which recombined, give a foundation for competitive advantage (Barney 1991).

Understanding resources exchanged in crowdfunding

Crowdfunding is a critical new area of study as it is a computer-mediated phenomenon that changes the way people interact with each other. Greenberg *et al.* (2013) use resource exchange theory to examine the landscape of existing crowdfunding platforms and extrapolate their findings to suggest how crowdfunding platforms at large can foster interactions and exchanges.

In broad terms, crowdfunding platforms support the request for financial resources in exchange for a reward offered by a requester (Lambert and Schwienbacher 2010; Ward and Ramachandran 2010). More specifically, crowdfunding platforms must allow for:

a) Many individuals to offer financial support to realize ONE new venture
b) Individuals to raise and receive funds between the ideation and completion of the project
c) Voluntary financial contributions

Crowdfunding is normally carried out online and is the voluntary exchange of funds based on the exchange of many types of resources. Greenberg *et al.* (2013) explain how this phenomenon works using the resource exchange theory.

Table 4.1 Resources for exchange in RET

Resource	Description
Money	Any coin or token that has some standard of exchange value
Love	An expression of affectionate regard, warmth, or comfort
Information	Includes advice, opinion or instruction or enlightenment but excludes behaviours that could be classed as love or status
Status	An evaluative judgement conveying high or low prestige, regard or esteem
Goods	Tangible products, objects or materials
Services	Activities on the body or belongings of an individual that often constitute labour

Source: Greenberg *et al.* (2013)

The Resource Exchange Theory

Resource Exchange Theory (RET) originated from the work of Foa and Foa in 1971 in which they explained the exchange of resources. RET introduces money, goods and services into the definition of valuable resources as explored in the re-source-based theory. The central principle of RET is that six distinct categories of resources: love, status, information, money, goods and services are exchanged by humans (Foa 1971; Foa and Foa 1975) as illustrated in Table 4.1.

RET can be used as a framework to view computer mediated platforms for ex-change as it allows the understanding of different types of exchanges and potential pitfalls. Resource exchange theory can also be used to understand the motivations of exchange and to track exchange patterns within groups (Greenberg *et al.* 2013). The theory describes how similarities between types of resources influence the likelihood and appropriateness of exchange.

RET is useful particularly for explaining the exchange of multiple resources at the same time, which is currently an emergent trend on crowdfunding platforms. Apart from explaining the types of resources for exchange, RET also explains the role of cultural institutions in resource exchange. According to Foa (1971), cul-tural institutions such as markets and retail operations foster voluntary exchanges by bringing together combinations of individuals with reciprocal motivations for exchanging resources. For example, a retail operation brings together a seller (pos-sessors of goods) with a buyer (possessors of money) in the correct setting for each role player to broker an exchange (Greenberg *et al.* 2013).

In the same direction are online communities, which are defined as a virtual space where people come together with others to converse, exchange informa-tion or other resources, learn, play, or just be with each other (Kraut and Resnick 2011). While the focal activity on crowdfunding platforms is often the exchange of financial resources to realize new ventures, in actuality crowdfunding platforms are virtual spaces where people come together with others to communicate, exchange information and learn (Greenberg *et al.* 2013). In their conference paper, Gerber *et al.* (2012) argue that the project page remains a platform for project creators to remain in communication with financial backers until the completion of the pro-ject. Therefore, through the resource exchange theory, our understanding of how resources are exchanged is enhanced.

Table 4.2 Attributes in online crowdfunding

Attributes	Sub-attributes
Mechanisms	Mediated (*platform*)
	Unmediated (*personal platform*)
	Hybrid (*combination*)
Directness of exchange	Direct (*one party to another via platform*)
	Indirect (*screened by platform*)
	Inaccessible (*no contact between members*)
Individual roles on platforms	Requestor (*project creator/founders*)
	Respondent (*backer/funder*)
	Community (*crowd*)
	Member (*potential contributor*)
Requestor resources received	Money
	Information (*comments about project*)
	Love
Respondent resources received	Status (*backer*)
	Love (*gratitude*)
	Money
	Goods
	Services
	Information (*information on projects/updates*)
Members and general public resources received	Information

Source: Adapted from Greenberg *et al.* (2013).

Crowdfunding through the lens of Resource Exchange Theory

Looking at crowdfunding through the lens of RET, Greenberg *et al.* (2013) suggest the attributes in online crowdfunding. These attributes are the mechanisms, directness of exchange, individual roles on platforms, requestor resources received, respondent resources received, members and general public resources received. These attributes with their corresponding attributes are presented in Table 4.2.

1 Platform mechanisms

The mechanisms discuss the process through which the resource exchange takes place. The process can be categorized as *mediated, unmediated* and *hybrid*. The mediated process is the process where an established platform such as Kickstarter is used for the exchanges. Therefore, Kickstarter is the best example of a mediated platform, since all communication must go through official Kickstarter channels. The unmediated process is the process where a user creates a personal platform by using their own website in coordination with PayPal or other payment handlers. This means individuals can collect funds in a free-form manner, via PayPal payments or other independent means. The hybrid process is a combination of the other two processes.

2 Directness of resource exchange

Access to participants in crowdfunding is very crucial and, therefore, the directness of access on platforms is an important factor in the crowdfunding process (Cummings 2002; Kraut and Resnick 2011). Using the RET perspective, Greenberg *et al.* (2013) categorized crowdfunding platforms based on how direct and transparent the means of resource exchange, namely *direct, indirect* and *inaccessible* was. A direct platform is one where exchanges are sent directly from one party to another and are transferred by the platform. Platforms such as Kickstarter allow direct exchange because they allow people to communicate with each other without impediment. An indirect platform, on the other hand, is one where the exchanges are screened and approved by the platform. An example of this type of platform is Kiva which only allows for indirect exchange because messages between individuals are mediated by platform moderators. In the case of inaccessible platform, exchanges are not possible. An example includes platforms such as Zidisha which do not allow contact between members and exchange is inaccessible.

3 Individual roles on platforms

In most online crowdfunding platforms, participants perform different roles and provide different types of resource exchange. For example, on Kickstarter, only users who are defined as *project backers* can post a comment on projects, while on a competing platform, such as RocketHub, any member of the general public can post a comment on any project (Greenberg *et al.* 2013). Therefore, the roles played by participants on online crowdfunding can be described as *requestor, respondent, site manager,* and *general public*.

The requestor is the individual who is requesting for funds to carry out or complete a project or a person who is running the crowdfunding campaign. This role is common to all crowdfunding platforms. The term *requestor* may be used interchangeably with the term *project creator*. The role of the requestor may be carried out by more than one person, especially if the project is a big one or a team project.

The respondent is any individual who commits funds towards the completion of a crowdfunding project. Simply put, these are individuals who have contributed funds to a crowdfunding campaign. Like the requestor role, the respondent role is common in online crowdfunding platforms. This term *respondent* may be used interchangeably with backer, supporter or funder.

A member of the public or community member is a member of an online crowdfunding website who is a potential contributor to a crowdfunding campaign. They are neither requestors, respondents nor site managers. Some crowdfunding platforms allow registered users who are not backers of projects to communicate with requestors, while others do not. Requestors and respondents are subsets of the larger group of community members. A member of the general public is an individual who has not registered as a user. In some platforms such as CircleUp, which is a crowdfunding website where backers purchase equity in start-ups, the general public are not allowed to even browse the list of projects (Greenberg and Gerber 2014).

4 Requestor resources received

The resources received by requestors on online crowdfunding platforms include money, information and love. See Table 4.2 for the definition and description of each of these resources. Requestors or creators are bound to disclose the information about their project. In return, funders provide small pecuniary contributions, and as the monetary goals are reached, the campaign is successful. Also, funders and potential funders can post comments about projects, often expressing enthusiasm or displeasure. Requestors or managers promote democratic practices to encourage trust, involvement and cooperation using different strategic options to increase the "right participation" through their platforms' purpose and mission statements (Ramos 2014).

The ability to exploit as well as acquire and act on information is described as absorptive capacity (Cohen and Levinthal 1990; Zahra and George 2002). In other words, absorptive capacity is a firm's ability to acquire, process and exploit information. Situations of uncertainty, such as the post-GFC environment, place a premium on a firm's ability to process information and adapt (e.g. financing models) or pivot (e.g. innovations) accordingly (Owen and Mason 2019).

The RBT and social embeddedness approaches to entrepreneurship suggest that factors such as access to information and networks, skill sets of management and staff, ability to process information and to learn from experience all contribute to determining when an innovative firm will be aware of, and seek, different forms of external finance and their ultimate chances of application success (Owen *et al.* 2019)

5 Respondent resources received

The resources received by respondents on crowdfunding platforms can be categorized to include information (updates), status (backer), love (gratitude), services and goods. Again, further descriptions of these resources are in Table 4.2. Updates are information which founders are encouraged to post about their projects during and after the fundraising event. Updates represent efforts by founders to reach out to current and potential funders, and to inform interested backers about developments in a project (Mollick 2014). To be successful, a crowdfunding campaign must offer frequent updates and reminders to keep the campaign supporters in the loop about the campaign progress. This may include providing backers with updates each time a new funding milestone is reached.

Backers are the number of funders supporting the project. Owen *et al.* (2019) argue that from a resource perspective, small innovative firms may face finance gaps that arise out of information asymmetries. Innovative firms' resources are often intangible assets (such as intellectual property rights – "IPR"), but these present evaluation and risk issues for potential funders. For example, credit providers will discount intangible assets and equity providers must judge the risk of such investments when information on market value is limited. However, such information gaps may be mitigated by higher quality of human and social capital (Owen *et al.* 2019).

6 Members and general public resources received

Information is the only resource received by the general public which may include viewing project pages. Research studies such as SQW (2009) have pointed out that high technology sectors of entrepreneurship experience persistent capital financing gaps. Hall and Lerner (2010) suggest this is due to heightened information asymmetries relating to the raised levels of investor uncertainty.

Crowdfunding: resources, capabilities and stakeholders

Stakeholders of an organization, especially financiers provide important resources for an entrepreneurship. Therefore, this section focuses on the role and meaning of these resources in the innovation and entrepreneurship process.

For entrepreneurship to flourish, it may involve developing and expanding competences (Floyd and Lane 2000). Taking the resource-based view lens, Leonard-Barton (1992) found that a firm's capabilities and resources generally speaking enhance product innovation and entrepreneurship, but may also impede innovativeness. Hence, there is an increasing need for firms to continuously acquire new resources, bundle and reconfigure them in a creative way, so that they become a source of new, original capabilities (Eisenhardt and Martin 2000). This notion is also known as developing dynamic capabilities (Teece *et al.* 1997), which over time become a source of new ideas, embedded in developing more innovative products (Eisenhardt and Martin 2000).

Stakeholder theory and crowdfunding

Stakeholder theory deals with the nature of the relationship between entrepreneurship and stakeholders. Stakeholders can be defined as any group or individual who can affect or is affected by the achievement of an organization's objectives (Freeman 1984). It is thus important for firms to pay attention to stakeholder influence for normative and instrumental reasons (Bakker-Rakowska 2014). According to Mitchell *et al.* (1997), normative accounts of stakeholder theory move firm–stakeholder relations into an ethical domain, proposing that managers should consider the interests of those who have stakes in the organization. Therefore, stakeholders have a legitimate interest in the firm's actions or products which generates intrinsic values (Donaldson and Preston 1995). Correspondingly, managers of an enterprise have a moral obligation towards the stakeholders, whether social or cultural (Freeman and Philips 2002).

Frooman (1999) suggests that there are several types of stakeholder influence and four types of resource relationship. Consequently, Rowley (1997) argues that an organization should focus on managing the multiple influences of stakeholders. This is because managing stakeholders' interests will maximize a firm's performance (Berman *et al.* 1999).

Bakker-Rakowska (2014) indicates that the identification of an organization stakeholders can pose a challenge. Clarkson (1995) classifies stakeholders into two groups, namely, primary and secondary groups. The primary group includes stakeholders who are essential for the business to exist. The examples of this group of stakeholders include owners, employees, customers or supplies. The secondary group of stakeholders consists of social and political stakeholders who play a vital role in achieving the business's credibility and acceptance of its activities. The examples of this group of stakeholders include non-governmental organizations (NGOs), communities, governments and competitors.

Mitchell *et al.* (1997) suggest that when stakeholders have been identified the next objective for the management of an organization is to develop strategies to deal with them. Developing strategies to deal with stakeholders may be a difficult task because of the different and contrasting interests of stakeholders as well as their contradicting goals and diverse priorities. Therefore, successful management practices chosen will depend on the strategic importance of a stakeholder to a firm (Harrison and St. John 1996). Harrison and St. John (1996) suggest that traditional stakeholder management techniques, such as buffering, and satisfying stakeholders' needs while partnering activities will enhance the bridge-building and pursuit of common goals.

Crowdfunding: stakeholder analysis and involvement

If stakeholders' involvement and their role in the organization must be recognized, it is important to develop a strategy for stakeholder management process. Such process must start with identifying critical stakeholders (Ansoff 1965). This means that management should, first and foremost, understand the needs of stakeholders. This is only possible if management recognizes and integrates the interests of all its stakeholders and incorporates these into the operations of the organization. Mitroff and Mason (1982) suggest that the importance of stakeholders in an organization should be determined through an environmental scan. This involves grouping stakeholders according to their roles and influence and placing them in primary or secondary categories as discussed earlier in the stakeholder theory.

There are various techniques an organization can use to manage their stakeholders. As suggested by Bryson (2004), the most frequently used techniques of stakeholder identification are:

1 The power versus interest grid
2 Stakeholder influence diagram
3 Participation planning matrix

The power versus interest grid was developed by Eden and Ackermann (1998) and focuses merely on stakeholders' interest in an organization and their power to affect it. They distinguish four categories of stakeholders, namely:

1 Players – this group of stakeholders has both significant interest and power.
2 Subjects – these are a group of stakeholders with significant interest but little power.
3 Context settlers – with little interest but significant power.
4 Crowd – with both little interest and power.

Bryson (2004) argues that this type of analysis helps in developing different strategies for including the interests of the various groups into the operations of the organization.

The stakeholder influence diagram is used when an organization intends to find out how stakeholders on the power vs. interest grid influence each other (Eden and Ackermann 1998). According to Eden and Ackermann (1998), after carrying out the power vs. interest grid, a modification is made by adding information about where influence relationships exist and what is the direction of the influence.

The participation planning matrix focuses on establishing a closer contact or communication with the most essential stakeholders of the organization (Bryson 2004). The aim is to engage in partnerships with stakeholders who have influence on decision making (Eden and Ackermann 1998). This technique encourages the creation of a new direction for the organization with regards to the relation between the firm and the environment. Therefore, a proper stakeholder analysis may influence a firm's survival positively and lead to success through the integration of multiple relationships and objectives (Bakker-Rakowska 2014).

Harrison and St. John (1996) suggest that in managing stakeholders, two basic techniques must be distinguished, namely, buffering and bridging. Buffering is a technique aimed at containing the effects of stakeholders on the firm by carrying out market research, engaging in public relations and planning. By contrast, bridging involves forming strategic partnerships by recognizing common goals and lowering the barriers between the organization and its external stakeholders.

However, in managing stakeholders either through buffering or bridging, it is important to invest sufficient resources in communication with stakeholders (Bakker-Rakowska 2014). This clarifies the intentions of the firm and enhances mutual understanding between the organization and its stakeholders (Harrison and St. John 1996).

Crowdfunding: the role of financiers

Hyytinen and Toivanen (2005) indicate that financiers have significant influence in new ventures as important stakeholders. The role of financiers in entrepreneurship provides understanding of crowdfunding which involves contributions from many funders whose motivations vary from acquiring a new product to offering support to novice entrepreneurs (Agrawal *et al.* 2013).

Due to information asymmetries and uncertainty about the acceptance of the product or service offering in the market, entrepreneurial ventures face higher cost of capital than the larger competitors (Hyytinen and Toivanen 2005). Consequently, there is a need for financing the products and services from both monetary and non-financial resources (Hall and Martin 2005).

A large number of studies have been conducted into the impact of venture capitalists on entrepreneurship development. Many of these studies have reported on the superiority of venture capital in the provision of resources over the more traditional institutions such as banks (Owen *et al*. 2019; Baldock 2016; Mole *et al*. 2016; Owen *et al*. 2016; Harrison and Baldock 2015; Baldock and North 2015; Baldock 2015). Without doubt, venture funding has a strong positive impact on new venture creation. (Kortum and Lerner 2000).

Venture capital (VC) is defined as equity or equity-linked investments in young, privately held companies, where the investor is a financial intermediary who is typically active as a director, advisor, or even a manager of the firm (Kortum and Lerner 2000). Venture capital can play a crucial role in assisting potential high growth innovative venture start-ups and scale up, and their contribution to economic growth (Lerner 2010; Baldock and Mason 2015; Colombo *et al*. 2016; Owen and Mason 2019).

Auderetsch and Lehmann (2004) discussed the role of debt-based financiers in the entrepreneurship process and found that institutions, such as banks, are able to create a milieu favourable for novel ideas, since their role is similar to that of venture capitalists in a bank-based system. Therefore, it can be assumed that the benefits brought by VCs to the companies are as relevant as the financial assistance provided by banks.

Since financiers are likely to have a positive impact on new ventures, it is important to understand their role and how they work. Brophy and Verga (1992) found that ventures with VC backing were found to outperform firms without similar connections and that such ventures benefited from the prestige brought about by their VC underwriter. Sapienza (1992) argues that venture capitalists are more likely to bring benefits such as being strategic, supportive and having networking as well as being a sounding board, mentor and financier. Venture capitalists offer an opportunity of high returns and are aware of their boundary-spanning functions in a milieu with information deficiencies (Gomez-Mejia and colleagues 1990). Thus, they provide valuable knowledge and service to the entrepreneur which can be used to create competitive edge (Owen and Mason 2019; Sapienza and Timmons 1989). They also provide credibility with suppliers and customers (Timmons and Bygrave 1986).

The characteristics of stakeholders and resource exchange process in crowdfunding

Crowdfunding is an initiative to raise money from the crowd for a new project proposed by an entrepreneur. Therefore, the process involves many possible funders. The resource-based theory advocates that firms with VRIN resources have a sustained competitive advantage (Barney 1991). Competitive advantage enhances innovation (Frankelius 2009). Therefore, in the model discussed here, there is a relationship between resource acquisition (whether pecuniary or non-pecuniary resources) and the effect on the success of innovation in the process of crowdfunding.

In the crowdfunding process, two major parties can be distinguished, namely, project creators and project backers. Thus, there is need to satisfy the expectations of many stakeholders in crowdfunding campaigns if the creators will succeed in financing their ventures (Ordanini *et al.* 2011). This involves providing them with updates and adequate, timely rewards for their contributions, which is a complex process (Bakker-Rakowska 2014).

The concept of stakeholder management suggests reconciling different demands from various interest groups which is an important factor in entrepreneurship and innovations (Hall and Martin 2005). Since there is uncertainty involved in new venture creation, entrepreneurship and innovation, it is important to have all essential interest groups on board to foster success (Tipping *et al.* 1995). Therefore, Afuah (1998) argues that including stakeholders in new venture creation is more likely to enhance trust in the entrepreneurship, enrich the social capital of the entrepreneur and deliver strategic knowledge necessary for product launch. However, the right involvement of interest groups by using specific techniques is the key to greater understanding between the organization and its stakeholders. Also, Freeman (1994) indicates that establishing a value-exchange relationship between the organization and its stakeholders may lead to the organization's better performance.

Although crowdfunding enables entrepreneurs to acquire new resources (Ordanini *et al.* 2001), it is not enough to ascertain that the necessary VRINO criteria will be satisfied (Teece *et al.* 1997). Resources need to be bundled and reconfigured in a creative way, so that they become a source of new, original capabilities (Eisenhardt and Martin 2000). This notion is also known as developing dynamic or innovative capabilities (Teece *et al.* 1997), which over time become a source of new ideas, embedded in developing novel products.

Summary

This chapter has dealt with the resource exchange theory and how it can be used to view crowdfunding as far as exchange of resources is concerned. The chapter has also explained the concept of the resource-based theory. The RBT is a strategy method that focuses on the actual resources available to a company.

Resource-based theory suggests that resources that are valuable, rare, difficult to imitate, and non-substitutable best position a firm for long-term success. These strategic resources can provide the foundation to develop firm capabilities that can lead to superior performance over time. Capabilities are needed to bundle, manage and otherwise exploit resources in a manner that provides value added to customers and creates advantages over competitors.

Instead of focusing on external factors, trends or deficiencies, this method highlights what a company has in its possession, which is its resources, and defines an action framework based on it. The RBT proposes an introspective approach, whilst other tools concentrate on the competitors or the market generally.

However, the chapter concludes that since this method focuses on internal factors, it is appropriate to use it in combination with other strategies that use broader approaches. By focusing on the actual resources of a company, it is suggested that strategy is more coherent, easier and more realistic. This is because when managers generally define strategies, they focus more on what the company should have rather than what it actually has in its possession. Therefore, when developing a resource-based view strategy it is advisable to focus on the current resources of the company.

The core thesis of a resource-based theory is that before managers begin to study what their competitors have or what they think the company should have to be successful or achieve a competitive advantage, they should first of all consider what the company currently has and what the company can offer. Finally, the RBT perspective suggests that previous management experience, networking connections, the existence of close relationships and the use of appropriate advice would lead to quicker and more successful outcomes (Owen *et al.* 2019).

Discussion questions

1 What is resource-based theory, and why is it important to organizations?
2 What are the characteristics of strategic resources?
3 What are the characteristics of stakeholders and the resource exchange process in the crowdfunding?
4 How does stakeholder involvement influence innovation in the process of crowdfunding?

Test questions

1 In what ways can intellectual property serve as a value-added resource for organizations?
2 Identify a particular resource of a company of your choice and evaluate how the resource enhances the competitive advantage of the company.

Glossary of key terminologies

B2B Business to business.
Intangible assets Resources with long-term financial value to a business. They are not material objects and cannot be touched or physically seen.
KBR Knowledge-based resources.
PBR Property-based resources.
PLC Product life cycle.
RBT Resource-based theory.
RET Resource exchange theory.
SMEs Small and medium-sized enterprises.
Tangible assets Physical items with a clear purchase value used by a business to produce goods and services.
VC Venture capital – equity or equity-linked investments in young and privately owned companies.

VRIN Attributes of resources: valuable, rare, imperfectly imitable and non-substitutable.

VRIO VRIN further revised as: valuable, rare, imperfectly imitable and organized to add value.

Recommended reading

Barney, J.B., and Clark, D.N., 2007. *Resource-based theory: Creating and sustaining competitive advantage*. Oxford: Oxford University Press.

Edwards, J., 2014. *Mastering strategic management*, 1st Canadian Edition, Victoria: BC Campus.

Montgomery, C.A., 1995. *Resource-based and evolutionary theories of the firm: Towards a synthesis*. Norwell, MA: Kluwer Academic Publishers.

Penrose, E., 2020. *The growth of firms, middle east oil and other essays*. London: Routledge.

Teece, D.J., 2011. *Dynamic capabilities and strategic management: Organizing for innovation and growth*. Oxford: Oxford University Press.

Wernerfelt, B., 2016. *Adaptation, specialization, and the theory of the firm: Foundations of the resource-based view*. Cambridge: Cambridge University Press.

References

Adegbile, A.S., 2018. *Linking resource mobilization approaches and performance in entrepreneurial ventures: A social network perspective* (Doctoral dissertation). Europa-Universität Viadrina Frankfurt.

Afuah, A., 1998. *Innovation management strategies, implementation and profits*. Oxford: Oxford University Press.

Agrawal, A.K., Catalini, C., and Goldfarb, A., 2013. *Some simple economics of crowdfunding* [NBER Working Paper]. Available from: www.nber.org/papers/w19133 [Accessed 26 July 2013].

Ahlstrom, D., and Bruton, G.D., 2002. An institutional perspective on the role of culture in shaping strategic actions by technology-focused entrepreneurial firms in China. *Entrepreneurship: Theory & Practice*, 26 (4), 53.

Alvarez, S.A., and Busenitz, L.W., 2001. The entrepreneurship of resource-based theory. *Journal of Management*, 27 (6), 755–775. Available from: https://doi.org/10.1177/014920630102700609

Ansoff, I., 1965. *Corporate strategy*. New York: McGraw Hill.

Auderetsch, D.B., and Lehmann, E.E., 2004. Financing high – Tech grow: The role of banks and venture capitalists. *Schmalenbach Business Review*, 56, 340–357.

Bakker-Rakowska, J., 2014. *Crowdfunding for innovation: A qualitative research on resources, capabilities and stakes*. Thesis (Master). Enschede: University of Twente.

Baldock, R., 2016. An assessment of the business impact of the UK enterprise capital funds. *Environment and Planning C: Government and Policy*. Available from: https://doi.org/10.1177/0263774X15625995

Baldock, R., and Mason, C.M., 2015. Establishing a new UK finance escalator for innovative SMEs: The roles of the enterprise capital funds and angel co-investment fund. *Venture Capital: An International Journal of Entrepreneurial Finance*. Available from: https://doi.org/10.1080/13691066.2015.1021025

Baldock, R., and North, D., 2015. The role of UK government hybrid venture capital funds in addressing the finance gap facing innovative SMEs in the post 2007 financial crisis era. *In*: J. Scott and J.G. Hussain, eds. *International research handbook on entrepreneurial finance*. Cheltenham: Edward Elgar.

Barney, J., 1991. Firm resources and sustained competitive advantage. *Journal of Management*. 17 (1), 99–120.

Barney, J.B., 1997. *Gaining and sustaining competitive advantages*. Reading, MA: Addison Wesley.

Berman, S.L., Wicks, A.C., Kotha, S., and Jones, T.M., 1999. Does stakeholder orientation matter? The relationship between stakeholder management models and the firm's financial performance. *Academy of Management Journal*, 42 (5), 488–506.

Brophy, D.J., and Verga, J.A., 1992. More than money? The Influence of venture capitalists on initial public offering. *Journal of Business Venturing*, 7 (1), 9–27.

Bryson, J.M., 2004. what to do when stakeholders matter. *Public Management Review*, 6 (1), 21–53.

BusinessBalls, 2019. *Resource-based view: What is a resource-based view?* Available from: www.businessballs.com/strategy-innovation/resource-based-view/ [Accessed 29 January 21].

Cardeal, N., and António, N., 2012. Valuable, rare, inimitable resources and organization (VRIO) resources or valuable, rare, inimitable resources (VRI) capabilities: What leads to competitive advantage? *African Journal of Business Management*, 6 (37), 10159–10170.

Chen, X.P., Yao, X., and Kotha, S., 2009. Entrepreneur passion and preparedness in business plan presentations: A persuasion analysis of venture capitalists' funding decisions. *Academy of Management Journal*, 52, 199–214.

Cho, Y.S., and Linderman, K., 2020. Resource-based product and process innovation model: Theory development and empirical validation. *Sustainability*, 12 (3), 913. Available from: https://doi.org/10.3390/su12030913.

Ciabuschi, F., Perna, A., and Snehota, I., 2011. Assembling resources when forming a new business. *Journal of Business Research*, 65 (2), 220–229.

Clarkson, M.B.E., 1995. A stakeholder framework for analysing and evaluating corporate social performance. *Academy of Management Review*, 20 (1), 92–117.

Cohen, W.M., and Levinthal, D.A., 1990. Absorptive capacity: A new perspective on learning and innovation. *Administrative Science Quarterly*, 35, 128–152.

Colombo, M.G., Cumming, D.J., and Vismara, S., 2016. Governmental venture capital for innovative young firms. *The Journal of Technology Transfer*, 41, 10–24.

Cummings, J.N. Butler, B., and Kraut, R.E., 2002. The quality of online social relationships. *Communications of the ACM*, 45 (7), 103–108.

Dalziel, T., Gentry, R.J., and Bowerman, M., 2011. An integrated agency-resource dependence view of the influence of directors' human and relational capital on firms' R&D spending. *Journal of Management Studies*, 48 (6), 1217–1242.

Delmar, F., and Shane, S., 2004. Legitimating first: Organizing activities and the survival of new ventures. *Journal of Business Venturing*, 19 (3), 385–410.

Donaldson, T., and Preston, L.E., 1995. The stakeholder theory of the corporation: Concepts, evidence and implications. *Academy of Management Review*, 20 (1): 65–91.

Drummond, C., McGrath, H., and O'Toole, T., 2018. The impact of social media on resource mobilisation in entrepreneurial firms, *Industrial Marketing Management*, 70 (2018), 68–89.

Eden, C., and Ackermann, F., 1998. *Making strategy. The journey of strategic management.* London: Sage Publications.

Eisenhardt, K.M., and Martin, J.A., 2000. Dynamic capabilities: What are they? *Strategic Management Journal*, 21, 1105–1121.

Floyd, S.W., and Lane, P.J., 2000. Strategizing throughout the organization: Managing role conflict in strategic renewal. *Academy of Management Review*, 25 (1), 154–177.

Foa, U.G., 1971. Interpersonal and economic resources. *Science*, 171 (3969), 345–351.

Foa, U.G., and Foa, E.B., 1975. *Resource theory of social exchange.* New York: General Learning Press.

Frankelius, P., 2009. Questioning two myths in innovation literature. *Journal of High Technology Management Research*, 20, 40–51.

Freeman, R.E., 1984. *Strategic Management: A Stakeholder Approach.* Boston: Pitman.

Freeman, R.E., 1994. The politics of stakeholder theory: Some future directions. *Business Ethics Quarterly*, 4 (4), 409–421.

Freeman, R.E., and Philips, R.A., 2002. Stakeholder theory: A libertarian defence. *Business Ethics Quarterly*, 12 (3), 331–349.

Frooman, J., 1999. Stakeholder influence strategies. *Academy of Management Review*, 24 (2), 191–205.

Frydrych, D., and Bock, A., 2013. *An analysis of reward-based crowdfunding as an entrepreneurial resource assembly process – A resource-based view and agency theory perspective.* London: British Academy of Management.

Gerber, E.M., Hui, J.S., and Kuo, P.Y., 2012. Crowdfunding: Why people are motivated to post and fund projects on crowdfunding platforms. *In: Proceedings of the international workshop on design, influence, and social technologies: Techniques, impacts and ethics* (Vol. 2, No. 11). February 2012, 10.

Gomez-Mejia, L.R., Balkin, D.B., and Welboume, T.M., 1990. Influence of venture capitalists on high tech management. *Journal of High Technology Management Research*, 1, 103–118.

Greenberg, M.D., and Gerber, E.M., 2014. *Understanding resource exchange in crowdfunding platforms, collective intelligence.* Evanston: Northwestern University.

Greenberg, M.D., Hui, J., and Gerber, E., 2013. Crowdfunding: A resource exchange perspective. *In: ACM conference on human factors in computing systems.* New York: ACM Press.

Grigoriou, N., Davcik, N., and Sharma, P., 2016. Exploring the influence of brand innovation on marketing performance using signaling framework and Resource-Based Theory (RBT) approach. let's get engaged! *Crossing the Threshold of Marketing's Engagement Era*, 813–818. Available from: https://doi.org/10.1007/978-3-319-11815-4_238.

Hall, B.H., and Lerner, J., 2010. The financing of R&D and innovation. *In: Handbook of the economics of innovation* (Vol. 1). North-Holland: Elsevier, 609–639.

Hall, J.K., and Martin, M.J.C., 2005. Disruptive technologies, stakeholders and the innovation value added chain: A framework for evaluating radical technology development. *R&D Management*, 35 (3), 273–283.

Harrison, J.S., and St. John, C.H., 1996. Managing and partnering with external stakeholders. *Academy of Management Executive*, 10 (2), 46–60.

Harrison, R., and Baldock, R., 2015. Financing SME growth in the UK: Meeting the challenges after the global financial crisis. *Venture Capital: An International Journal of Entrepreneurial Finance.* Available from: https://doi.org/10.1080/13691066.

Holdford, D.A., 2018. Resource-based theory of competitive advantage – A framework for pharmacy practice innovation research. *Pharmacy Practice (Granada)*, 16 (3), 1351. doi: 10.18549/PharmPract.2018.03.1351

Hunt, S.D., 2013. A general theory of business marketing: R-A theory, alderson, the isbm framework and the IMP theoretical structure. *Industrial Marketing Management*, 41, 283–293.

Hyytinen, A., and Toivanen, O., 2005. Do financial constraints hold back innovation and growth? Evidence on the role of public policy. *Research Policy*, 34, 1385–1403.

Kamasak, R., 2015. Determinants of innovation Performance: A Resource-based Study. *Procedia – Social and Behavioral Sciences*, 195, 1330–1337. Available from: https://doi. org/10.1016/j.sbspro.2015.06.311

Kim, Y., Li, H., and Li, S., 2014. Corporate social responsibility and stock price crash risk. *Journal of Banking & Finance*, 43, 1–13.

Kortum, S., and Lerner, J., 2000. Assessing the contribution of venture capital to innovation. *RAND Journal of Economics*, 31 (4), 674–692.

Kraaijenbrink, J., Spender, J.C., and Groen, A.J., 2010. The resource-based view: A review and assessment of its critiques. *Journal of Management*, 36 (1), 349–372. Available from: https://doi.org/10.1177/0149206309350775 (First Published December 28, 2009).

Kraut, R.E., and Resnick, P., 2011. *Building successful online communities: Evidence-based social design*. Cambridge, MA: The MIT Press.

Lambert, T., and Schwienbacher, A., 2010. An empirical analysis of crowdfunding. *Social Science Research Network*, 1578175 (1), 1–23.

Leonard-Barton, D., 1992. Core capabilities and core rigidities: A paradox in managing new product development. *Strategic Management Journal*, 13, 111–125.

Lerner, J., 2010. The future of public efforts to boost entrepreneurship and venture capital. *Small Business Economics*, 35, 255–264.

Lewis, V.L., and Churchill, N.C., 1983. The five stages of small business growth. *Harvard Business Review*, 3 (3), 1–12.

Lounsbury, M., and Glynn, M.A., 2001. Cultural entrepreneurship: Stories, legitimacy, and the acquisition of resources. *The Strategic Management Journal*, 22, 545–564.

Mitchell, R.K., Agle, B.R., and Wood, D.J., 1997. Toward a theory of stakeholder identification and salience: Defining the principle of who and what really counts. *Academy of Management*, 22 (4), 853–856.

Mitroff, I.I., and Mason, R.O., 1982. Business policy and metaphysics: Some philosophical considerations. *Academy of Management Review*, 7 (3), 361–371.

Mole, K., North, D., and Owen, R., 2016. Which SMEs seek external support? Business characteristics, management behaviour and external influences in a contingency approach. *Environment and Planning C: Government and Policy*. Available from: https:// doi.org/10.1177/0263774X1666536

Mollick, E., 2014. The Dynamics of crowdfunding: An exploratory study. *Journal of Business Venturing*, 29 (1), 1–16.

Mollick, E.R., 2012. The dynamics of crowdfunding: Determinants of success and failure. *Journal of Business Venturing*, 29 (1), 1–16.

Nahapiet, J., and Ghoshal, S., 1998. Social capital, intellectual capital and organizational advantage. *Academy of Management Review*, 23 (2), 242–266.

Newbert, S.L., 2007. Empirical research on the resource-based view of the firm: An assessment and suggestions for future research. *Strategic Management Journal*, 28 (2), 121–146.

Ordanini, A., Micel, L., Pizzetti, M., and Parasuraman, A., 2011. Crowd-funding: Transforming customers into investors through innovative service platforms. *Journal of Service Management*, 22 (4), 443–470.

Owen, R., Deakins, D., and Savic, M., 2019. Financing pathways for young innovative small- and medium-size enterprises: A demand-side examination of finance gaps and policy implications for the post-global financial crisis finance escalator. *Strategic Change*, 28 (1), 19–36.

Owen, R., and Mason, C., 2019. Emerging trends in government venture capital policies in smaller peripheral economies: Lessons from Finland, New Zealand, and Estonia. *Strategic Change*, 28 (1), 83–93.

Owen (Baldock), R., and Mason, C., 2016. The role of government co-investment funds in the supply of entrepreneurial finance: An assessment of the early operation of the UK Angel Co-investment Fund. *Environment and Planning C: Government and Policy*. Available from: https://doi.org/10.1177/0263774X16667072

Penrose, E., 1959. *The theory of the growth of the firm*. Oxford: Basil Blackwell.

Peteraf, M.A., 1993. The cornerstones of competitive advantage: A resource-based view. *Strategic Management Journal*, 14 (3), 179–191. Available from: https://doi.org/10.1002/smj.4250140303

Pollack, J.M., Rutherford, M.W., and Nagy, B.G., 2012. Preparedness and cognitive legitimacy as antecedents of new venture funding in televised business pitches. *Entrepreneurship: Theory & Practice*, 36 (5), 915–939.

Prahalad, C.K., and Hamel, G., 1990. The core competence of the corporation. *Harvard Business Review*, 68 (3), 79–91.

Ramos, J., and Stewart, J., 2014. Crowdfunding and the role of managers in ensuring the sustainability of crowdfunding platforms. *JRC Scientific and Policy Reports*, 85752.

Rodriguez, M.A., Ricart, J.E., and Sanchez, P., 2002. Sustainable development and the sustainability of competitive advantage: A dynamic and sustainable view of the firm. *Creativity and Innovation Management*, 11 (3), 135–146.

Rowley, T.J., 1997. Moving beyond dyadic ties: A network theory of stakeholder influences. *Academy of Management Review*, 22 (4), 887–910.

Sapienza, H.J., 1992. When do venture capitalists add value? *Journal of Business Venturing*, 7 (1), 9–27.

Sapienza, H.J., and Timmons, J.A., 1989. The roles of venture capitalists in new ventures: What determines their importance? *In: Academy of Management Proceedings* (Vol. 1989, No. 1). Briarcliff Manor, NY: Academy of Management, 74–78.

Schlangenstein, M., and Hughes, J., 28 September 2010. *Southwest risks keep-it-simple focus to spur growth*. Available from www.washingtonpost.com/wp-dyn/content/article/2010/09/28/AR2010092801578.html

Schoonhoven, C.B., and Romanelli, E., 2001. *The entrepreneurship dynamic: Origins of entrepreneurship and the evolution of industries*. Stanford, CA: Stanford University Press.

Shane, S., and Cable, D., 2002. Network ties, reputation, and the financing of new ventures. *Management Science*, 48, 364–381.

Soni, P., and Krishnan, R., 2014. Frugal innovation: Aligning theory, practice, and public policy. *Journal of Indian Business Research*, [online] 6 (1), 29–47.

Sorescu, A., Shankar, V., and Kushwaha, T., 2007. New product preannouncements and shareholder value: Don't make promises you can't keep. *Journal of Marketing Research*, 44 (3), 468–489.

SQW Consulting, 2009. *The supply of equity finance to SMEs: Revisiting the equity gap*. London: Department for Business, Innovation and Skills, URN 09/1573.

Suardhika, I.N., Yuesti, A., and Sudja, I.N., 2018. Innovation strategy based on resource-based theory perspective and its impact on small and medium business performance. *International Journal of Contemporary Research and Review*, 9 (11), 21109–21126.

Svendsen, A.C., Boutilier, R.G., Abbott, R., Wheeler, D., 2001. *Measuring the business value of stakeholder relationships*. Vancouver, BC: Simon Fraser University.

Teece, D.J., 2007., Explicating dynamic capabilities: The nature and microfoundations of (sustainable) enterprise performance. *Strategic Management Journal*, 28, 1319–1350.

Teece, D.J., Pisano, G., and Shuen, A., 1997. Dynamic capabilities and strategic management. *Strategic Management Journal*, 18 (7), 509–533.

Timmons, J.A., Bygrave, and W.D., 1986. Venture capital's role in financing innovation for economic growth. *Journal of Business Venturing*, 1 (2), 161–176.

Tipping, J., Zeffren, D., and Fusfeld, A., 1995. Assessing the value of technology. *Research Technology Management*, 38 (5), 22–39.

Tsai, W., and Ghoshal, S., 1998. Social capital and value creation: The role of intrafirm networks. *Academy of Management Journal*, 41 (4), 464–476.

Ward, C., and Ramachandran, V., 2010. Crowdfunding the next hit: Microfunding online experience goods. *In: Workshop on Computational Social Science and the Wisdom of Crowds at NIPS2010*, 1–5.

Wernerfelt, B., 1984. A resource-based view of the firm. *Strategic Management Journal*, 5 (2), 171–180.

Zahra, S.A., and George, G., 2002. Absorptive capacity; A review, re-conceptualisation and extension. *Academy of Management Review*, 27 (2), 185–203.

5 Reducing the risk of information asymmetry in crowdfunding

Learning objectives

- Discuss the meaning of information asymmetry
- Discuss the challenges of information asymmetry on crowdfunding
- Explore how information asymmetry can be mitigated to achieve crowdfunding success
- Examine the role of feedback in resolving information asymmetry in crowdfunding

Introduction

In recent years, crowdfunding has become a veritable source of finance for entrepreneurship, providing entrepreneurs the opportunity to draw on small contributions from a large number of people (the crowd) through the internet to fund their ventures (Belleflamme et al. 2014). This new source of entrepreneurial finance has started an expanding academic and professional debate on various consequences of crowdfunding in terms of technicalities and legal implications as well as its impact on financial markets and wealth distribution in the society (Firoozi et al. 2017). Although crowdfunding has made significant strides as an alternative source of entrepreneurial finance, it presents some challenges for both entrepreneurs and potential funders as a result of information asymmetry between them (Courtney 2018). A few existing research studies have highlighted the prospect of a rise in opportunity for fraud as a consequence of information asymmetry between venture capital seekers and crowd investors (Firoozi et al. (2017).

Firoozi et al. (2017) suggest that the main concern that has been almost universally stated in the debates on crowdfunding is related to signalling and information asymmetry indicating that the crowd is not as fit as the traditional lenders to evaluate the true risks and prospects of a new venture and thus may fall in the trap of false signals sent by entrepreneurs seeking funds or inability to assess the signals correctly. The major concern highlighted in the literature is misinformation or fraud that can be inflicted on a non-expert crowd by fund seekers because of information asymmetry. These concerns arise mainly because founders seeking

DOI: 10.4324/9781003193975-5

crowdfunding may have previously failed to secure funding from the traditional sources and also because the crowd investors do not have the expertise to correctly evaluate the risks and prospects associated with the crowdfunding projects, whether the crowdfunding is in the form of debt or equity.

Therefore, because of the information asymmetry which exists between business owners and potential backers, the former has to provide credible information to the latter to enable them to evaluate the projects to be funded through crowdfunding (Ahlers *et al.* 2015). This chapter explores how information asymmetry can be mitigated to enhance a successful crowdfunding. It also explores the role of feedback in the crowdfunding process (Courtney 2018). The lack of information or inadequate information (information asymmetry) between entrepreneurs and financiers oftentimes leads to difficulties in attracting external finance (Li and Chi 2013).

The chapter also examines when signals and endorsements obtained from multiple information sources enhance or diminish one another's effects. The chapter suggests that project signals through the use of media and the crowdfunding experience of the founder can mitigate information asymmetry in relation to the project quality and founder credibility, thus enhancing the project's likelihood of obtaining finance.

What is information asymmetry?

Information asymmetry occurs when one party to an economic transaction possesses greater material knowledge or more or superior information than the other party (Myers and Majluf 1984). It can also be referred to as information failure. This typically takes place when the seller of a good or service possesses greater knowledge than the buyer. The reverse dynamic, however, can also be true. Information asymmetry can be observed in almost all economic transactions.

Therefore, where one party in a deal between a seller and a buyer is able to take advantage of another, information asymmetry is said to exist in the transaction. Take a homeowner who wants to sell their house as an example. The homeowner would obviously have more information about the house than the buyer; such as creaky floorboards or noisy neighbours or the home getting too cold in winters. This is information which the buyer would only get to know after buying the house and moving in. The buyer may not have bought the house or pay as much as they paid if they had this information in the first place.

Information asymmetry can also be viewed in terms of specialization and division of knowledge, which can be applicable in any economic trade. For example, teachers typically know more about their subjects than their students because teachers have more educational backgrounds than students. This principle is also applicable to medical doctors, architects, lawyers, engineers and other trained professionals. In this regard, information asymmetry can be beneficial to an economy and a society in increasing efficiency (Bloomenthal 2021).

Advantages and disadvantages of information asymmetry

Advantages

In the context of specialization, Bloomenthal (2021) suggests that asymmetric information is not necessarily a bad thing since growing asymmetrical information is the desired outcome of a healthy market economy. He argues that as workers strive to become increasingly specialized in their chosen fields, they become more productive, and can consequently provide greater value to workers in other fields. For example, on the one hand, a stockbroker's knowledge is more valuable to a non-investment professional, such as a farmer, who may be interested in confidently trading stocks to prepare for retirement. On the other hand, the stockbroker does not need to know how to grow crops or tend to livestock to feed themselves, but rather can purchase the items from a grocery store that are provided by the farmer. In each of their respective trades, both the farmer and the stockbroker hold superior knowledge over the other, but both benefit from the trade and the division of labour.

One alternative to ever-expanding information asymmetry is for workers to study all fields, rather than specialize in fields where they can provide the most value. However, this is an impractical solution, with high opportunity costs and potentially lower aggregate outputs, which would lower standards of living (Bloomenthal 2021).

Disadvantages

In some circumstances, information asymmetry may have near fraudulent consequences, such as adverse selection, which describes a concept where an insurance company encounters the probability of extreme loss due to a risk that was not disclosed at the time of sale of the policy. In certain information asymmetry models, one party can retaliate for contract breaches, while the other party cannot.

For example, if the insured hides the fact that they are a heavy smoker and frequently engages in dangerous recreational activities, this asymmetrical flow of information constitutes adverse selection and could raise insurance premiums for all customers, forcing the healthy to withdraw. The solution is for life insurance providers to perform due diligence or thorough actuarial work and conduct detailed health screenings, and then charge different premiums to customers based on their honestly disclosed risk profiles (Bloomenthal 2021).

Information asymmetry in crowdfunding

Information asymmetry deals with the study of decisions in transactions where one party has more or better information than the other. This means that both parties are not in identical positions which creates an imbalance of power in the transaction. This imbalance can sometimes cause the transaction to be askew. It can lead to inefficient exchanges which can potentially result in market failure (Akerlof 1970). Information asymmetry is common in sectors where the level of uncertainty is relatively high, such as in the realm of crowdfunding where underdeveloped products and services are more likely (Belleflamme *et al.* 2014). Projects that are in the early stages of development often experience the liability of newness, a high level of uncertainty and risk which can increase information asymmetry (Cumming 2007; Olsson and Wahlberg 2018).

Information asymmetry is a challenge within crowdfunding and often leads to inefficient exchanges between the founders seeking funding and the crowd of investors on the platforms (Courtney *et al.* 2017; Belleflamme *et al.* 2015). Inefficient informational exchanges can create difficulties for the crowd of investors to evaluate the project founders seeking funding and can lead to opportunistic and irrational behaviour in investment situation (Cohen and Dean 2005; Olsson and Wahlberg 2018). Thus, it puts founders seeking finance in a disadvantage and limits the credibility of being able to deliver on the products and services (Ahlers *et al.* 2015; Mollick 2014).

In the context of crowdfunding, potential backers usually possess incomplete and imperfect information about the prospect of a project as compared with the entrepreneur. As a result, backers face the economic risk of investing in the project (Akerlof 1970) and entrepreneurs face the challenge of credibly informing potential backers about the viability of the project which results in a finance gap. Finance gaps are often interpreted as being the result of the information asymmetry problem. This means that entrepreneurs know more about themselves and their businesses than the lending organizations. This problem reflects difficulties in communication and credibility. Notably, younger innovative businesses, which do not have trading track records often face information asymmetries for which effective due diligence is prohibitively expensive for prospective financiers to undertake and invest (Ekanem *et al.* 2019). This results in Modigliani and Miller's (1958) finance market imperfections which lead to finance supply gaps along the finance escalator (Ekanem *et al.* 2019).

In financial markets, information asymmetry leads to two problems, namely "adverse selection" and "moral hazard", both of which lead to increased monitoring costs (Bebczuk 2003). The finance market for entrepreneurship is imperfect (Modigliani and Miller 1958) and information asymmetry is considered to be the main cause of market failure and finance gaps (Akerlof 1970; Myers and Majluf 1984; Lean and Tucker 2000). This is due to the lack of, or insufficient, information between the finance provider and the business owner, which means that entrepreneurs know about themselves and their businesses than the lending organizations. This problem becomes more serious for young innovative businesses which do not have track records to demonstrate their market traction and value, and often lack sufficient collateral. These businesses require risk equity finance, but face problems of adverse selection and moral hazard (Carpenter and Peterson 2002), which result from the prohibitively high cost of due diligence for relatively small-scale seed and early stage investments and is reflected in the resultant poor performance of these equity markets in recent years (Mason *et al.* 2010; BVCA 2013).

Adverse selection arises when a venture capitalist is unable to verify what the entrepreneur knows before signing a contract and the quality of the investment opportunity (Lahti 2014). This results in either the investor providing finance for a business that subsequently fails or refusing to provide finance for a business that would have been successful (Deakins and Freel 2012). Therefore, VCs invest heavily in mitigating the risk of adverse selection (Arthurs and Busenitz 2003).

Moral hazard occurs when it is impossible to observe entrepreneur behaviour in the venture, so they may act opportunistically by not putting forth the agreed effort required to run the business operation successfully (Lahti 2014). This implies that business owners are using the company's resources for their own benefit. In other words, moral hazard is the difficulty of the funder to monitor the activities of an entrepreneur once the finance is raised as there is no guarantee that the entrepreneur will act in the best interests of the funder (Deakins and Freel 2012).

In crowdfunding, Wessel (2016) suggests that project creators will, in most cases, have considerably more information about their project and its quality than the crowd or backers. Backers are only aware that some projects on the platform are of good quality, while the rest are of bad quality (Akerlof 1970). Compared to other contexts where there are two-sided markets, the problem of information asymmetry is, however, more severe in the crowdfunding context giving rise to two main issues. In the first instance, all investment decisions on crowdfunding platforms are being made before the actual quality of the project can be effectively evaluated after the campaign has ended. Wessel (2016) argues that it is therefore particularly difficult for backers to distinguish between low-quality and high-quality projects, as they are unable to assess the true quality and could thus make suboptimal choices due to the potentially biased information provided by project creators.

Secondly, project creator incompetence and general project risks can be considered to be more serious issues (Tomboc 2013; Agrawal *et al.* 2014). Similarly, outright fraud occurs on crowdfunding platforms as project creators make use of the high level of information asymmetry by overstating quality or withholding information, thus passing off a low-quality project as a higher-quality one. This is because with the exception of equity-based crowdfunding, raising funds through crowdfunding platforms is still subject to little regulation (Wessel 2016).

Recent studies have started to examine information challenges in crowdfunding (Courtney 2018) as crowdfunding presents unique information challenges (Ahlers *et al.* 2015; Mollick 2014). This is so because crowdfunding takes place online and over a short period of time (Courtney 2018). Furthermore, crowdfunding projects are oftentimes at their early stages of development where there are prevalent uncertainties about their viability (Belleflamme *et al.* 2014).

As defined earlier, information asymmetry becomes critical when one party lacks information about the quality of another party or when one party is concerned about another party's behavioural tendency (Courtney *et al.* 2017; Stiglitz 2000). In crowdfunding, the entrepreneur may know more about the underlying quality of the project than potential backers and the backers can be informationally disadvantaged with regard to the founder's credibility to produce and deliver the product or service as promised (Ahlers *et al*. 2015; Mollick 2014). The quality of the project depends on both the technical feasibility and market viability of the project's product or service. Courtney (2018) argues that the viability of the project cannot be ascertained until the backer receives and experiences the product or service, but it can be reflected, among other things, through the physical attributes of the product, product functionality and the development stage of the project. Courtney further indicates that the credibility of the founder depends on the trust that potential backers place in the founder's promise to produce and deliver a product or service as specified. Therefore, while quality is more related to the functional aspects of the product or service, credibility is more related to the behavioural predisposition of the founder.

Causes of information asymmetry

Existing literature has given three reasons as being main causes of information asymmetry. Cumming (2007) suggests that information asymmetry arises because of the associated high level of uncertainty and risk. Dehlen (2014) indicates that it arises when companies make use of their informational advantage to obtain funding, while Courtney (2018) suggests that it arises when there is a misunderstanding of information and signals between the crowd of investors from whom the companies are seeking funding. However, the empirical findings in Olsson and Wahlberg (2018), a study on "Impacting Information Asymmetry within the Swedish Equity Crowdfunding Market", show that there are five main recurring platform perceptions that explain how information asymmetry arises within the market as presented in the following paragraphs.

(i) The environmental setting of high-risk investments

This is particularly relevant to equity crowdfunding. Information asymmetry arises because the equity crowdfunding market is associated with high risk investments. The high level of risk makes it challenging for the crowd investors to evaluate companies seeking funding (Olsson and Wahlberg 2018). The evidence in the study suggests that there is risk when investing in established public companies, however in equity crowdfunding the level of risk-taking is increased as the companies are in earlier stages of development. There is also a high level of risk in equity crowdfunding because there is a low level of liquidity. This means that it is challenging for the crowd investors to trade their shares because neither the companies seeking funding, nor the crowd investors can have guarantees that the investment will be successful.

(ii) Information asymmetry between the platforms and the crowd of investors

Information asymmetry is perceived to arise between crowdfunding platforms in the market and the crowd of investors because crowd investors lack knowledge about investing in the equity crowdfunding market and about the functioning of platform processes (Olsson and Wahlberg 2018). The study also indicates that small nonprofessional investors often invest because they know or like the product or service that the company provides and stresses that there is a need for education about equity crowdfunding and how the investment situations function.

(iii) Information asymmetry arises because of informational advantage

The empirical findings in Olsson and Wahlberg (2018) demonstrate that information asymmetry is also perceived to arise between project funders and the crowd investors on crowdfunding platforms when project founders seeking funding make use of their informational advantage with the intention to receive funding. The study stresses that the problem is exacerbated when platforms are governed and controlled to ensure a high quality of the companies seeking funding. However, governing and controlling the market can also have the effect of mitigating fraud by the companies seeking funding.

(iv) Information asymmetry arises because of lack of shared information

Information asymmetry is also perceived to arise in crowdfunding markets because of lack of shared information between companies seeking funding and the crowd investors. Olsson and Wahlberg (2018) stress that platforms should develop internal informational requirements that companies seeking funding need to communicate and should also assist companies seeking funding in developing their communicational material and provide channels for communication. It is important to present as much information as possible to give the investor the opportunity to make a rational investment decision (Olsson and Wahlberg 2018).

(v) Information asymmetry arises because of company valuation

The empirical findings in Olsson and Wahlberg (2018) show that information asymmetry is perceived to arise in the Swedish equity crowdfunding market because of the lack of information and understanding of company valuation by the crowd of investors. This is a problem in the market as the companies seeking funding and the crowd investors have different motivations for company valuation. The study suggests that the companies seeking funding want to have high company valuation and will try to adjust their communication to sell their company with a high valuation.

Case study of the effects of fake social information in crowdfunding

The study in Wessel (2016) has revealed that social information such as social buzz has a significant effect on decision making in the crowdfunding context as it allows backers to better assess the quality of campaigns before investing. This effect might, however, also incentivize project creators to manipulate the system by creating fake data in favour of their own campaign in order to deliberately mislead backers. The study contributes to signalling theory by showing why non-genuine social information might have an effect on consumer decision making. The study is concerned with the emergence and effects of fake social information in the form of non-genuine Facebook Likes in the crowdfunding context. Specifically, it captured unnatural, artificially created peaks in the number of Facebook Likes that a specific crowdfunding campaign received and observed subsequent campaign performance. Analyzing more than 35,000 campaigns on the platform Kickstarter, the study found that 1.6% of all campaigns receive fake Facebook Likes. The results show that fake Facebook Likes have a very short-term positive effect on the number of backers funding the respective crowdfunding campaign.

However, this short-term peak is followed by an immediate, sharp drop in the number of backers funding the campaign reaching levels that are lower than prior to the occurrence of the non-genuine social information. Though the analysis shows that non-genuine social information does, in fact, influence the investment decisions of backers, overall, manipulation activities have a negative effect on backing behaviour. Thus, creating non-genuine social information can virtually backfire, as the campaign creators achieve the opposite of what they originally intended. This study therefore demonstrates that signals, which are expected to reduce information asymmetries between project creators and backers, can be manipulated but the manipulation might not have the intended effects.

Source: Adapted from Wessel (2016)

Strategies for reducing information asymmetry in crowdfunding

In crowdfunding two groups of investors can be distinguished, namely, traditional accredited investors who are mainly large investors and investment banks, and another group consisting of non-accredited small crowdfunding investors, the crowd (Firoozi *et al.* 2017). Both groups of investors have access to all relevant information available. However, there is still no level playing field in the capital market which results in the parity of information between the accredited traditional investor group and non-accredited crowd investor group. Firoozi *et al.* (2017) define non-accredited crowd investors to consist of small investors that are not as resourceful and typically have less capital and less investing experience relative to accredited traditional investors.

Accredited traditional investors, on the other hand, "are typically in a position of having access to private resources that allow them to have a deeper financial and operational knowledge and thus are in a position of making a better risk assessment regarding a prospective project relative to non-accredited crowd investors" (Firoozi *et al.* 2017, p. 4). These information parities have important implications for risk assessment and investment decisions. Typically, a new project sends signals to potential investors regarding the prospects of its management, product line, marketing and financial plans. The signals from the project founders are likely to be more accurately interpreted by accredited traditional investors than non-accredited crowd investors. These differences are referred to as information parities.

The emerging ideas in the literature suggest ways which will enable non-accredited crowd investors to behave in exactly the same skilful and well-informed way as the accredited traditional investors. Agrawal *et al.* (2013) suggest the use of feedback systems and skilled intermediaries by the non-accredited crowd groups in order to close the gaps in information asymmetries. Firoozi *et al.* (2017, p. 7), on the other hand, argue that "a market in which crowd investors can only safely invest through skilled representative investment firms is not a crowdfunding market in a full sense anymore". However, existing literature agrees that there is information asymmetry between the founders and non-accredited crowd investors that can expose the crowd to misinformation and fraud by fund seekers. In view of this possible exposure, reducing the risk of information asymmetry between fund seekers and the crowd is vital.

Typically, crowdfunding projects are always in their early stage of development and therefore, the actions of the entrepreneur are essential to demonstrate the project quality and the founder credibility. The entrepreneurial actions and information provided help to attract backers and increase the success of crowdfunding.

A broad range of market designs have been suggested and deployed in crowdfunding and other online market settings in an attempt at reducing information-related market failures (Torabi and Mirakhor 2018). These are signals from projects, endorsement from third party, reputation mechanism, pure and hybrid crowds, due diligence and deal screening. At this stage, we discuss the various market designs.

1 Signals from projects

This is information which originates from the project itself which helps to convey what the project is about, at what stage the project is, the outcome of the project, and what need it fulfils (Courtney 2018). A number of studies have provided insights into how signals reveal information to potential investors about the prospects of business projects (Baum and Silverman 2004; Hsu 2007). Studies have suggested that project patents can provide a credible signal about the quality of the project (Hsu and Ziedonis 2013) and attract attention from potential investors such as venture capitalists and business angels (Mann and Sager 2007). Signals from projects usually originate from two sources: use of media and founders' crowdfunding experience.

(a) Use of media

Courtney (2018) suggests that one potential source of information signals is the use of media such as videos and images to communicate the attributes and characteristics of the project and the stage of development. Such attributes include the product's technical feasibility and the market readiness of the project that help potential backers to establish with certainty the quality of the project. The inclusion of the video and images of the project suggests that the project is at a more developed stage and has met at least minimum preparation for crowdfunding (Mollick 2014). It is also more likely that the founder will develop and deliver the product with the specified functionality in the specified time. This enhances potential backers' trust in the founder's ability to live up to expectations (Courtney 2018). Therefore, the use of media is an information tool which demonstrates the level of preparedness and signals both project quality and founder credibility.

Courtney (2018) argues that although low quality projects can imitate the video and images of high-quality projects, it is not without costs. It is also argued that although the monetary expenses in making a video or creating an image can be marginal, the real cost incurred to demonstrate project preparedness pertains to the founder's ability and efforts to lead the project to the development stage that enables a high-quality project to use appropriate media tools to display a working model or prototype of the product (Courtney 2018).

The use of video is one feature that can make a successful crowdfunding campaign by reducing information asymmetry. Most crowd-based funding projects use the video approach to reach backers and potential supporters. The video also tells a story which can be shared with the crowdfunding community. This can be in the form of a short commercial for the initiative which enables participants to watch, thus attracting millions of attentions.

We can conclude that although crowdfunding projects are different in their use of media, the use of media can convey useful information to backers regarding the quality of the projects and the founder's credibility to successfully develop and deliver the product. Thus, it has a positive effect on reducing information asymmetry and enhancing crowdfunding success.

(b) Founders' crowdfunding experience

Another important potential source of information signal is the founders' experience which can influence investors' funding decisions (Hsu 2007; Kaplan and Strömberg 2004). Courtney (2018) postulates that founders differ in their crowdfunding experience. Some have more experience in successfully raising crowdfunding finance than others. Such experience can be a credible signal of project quality and founder credibility. Potential backers can draw meaningful inferences from founders' past success about the quality of the current project. In addition, if a founder has experience in launching and managing crowdfunding projects successfully, it enhances the credibility of the founder to develop and deliver the current project.

Courtney (2018) further argues that it is difficult for founders with no past success to misrepresent their record or mislead potential backers because crowdfunding platforms such as Kickstarter maintain records of founders' past projects. Such records are observable to potential backers and cannot be manipulated. "To the extent that founders' past success correlates with the quality of the current project and reflects the founder's credibility, successful crowdfunding experience can be useful in distinguishing high-quality projects from low-quality projects" (Courtney 2018, p. 14).

2 Endorsements from third parties

Another solution to information asymmetry in crowdfunding is third-party endorsement. Apart from signals originating from the project as discussed earlier, information revealed through third-party endorsements can also help potential backers to ascertain project quality and founder credibility (Courtney 2018). Such endorsements may qualify as a signal of quality when the third-party endorsing the project or the product is a prominent entity such as the ISO quality certifications, FDA drug approvals and bond ratings (King *et al.* 2005; Stuart *et al.* 1999).

Courtney (2018) argues that some third-party endorsements may not be construed as credible signals when the third parties are not prominent entities. Nevertheless, such endorsements may also be useful in revealing discrete information about the assets of the company or the unique features of a product. For example, industry analyst reports on the capital market or online product reviews by consumers help in reducing the search costs for potential investors and customers (Mudambi and Schuff 2010; Zhu and Zhang 2010). Venture capital backing is another source of powerful third-party endorsement which can signal a project's quality and help potential backers to ascertain the value of the project (Plummer *et al.* 2015).

A unique source of third-party endorsement can originate from crowdfunding platforms through a collective set of backer comments. Oftentimes, backers leave comments about a project on the crowdfunding platform which can help other potential backers make up their minds before investing in projects in their early stages of start up which usually experience considerable uncertainty. The comments and opinions of backers are usually regarded as strong peer reviews which can influence the perceptions and opinions of others (Rindova *et al.* 2007). The overall positive comments from backers act as an external endorsement of the project quality and the founder's credibility (Courtney 2018).

There are two reasons why backers' comments may be a powerful source of third-party endorsement: First, they often contain information about the technical feasibility and market viability of the product with useful information about certain features unique to the product or even provide suggestions to improve the design and usability of the product. Second, backer comments can also carry information about the founders' credibility to develop and deliver the product as promised that further instils trust in backing the project (Courtney 2018).

Research studies have examined the varying effects of different signals and how they help in mitigating information asymmetry. Examples of these research studies include Pollock *et al.* (2010), Ozmel *et al.* (2013) and Plummer *et al.* (2015). Pollock *et al.* (2010) posit that there is a linear increase in the marginal effects of signalling through a firm's characteristics and reputation on IPO valuations while the marginal effects from signalling due to third-party endorsement is at a diminishing rate of increase. Ozmel *et al.* (2013) suggest that a project's endorsement from prominent VCs tends to have diminishing signalling effects on new projects. Whereas, Plummer *et al.* (2015) argue that endorsements from new venture development organizations would validate the signalling value of a project in seeking external funding. Therefore, there is the need to understand how different types of signals interact to reduce information asymmetry in crowdfunding.

The interplay of project signals and third-party endorsement

Since project signals from media and the crowdfunding experience of the founder can operate together with third-party endorsements, it is important to explore their interactions and how they influence the success or otherwise of crowdfunding (Courtney 2018).

(i) Interaction between project signals

Courtney (2018) argues that although differences exist in the information interpreted from the project through observing media and founders' past success, the two signals originate from the same source. Since they originate from the same source and convey information about project quality and founder credibility, they have the ability to offset each other's information value.

Courtney (2018, p. 18) then postulates that "the signalling value of media usage in determining crowdfunding success is a function of the level of the potential backers' information concerns with regard to both quality and credibility". If the founder does not have prior crowdfunding success, potential backers confront greater uncertainty regarding the potential of the project and the value of funding commitment. Consequently, they will have to rely more on media usage and other channels of information. Therefore, the signalling value of media usage will be higher. If, on the contrary, the founder has prior success in achieving crowdfunding goals, potential backers will have more trust in the unobservable quality of the project and the founder's promise to deliver. Consequently, the marginal value of media usage as a signal will be relatively lower which suggests that the positive effect of use of media on likelihood of achieving crowdfunding success decreases with the founder's past crowdfunding success.

(ii) Interactions between project signals and third-party endorsement

Courtney (2018) further suggests that while the signals originating from the project (use of media and founder crowdfunding experience) may reduce each other's effects, third-party endorsements can validate and complement the information conveyed by the founder. The explanation for this is that while information conveyed through media usage and founder crowdfunding experience are internal to the project, backer comments are external and are observed subsequently in the crowdfunding process after some individuals have pledged financial contributions. Since backers are aware of different project signals before making comments on a project, backers' positive comments help to validate the information signalled through the use of media and founders' crowdfunding experience. Also, any negative comments from backers can discourage some founders from misrepresenting the use of media.

Similarly, the information conveyed through backers' comments is capable of complementing the information obtained from the project (Courtney 2018). Furthermore, it is important to point out that backers can access information through other sources such as the internet and social media. This makes it possible for backers to be able to make judgements about the quality and credibility of the project provided that the information is consistent across different sources and in the same direction. Since backer comments and project signals originate from different sources, they are two distinct information mechanisms and are thus less likely to reflect redundant information or offset each other's effects. Therefore, positive information from backers is expected to strengthen the signalling benefits of media usage and founder crowdfunding experience (Courtney 2018).

3 Reputation mechanism

Torabi and Mirakhor (2018) suggest that one of the newest ways of solving the problem of information asymmetry is reputation mechanism. The main objective of a reputation mechanism is to enable efficient transactions in sectors where cooperation is compromised by post-contractual opportunism or information asymmetries (Torabi and Mirakhor 2018). Reputation mechanism is about the honesty and credibility of the participants. If the community follows a norm by punishing traders with an adverse track record of behaviour, by refusing to deal with them, and if the present value of punishment exceeds the gains from cheating, then the threat of public revelation of a trader's cheating behaviour provides rational traders with sufficient incentives to cooperate (Dellarocas 2015). Torabi and Mirakhor (2018) regard the role of reputation as an important mechanism to establish trust to address the risk of fraud in online transactions. While there are various mechanisms to deal with fraud, reputation is one of the best and more effective candidates (Torabi and Mirakhor 2018).

By the same token, Bloomenthal (2021) posits that financial markets rely on reputation mechanisms to prevent abuse of customers or clients by finance specialists. Financial advisors and fund companies that prove to be the most honest and effective stewards of their clients' assets tend to gain clients, while dishonest or ineffective agents tend to lose clients, face legal damages, or both (Bloomenthal 2021).

In their paper "Controlling Information Asymmetry in Equity Crowdfunding" Torabi and Mirakhor (2018) design an enhanced reputation mechanism called "Fame". "Fame" refers to the credibility of every individual who is a member of a crowdfunding system. Fame is systematic, countable and computable (implicit and explicit) reputation, a clear signal to other members of the social network of crowdfunding. This credibility is formed for all users of the system based on their banking (financial) credit, social credit, participation (activities) history, and track record of their success in previous transactions. Fame has been innovated in order to represent and monitor the reputation of the users in the social network of the crowdfunding system.

4 Pure and hybrid crowds in crowdfunding

As a result of the limitations raised in managing crowd investors by most projects creators, Chen et al. (2016) have suggested how crowds can be designed to avoid their common shortcomings and thus reduce information asymmetry. Two popular forms of crowd designs suggested are pure crowds and hybrid crowds.

(i) Pure crowds

This is a design where all investors in the crowd participate as equals (i.e. no one member assumes the formal role of the lead investor). A pure crowd design requires the crowd members to play many roles in a crowdfunding platform, including supplying funds, choosing and evaluating projects, gathering project information, and monitoring and promoting a project. However, Chen *et al.* (2016) argue that several barriers prevent an unorganized crowd from fulfilling some of these roles. First, some activities such as due diligence are "public goods" (p. 2) in the sense that efforts by one crowd member can benefit others. A common problem associated with the private provision of public goods is the "tragedy of the commons", where an individual member has insufficient incentives to carry out an activity that benefits others (Chen *et al.* 2016, p. 2). Furthermore, relying on the wisdom of the crowds has limitations for evaluating the merits of a project. This is because crowd members are not generally experts, but they infer project quality by observing the decisions made by their peers (Zhang and Liu 2012). A lack of independence undermines the wisdom of the crowds, causing biases and large uncertainties in the outcome (Salganik *et al.* 2006; Lorenz *et al.* 2011). Finally, when a project faces tens of hundreds of crowd investors, managing and communicating with crowd members becomes cumbersome and inefficient.

(ii) Hybrid crowds

Chen *et al.* (2016, p. 4) describe hybrid crowds as a design which uses lead investors, who are "well-versed and experienced investors who spend the time conducting due diligence on a venture, and invest a large amount in an equity crowdfunding campaign". Lead investors perform several roles in the crowdfunding process such as identifying projects and bringing them to the platform, conducting due diligence on projects, reporting to crowd investors, promoting a crowdfunding campaign, monitoring an ongoing project, and providing followers with project updates. Lead investors are also required to invest a significant proportion of the total investment amount to signal their commitment to and confidence in the project. Crowd investors often choose projects based on whether it is backed by a lead investor as well as what the lead investor says about the project. Therefore, lead investors perform many of the roles typically carried out by traditional financial intermediaries (e.g. banks, charity organizations, venture capitalists).

Chen *et al.* (2016) explain how hybrid crowds are designed: after a project is posted online, an investor, often an institutional investor, may apply to become the lead investor for the project. The platform delegates the task of choosing the lead investor to the project creator. If the project is successfully funded, the lead receives a small percentage, usually 2%, of the total amount raised as a service fee. After the project is successfully funded, the lead investor and his or her co-investors form a Limited Liability Partnership company with the lead playing the role of the General Partner and the rest serving as Limited Partners. When the project exits from the venture, by way of compensation for lead investors' efforts and the risk they take, they are often paid a proportion of the total exit profits (typically around 20%) referred to as "carry". Hence, lead investors serve as a catalyst for unlocking investment from others because the commitment and endorsement from a lead investor gives confidence to other crowd investors.

There are several differences between the two types as explained by Chen *et al.* (2016). First, lead investors are selected from the crowd; indeed, any accredited investor on platforms may become the lead. Further, lead investors supplement rather than replace direct investments by crowd members. The two coexist in a hybrid crowd (whereas some traditional financial intermediaries may preclude direct investments). Chen *et al.* (2016) argue that hybrid crowds are currently only seen and widely employed in equity-based crowdfunding.

A group of investors led by an expert lead investor can provide a good solution to overcome the limitation of pure crowds (Deschler 2014). Chen *et al.* (2016) argue that unlike smaller investors in the crowd, a lead investor is generally highly knowledgeable about valuing risky projects and ventures. Lead investors have the incentives because they get a share of profit from successful projects. They also have the expertise to carry out costly activities such as due diligence, project monitoring and brokering the communication between project creators and crowd investors.

Therefore, a hybrid crowd offers another way of alleviating information asymmetry (Chen *et al.* 2016). By crowdsourcing the due diligence and other necessary functions to lead investors, the crowdfunding platform can continue to function as an online platform. In this way, lead investors can fulfil the roles that an average crowd member is unwilling or unable to do. By investing significantly in a project, a lead investor can also boost investor confidence and increase the liquidity of crowdfunding markets.

(iii) Managing lead investors

In their study "Pure and Hybrid Crowds in Crowdfunding Markets", Chen *et al.* (2016) explain why it is important for crowdfunding platforms to manage lead investors. In a hybrid crowd, lead investors have a great impact on crowd investors, project creators and the crowdfunding platform. As information asymmetry always exists between crowd investors and project creators, crowd investors have to leverage the expertise of lead investors to reduce such asymmetry. The quality of jobs such as due diligence and risk disclosure conducted by lead investors has a direct impact on crowd investors' investment judgement. As for project creators, endorsement by a prominent lead investor serves as signal of quality and impacts project success because lead investors have good investment records and reputation. At the platform side, lead investors can attract more crowd investors and promote project success, which aligns with the platform's interests in maximizing revenue.

A further argument by Chen *et al.* (2016) in favour of managing lead investors is because crowd investors tend to place great trust in lead investors. Therefore, any imprudence, misrepresentation, or misconduct by lead investors may influence a crowdfunding market. Due to the elevated power of lead investors and strong financial incentives attached, the management and regulation of lead investors require special attention.

Lead investors may represent crowd investors (e.g. for conducting due diligence), project creators (e.g. for promoting and endorsing projects), and platforms (e.g. for identifying projects and promoting project success), so the management of lead investors can be analyzed by using the principle–agent framework. Hence, Chen *et al.* (2016) suggest that lead investors must be qualified and properly trained for their job through the use of selection and qualification mechanisms. Once they enter the role, they should be properly rewarded for desirable efforts and penalized for undesirable ones through disciplinary mechanisms.

(iv) Selection mechanisms

As explained by Chen *et al.* (2016), lead investor qualification is both a management issue and a domain of law. While no special laws specify qualifications for lead investors, laws for qualified investors do exist. In the United States, for example, according to the JOBS Act (Title III), investment by crowd investors is limited within a 12-month period: if an investor's annual income or net worth is less than $100,000, his or her investment limit is the greater of $2,000 and 5% the lesser of the investor's annual income or net worth; if both annual income and net worth are equal to or more than $100,000, then the investor's limit is 10% of the lesser of their annual income or net worth. Moreover, during the 12-month period, the aggregate amount of securities sold to an investor through all regulation crowdfunding offerings may not exceed $100,000 regardless of the investor's annual income or net worth. Although the JOBS Act enables more individuals in the United States to join crowdfunding, the barriers to entry globally are still high. For instance, in the UK a lead investor must be a "certified high net worth individual" within the meaning of article 48 of the Financial Promotion Order (FPO). It seems that to meet these financial criteria, accredited investors should be high-net-worth individuals such as business angels or institutions such as venture capitalists and wealth management groups.

Chen *et al.* (2016) indicates that a lead investor is supposed to work independently of the project in which he or she invests (just as auditors should be independent of the company they audit). Allowing a project creator to choose the lead grants the former implicit power to influence the lead (e.g. being influenced by flattery), thereby causing collusion concerns. Chen *et al.* (2016) argue that there may be fewer concerns if leads are selected by the platform, which also has vested interests in maximizing funding successes. A crowd-selected lead thus seems to better align the interests of lead investors with its primary principle, namely crowd investors.

(v) Compensation mechanisms

Chen *et al.* (2016) suggest that since lead investors are required to put in significant effort and take extra risk (e.g. 20% investments), they need to be compensated more. The most common components of lead compensation include a service fee and a *carry* (carried interest is a proportion of the proceeds from a successful exit). To earn the service fee, lead investors must conduct a set of duties for crowds such as carrying out due diligence, preparing investment documents, and disclosing risk.

The service fee is paid when project funding succeeds, and it is usually 2% of the total funds raised. The "carry" is paid from the exit profits, usually accounting for 20%. The balance between the service fee and carry is an important issue. Because the probability of successful exits is much lower and more remote than that of successful funding, leads may be incentivized to earn the service fee, which is faster and easier, than waiting for the "carry". Thus, this compensation structure may motivate the lead investor to conspire with the project creators to cheat money out of crowd investors. Another issue with the lead compensation design is that a performance evaluation on the lead is lacking. If the lead does a poor job in due diligence reports, he or she may still receive his or her service fee. Furthermore, because the service fee is contingent on project success, it incentivizes the lead to exaggerate the prospect of the project so that he or she is more likely compensated. In an ideal setting, therefore, the service fee would be paid upon the delivery of a satisfactory service regardless of project funding success, while the crowd should be the judge of whether the service is satisfactory.

(vi) Disciplinary mechanisms

Presently, lead investors are not penalized for inflating the prospects of a project or for producing a low-quality due diligence report (Chen *et al.* 2016). Chen *et al.* (2016) argue that indeed it may be difficult to verify ex post that a lead purposefully misled crowd investors because of the inherent uncertainty of the outcome. However, if a lead deliberately withholds facts that he or she knows or lies about certain aspects of the project, he or she may still be held accountable.

The major problem is that platforms have no framework for imposing such a penalty. One potential approach would be to involve reputation mechanisms and exploit the power of a professional society/association. If cases of cheating and misconduct are reported to the professional association, this may harm a person's reputation, creating a credible threat.

It is, however, rather unclear whether such "reputational concerns" could always be leveraged, given the emerging nature of lead investors. Chen *et al.* (2016) continue to indicate that certain dimensions of the lead investors' work such as the informativeness or thoroughness of their report may be readily assessable by crowd investors. Thus, their service fees may be tied to crowd investors' satisfaction. Currently, this is missing from the compensation design and crowds may also be involved in selecting the lead investors from many candidates. Rules could also require lead investors to disclose their relevant performance history and any conflict of interests with the platform or project creator to ensure that crowd investors are equipped with the pertinent information to choose lead investors. However, such disclosure is currently rather limited (Chen *et al.* 2016).

5 Due diligence

Information asymmetry can be reduced in crowdfunding through due diligence especially in equity crowdfunding. The equity crowdfunding platform can work to control the opportunities of the crowd of investors to execute due diligence pre-investment to thereby mitigate information asymmetry (Olsson and Wahlberg 2018). Investor due diligence is connected to evaluating a company seeking funding to make informed investment decisions. This means that the platform can work to control the disclosing of information to make information accessible for the crowd of investors. Due diligence is especially important because companies seeking funding in equity crowdfunding often are in early stages of development which can impact the level of risk and quality of disclosed information (Ley and Weaven 2011).

6 Deal screening

Deal screening can be used by equity crowdfunding platforms to control companies seeking funding to reduce information asymmetry. This means that platforms can work to evaluate the companies seeking funding pre-investment (Olsson and Wahlberg 2018). Deal screening can impact agency problems and information asymmetry by mitigating hidden informational problems to make sure that unsuitable companies are rejected access to seek funding (Ley and Weaven 2011).

Summary

The argument in this chapter is that both project-originated signals (which consist of the use of media and founders' prior crowdfunding success and experience) and third-party endorsements (which are positive comments from backers) reduce information asymmetry in crowdfunding by mitigating concerns about project quality and founder credibility. It is also argued in this chapter that while the two project signals (i.e. media usage and founders' previous successful experience) offset each other, third-party endorsements complement and validate project generated signals (Courtney 2018). Courtney (2018) also argues that media usage is more beneficial when project founders do not have previous crowdfunding successful experience. Therefore, information generated from media usage can be as useful to backers as information generated through patents, trademarks and other intellectual property.

The chapter has demonstrated that in the context of crowdfunding the language used by those seeking funding can send signals to the market, which can ultimately reduce information asymmetries (e.g. Loughran and McDonald 2013; Wessel 2016). It has also been suggested that a reputation monitoring mechanism can provide a key to reducing information asymmetry. Since crowdfunding is a web 2.0-based platform, which is actually a closed system, the implementation of a reputation monitoring mechanism is appropriate (Torabi and Mirakhor 2018). Finally, hybrid crowd design offers another way of reducing information asymmetry in crowdfunding.

It is also suggested that the equity crowdfunding platforms should work to reduce information asymmetry by transparent, relevant, trustworthy and simplified investor communication. This means that the platforms should structure and develop the investor communication so that the crowd investors can interpret and understand the information (Olsson and Wahlberg 2018).

Discussion questions

1 What do you understand by information asymmetry?
2 What are the problems information asymmetry gives rise to?
3 How can information asymmetry be reduced in crowdfunding?
4 "Signals from projects usually originate from two sources." Discuss these sources.
5 Discuss the ways in which lead investors can be effectively managed.

Test questions

1 Students are split into two groups and asked to debate the advantages and disadvantages of information asymmetry.
2 How does adverse selection impact crowdfunding?
3 Apply the concepts of adverse selection and moral hazard to financial markets.

Glossary of key terminologies

Adverse selection   Giving finance to a business that subsequently fails or no finance for a business that would have been successful.

Collateral   An asset that a lender accepts as security for a loan.

Deal screening   Evaluating the companies seeking funding before investment.

Due diligence   A systematic investigation and analysis to mitigate risk from a business or investment decision.

Equity finance   A method of raising funds by selling shares of the company to public, institutional investors, or financial institutions.

Finance gap   The difference when the demand for finance is greater than the willingness of financial institutions to supply it at current market conditions.

Hybrid crowds   A design which uses lead investors, who are well-versed and experienced and who spend time conducting due diligence on a venture, and invest a large amount in an equity crowdfunding campaign.

Information asymmetry   One party in a contract has more or better information than the other.

Information parity   Information parity is the difference in the level of information and interpretation between accredited investors and non-accredited crowd investors.

IPO   Initial public offering.

Moral hazard   Is a monitoring problem; where the entrepreneur is not acting in the best interests of the funder or the company once finance is raised.

Pure crowds   All investors in the crowd participate as equals.

VC   Venture capital.

Recommended reading

Gaul, L., and Steburnovs, V., 2015. *Ownership and asymmetric information problems in the corporate loan market: Evidence from a heteroskedastic regression, createspace.* Independent Publishing Platform, London.

Hillier, B., 1997. *The economics of asymmetric information*. London: Palgrave.

Masroianni, F., 2017. *Asymmetric information relating to initial public offering underpricing*. Munich: GRIN Publishers.

Schwienbacher, A., and Larralde, B., 2010. *Crowdfunding of small entrepreneurial ventures. Handbook of entrepreneurial finance*. Oxford: Oxford University Press.

Voorbraak, K.J.P.M., 2011. *Crowdfunding for financing new ventures: Consequence of the financial model on operational decisions*. Eindhoven: Eindhoven University of Technology.

Zavadskas, E.K., Turkis, Z., and Antucheviciene, J., 2019. Solution models based on symmetric and asymmetric information. *Symmetry*, 11 (4), 500.

References

Agrawal, A., Catalini, C., and Goldfarb, A., 2013. The simple economics of crowdfunding. *Policy Economics*, 14, 1–46.

Agrawal, A., Catalini, C., and Goldfarb, A., 2014. Some simple economics of crowdfunding. *Innovation Policy and the Economy*, 14 (1), 63–97.

Ahlers, G.K., Cumming, D., Günther, C., and Schweizer, D., 2015. Signaling in equity crowdfunding. *Entrepreneurship Theory and Practice*, 39 (4), 955–980.

Akerlof, G.A., 1970. The market for "lemons": Quality uncertainty and the market mechanism. *The Quarterly Journal of Economics*, 84 (3), 488–500.

Arthurs, J., and Busenitz, L., 2003. The boundaries and limitations of agency theory and stewardship theory in the venture capitalist/entrepreneur relationship. *Entrepreneurship Theory & Practice*, 28 (2), 145–162.

Baum, J.A., and Silverman, B.S., 2004. Picking winners or building them? Alliance, intellectual, and human capital as selection criteria in venture financing and performance of biotechnology startups. *Journal of Business Venturing*, 19 (3), 411–436.

Bebczuk, N.R., 2003. *Asymmetric information in financial markets. Introduction and applications*. Cambridge: Cambridge University Press.

Belleflamme, P., Lambert, T., and Schwienbacher, A., 2014. Crowdfunding: Tapping the right crowd. *Journal of Business Venturing*, 29 (5), 585–609.

Belleflamme, P., Omrani, N., and Peitz, M., 2015. The economics of crowdfunding platforms. *Information Economics and Policy*, 33, 11–28.

Bloomenthal, A., 2021. Asymmetric information. *Investopedia*. Available from: www.investopedia.com/terms/a/asymmetricinformation.asp [Accessed 2 April 2021].

BVCA, 2013. *BVCA private equity and venture capital report on investment activity 2012*. London: British Venture Capital Association.

Carpenter, R.E., and Peterson, B.C., 2002. Capital market imperfections, high-tech investment, and new equity financing. *The Economic Journal*, 112, F54–F72.

Chen, L., Huang, Z., and Liu, D., 2016. Pure and hybrid crowds in crowdfunding markets, *Financial Innovation*, 2 (19), 1–18.

Cohen, B., and Dean, T., 2005. Information asymmetry and investor valuation of IPOs: Top management team legitimacy as a capital market signal. *Strategic Management Journal*, 26 (7), 683–690.

Courtney, C., Dutta, S., and Li, Y., 2017. Resolving information asymmetry: Signaling, endorsement, and crowdfunding success. *Entrepreneurship Theory and Practice*, 41 (2), 265–290.

Courtney, C.M., 2018. *Essays on crowdfunding: Information asymmetry, signalling and feedback*. Thesis (PhD). University of Buffalo, State University of New York.

Cumming, D.J., 2007. Government policy towards entrepreneurial finance: Innovation investment funds. *Journal of Business Venturing*, 22 (2), 193–235.

Deakins, D., and Freel. M., 2012. *Entrepreneurship and small firms*. 6th ed. London: McGraw-Hill.

Dehlen, T., Zellweger, T., Kammerlander, N., and Halter, F., 2014. The role of information asymmetry in the choice of entrepreneurial exit routes, *Journal of Business Venturing*, 29, 193–209.

Dellarocas, C., 2015. *Reputation mechanisms*. Mowatt Lane: R.H. Smith School of Business University of Maryland.

Deschler, G.D., 2014. Wisdom of the intermediary crowd: What the proposed rules mean for ambitious crowdfunding intermediaries. *Saint Louis University Law Journal*, 58, 1145–1187.

Ekanem. I., Owen, R., and Cardoso, A., 2019. The influence of institutional environment on venture capital development in emerging economies: The example of Nigeria. *Strategic Change*, 28 (1), 95–107. Available from: https://doi.org/10.1002/jsc.2249

Firoozi, F., Jalilvand, A., and Lien, D., 2017. Information asymmetry and adverse wealth effects of crowdfunding. *The Journal of Entrepreneurial Finance*, 18 (1), 1–8.

Hsu, D.H., 2007. Experienced entrepreneurial founders, organizational capital, and venture capital funding. *Research Policy*, 36 (5), 722–741.

Hsu, D.H., and Ziedonis, R.H., 2013. Resources as dual sources of advantage: Implications for valuing entrepreneurial-firm patents. *Strategic Management Journal*, 34 (7), 761–781.

Kaplan, S.N., and Strömberg, P.E., 2004. Characteristics, contracts, and actions: Evidence from venture capitalist analyses. *The Journal of Finance*, 59 (5), 2177–2210.

King, A.A., Lenox, M.J., and Terlaak, A., 2005. The strategic use of decentralized institutions: Exploring certification with the ISO 14001 management standard. *Academy of Management Journal*, 48 (6), 1091–1106.

Lahti, T., 2014. The value-added contribution of advisors in the process of acquiring venture capital, *International Small Business Journal*, 32 (3), 307–326.

Lean, J., and Tucker, J., 2000. Information asymmetry and small firm finance. *In: Paper presented to the 23rd ISBA national small firms conference, small firms: Adding the spark*, 15–17 November. Aberdeen: The Robert Gordon University.

Ley, A., and Weaven, S., 2011. Exploring agency dynamics of crowdfunding in start-up capital Financing. *Academy of Entrepreneurship Journal*, 17 (1), 85–110.

Li, Y., and Chi, T., 2013. Venture capitalists' decision to withdraw: The role of portfolio configuration from a real options lens. *Strategic Management Journal*, 34 (11), 1351–1366.

Lorenz, J., Rauhut, H., Schweitzer, F., and Helbing, D., 2011. How social influence can undermine the wisdom of crowd effect. *PNAS Proceedings of the National Academy of Sciences of the United States of America*, 108 (22), 9020–9025. Available from: https://doi.org/10.1073/pnas.1008636108

Loughran, T., and McDonald, B., 2013. IPO first-day returns, offer price revisions, volatility, and form S-1 language. *Journal of Financial Economics*, 109 (2), 307–326.

Mann, R.J., and Sager, T.W., 2007. Patents, venture capital, and software start-ups. *Research Policy*, 36 (2), 193–208.

Mason, C.M., Jones, L., and Wells, S., 2010. *The City's role in providing for the public equity financing needs of UK SMEs* (Report to the City of London by URS Corporation, March 2010). London: City of London.

Modigliani, F., and Miller, M.H., 1958. The cost of capital, corporation finance and the theory of investment. *The American Economic Review*, 48 (3), 261–297.

Mollick, E., 2014. The dynamics of crowdfunding: An exploratory study. *Journal of Business Venturing*, 29 (1), 1–16.

Mudambi, S.M., and Schuff, D., 2010. What makes a helpful review? A study of customer reviews on Amazon. com. *Mis Quarterly*, 34 (1), 185–200.

Myers, S.C., and Majluf, N.S., 1984. Corporate financing and investment decisions when firms have information that investors do not have. *Journal of Financial Economics*, 13 (2), 187–221. Available from: https://doi.org/10.1016/0304-405X(84)90023-0

Olsson, A., and Wahlberg, N., 2018. *Impacting information asymmetry within the swedish equity crowdfunding market – An aggregated approach on how equity crowdfunding platforms work to govern, control and reduce information asymmetry*. Uppsala: Uppsala University.

Ozmel, U., Reuer, J.J., and Gulati, R., 2013. Signals across multiple networks: How venture capital and alliance networks affect interorganizational collaboration. *Academy of Management Journal*, 56 (3), 852–866.

Plummer, L.A., Allison, T.H., and Connelly, B.L., 2015. Better together? Signaling interactions in new venture pursuit of initial external capital. *Academy of Management Journal*, 2013, Article 0100.

Pollock, T.G., Chen, G., Jackson, E.M., and Hambrick, D.C., 2010. How much prestige is enough? Assessing the value of multiple types of high-status affiliates for young firms. *Journal of Business Venturing*, 25 (1), 6–23.

Rindova, V.P., Petkova, A.P., and Kotha, S., 2007. Standing out: How new firms in emerging markets build reputation. *Strategic Organization*, 5 (1), 31–70.

Salganik, M.J., Dodds, P.S., and Watts, D.J., 2006. Experimental study of inequality and unpredictability in an artificial cultural market. *Science*, 311 (5762), 854–856.

Stiglitz, J.E., 2000. The contributions of the economics of information to twentieth century economics. *Quarterly Journal of Economics*, 1441–1478.

Stuart, T.E., Hoang, H., and Hybels, R.C., 1999. Interorganizational endorsements and the performance of entrepreneurial ventures. *Administrative Science Quarterly*, 44(2), 315-349.

Tomboc, G.F.B., 2013. The lemons problem in crowdfunding. *The John Marshall Journal of Information Technology & Privacy Law*, 30 (2), 253–279.

Torabi, O., and Mirakhor, A., 2018. Controlling information asymmetry in equity crowdfunding. *Journal of Economic and Social Thought*, 5 (1), 32–41.

Wessel, M., 2016. *Crowdfunding: Platform dynamics under asymmetric information*. Thesis (PhD). Technische Universität Darmstadt.

Zhang, J., and Liu, P., 2012. Rational herding in microloan markets. *Management Science*, 58 (5), 892–912.

Zhu, F., and Zhang, X., 2010. Impact of online consumer reviews on sales: The moderating role of product and consumer characteristics. *Journal of Marketing*, 74 (2), 133–148.

6 The trends in the market of digital finance

Learning objectives

- Examine the trends in the market of digital finance
- Discuss how financial services are rapidly digitizing
- Explore how the trend in digital finance represent a significant change in financial services market
- Examine the implications of these shifts for crowdfunding
- Discuss the concept of financial inclusion

Introduction

The European Commission (2020) defines digital finance as the term used to describe the impact of new technologies on the financial services industry. It includes a variety of products, applications, processes and business models that have transformed the traditional way of providing banking and financial services.

Although technological innovation in finance is not new, investment in new technologies has developed substantially and exponentially in recent years. It has become possible to interact with our bank using mobile technology. Payments, investments, and transfer of money can now be made using a variety of new tools that were hitherto not available. Established financial services institutions have seen new services and business models through the use of artificial intelligence, social networks, machine learning, mobile applications, distributed ledger technology, cloud computing and big data analytics.

The European Commission (2020) argues that these technologies can benefit both consumers and companies by enabling greater access to financial services, offering wider choice and increasing efficiency of operations. These technologies can also contribute to breaking national barriers and speed up competition in areas such as online banking, online payment and transfer services, peer-to-peer lending and personal investment advice and services.

In recent years customers are able to demand intelligent and easy-to-use financial services irrespective of their locations and time and at decreasing costs (Gomber *et al*. 2017). This is because of the ease with which the internet is used for economic purposes and new and increased usage of mobile devices among

DOI: 10.4324/9781003193975-6

different age and economic groups, thus promoting financial inclusion. However, digital finance provides challenges to existing financial service providers, such as established banks or insurance providers, due to new competition by FinTech companies, while offering new opportunities for the incumbents to reach their younger and more technology-savvy clientele (Gomber *et al.* 2017).

The concept of financial inclusion

Financial inclusion can be defined as the attainment of effective access to financial products and services from credit, savings, insurance and remittance for vulnerable and low-income groups (Jong-Hee 2016). However, Jong-Hee (2016) argues that these services should be economically reasonable for end users and viable for the service providers with the end result of integrating poor people into the formal financial system. Where low-income earners are unable to have access to or afford financial services, it can result in financial exclusion. This group of people are often referred to as "unbankable" and are excluded from the formal financial system because of the high risk of lending (Ebimoghan 2021).

According to Ebimoghan (2021) a group might be unbanked due to discrimination on social, religious or ethnic prejudice; while Jong-Hee (2016) argues that information asymmetry can foster financial exclusion of low-income groups. World Bank Group (2008) indicates that the high cost of financial services may prevent low-income groups and small enterprises from accessing financial services because lower costs may not be economically sustainable for financial institutions.

Financial inclusion is important because of its implications for reducing poverty and boosting shared prosperity (World Bank 2014). When finance becomes affordable, the poor are able to participate effectively in economic activities and are able to close the income inequality gaps (Cnaan *et al.* 2012). Research studies such as Ebimoghan (2021) and Jong-Hee (2016) suggest that finance is a pivotal tool for poverty reduction as countries with higher rates of financial integration and development record quicker reduction in poverty. Financial inclusion enables empowerment, economic advancement, social inclusion and poverty reduction (Solo 2008). Therefore, improved access to finance can bolster poverty alleviation (Ebimoghan 2021).

The concept of financial inclusion involves a combination of traditional banking services and digital finance services and therefore can be regarded as multifaceted (Cnaan *et al.* 2012). Financial inclusion provides indiscriminate access to financial products for everybody or organizations at a transparent and affordable cost (Solo 2008). Therefore, Fuller and Mellor (2008) argue that welfare-directed financial services instead of dividend-based services depict financial inclusion, whilst Alpana (2007) presents financial inclusion as a commercial tool for poverty reduction. Ebimoghan (2021) asserts that financial inclusion alleviates low-income and vulnerable groups from poverty and addresses the risks of financial exclusion.

Financial inclusion is positioned prominently by UNCDF (2020) as an enabler of other developmental goals in the 2030 Sustainable Development Goals, where it is featured as a target in eight of the seventeen goals. These include SDG1 – eradicating poverty; SDG 2 -ending hunger, achieving food security and promoting sustainable agriculture; SDG 3 – profiting health and well-being; SDG 5 – achieving gender equality and economic empowerment of women; SDG 8 – promoting economic growth and jobs; SDG 9 – supporting industry, innovation and infrastructure; and SDG 10 – reducing inequality. In addition, UNCDF (2020) indicates that in SDG 17, on strengthening the means of implementation, there is an implicit role for greater financial inclusion through greater savings mobilization for investment and consumption that can spur growth.

According to Ebimoghan (2021), financial inclusion is aimed at providing affordable access to a broad range of financial services for vulnerable and low-income groups. Klapper (2016) suggests that it is also aimed at promoting consumer trust and competition between service providers to limit potential monopoly and to provide credible financial institutions with transparent and efficient regulations. By the same token, Nageswara (2018) posits that it also helps entrepreneurs and small business owners with recurring expenditure and to address unexpected emergencies.

Financial exclusion is still presenting difficulties which limit access to financial services to the underprivileged or low-income earners (Ebimoghan 2021). Ebimoghan (2021) argues that through financial inclusion, disadvantaged and low-income groups can access financial products and services to improve their living standards. For Mitton (2008) the inability to access financial services can result in social marginality and poverty. Ebimoghan (2021) concludes that in order to manage daily financial transactions, credit flows, expenditures and profits, financial inclusion is crucial.

To demonstrate that financial exclusion is still a challenge, Ebimoghan (2021) argues that in 2016, over 37 million European Union adult citizens lacked access to formal financial services, whilst in Africa digital solutions are critical for financial inclusion (Stijns 2017). Consequently, Demirguc-Kunt *et al.* (2015) posit that over 350 million adults in Sub-Saharan Africa are financially excluded. Using the Global Findex data they show that more women and youths in rural areas are financially excluded due to the absence of bank branches in low-population density areas. Ebimoghan (2021) suggests that this gap is increasingly filled by digital finance service providers who utilize electronic payment methods to improve financial inclusion in rural areas. As a result, over 40% of the adult population in Kenya, Tanzania, Zimbabwe, Ghana, Uganda, Gabon and Namibia have access to financial services through digital platforms (Ebimoghan 2021).

The Mckinsey Global Institute suggests that financial exclusion does not only affect the poor, it also affects the middle class (MGI 2016). The institute posits that in emerging economies as a whole, 45% of adults (or two billion individuals) do not have a financial account at a bank or another financial institution, or with a mobile money service. The institute argues that the share of financial exclusion is higher in Africa, the Middle East, Southeast Asia, and South Asia, and is particularly high among poor people, women and those living in rural areas, but many middle-class people are also affected. The institute stresses:

> Even those people who do have basic financial accounts lack access to the broad range of financial services that those in developed countries take for granted, such as different types of savings accounts, loans, and insurance products. As a result, the majority of people in emerging economies rely on informal financial solutions that are often less flexible and more expensive than formal alternatives and frequently fail to deliver when needed the most. These include saving in the form of livestock, gold, or through informal savings groups, and borrowing from family, employers, or money lenders.
>
> (MGI 2016, p. 2)

The World Bank Group looks at financial inclusion as a catalyst for poverty reduction and plays a critical role in providing access to finance through its financial sector expertise since close to 1.7 billion adults are still unbanked (World Bank 2018). It helps in the financial inclusion process by promoting innovations in payment methods from cash to digital payments and support through efficient legal framework for access to finance for SMEs. It also helps the Women Entrepreneurs Finance Initiative (We-Fi) to be able to address the financial challenges of SMEs owned by female entrepreneurs. Other initiatives which the World Bank helps include the Digital Economy for Africa (DE4A). This is an initiative that provides support to build a sustainable digital ecosystem in Africa (World Bank 2018). The World Bank is committed to improving the reach of financial services to 1 billion adults in 25 countries with the highest rate of financial exclusion and instrumental in providing reforms in payment systems to facilitate innovations in payment services through electronic payment methods (Ebimoghan 2021).

Digital finance

Digital finance is defined as financial services delivered over digital infrastructure, including mobile and internet with low use of cash and traditional bank branches (MGI 2016). MGI (2016) explains that mobile phones, computers, or cards use point-of-sale (POS) devices to connect individuals and businesses to a digitized national payments infrastructure, enabling seamless transactions across all parties.

Therefore, digital finance is about the digitalization of the financial industry. It consists of all electronic products and services of the financial sector, e.g. credit and chip cards, electronic exchange systems, home banking, and home trading services including automated teller machines (ATMs) and all mobile and app services (Gomber *et al.* 2017). Digital finance can provide access to banks and their services particularly in developing countries. Examples of these services include payment systems and credits which could not otherwise have been reached (Rizzo 2014).

The Digital Finance Institute describes digital finance as a new and emerging area of finance, which encompasses the areas of financial technology, digital payment systems and digital financial products such as digital derivatives, digital securities, digital carbon credits and a wide variety of digital forms of traditional financial products (DFI 2015). The Digital Finance Institute also indicates that there is a growing global support for digital finance ecosystem start-ups, entrepreneurs and investor communities that are integrating distributed digital banking, mobile transactions and cryptocurrency solutions and delivery platforms; and also support for participation in the emerging digital economy market areas such as microfinance, peer-to-peer lending, diaspora remittances, socially and environmentally motivated initiatives, etc.

Nevertheless, Gomber *et al.* (2017) argue that new technologies and services are not reserved for start-ups only as established service providers also strive intensively to engage in this field. Gomber *et al.* (2017) also argue that while parts of the digital processes and services stated here are well-established (e.g. ATMs), there exist other services and business models that are novel, not widely adapted, and bear disruptive potential for the financial industry. These innovative services and business models that are based on new technologies are often referred to as FinTech solutions (Gomber *et al.* 2017).

The Digital Finance Institute indicates that the digitization of the financial sector is transformative because it reduces costs of services and distribution and creates purely digital financial products and services, some of which are entirely new, and others of which may not be new but are delivered on international digital platforms that are new. These technological changes create significant new opportunities for new financial technology, and many new opportunities for governments and companies to drive growth and innovation, opening the door to greater participation by entrepreneurs (DFI 2015).

Types of digital finance

In this section, we discuss different types of digital finance in more detail. As mentioned earlier, these include (i) digital financing, (ii) digital investments, (iii) digital money, (iv) digital payments, and (v) digital insurances.

(i) Digital financing

Digital financing is quite different from digital finance. Therefore, the two terms should not be confused with one another. While *digital financing* focuses on financing aspects, *digital finance* is the superordinate term embracing all business functions, including financing (Gomber *et al.* 2017).

The traditional source of finance for both businesses and individuals is the bank. However, other sources of finance for businesses and start-ups include venture capital, business angel finance and government financing initiatives (Klöhn and Hornuf 2012). Digital financing allows individuals, businesses, and start-ups to become independent from these traditional ways by using the internet to acquire the necessary financing (Gomber *et al.* 2017). Digital financing includes all digital types of finance which are available to businesses as financial capital. Gomber *et al.* (2017) suggest that various platforms offer digitalized services in the area of factoring, invoicing, leasing and crowdfunding.

Factoring can be described as a type of supplier financing in which firms sell their creditworthy accounts receivable or debtors at a discount (generally equal to interest plus service fees) and receive immediate cash (Klapper 2006). In factoring, a complete portfolio of debtors is sold by the original creditor to a factor. The mixed portfolio of debtors diversifies the risk that originates from each debtor of the creditor (Gomber *et al.* (2017). In reverse factoring, the lender purchases accounts receivables only from specific informationally transparent, high-quality buyers (Klapper 2006). Here, a supplier's customer is the initiator of the factoring process. Reverse factoring helps suppliers to be provided with financial resources to serve the customer with products or services. Gomber *et al.* (2017) suggest that electronic factoring via online platforms has facilitated the initiation of such factoring relationships tremendously.

Electronic invoicing is another type of digitized service which offers fast, simple and reliable services in order to transmit invoice data electronically in a structured and standardized format that allows for automated processing (Penttinen and Tuunainen 2011). It provides a better coordination of invoices, better overviews, faster transmission and account settling which help to shorten the length of credit by acting as an inducement to customers to settle their accounts.

Leasing can be defined as an implied or written agreement specifying the conditions under which a lessor accepts to let out a property to be used by a lessee. The agreement promises the lessee use of the property for an agreed length of time while the owner is assured consistent payment over the agreed period. Both parties are bound by the terms of the contract, and there is a consequence if either fails to meet the contractual obligations. Leasing helps individuals or businesses that are not endowed with sufficient liquidity to pay for assets such as machinery, equipment and vehicles. The user is immediately allowed to use the asset while it remains in the possession of the lessor-financier. Gomber *et al.* (2017) argue that various service offers concerning lease-financing can be found online nowadays. As a result, electronic leasing has become a simple method for individuals and firms to acquire the necessary assets without paying the full price at once (Gomber *et al.* 2017).

Crowdfunding is a growing segment of digital financing which as defined by Belleflamme *et al.* (2014) is an open call, mostly through the internet, for the provision of financial resources either in the form of donation or in exchange for the future product or some form of reward to support initiatives for specific purposes. On crowdfunding platforms, special project websites are created to present the campaign and to collect money from the internet community or the "crowd". Hence, not a single intermediary or a small group of experienced investors is addressed as in traditional financing, but a considerable amount of people that support an initiative by relatively small contributions (Gomber *et al.* 2017). The basic idea of financing through many little contributions is not new but the internet has lowered transaction costs as well as transaction time and simplified bringing together people who seek money and people who are willing to provide money (Zhang and Liu

2012). Crowdfunding is rather powerful because amazingly high sums of money can be reached when many contributors support an initiative (Gomber *et al.* 2017).

(ii) Digital investments

Digital investments support individuals or institutions in investment decisions and in arranging the required investment transactions on their own with the use of the respective devices and technologies. Digital investments include mobile trading, social trading, online brokerage and online trading in the B2C area and high-frequency and algorithmic trading in the B2B context (Gomber *et al.* 2017).

Mobile trading refers to the trading of securities through mobile devices, such as smart phones or tablets, through special software and applications. Platforms for mobile trading offer real-time access to financial markets and the possibility to trade independently from location and human advisors or brokers (Gomber *et al.* 2017; Tai and Ku 2013; Zhang and Teo 2014). Mobile trading is still at its infancy compared to other mobile devices (Tai and Ku 2013). Several factors such as small displays of smart phones or bad image resolution, difficult data input, and low computing power make mobile trading less convenient than trading on desktop computers (Gomber *et al.* 2017; Kim *et al.* 2007; Tai and Ku 2013).

Social trading describes securities trading using internet platforms that combine social media networking with investment strategies (Kromidha and Li 2019). Besides offering products that are tradable on traditional exchanges, social trading platforms also focus on over-the-counter products, like foreign exchange or commodities (Doering *et al.* 2015; Pan *et al.* 2012). Social trading evolved as a promising alternative to banks and investment advisers, specifically as the 2008 financial crisis challenged investors' confidence in traditional service providers (Gomber *et al.* 2017). The search for investment information and strategies shifted partly to social media platforms, such as Facebook and Twitter. Building upon the idea of investment information exchange among individuals, entrepreneurs founded the first social trading network start-ups (Doering *et al.* 2015; Gomber *et al.* 2017) that offer three main functions (eToro Ltd 2021; Ayondo markets Ltd 2021; Pan *et al.* 2012). Gomber *et al.* (2017) explain the three functions as follows:

> First, the possibility to observe trading strategies of traders that want to share information on their investments; second, the function of following one or multiple traders as known from other social media platforms, i.e. selecting and subscribing to traders in order to monitor details and changes of their investment strategies; and, third, copying the investment strategies of traders to one's own portfolio, i.e. performing buying and selling operations in real-time and precisely according to the selected traders investments (the core function of social trading platforms). Traders serve a similar function to a portfolio manager and receive a monetary compensation (Doering *et al.* 2015). Still, each investor takes responsibility for his own portfolios and for the selection of traders to follow – under exclusion of followees' liability for following traders as well as claims for financial damages against followed

traders. Ultimately, social trading constitutes a promising alternative to individual investment decisions because investors that follow experienced traders can reach impressive above-average returns (Gottschlich and Hinz 2014).

Online brokers fulfil the same tasks as human brokers but operate independently from time and location and need less staff and can accomplish more orders at lower costs than traditional "brick-and-mortar" brokers (Gomber *et al*. 2017). Retail investors use specialized trading software provided by the broker to access multiple markets including charts, economic and stock specific information, analytics and trading tools comparable to professional trading software (Kromidha and Li 2019; Lechner and Nolte 2007; OANDA 2021). In online brokering, there are no face-to-face interactions between the customer and the broker concerning additional agreements, special instructions, or custom execution conditions. This can lead to imprudent decisions and self-directed trading, and can cause overconfidence regarding their abilities and competence (Barber and Odean 2001, 2002; Kromidha and Li 2019).

(iii) Digital money

Digital money can be defined as a type of currency that fulfils (more or less) all typical functions of money but exists only electronically and is mainly used on the internet (Gomber *et al*. 2017). It includes digital currency, virtual currency, e-money and cryptocurrency. Digital money serves as a medium of exchange, unit of account and store of value but unlike traditional money it exists only digitally (Dodgson *et al*. 2015; Gomber *et al*. 2017). According to the European Central Bank, virtual currencies are non-regulated digital money that is distributed from and controlled by their creators. Usually, there is no central representative (like a central bank) but the currency is based on an organized network that is decentralized (European Central Bank 2012).

Cryptocurrencies are decentralized, freely convertible, virtual currencies that are based on encryption technology (FATF 2014). The use of cryptography ensures a secure currency system that enables an exchange of currency units without a mediating instance (Gomber *et al*. 2017; Nakamoto 2008). Its value is based on demand and supply on respective digital currencies exchanges and is not regulated through decisions of a superordinate instance, like a central bank (Velde 2013).

Bitcoin is a type of cryptocurrency which was introduced in 2008. It is not backed by assets or commodities, e.g. gold, and its emission is not controlled by any central institution (Grinberg 2012). However, the cryptographic mechanisms ensure a decentralized control of circulating currency units and a verification of transactions (Nakamoto 2008). This is achieved by a public transaction system and a shared ledger which comprises all encrypted account numbers and balances, i.e. it provides information on who owns how many bitcoins. This data is updated by a decentralized network consisting of private computers of individuals that participate in the bitcoin network (Kaplanov 2012). Similarly, the ledger is not centrally managed but stored at many nodes in the network (Gomber *et al*. 2017).

(iv) Digital payments

Digital payments are electronic payments (or e-payments) which are defined as all payments that are initiated, processed and received electronically (Hartmann 2006). Digital payments include mobile payments, peer-to-peer payments, person-to-person payments, and private-to-private (P2P) payments. Gomber *et al.* (2017) posit that the demand for e-payment has emerged due to the rise of online shops. This is because electronic payment solutions, such as online banking, are strongly inspired by the established account-based bank transfer. From then on, there have been innovative and easy-to-use solutions that better fit the needs of merchants and customers (Dahlberg *et al.* 2008). The process of e-payments covers the transfer of a certain amount of money from the payer to the payee through an electronic, location-independent payment mechanism (Gomber *et al.* 2017; Lim 2008; Weir *et al.* 2006).

Mobile payment is a sub-category of e-payments and can be defined as a transfer of funds in return for a good or service, where the mobile phone is involved in both the initiation and confirmation of the payment (Dennehy and Sammon 2015). Dennehy and Sammon (2015) further suggest that the location of the payer and supporting infrastructure are not important because they do not necessarily have to be "mobile" or "on the move" or at a Point of Sale (PoS). Similarly, Mallat (2007) defines mobile payment as the use of a mobile device to conduct a payment transaction in which money or funds are transferred from payer to receiver via an intermediary, or directly, without an intermediary. Gomber *et al.* (2017) explain that the initial focus on deploying mobile devices for using existing online banking and shopping opportunities has now shifted towards the introduction of new mobile applications that function as a substitute for established payment structures, such as cash, card payment, or cheques. It is worth mentioning that it is not only financial institutions that engage in new mobile payment structures but big internet companies, such as Google or Amazon are also engaging in it (Contini *et al.* 2011). This is a particularly interesting development for less developed countries where mobile banking is a promising and feasible alternative to non-reliable bank structures (Contini *et al.* 2011; Merritt 2010).

Peer-to-peer payments, person-to-person payments and P2P payments are another sub-category of digital payments. These terms are used to denote payments between private individuals such as family members or friends (Gomber *et al.* 2017; Hartmann 2006). An example of this type of payments is PayPal which was originally introduced to execute and verify payments on eBay. To illustrate the speed of this type of transaction, Gomber *et al.* (2017) state that

> while money transfers to a bank account take some time, P2P payments provide immediate transactions. The moment the payment has been initiated, the service provider validates the payment so that the receiver can trust in receiving the money although it has not yet been added to the bank account. Further, there is no need to distribute bank account data and banking information to unknown people anymore, which increases the perceived level of security.
>
> (p. 9)

Bradford and Keeton (2012) distinguish between three models of peer-to-peer payments. First, a *nonbank-centric model* where an individual instructs a nonbank intermediary such as PayPal to transfer funds to another consumer. A disadvantage of this model is the fact that customers need to sign up and register using their real banking information which may result in additional work and safety concerns towards a yet unknown service provider. Second, a *bank-centric model* where the individual interacts directly with a bank to request a transfer from the bank account of the individual to the bank account of the recipient. In this case, users do not need to sign up with another service provider but make use of services of their bank so that safety concerns are rather low. However, customers of banks that do not offer such services would have to change their bank. Third, a *card-centric model* where the payment is processed entirely over a credit card or debit card network. A disadvantage of this model is that both parties of a transaction need to have a card that works with the network on which the service is based.

Other types of digital payments are e-wallets and digital wallets. E-wallet is a type of electronic card which is used for transactions made online through a computer or a smartphone (Economic Times 2021). Its utility is the same as a credit or debit card. An e-wallet needs to be linked with the individual's bank account to make payments. The *Economic Times* (2021) describes e-wallet as a type of prepaid account in which a user can store his/her money for any future online transaction and is protected with a password. With the help of an e-wallet, one can make payments for groceries, online purchases and flight tickets, among others.

Digital wallets and e-wallets are designed for the same function of assisting online transactions. SMEBOOK (2020) suggests that both are similar in nature but with only two differences:

- Digital wallets store all payment information and back it up on the cloud which can be accessed and used anywhere and anytime to conduct transactions. The user's money still stays within the bank account unless and until a transaction is carried out.
- E-wallets are prepaid wallets that store the user's money to carry out transactions. Money can be loaded in e-wallets and used as and when needed.

Similarly, Gomber *et al.* (2017) argue that both e-wallet and digital wallet describe a digital storage for money that fulfils most tasks of a physical wallet: holding identification information (e.g. ID card, driver's license), facilitating cash and credit payments, and storing temporary tokens (e.g. vouchers, bus tickets). Ebringer *et al.* (2000) explain that these functions can be implemented digitally so that an e-wallet is able to replace a physical wallet. A digital wallet integrated to a mobile device, e.g. a smart phone, has the potential to replace not only traditional payment functions but also analog wallet items, like identity cards, tickets, and other content items (Contini *et al.* 2011; Shetty *et al.* 2014).

(v) Digital insurances

The concept of *digital insurance* is an umbrella term that encompasses the vast amount of new technologies that have changed the way nearly every carrier operates (Wargin 2021). Wargin (2021) defines digital insurance as any company using a technology-first business model to sell and manage insurance policies. Many insurance companies today have a digital insurance arm of their business in addition to traditional insurance practices. Digital insurance differs from the traditional insurance in the following respects:

- Omni-channel experiences which allow people to research, compare and purchase insurance online or through an app without having to speak directly to an agent in person or over the phone.
- Pricing, risk evaluation and/or claims handling rely on modern, open software platforms connected to the *insurtech* ecosystem (new insurance-specific technology).
- Coverage options are simplified to cater to individuals or families with less robust insurance needs.

Therefore, digital insurance provides the speed, agility, accessibility and ease of use that enables carriers to compete in today's evolving insurance industry. This means offering a bevy of services on the customer-facing side of operations that are entirely online, which is a sharp deviation from the traditional insurance model. Other features of digital insurance include live chat, customer self-service portals and online claims filing which are all made possible by digital insurance applications and technologies, and which are growing and expanding at an ever-increasing rate (Wargin 2021).

The benefits of digital finance

In this section, two main benefits of digital finance are discussed which include financial inclusion and new business opportunities.

(i) Digital finance enables financial inclusion

The Mckinsey Global Institute argues that digital finance allows for financial inclusion because for financial-services providers, the cost of offering customers digital accounts can be 80 to 90% lower than using physical branches (MGI 2016). This promotes efficiency as it enables providers to serve many more customers profitably, with a broader set of products and lower prices. The Mckinsey Global Institute also suggests that over time, many individuals may begin to use their digital accounts to save money for the future. The institute argues that as individuals and businesses make digital payments, they create a data trail of their receipts and expenditures, that enables financial service providers to assess their credit risk. The information allows providers to underwrite loans and insurance policies for a larger set of borrowers with greater confidence. Financial services providers can also collect digital repayments on an automated basis and send text messages to prompt borrowers when they have missed a payment. This promotes cost-effectiveness in savings, credit and insurance products and provides even for people at low incomes and for very small businesses.

(ii) Digital finance unlocks new business models

Apart from enhancing financial inclusion, digital finance has other advantages. The benefit of digital finance extends beyond expanding access, driving down costs, and increasing the convenience of transactions (MGI 2016). The Mckinsey Global Institute describes digital finance as an infrastructure and likens it to electricity or roads: "Like electricity or roads, a digital-payment network is part of the basic infrastructure of an economy that enables individuals and businesses to transact with one another seamlessly (MGI 2016, p. 14).

The Institute postulates that it can also underpin a broader and more innovative array of business activities. For example, the increased transparency and information about users generated by digital payments can give rise to new types of financial services. These can include new credit-scoring models that assess user data and help lenders assess the credit risk of a broader set of customers (MGI 2016).

Another example of the type of business activity that can emerge from digital finance is peer-to-peer (P2P) lending platforms. An example of this is the Kubo. financiero in Mexico which matches middle class and wealthier savers with small businesses and households looking for credit (MGI 2016). The Mckinsey Global Institute explains how it works: "Borrowers submit requests that are automatically risk-assessed along with their profiles, and lenders can select the borrowers they want to fund. Text messages prompt borrowers when they miss a payment, and delinquency rates have been lower than at MFIs . . . providing lenders with double-digit returns" (MGI 2016, p. 14). Other examples include new apps and digital tools that can help businesses analyze their digital sales to improve operations and gain access to cash-advance facilities (MGI 2016).

Digital finance also creates small business opportunities through digital payments which allow people to transact in small amounts. This creates new business opportunities based on so-called micro-payments (MGI 2016). The examples of this include pay-as-you-go solar power for households, irrigation systems purchased on layaway plans, and school tuition fees broken into small, frequent payments (MGI 2016). The Mckinsey Global Institute illustrates this in a Kenyan context: "In Kenya, M-Kopa Solar utilizes a pay-as-you-go model with payment made over the M-Pesa mobile-money platform; through this, 375,000 homes across East Africa now have solar electricity, and they will save an estimated $280 million over the next four years on their utility bills" (MGI 2016, p. 14).

The Institute also argues that over a long term, digital payments can enable development of e-commerce and on-demand services. The Institute remarks that most e-commerce in emerging economies relies on cash payment on delivery. But digital payments allow more rapid growth, given their greater convenience and in turn e-commerce can release consumer spending, especially in areas where retail options are limited (MGI 2016). The Institute also draws attention to on-demand services which can enable individuals to tap directly into the labour market to find out where their services are most valued. These services include taxi drivers, daily labourers and specialized workers in technology.

FinTech

Technological advances and digital transformation imply a paradigm shift in the financial sector. The basis of this revolution is innovation in business models based on emerging technologies at the customer's service (Abad-Segura *et al.* 2020).

The term *FinTech* is a new term and originates from two words *financial* and *technology*. FinTech or financial technology is a relatively new subject in the literature but commonly cited as one of the most important innovations in the financial industry (Iman 2020). It describes in general the connection of modern and, mainly, internet-related technologies (e.g. cloud computing, mobile internet) with established business activities of the financial services industry (e.g. money lending, transaction banking) (Gomber *et al.* 2017). Gomber *et al.* (2017) indicate that FinTech refers to innovators and disruptors in the financial sector that make use of the availability of ubiquitous communication, specifically via the internet and automated information processing. Lee (2015a) explains that such companies have new business models that promise more flexibility, security, efficiency and opportunities than established financial services. The innovator can be either a start-up, an established technology company, or an established service provider (Gomber *et al.* 2017). Lee (2015b) distinguishes between innovators and disruptors. Lee (2015b) defines innovators as "sustaining FinTech", such as established financial services providers that try to protect their market position by the use of information technologies, while a "disruptive FinTech" is defined as new companies and start-ups that challenge established providers by offering new products and services.

The term *FinTech* is used and defined differently by various people (Zavolokina *et al.* 2016). Both Gomber *et al.* (2017) and Zavolokina *et al.* (2016) explain that information technology was hitherto regarded as a tool in the financial industries context. However, in recent years FinTech start-ups or established IT companies entering the financial domain gain ground in the financial sector and seize customers that traditionally have been served by established providers. These researchers suggest three main reasons for the occurrence:

First, FinTech companies offer new products and solutions which fulfil customers' needs that have previously not or not sufficiently been addressed by incumbent financial service providers. One example is the introduction of a card-reader unit for smart phones and tablets that makes it possible for street merchants and traveling salesmen to accept cash cards and credit cards.

Second, FinTech companies have created novel opportunities for selling products and services through the application of novel technologies and concepts. MarketInvoice, for example, offers small-and medium-sized companies the possibility of selling their invoices in order to attain higher working capital by not depending anymore on the final payment of invoices (Lee 2015b).

Third, companies with an IT background are relatively better suited to provide services in a highly innovative environment. This is because changes and developments in the domain of communication and information technologies can be very quick and dynamic, and therefore companies in this field need to be agile and innovative. Consequently, such IT companies often have a culture that is distinctively different from established financial service providers. They are agile and innovative enough to set these established players under pressure. FinTech companies concentrate on affordable and cost-efficient internet-based business models in order to attack established financial services providers. Some experts in the field even believe that one day banks may only be used for deposits while everything else will be done by use of FinTech company services (Hemmadi 2015).

For the rapid development of FinTech, both Gomber *et al.* (2017) and King (2014) argue that founders of FinTech companies are often former bank employees who have been relieved of their jobs in the aftermath of the 2008 crisis. They possess the relevant expertise as well as the knowledge and have managed to connect financial services with new technologies to launch innovative companies and/or create new business models. Such experts are often specialized in specific tasks within, for example, a bank. Thus, they create point solutions for services which are only small parts of the whole range of services of big financial service providers (Gomber *et al.* 2017; King 2014). As a result, they can concentrate on optimizing these offered services. However, Dapp (2014) emphasizes that FinTechs usually do not evolve from the traditional financial sector but have a technology background. The trend towards FinTechs seems to be kept up as the development and improvement of mobile devices, big data analysis as well as cloud processing and data storage continues and new possibilities of simplification, adaptability and individualization evolve (Dapp 2014; Gomber *et al.* 2017). Gomber *et al.* (2017) conclude that FinTech companies, whether start-ups or established IT companies entering the financial domain, evolve at the intersection of information and communication technology and finance. They focus on business model innovations and new solutions for existing challenges in the financial industry.

Digital technologies enable financial inclusion

Mobile and digital technologies, which are rapidly expanding round the world enable financial inclusion (MGI 2016). The Mckinsey Global Institute suggests that in emerging economies, the next frontier is finance: "For most people in these countries, the story begins in the palm of their hand, with a mobile phone. This can provide easy access to a digital wallet that could be used for all payment transactions, such as receiving remittances, wages, and government subsidies, making purchases at stores, or paying utility bills and school fees" (MGI 2016, p. 6).

   The Mckinsey Global Institute argues that using a mobile phone rather than cash saves considerable travel time and cost, reduces the risk of theft, and boosts convenience. It also gives access to a broader range of financial services that can be delivered digitally, such as savings accounts or loans. Mobile phones are becoming ubiquitous as networks increase coverage and quality. The Institute provides the flowing statistics: "Mobile networks now reach more than 90 percent of people in emerging economies. Phone ownership still lags behind network coverage, but it too is growing rapidly. In 2014, nearly 80 percent of adults in emerging economies had mobile subscriptions, compared with 55 percent who had a financial account. Mobile phone ownership is projected to reach over 90 percent of adults by 2020" (MGI 2016, p. 6).

FinTech trends

The demand for Fintech and digital banking products is likely to gain ground in years to come (Shumsky 2021). Shumsky (2021) also argues that it is expected that virtual payment and banking solutions will take the lead in the financial services industry in 2021 due to the following reasons:

(i) 5G taking digital banking to a new level

The roll-out of 5G in 2021 has triggered a step-change in what digital banking solutions are capable of during the years ahead. The 5G network has fostered accelerated innovation and digital transformation in mobile digital banking products and services because the network allows a higher density of mobile broadband and lower battery consumption and can process high volumes of data with minimal delay. As a result of the speed of 5G networks, complex processes are performed much more quickly, which reduces turnaround times.

The network has also improved the functionality of mobile banking and payment apps, with less downtime or technological glitches and faster and simpler payment options that increase their appeal to a broader audience. Another advantage of 5G is that it enables proactive fraud prevention by processing data, verifying the nature of transactions, confirming transaction amounts and funds availability, consulting multiple data instances in real-time, coupled with customer geolocation and merchant ID. These help to reduce fraud detection errors and false positives, thereby protecting consumers and the bank's bottom line.

(ii) The growth in cryptocurrency wallets

The growing number of digital banking apps that support cryptocurrencies positions cryptocurrency wallets at the centre of the transformation of the payment industry. Cryptocurrency wallets do not only offer the robust security of blockchain-based technology but they also lower costs as a result of removing the middle-man in payment processes.

Furthermore, Shumsky (2021) suggests that blockchain enables a layer of security known as tokenization. Tokenization is a process by which the user's personal data is stored in a digital account, with the provider sending payment information to vendors as a token that holds only enough information to associate the transaction with the cryptocurrencies stored in the wallet. Shumsky (2021) further suggests that the number of people using cryptocurrency wallets has grown steeply over the last few years and is expected to continue doing so.

(iii) Smart voice payments

Smart speakers and home assistants have become part of daily life for many individuals around the world. They help people find restaurants, write up shopping lists and find out what the weather is likely to be that day. From Amazon's Alexa through to Google's Smart Assistant and Siri, the number of internet users who made at least one purchase via smart speaker amounted to 18.3 million in 2019 (Shumsky 2021). Shumsky (2021) also suggests that some 23.5 million US consumers are expected to buy smart speakers in 2021 and that Internet of Things payments, which includes voice payments, will experience exponential growth from $24.5 billion in 2018 to $410 billion in 2023. However, security concerns have slowed down this verbal form of digital banking but as artificial intelligence bolsters security measures and improves the ability to identify and thwart cyber-security breaches and fraudulent transactions, using smart speakers as a banking solution is likely to become commonplace (Shumsky 2021).

(iv) The impact of Covid-19

While the long-term effects of the Covid-19 pandemic are yet to be determined, its immediate impact on crowdfunding is nonetheless significant (Wang *et al.* 2022). Using a unique dataset of all GoFundMe campaigns published over the past two years, the analysis suggests changes in significant features influencing crowdfunding success before and after the Covid-19 outbreak. Wang *et al.* (2022) suggest a significant racial disparity in crowdfunding success. In addition, sad emotions expressed in a campaign's description became significant after the Covid-19 outbreak.

In relation to digital finance, the impact of Covid-19 propels the preference for contactless payments. Shumsky (2021) argues that the predominant form of payment is fast becoming contactless, near field communication (NFC)-based wallet payments, such as Google Pay, Samsung Pay and Apple Pay. Covid-19 has accentuated the benefits of this mode of payment, highlighting the convenience, speed and personal safety of making proximity mobile payments.

(v) Social and seamless online payments

Social and seamless shopping is likely to become ubiquitous in 2021 and digital banking is also likely to be the engine behind a "shop-until-you-drop" online experience (Shumsky 2021). Shumsky (2021) stresses that Facebook and Instagram viewers who are scrolling through their accounts now find themselves easily diverted into shopping online without even knowing whether it was Facebook or Instagram that took them onto the retailer's online store.

(vi) Artificial intelligence (AI) and machine learning (ML)

AI/ML-driven systems are enabling companies to put big data to effective use in monitoring customer behaviour and detecting anomalies and opportunities they can factor into their services and product offerings. Whereas banks have traditionally relied on the scale of assets, the financial services players of the future, namely

FinTech companies, depend on the scale of data. Instead of treating customers as the masses, FinTech companies differentiate themselves by providing a highly personalized, customized service to their clients. This is made possible by combining the best of technology and human skills in what Shumsky (2021) refer to as "augmented performance versus dependence on human ingenuity" (p. 2).

The areas where AI/ML is becoming particularly prevalent is in the detection of fraud, banking chatbots, algorithmic trading, regulations and policy. AI/ML is helping banks in their anti-money laundering and terrorism financing efforts. The use of the technology is turning the tide on the ineffective investments they have been making into compliance departments to meet increasingly demanding regulatory requirements. The incorporation of AI/ML is expected to improve the return on investment in compliance departments and slow the annual growth in compliance expenses. However, the downside is the organizations do not properly manage the incorporation of AI/ML into their processes. These include bias in input data, process and outcome when profiling customers and scoring credit, as well as due diligence risk in the supply chain.

(vii) Blockchain technology

Blockchain is a robust technology for the new emerging financial ecosystem because it offers transparency and security, removing the reliance on doing business with trusted financial services companies, as in the past. Instead, transactions are facilitated by smart contracts and tokens, which effectively become the digital middlemen and allow individuals to transfer anything of value transparently (PWC 2016). Blockchain technology is explored in greater detail in Chapter 11.

(viii) Predictive analytics

Predictive analytics is expected to play a central role in strengthening cybersecurity measures and preventing fraud as cyber-security is cited as one of the biggest challenges likely to confront businesses in the years ahead. However, Protiviti (2021) suggests that for small- and medium-sized players and new entrants, such as FinTech companies, predictive analytics provide a significant competitive advantage. Predictive analytics uses big data, algorithms and machine learning to assess the likelihood of things happening in the future based on past behaviour. It is a relatively new branch of data science and favours a wide range of applications, particularly in the FinTech industry where technology facilitates cost-effective, efficient and scalable outcomes.

In addition to combating fraud, predictive analytics prove valuable in improving customer experiences, identifying employees who are most likely to add value to organizations, and improving operational processes with the foresight offered by the analytics' forward-looking nature. From the customer perspective, predictive analytics enables companies to monitor and measure customer behaviour both in their interactions with the company and across digital and social platforms. They can measure, for instance, average spend, purchasing patterns, loyalty, and customer feedback, and use this data to model customer behaviour and use the insights generated to enhance customer experiences, marketing strategies and brand awareness.

Example of FinTech trend: decentralized finance

Decentralized Finance (DeFi) is experiencing exponential growth in recent years, highlighting how well-positioned this emerging technology is becoming to revolutionize the finance industry forever.

DeFi is finding favour because it operates outside the centralized regulatory financial structures, cuts out intermediaries and effectively democratizes finance for the vast proportion of people who are currently not well serviced by the existing financial incumbents. As its name suggests, DeFi's common goal is to decentralize financial services. It does so by removing bank, payment and investment intermediaries and replacing these with services that operate within the blockchain network.

Blockchain is a robust alternative base for this disruptive emerging financial ecosystem because it offers transparency and security, removing the reliance on doing business with trusted financial services companies, as in the past. Instead, transactions are facilitated by smart contracts and tokens, which effectively become the digital middlemen and allow individuals to transfer anything of value transparently.

Research has shown that the demand for the DeFi market has grown by almost 1000% in 2021, from about $680 million at the beginning of 2020 to some $6.7 billion by August 2021. Growth is picking up exponentially on a month-by-month basis, with the total value locked into the system almost doubling from $3.5 billion to $6.68 billion in one month alone.

It is predicted that the sectors most likely to be affected by the DeFi revolution are lending, decentralized exchanges, asset management, financial data and insurance.

Meanwhile, Deltec Bank also sees DeFi predominating in the savings industry, trading platforms and asset management industry. It points out that whereas in the past, interest was not earned on cryptocurrencies, with the advent of DeFi, interest on deposits is now available, and individuals can compare interest rates on loanscan.io. Deltec Bank says finance is one of the biggest players, with a total of $1.5 billion earning interest of up to 3.8% across nine crypto markets.

The one challenge that stands in the way of DeFi becoming as ubiquitous as AI/ML is its complexity. Getting to the 25% of unbanked potential customers globally will require educational initiatives that help them understand DeFi and why it can offer them so much more than traditional financial services.

Source: Shumsky (2021)

Summary

This chapter has discussed financial inclusion and its objective which is the promotion of easy and safe access to financial services for consumers, including the vulnerable and low-income groups and how these groups of people can be integrated into formal financial systems. It has also discussed the link between financial inclusion and the SDGs and how the achievement of financial inclusion enables access to formal financial services and how it can facilitate poverty reduction and income inequalities. The chapter has also shown that digital finance service promotes financial inclusion such that through bank-led and non-bank-led models via internet channels remote groups can access financial services and foster their economic development (Ebimoghan 2021).

The chapter demonstrates that the financial industry has a lot of challenges including emerging competitors, shifting demographics, rising customer expectations and changing regulations. As suggested by PWC (2016), technology offers solutions by allowing financial institutions to cut costs and become more efficient.

The trend in the market of digital finance has had a tremendous influence on current industry dynamics. With the rapid development in technology and changing economic environment, the financial services industry is facing a substantial transformation. Consequently, the clientele is becoming more technology-savvy and the industry players are designing customized, intelligent and flexible financial products and services in order to attend to new levels of customer experience.

As digital finance is a recent phenomenon, there is an enormous research gap in this area for research especially, to explore the specific roles of FinTech companies and traditional service providers in digital finance. It seems like in going forward FinTech will require collaboration with traditional financial institutions such as banks to address the problem of FinTech as a disruptive technology. Also, banks need FinTech as a strategic partner because FinTech is considered to be faster in following digital transformation (Suryono *et al.* 2020).

Discussion questions

1 Discuss the concept of financial inclusion.
2 What are the benefits of digital finance and how does it enable financial inclusion?
3 Discuss the different types of digital finance.
4 How do digital technologies impact financial inclusion?

Test questions

1 How are traditional financial institutions facing new digital competitors?
2 What tips for digitization would you give to your organization?
3 Students should be allocated to small working groups to discuss the future of digital finance.

Glossary of key terminologies

AI Artificial intelligence.

ATMs Automated teller machines.

Bitcoin A decentralized digital currency, without a central bank or single administrator, that can be sent from user to user on the peer-to-peer bitcoin network without the need for intermediaries.

Blockchain technology A robust technology for the new emerging financial ecosystem which offers transparency and security.

Cryptocurrency A digital currency that can be used to buy goods and services, but uses an online ledger with strong cryptography to secure online transactions.

DFI Digital Finance Institute.

Digital finance A term used to describe the impact of new technologies on the financial services industry.

Digitalization The use of digital technologies to change a business model and provide new revenue and value-producing opportunities.

Factoring A financial transaction in which a business sells its accounts receivable (or invoices) to a third party (a factor) at a discount.

Financial inclusion Financial inclusion is the availability and equality of opportunities to access appropriate, affordable and timely financial products and services by individuals and businesses.

FinTech A new financial technology which connects modern and, mainly, internet-related technologies with established business activities of the financial services industry.

ICT Information and communications technology.

Leasing A written agreement specifying the conditions under which a lessor accepts to let out a property to be used by a lessee for instalment payments and at the end of which the property reverts to the lessor.

Mobile trading Mobile trading is the use of wireless technology such as telephones to access trading platforms rather than being confined to traditional trading methods via computer.

Social trading A form of investing that allows investors to observe the trading behaviour of their peers and expert traders.

Recommended reading

Arslanian, H., and Fischer, F., 2019. *The future of finance: The impact of FinTech, ai, and crypto on financial services hardcover*. London: Palgrave Macmillan.

Beaumont, P.H., 2020. *Digital finance: Big data, start-ups, and the future of financial services*. Oxon: Routledge.

Hermes, N., and Lensink, R., 2013. *Financial development and economic growth: Theory and experiences from developing countries*. London: Routledge.

Mbiti, I., and Weil, D.N., eds., 2016. *Mobile banking: The impact of M-Pesa in Kenya*. Chicago: University of Chicago Press.

Nicoletti, B., 2017. *Financial services and FinTech. In the future of FinTech*. London: Palgrave Macmillan.

Panzarino, H., and Hatami, A., 2020. *Reinventing banking and finance: frameworks to navigate global FinTech innovation.* London: Kogan Page.
Pedersen, N., 2020. *Financial technology: Case studies in FinTech innovation.* London: Kogan Page.

References

Abad-Segura, E., Gonzalez-Zamar, M., Lopez-Meneses, E., and Vazquez-Cano, E., 2020. Financial technology: Review of trends, approaches and management. *Mathematics,* 8, 951.
Alpana, V., 2007. Promoting financial inclusion: An analysis of the role of banks. *Indian Journal of Social Development,* 7 (1), 107–126.
Ayondo markets Ltd, 2021. *Social trading: Innovative network trading.* Available from: https://socialtradingguru.com/networks/ayondo [Accessed 28 May 2021].
Barber, B.M., and Odean, T., 2001. The Internet and the Investor, *Journal of Economic Perspectives* 15 (1), 41–54.
Barber, B.M., and Odean, T., 2002. Online investors: Do the slow die first? *The Review of Financial Studies,* 15 (2), 455–487.
Belleflamme, P., Lambert, T., and Schwienbacher, A., 2014. Crowdfunding: Tapping the right crowd. *Journal of Business Venturing,* 29 (5), 585–609.
Bradford, T., and Keeton, W.R., 2012. New person-to-person payment method: Have checks met their match. *Economic Review,* 97 (3), 41–77.
Cnaan, R.A., Moodithaya, M.S., and Handy, F., 2012. Financial inclusion: Lessons from rural South India. *Journal of Social Policy,* 41 (1), 183–205.
Contini, D., Crowe, M., Merritt, C., Oliver, R., and Mott, S., 2011. Mobile payments in the united states: Mapping out the road ahead. *Federal Reserve Bank of Atlanta and Boston, White Paper,* March 2011. Boston, USA: Federal Reserve Bank of Boston.
Dahlberg, T., Mallat, N., Ondrus, J., and Zmijewska, A., 2008. Past, present and future of mobile payments research: A literature review. *Electronic Commerce Research and Applications,* 7 (2), 165–181.
Dapp, T., 2014. *FinTech – Die digitale (R)evolution im Finanzsektor: Algorithmenbasiertes Banking mit human touch.* Frankfurt: Deutsche Bank Research.
Demirguc-Kunt, A., Klapper, L., Singer, D., and Oudheusden, P.V., 2015. *The global findex database 2014:* Measuring financial inclusion around the world. *World Bank Policy Research Working Paper* (7255). Washington, DC: World Bank.
Dennehy, D., and Sammon, D., 2015. Trends in mobile payments research: A literature review. *Journal of Innovation Management,* 3(1), 49–61.
DFI, 2015. *Innovation: Innovation matters, Digital finance institute.* Available from: http:// digifin.org/digital-finance-innovation/ [Accessed 25 May 2021].
Dodgson, M., Gann, D., Wladawsky-Berger, I., Sultan, N., and George, G., 2015. Managing digital money, *Academy of Management Journal,* 58 (2), 325–333.
Doering, P., Neumann, S., and Paul, S., 2015. A primer on social trading networks – Institutional aspects and empirical evidence. Presented at *EFMA Annual Meetings 2015,* 5 May 2015. Bochum, Germany: University of Bochum, Department of Finance and Banking, Universitätsstrasse 150, 44801.
Ebimoghan, E.A., 2020. *Financial inclusion through innovations-improving consumer protection in digital financial services.* Belgrade, Serbia: Union University Law School Review. Available from: http://www. pravnizapisi. rs/en/about/about-the-review [Accessed 12 January 2023].

Ebringer, T., Thorne, P., and Zheng, Y., 2000. Parasitic authentication to protect your e-wallet. *Computer*, 33 (10), 54–60.

Economic Times, 2021. *Definition of E-wallets*. Available from: https://economictimes. indiatimes.com/definition/e-wallets [Accessed 29 May 2021].

eToro Ltd, 2021. *eToro brings the promise of social trading to the world*. Available from: www.etoro.com/trading/social/ [Accessed 28 May 2021].

European Central Bank, 2012. *Virtual currency schemes*. Frankfurt-on-Main: European Central Bank.

European Commission, 2020. *Digital finance, European commission*. Available from: https://ec.europa.eu/info/business-economy-euro/banking-and-finance/digital-finance_en [Accessed 23 May 2021].

FATF, 2014. Virtual currencies: Key definitions and potential AML/CFT Risks. *Financial Action Task Force*. Available from: https://www.fatf-gafi.org/content/dam/fatf-gafi/ reports/Virtual-currency-key-definitions-and-potential-aml-cft-risks.pdf [Accessed 23 May 2021].

Fuller, D., and Mellor, M., 2008. Banking for the poor: Addressing the needs of financially excluded communities in Newcastle upon Tyne. *Urban Studies*, 4 (7), 1505–1524.

Gomber, P., Koch, J.A., and Siering, M., 2017. Digital finance and *FinTech*: Current research and future research directions. *Journal of Business Economics*, 87, 537–580.

Gottschlich, J., and Hinz, O., 2014. A decision support system for stock investment recommendations using collective wisdom. *Decision Support Systems*, 59, 52–62.

Grinberg, R., 2012. Bitcoin: An innovative alternative digital currency. *Hastings Science & Technology Law Journal*, 4 (1), 160–208.

Hartmann, M.E., 2006. E-payments evolution. *In*: T. Lammer, ed. *Handbuch E-Money, E-payment & M-payment*. Heidelberg: Physica-Verlag.

Hemmadi, M., 2015. FinTech is both friend and FOE. *Canadian Business*, 88 (6), 10–11.

Iman, N., 2020. The rise and rise of financial technology: The good, the bad, and the verdict. *Cogent Business & Management*, 7 (1), 1725309.

Jong-Hee, K., 2016. A study on the effect of financial inclusion on the relationship between income inequality and economic growth. *Emerging Markets Finance and Trade*, 2 (52), 498.

Kaplanov, N., 2012. Nerdy money: Bitcoin, the private digital currency, and the case against its regulation. *Loyola Consumer Law Review*, 25 (1), 111–174.

Kim, H., Chan, H.C., and Gupta, S., 2007. Value-based adoption of mobile internet: An empirical investigation. *Decision Support Systems*, 43 (1), 111–126.

King, A., 2014. *FinTech: Throwing down the gauntlet to financial services*. Available from: www.unquote.com/unquote/analysis/74596/fintech-throwing-down-the-gauntlet-to-financial-services [Accessed 26 May 2021].

Klapper, L., 2006. The role of factoring for financing small and medium enterprises. *Journal of Banking & Finance*, 30 (11), 3111–3130.

Klapper, L., 2016. *Financial inclusion has a big role to play in reaching the SDGs*. Available from: https://www.cgap.org/blog/financial-inclusion-has-big-role-play-reaching-sdgs [Accessed 24 May 2021].

Klöhn, L., and Hornuf, L., (2012). Crowdinvesting in Deutschland: Markt, Rechtslage und Regulierungsperspektiven. *Zeitschrift für Bankrecht und Bankwirtschaft*, 24 (4), 237–266.

Kromidha, E., and Li, M.C., 2019. Determinants of leadership in online social trading: A signaling theory perspective. *Journal of Business Research*. Available from: https://doi. org/10.1016/j.jbusres.2019.01.00.

Lechner, S., and Nolte, I., 2007. *Customer trading in the foreign exchange market empirical evidence from an internet trading platform* [CoFE Discussion Papers 07/03]. Konstanz: University of Konstanz, Center of Finance and Econometrics (CoFE).

Lee, P., 2015a. The *FinTech* entrepreneurs aiming to reinvent finance. *Euromoney (UK)*, 46 (552), 42–48.

Lee, S., 2015b. *FinTech* and Korea's financial investment industry. *KCMI – Capital Market Opinion*. Available from: https://www.semanticscholar.org/paper/Fintech-and-Korea%E2%80%99s-financial-investment-industry-Lee/c748223e433bcf1f0c1aaae-ba3e324983748bb53 [Accessed 23 May 2021].

Lim, A.S., 2008. Inter-consortia battles in mobile payments standardisation. *Electronic Commerce Research and Applications*, 7 (2), 202–213.

Mallat, N., 2007. Exploring consumer adoption of mobile payments – A qualitative study. *The Journal of Strategic Information Systems*, 16 (4), 413–432.

Merritt, C., 2010. *Mobile money transfer services: The next phase in the evolution in person-to-person payments, retail payments risk forum white paper*. Atlanta: Federal Reserve Bank of Atlanta.

MGI, 2016. *Digital finance for all: Powering inclusive growth in emerging economies, executive summary, mckinsey global institute*. Available from: www.mckinsey.com/mgi [Accessed 25 May 2021].

Mitton, L., 2008. *Financial Inclusion in the UK: Review of policy and practice*. Available from: www.jrf.org.uk/report/financial-inclusion-uk-review-policy-and-practice [Accessed 24 May 2021].

Nageswara, R.D., 2018. The global digital financial services: A critical review to achieve for digital economy in emerging markets. *International Research Journal of Human Resources and Social Sciences*, 5 (1), 159–160.

Nakamoto, S., 2008. Bitcoin: A Peer-to-peer electronic cash system. ResearchGate. Available from: https://www.researchgate.net/publication/228640975_Bitcoin_A_Peer-to-Peer_Electronic_Cash_System.

OANDA, 2021. *OANDA retail trading platforms*. Available from: www.oanda.com/forex-trading/platform/ [Accessed 28 March 2021].

Pan, W., Altshuler, Y., and Pentland, A., 2012. Decoding social influence and the wisdom of the crowd in financial trading network. *In: 2012 International Conference on Privacy, Security, Risk and Trust and 2012 International Conference on Social Computing*. Massachusetts Institute of Technology, USA: IEEE, 203–209.

Penttinen, E., and Tuunainen, V.K., 2011. Assessing the effect of external pressure in inter-organizational IS adoption – Case electronic invoicing. *In*: W. van der Aalst, J. Mylopoulos, N.M. Sadeh, M.J. Shaw, C. Szyperski, R. Sharman, H.R. Rao and T.S. Raghu, eds. *Exploring the Grand Challenges for Next Generation E-Business* (Vol. 52). Berlin and Heidelberg: Springer Berlin Heidelberg, 269–278.

Protiviti, 2021. *Innovation in predictive analytics*. Available from: www.protiviti.com/US-en/insights/innovation-predictive-analytics [Accessed 29 May 2021].

PWC, 2016. *Financial services technology 2020 and beyond: Embracing disruption*. Available from: www.pwc.com/gx/en/financial-services/assets/pdf/technology2020-and-beyond.pdf [Accessed 29 May 2021].

Rizzo, M., 2014. *Digital finance: Empowering the poor via new technologies*. Available from: www.worldbank.org/en/news/feature/2014/04/10/digital-finance-empowering-poor-new-technologies [Accessed 24 May 2021].

Shetty, S., Shetty, T., and Amale, R., 2014. QR-Code based digital wallet. *International Journal of Advanced Research in Computer Science*, 5 (7), 105–110.

Shumsky, P., 2021. *Digital Banking and FinTech Trends in 2021*. Available from: www. finextra.com/blogposting/19917/digital-banking-and-fintech-trends-in-2021 [Accessed 27 May 2021].

SMEBOOK, 2020. *Digital wallet vs. E-wallet*. Available from: https://smebook.eu/knowledge-base/digital-wallet/digital-wallet-vs-e-wallet/ [Accessed 29 May 2021].

Solo, T.M., 2008. Financial exclusion in Latin America – Or the social costs of not banking the urban poor. *Environment and Urbanization*, 20 (1), 47–66.

Stijns, J.P., 2017. *Digital financial inclusion in sub-saharan Africa (European Investment Bank) round table proceedings*. Available from: www.eib.org/attachments/general/events/africa_day_2017_roundtable_proceedings.pdf?cid=sn_twitter_Report-book_2017-10-18-01_en_na_Region-Africa_InternationalDevelopment-outsideEU [Accessed 24 May 2021].

Suryono, R.R., Budi, I., and Purwandari, B., 2020. Challenges and trends of financial technology (*FinTech*). *A Systematic Literature Review, Information*, 11, 590. Available from: https://doi.org/10.3390/info11120590.

Tai, Y., and Ku, Y., 2013. Will Stock investors use mobile stock trading? A benefit-risk assessment based on a modified utaut model. *Journal of Electronic Commerce Research* 14 (1), 67–84.

UNCDF, 2020. *Financial Inclusion and the SDGs*. Available from: www.uncdf.org/financial-inclusion-and-the-sdgs [Accessed 24 May 2021].

Velde, F.R., 2013. *Bitcoin: A primer, Chicago Fed Letter*. Chicago: Federal Reserve Bank of Chicago.

Wang, J., Luo, J., and Zhang, X., 2022. How COVID-19 has changed crowdfunding: Evidence from GoFundMe. *Frontiers in Computer Science*, 4, 1–10. Available from: https://doi.org/10.3389/fcomp.2022.893338

Wargin, J., 2021. *Digital insurance & you: Understanding the new industry standard*. Available from: www.duckcreek.com/blog/digital-insurance/ [Accessed 29 May 2021].

Weir, C.S., Anderson, J.N., and Jack, M.A., 2006. On the role of metaphor and language in design of third-party payments in eBanking: Usability and quality. *International Journal of Human-Computer Studies*, 64 (8), 770–784.

World Bank, 2014. *Global financial development report 2014: Financial inclusion*. Washington, DC: World Bank. Available from: https://openknowledge.worldbank.org/handle/10986/16238 License: CC BY 3.0 IGO [Accessed 24 May 2021].

World Bank, 2018. *Financial Inclusion: Financial inclusion is a key enabler to reducing poverty and boosting prosperity*. Available from: www.worldbank.org/en/topic/financial-inclusion/overview [Accessed 24 May 2021].

World Bank Group, 2008. Finance for all? Policies and pitfalls in expanding access. *Policy Research Report*. The World Bank. Available from: https://pure.uvt.nl/ws/portalfiles/portal/1107575/Financeforall.pdf

Zavolokina, L., Dolata, M., and Schwabe, G., 2016. The FinTech phenomenon: Antecedents of financial innovation perceived by the popular press. *Financial Innovation*, 2 (1), 1–16.

Zhang, J., and Liu, P., 2012. Rational herding in microloan markets. *Management Science*, 58 (5), 892–912.

Zhang, Z., and Teo, H.H., 2014. The impact of mobile trading technology on individual investors' trading behaviors: The "two-edged sword" effect. *In: Proceedings of the Twenty Second European Conference on Information Systems* (ECIS 2014), Tel Aviv: ECIS.

7   The features of a good crowdfunding campaign

Learning objectives

- Discuss the features of a crowdfunding campaign
- Discuss the strategies to be deployed in crowdfunding
- Explore the composition of the pitch
- Examine the role of effective communication

Introduction

The subject of how precise project qualities need to be described in order for a project to be funded successfully has already been considered by previous studies. For example, it has been discovered that the extent to which a project is described (Xiao *et al*. 2014) and the quantity of money that is asked (Mollick 2014) both have an impact on whether or not funding is obtained.

Other studies have centred on the subject of whether or not the information about the project founder has an effect on the amount of financing that is received for subsequent ventures (Zvilichovsky *et al*. 2015). According to the findings of studies, the success of a funding campaign is influenced not only by project-related factors but also by founder-related factors. For instance, the success of obtaining funding is positively influenced by the addition of further information to the web of project description in the form of texts, photographs, or videos. It is interesting to note that projects whose founders have participated in the funding of other projects in the past have a higher chance of receiving successful funding compared to projects whose founders have not participated in the funding of other projects (Koch and Siering 2015).

Founders that engage in crowdfunding are motivated by numerous factors, the most obvious being fundraising or capitalization. Marketing, exposure, proof of concept and feedback are further factors. As a result, crowdfunding success must be defined in terms of the exercise's objective, as acquiring the complete amount required for a project cannot be the sole indicator of success.

Most studies have highlighted crowdfunding as a viable technique for businesses to seek investment (e.g. Burtch *et al*. 2013; Mollick 2014). These studies follow the same standard of evaluating a project's performance based on whether or not it achieves its monetary financing objective.

DOI: 10.4324/9781003193975-7

The approach of defining crowdfunding success as successful fundraising is consistent with the industrial definition offered by crowdfunding platforms. In addition to this operational definition, academics have devised various metrics of success, such as attaining absolute fundraising amount (Ahlers *et al.* 2015), capital per funder (Mollick 2014), and time taken to accomplish financing target (Ahlers *et al.* 2015; Burtch *et al.* 2013). Therefore, fundraising success is the first dimension of crowdfunding success.

When determining whether or not a crowdfunding campaign was successful, it has been suggested that idea generation be taken into account. This recommendation is conditional on the founders' intended outcomes (Schwienbacher and Larralde 2010). Crowdfunding is frequently used as a pre-sale marketing strategy (Belleflamme *et al.* 2014). This allows businesses to directly engage customers in order to learn more about their ideas and preferences (Younkin 2016). Crowdfunding is one method by which entrepreneurs hope to obtain feedback from customers (Gerber *et al.* 2012; Mollick and Kuppuswamy 2014). For the continued development of the product, both positive and negative feedback is valued equally. As a consequence of this, collecting feedback in an efficient manner is another indicator of successful crowdfunding.

In practice, companies use crowdfunding as an innovative form of marketing while they are preparing to launch new products into markets that have not been fully explored (Ordanini *et al.* 2011; Mollick and Kuppuswamy 2014). As a consequence of this, garnering the interest of members of the general public may be regarded as yet another essential objective of founders. Entrepreneurs can improve their market share by using crowdfunding to access a previously untapped market and to test product prices, poll the crowd for the optimal price point, product name, and other potential uses of the product (Gerber and Hui 2013; Mancuso and Stuth 2014).

In their study, Belleflamme *et al.* (2013) stated that due to the growing popularity of crowdfunding, it is increasingly being used as a marketing tool to acquire worldwide awareness for creative projects. Using crowdfunding, founders launch a campaign to enlist as many participants as possible in support of their ideas.

An early audience for the marketing campaign can help reduce the amount of time needed for the product to achieve market acceptability when the finished goods are finally brought to the market in an official capacity (Urban *et al.* 2000). Consequently, the capacity to attract investors through marketing is yet another indicator of crowdfunding success. Therefore, a good crowdfunding campaign should be a project that has a solid measure of the three aforementioned dimensions of success, namely fundraising success, funder attraction success, and feedback collection success.

Empirical studies

Many research works on crowdfunding have examined project success factors. Factors including the size of the social network, non-profit status, the location of the creator, details of the project, language and exit strategy have been identified. Various other factors of crowdfunding have been examined, and entrepreneurs should consider these before a campaign to ensure a successful outcome. Valančienė and Jegelevičiūtė (2014) found that all stakeholders' interests must be satisfied in order to have successful crowdfunding. Several studies have identified the optimal project timeline to be between 40 and 60 days (Boeuf *et al*. 2014).

On Kickstarter, there were 174,267 projects as of September 2014, and of those, 39.69% had raised more than $1.3 billion (Profatilov *et al*. 2015). Over the course of time, crowdfunding and the economic benefits it offers has proved to be successful. Over 90% of successful ventures continued to operate between one and four years after the campaign, with one-third of those generating annual revenue of more than one hundred thousand dollars. Additionally, Mollick and Kuppuswamy (2014) reported a 2.2% rise in the number of employees. There are a variety of aspects of a project that can affect its likelihood of being successful, including its scope, product quality, exit strategy and financial goals (Cohen 2017).

Mollick (2014) identified an extensive social network, strong quality signals such as audio-visuals and regular updates. He also related the success of a project to the location of its founders within the United States. Hui *et al*. (2014) discovered, through interviews with 58 project founders, that having a massive fan following was a significant predictor of enormous financing success. Zheng *et al*. (2014) investigated reward-based projects and looked at the data available on Kickstarter. They found a significant correlation between the size of an entrepreneur's social network and the success of the project they were working on. Similarly, Colombo *et al*. (2015) analyzed 699 different Kickstarter campaigns and found that the number of investors and the ratio of early fundraising to aim are both good indicators of the success of a campaign. On the other hand, Belleflamme *et al*. (2013) discovered that the amount of money raised for charitable causes was not increased by the utilization of social networks. Riedl (2013) discovered that technological projects whose worth is recognized and whose final product appeals to a broad range of users were more successful.

Antonenko *et al*. (2014) found that 90% of the crowdfunding initiatives raised $6,000 or less, although five of these projects exceeded their crowdfunding goal by raising up to $20,000. Research has also shown that creators who had previous experience with crowdfunding set lower targets (Boeuf *et al*. 2014) and these results suggest that crowdfunding projects that set lower targets were more successful than the projects with bigger targets (Antonenko *et al*. 2014). Firms that did not provide financial projections and disclaimers were found to raise less capital or took longer to achieve their targets or attracted fewer contributors (Ahlers *et al*. 2015).

Barbi and Bigelli (2017) analyzed all 123,467 Kickstarter projects from April 2009 to December 2013 and determined that the success variables in the United States and elsewhere are substantially identical. The variables include factors such as the inclusion of audio-visuals, a lower funding target, more or greater rewards and brief campaigns. They observed that crowdfunding success was further enhanced with lower monetary targets and provision of brief information in the prescribed manner (Barbi and Bigelli 2017).

While researching the Chinese crowdfunding platform, Xu *et al.* (2014) found that investor satisfaction was positively correlated with project owners achieving their crowdfunding goals. This satisfaction was facilitated through timely delivery, quality of the product, project novelty, and the active participation of project creators and sponsors' participation and demographics.

Language that emphasized human interests resulted in significantly faster funding than language that emphasized rewards and risk-taking. This was the conclusion reached by Allison *et al.* (2015), who investigated project description languages on 36,665 Kiva loans using a considerably bigger data set to establish the language that leads to the most successful funding.

Furthermore, the findings indicated that both intrinsic and extrinsic language were significant determinants of the decisions made by funders. They found that the effect that was caused internally was five times more powerful than the effect that was caused externally (Allison *et al.* 2015). On the other hand, Cholakova and Clarysse (2015) discovered that intrinsic motivations, which do not involve financial gain, are not significant predictors.

Trust serves as another critical factor for success since both funder and founder are probably never going to meet one another. Crowdfunding projects are prone to the signalling effects of stability and investability (Ley and Weaven 2011). Specifically, venture capital firms will invest in sterling opportunities and in cases where investors are seasoned, as this enhances the opportunities' trustworthiness (Ley and Weaven 2011). Cholakova and Clarysse (2015) found that individuals' decisions to support and the actual quantity contributed to reward-based projects were directly related to their trust in the project owner and the prizes being offered.

According to the findings of Colombo *et al.* (2015), early support, which was defined as the number of supporters and the percentage of the fundraising goal that was raised in advance, are both positive indications of success. Early-stage funding helps to reduce uncertainty by providing indirect indicators of project quality, boosting word-of-mouth, and possibly allowing early backers to provide recommendations, comments and feedback on the project (Colombo *et al.* 2015).

Mollick (2014) discovered that projects either succeed by a narrow margin or fail by a significant margin, and that higher-quality ventures have a greater chance of obtaining funding. According to Cordova *et al.*'s (2015) research on the factors that determine whether or not a technology project is successful, increasing the project's financing objective was found to be associated with a lower probability of success, while increasing the project's duration was found to increase the success rate. They also noticed that success was strongly correlated with daily donation amounts and that the success rate reduced by five to six times for every 1% increase in funding targets (Cordova *et al.* 2015). These findings corroborated those of Mollick (2014), but were based on a considerably bigger data set that included information from Kickstarter, Indiegogo, Ulule and Eppela (Cordova *et al.* 2015).

It is a common misconception that the internet and social networks have eliminated all barriers, but in reality, geography still plays a significant role in the success of fundraising efforts. According to the findings of research carried out by Burtch *et al.* (2014) on Kiva.org, physical distance and cultural differences have a significant negative correlation with lending. Specifically, the researchers found that banks lend less money as geographical distance increases. As a result, the owners of projects ought to promote themselves, their projects and their products to investors who are either geographically close to them or with whom they have strong cultural or communal ties (Burtch *et al.* 2014). According to the findings of a study that was conducted by Antonenko and colleagues (2014), the majority of the most successful educational technology initiatives were situated in or close to major metropolitan areas. Mollick (2014) found that location plays a role in determining the success of crowdfunding in certain regions that have significant cultural preferences. According to the findings of Belleflamme *et al.* (2013), direct participation with the crowd is positively correlated with the amount of funds raised, and projects that manufacture items as opposed to providing services raised more money overall. Both Belleflamme *et al.* (2013) and Boeuf *et al.* (2014) investigated 875 theatrical projects that were funded through Kickstarter in 2011. They made the discovery that founders who support other projects have a positive effect on supporters' willingness to give to their own initiative. On the other hand, they found that support decreases as founders launch successive projects, which suggests that donors become fatigued (Boeuf *et al.* 2014).

It is a widespread fallacy that the internet and social networks have removed all barriers; however, in practice, physical distance and cultural differences have a significant negative correlation with lending, as demonstrated by the findings of research conducted on Kiva.org by Burtch *et al.* (2014). More specifically, the researchers discovered that a greater geographical distance results in a decrease in the amount of money that banks are willing to lend. As a consequence of this, the owners of projects ought to promote themselves, their projects and their products to investors who are either geographically close to them or with whom they have strong cultural or communal ties. In either case, this should be done to investors who have strong ties to the community (Burtch *et al.* 2014).

The majority of the most successful educational technology initiatives were located in major metropolitan areas or in close proximity to those areas, according to the findings of a study that was carried out by Antonenko and colleagues (2014). Mollick (2014) discovered that the location of the crowdfunding project plays a role in determining how successful the project will be in certain regions that have significant cultural preferences. According to the findings that Belleflamme *et al.* (2013) uncovered, direct participation with the crowd is positively correlated with the amount of funds raised, and projects that manufacture items as opposed to providing services raised more money overall. In 2011, Kickstarter was used to fund 875 different theatrical projects. Belleflamme *et al.* (2013) and Boeuf *et al.* (2014) each investigated these projects. They made the discovery that founders who support other projects have a positive effect on the willingness of supporters to give to their own initiative, and this effect can be positive or negative. On the other hand, they discovered that the level of support drops as the founders of the organization launch successive projects. This indicates that donors become tired of giving (Boeuf *et al.* 2014).

A critical factor in crowdfunding success is communication. Coleman (2015) observed that creators who frequently shared updates and posted about the relevant project and personal desires and pleasures and related to funders were more successful than those who failed to do so. Antonenko *et al.* (2014) found that posting of regular updates, including milestones and deadlines and other project information were features of successful projects. In addition, Kuppuswamy and Bayus (2018) found that projects were more likely to reach their crowdfunding goals in the last week if project authors provided regular updates and replied quickly to questions and comments. At the same time, the presence of special offers for early backers and showing commitment in the platform by helping other projects are two good mediators influencing the relationship between the number of purchases of the product and the rate of funding (Marelli and Ordanini 2016). Finally, McSweeney *et al.* (2022) found that both male and female entrepreneurs' pitch assertiveness was associated with crowdfunding success, further stressing the importance of communication in the crowdfunding campaign.

The ten commandments of crowdfunding

The concept of finance has been rethought as a result of crowdfunding. It has emerged as a practical choice for funding creative endeavours, new businesses and seed capital in recent years. Numerous crowdfunding platforms based on the internet are currently operational on all seven continents. These platforms have made it possible for the leaders of creative business, and/or social projects to raise billions of euros through donations, subscriptions, equity holdings and/ or financial loans.

It is essential for the success of a crowdfunding campaign to have the participation of the project's owners, not only during the critical planning and preparation phase but also throughout the entirety of the campaign itself. On the other hand, the choice of whether or not to participate in crowdfunding can be a difficult one for potential project owners. Inadequate expertise, a lack of time to commit to a possible campaign initiative, and reluctance on how to use the instrument are all potential challenges that could arise. Before moving on to the more important phase of campaign preparation, potential project leaders need to have a complete understanding of the prerequisites that are associated with the crowdfunding concept. They also need to evaluate whether or not it is compatible with their project, personality and hobbies. The self-evaluation method known as "The Ten Commandments of Crowdfunding", which was proffered by Eversheds Southerland (2013) and developed by Gura (2018), is an approach that includes essential rules that should be considered when deciding whether or not to use crowdfunding as a strategy for marketing and funding. During the process of self-evaluation, factors such as community, ethics, adhesion, involvement, interaction, readjustment, planning, confidence, transparency and emotion are taken into account.

Using this instrument to conduct a thorough self-evaluation, project creators will be able to determine whether or not they should use crowdfunding to raise funds for their projects if they use this instrument to conduct an in-depth self-evaluation and then use the results of that evaluation to make their decision. It is a test to determine how well prepared they are.

The "ten commandments" of crowdfunding

1 **Thou shall have no other mission other than crowdfunding**. To run a successful campaign, it is crucial to commit to it as a fulltime job. If this is impossible, it may be necessary to get fulltime help. Keeping the campaign length relatively short (30–45 days), may help to ensure the entrepreneur's ability to fully attend and nurture their campaign.

2 **Thou shall not make idols out of any one crowdfunding platform**. Neither Indiegogo, nor Kickstarter, nor Headstarter is a God. None of them will, nor can, guarantee a successful campaign. There are more and perhaps lesser known crowdfunding platforms in existence with differentiating guidelines and parameters that you should consider. The entrepreneur must do their homework and choose wisely. By the same token, they should not speak ill of their crowdfunding platform. Whether they reach their goal or not, they must not speak poorly of their platform of choice. If they are not 100% pleased with the platform they chose, they should consider looking in to another platform for the next time. If they were pleased, they should do them a favour and sing their praises!

3 **Thou shall not assume people will react after one email**. During project creators' "soft launch", they should not expect to hear back from all of their family and friends. While this campaign is on the forefront of creators' mind, it is probably not on theirs. By adding "please let me know either way" to creators' initial message, creators should have an excuse to reach out to them a second time or even a third time without feeling like they are badgering them.

4 **Remember the Sabbath day**. Entrepreneurs should consider taking a "day of rest" during their campaign. Crowdfunding is a full-time job which can lead to mental and emotional enslavement as well as burn out. There is great wisdom in abstaining from computer devices and avoiding the campaign for 24 hours. They should go on a hike, smell the roses and read to their children.

5 **Honour your neighbours as yourself**. Project creators should accept everyone's choices as to whether they choose to contribute or support the campaign. Project creators should not depend on their friends or contributors to spread the word. When creators are moving beyond their inner circles, they should always approach people with respect and when/if they do contribute, keep them inspired and enthusiastic about the campaign. Contributors should be thanked regularly for their support, for without them, the potential success of the campaign would not be achieved. The potential success of the campaign is due in part, to them.

6 **Thou shall not go in this alone**. Even if entrepreneur is a sole trader (or a solopreneur), they should consider creating a team for the project. There is an art and science to leading a successful crowdfunding campaign, and by working alongside others, the entrepreneur will be able to prepare better,

work more efficiently, and strategically reach and capture the attention of a much broader audience than from his/her network alone.

7 **Thou shall not spam.** While it may be tempting to post the campaign to the thousands of members in a particular Facebook group, it should not be done. There is need to be casual and subtle. If someone specifically asks about the campaign, that person should be privately messaged, rather than posting in the comments.

8 **Thou shall not steal intellectual property.** When project creators send updates to their contributors, they should not create fictitious remarks about the campaign. Rather, they should utilize actual responses, quotes and praises from targeted efforts made.

9 **Thou shall not hold a grudge.** The entrepreneur should remember that not everyone they reach out to will contribute to the campaign – not even the person on the entrepreneur's list whom they consider to be the most likely one to contribute or who the entrepreneur believes needs his/her product the most. Entrepreneurs should stay positive and stay open-minded because they may be pleasantly surprised that the person who is least likely to contribute to the campaign may do so.

10 **Thou shall not covet your crowdfunding neighbour.** Entrepreneurs should not be tempted to peek at the campaign next to theirs. The other person's campaign may have secured more funds, may have a greater number of contributors, or may be closer to its goal than the entrepreneurs', but getting stuck on jealousy or desire is not going to help their campaign in any way. Project creators should stay in their own lane, mind their business and remain focused and continue with their mission.

NOTE: While these ten commandments will support and guide entrepreneurs on their path, they cannot guarantee any success. Therefore, it is important for the entrepreneur to stay goal-oriented and have "Plan B" prepared in advance.

Source: Adapted from Gura (2018).

Crowdfunding campaign timelines

There are three distinct phases that make up a crowdfunding campaign, and they are the pre-launch, the campaign proper, and the post-campaign phase. Each of these phases/stages require skilful planning and management. It is how each of these stages is planned and managed that will determine whether or not the process is successful.

(i) Pre-launch

Every successful crowdfunding campaign includes a significant contribution from the campaigner's family, friends and other supporters. Therefore, the time leading up to the launch should be spent building email lists. A list of all the people in the initiator's circle who are "wired", should be compiled during the pre-launch phase, including friends, relatives, friends of friends, colleagues and co-workers. A time of crowdfunding is not the ideal time to be distant and removed. Everyone should be informed about the upcoming "big" event.

Twitter in particular is a significant factor in determining whether or not a crowdfunding project will be successful in the modern era. During the pre-launch phase of the campaign, which occurs well in advance of the campaign itself, all of the social media platforms that are currently available, including Facebook, Snapchat and Tiktok, should be utilized. Build a network and start recruiting people for the upcoming project by collecting email addresses, creating tweets and postings for others, liking and following other people's content, and so on.

During the pre-launch phase, the time is used to plan and construct the rewards, as well as "back-ups" that may be substituted for ones that do not attract sufficient subscription. In addition, the pre-launch period is the time to create the pitch, whether in the form of a video or a written document, and to ensure that the content is submitted to the platform of choice for verification and is ready for "Launch Day". Sharing a project preview link with friends and colleagues is a good way of getting feedback that the project is ready to go "Live". Finally, a press release would have to be sent to the crowd by email and other social media handles to inform them on the campaign kick-off and this should be done approximately one week before the start date. It is important to keep in mind that the length of a campaign is not nearly as significant as how well prepared it is. Sufficient support can be guaranteed for the initiative if enough time and effort is put into planning the pre-launch. Efforts should therefore be directed toward creating and expanding the "crowd".

(ii) Campaign launch day

Campaign launch day is the most important as well as exciting day of any crowdfunding campaign. It is the day that the project is unveiled to the public and reactions garnered. The goal of any campaign should be to attain 100% funding within the first 24 hours of launch (Stanislovatis 2019). However, this is determined well ahead of time; in the pre-launch period when leads are generated and contacts made preparatory to the launch.

Immediately after launch activities include: send newsletter to potential backers on the mailing list; send private messages to friends, family and colleagues through normal communication channel; send emails to bloggers, journalists and influencers previously informed on the project; make posts in all available social media platforms using both personal and project profiles and re-direct all visitors to the campaign using appropriate links. All necessary communication should be created in advance and scheduled to reduce early launch hour pressures. Be responsive and review emails as soon as possible; communicate often and publish significant events including achieving milestones as updates. You may also add some analytics to track campaign traffic and analyze performance.

(iii) Post-campaign completion

Post-campaign events include more communication including "thank you" letters to everyone who helped in achieving the fund-raising target; share excitement/emotion with contributors and the team. A survey is also a post-campaign activity once the list of backers is known. Creating a survey will enable the entrepreneur to collect important information such as shipping addresses, colours, sizes and other details for fulfilment. Finally, communication with backers to keep them informed on the progress of the project until it is completely delivered is a sine-qua-non for a successful crowdfunding campaign.

The pitch

It has become very clear that a significant part of the success of a crowdfunding campaign lies in the pitch. The manner in which the entrepreneur presents his/her campaign will determine how noticeable it is. No matter the concept, creation, or innovation, the story behind it needs to be interesting enough to draw in the target audience. On the other hand, a campaign that is either too superficial or not adequately explained can have the complete opposite effect. Platforms for crowdfunding are available so that the entrepreneur can adequately describe the purpose of their campaign to a more substantial online audience. The delivery is the most important part. Campaigns that include a captivating pitch and details, along with captivating pictures and videos, are likely to attract more attention than campaigns that do not include these elements. The following are components of a compelling pitch:

(i) Simplicity

When writing a pitch, it is a lot simpler if the entrepreneur writes it from the perspective of the people who will be reading or watching it. The more questions that are addressed in the presentation, the better the chances will be of convincing potential backers to contribute to the cause. Keep it as simple as possible. A pitch for crowdfunding may be lengthy, but it does not have to be an epic in length. The pitch must be kept as straightforward as possible. Being succinct and to-the-point can help the project come across as more convincing. Backers are more likely to back the project when they understand the objectives and the usability of the product. Buzzwords and flowery language are not advised. It must be kept simple!

(ii) Title

The first things that a potential backer reads on a page for a crowdfunding campaign, are the project's title and a brief description. In addition to being clear and succinct, the title of the product should explain what the product is while the brief description should focus on the most important aspect of the product. The investor ought to be able to comprehend at least 50% of the campaign solely based on the title and the description.

(iii) Story

As a creator of a crowdfunding campaign, it is essential to explain to the audience why the entrepreneur chose to crowdfund and the story behind the campaign. The success rate of story-based pitches is higher than that of typical product description pitches. A story approach necessitates a description that discusses both the product and the project as a whole.

The more the campaign is discussed, the easier it is for the audience to trust the campaign and ultimately support it. Make use of different fonts and styles in addition to images, videos, charts in the process and be sure to describe everything in concise and direct language to facilitate reading. "The way the video content is presented can significantly alter campaign success" (Forbes and Schaefer 2017, p. 5). When the purpose is obvious, consumers comprehend the product's utility and are more willing to support it.

In using the "Story" approach, the pitch must address and respond to the following questions:

- Who are you: Include a brief description of yourself and your team.
- Why you are seeking to gather funds: Provide an overview of your initiative.
- When your project will be carried out: Create an approximate timetable detailing the tentative dates for each project phase.
- Where your project will take place: Select the crowdfunding site you plan to utilize and review their presentation style to ensure you adhere to their particular format.
- Why you are raising funds: Specify the rationale behind your crowdfunding campaign.
- Methods of participation: In addition to the standard incentives, you can make it more personal by including customized notes and pledges for your backers.

(iv) Facts and figures

As is the situation with conventional finance, information asymmetries occur in crowdfunding due to investors' lack of access to the necessary information for making investment decisions. There is a reason why the entrepreneur chooses to crowdfund his/her project, but regardless of how certain they are in their idea, potential backers require information in order to make the investment decision. To strengthen their credibility, entrepreneurs must support their product with substantial facts and data.

The entrepreneur must post a great deal of information in the public domain (the internet) in order to entice participants to contribute. Disclosure of important information is required to eliminate information asymmetry and encourage backers' participation in the project. The pitch should include necessary and sufficient information and data to achieve its purpose.

(v) Rewards

People back projects on crowdfunding platforms firstly because they are part of a community that supports creators and encourages them towards realizing their dreams. Secondly, backers anticipate a reward for their financial support. Rewards are therefore a very important component of any crowdfunding campaign and also of the crowdfunding pitch. Tangible rewards have been proven to be preferable to "gimmicky" things such as T-shirts and stickers (Forbes and Schaefer 2017). The rewards system should be planned and prepared well ahead of campaign launch. A crowdfunder must be very creative in the design of the reward system. The campaign pitch should include the reward title and description and it should be short and clear.

(vi) Project timeline

The project timeline is one of the most crucial components of a crowdfunding pitch. Even if they are mere estimates, project timetables should be clearly specified and communicated in written or graphical format. In either case, this increases the credibility of the campaign and clarifies the fulfilment and post-production information for the investors. Any modifications to plans should be communicated to investors in a timely manner. No rational investor would prefer to make an open-ended investment.

(vii) Plea

A pitch video, audio or text should always conclude with a plea; a "call to action" on the point of arrival. A pitch without a plea is an incomplete pitch and most likely to fail in achieving its objectives. The audience must understand the required action to take in order to actualize the campaign objective, which is, to galvanize the audience to invest in the project. Necessary links should be provided to enable investors to make their pledges or commitment, where possible.

(viii) Other considerations

The pitch should also consider the following researched predictors of success:

Social entrepreneurs are more to be trusted than non-social firms (Lehner 2013); while projects signalling empathy, warmth, conscientiousness are likely to attract sufficient interest while such loans, if obtained are more likely to be unpaid.

(Moss *et al.* 2015)

In addition, individuals who demonstrate autonomy, competitive aggression and risk-taking are more likely to acquire funding, whereas individuals who demonstrate proactiveness were less likely to repay the loan. Those who demonstrate risk-taking are more likely to acquire funding (Moss *et al.* 2015). Entrepreneurs who use Kiva should choose their words very carefully in order to maximize the sending of positive signals and the subsequent funding they receive. According to the findings of Belleflamme *et al.* (2014), the pre-sales model is favoured when the initial funding requirement is relatively low, whereas the profit-sharing model is preferred when the initial funding requirement is substantially high. Song and van Boeschoten (2015) found that 40% of all project initiators would use the pre-purchase model to test products in their social network. However, these project initiators did not have knowledge of crowdfunding and would not use it again due to the amount of time and effort that it required (Song and van Boeschoten 2015).

Crowdfunding projects that are transparent regarding their finances and their exit strategies are attracting a growing number of investors. According to the findings of Ahlers *et al.* (2012), start-ups that had listed exit strategies attracted more investors than those that did not have any. According to the findings of the study, businesses that did not present financial forecasts and disclaimers had a greater risk of attracting fewer investors and failing to raise the required amount of capital (2012). Before utilizing crowdfunding, entrepreneurs are required to evaluate all of these characteristics, and further study is necessary in order to expand upon these characteristics. In general, the people behind the project need to develop their campaigns in order to demonstrate their credibility and establish the demand for their products.

The role of effective communication

A critical factor in crowdfunding success is communication. Effective communication is required at every stage of the campaign (pre-launch, launch and post-launch) to keep the audience well informed, firstly, with the objective/purpose of the project and secondly, with the up-to-date progress and news related to the project.

Emails and messages may be received pre-launch from potential backers requesting information or from backers and potential backers who are wondering whether to support the project or not. These represent concerns or feedback and opportunity for the founder to influence their choice. Every query should be reviewed and attended as quickly as possible using the same channel of communication. Posting updates on the crowdfunding platform and all other communication channels detailing the project's accomplishments, such as notable milestones, blog or website reviews, and press coverage or mention ensures investors are kept abreast with developments on the project. Founders should also express their enthusiasm for the campaign through these channels. Many backers support projects because of an emotional connection to what founders do; therefore, exposing your feelings demonstrates your sensitivity and strengthens your connection with the community.

12 tips for running a successful crowdfunding campaign

    i Do not rush into a campaign – plan, plan, plan.
   ii Learn the rules and how to play the game
  iii Study and learn from other campaigns
  iv Learn timing – long campaigns do not work
   v Put a lot of thought and research into your funding goal
  vi Be pitch perfect
 vii Have a video – short but creative and credible story
viii Rewards are essential – tangible rewards preferable
  ix Family, friends and colleagues are critical to your success
   x List-building is a continuous process

xi Social media is essential

xii Create a "Call to Action" or plea

Source: *The Crowdfunding Guide for Authors and Writers* (Briles 2015)

Advantages and disadvantages of a crowdfunding campaign

Advantages:

- Pitching a business through online platforms can be a valuable form of marketing and results in media attention
- You can get feedback and expert guidance
- It is a good way to test the public's reaction to your product/idea
- Investors can track your progress – this may help you to promote your brand through their networks
- Ideas that may not appeal to conventional investors can often get financed more easily
- Your investors can often become your most loyal customers through the financing process
- It is an alternative finance option if you have struggled to get bank loans or traditional funding

Disadvantages:

- Not always easier compared to traditional ways of raising finance; not all projects applying get on a crowdfunding platform
- You need to do a lot of work in building up interest before the project launches
- If you don't reach your funding target, any finance pledged will usually be returned to your investors and you get nothing
- Failed projects risk damage to the reputation of your business
- If you haven't protected your business idea with a patent or copyright someone may see it on crowdfunding site and steal your concept
- It can be easy to give away too much of the business to investors

---

A case study of how Oculus VR crowdfunded their way to a $2 billion business (a 6-step checklist)

Crowdfunding is not a lottery, it is a process – and you can win if you prepare for it

The attraction of crowdfunding is that anyone can do it and because anyone can do it, anyone (in theory) can raise loads of money. In 2014, two years after launching their Kickstarter, Oculus Rift was bought by Facebook for $2 billion.

An entrepreneur may have an idea, and they think it is good, but there are many good ideas. What if nobody likes the idea? What if your campaign gets lost in the crowd?

Crowdfunding successfully does not mean asking for money at random. It means building a campaign as if building a business, and taking the power of the crowd into the creator's hands.

1 Figure out why people should care

Entrepreneurs get so deep in the weeds building their product that they often become totally incapable of describing why it actually matters.

Entrepreneurs have to be able to sell their product clearly and succinctly to be able to convince people to fund their idea. That does not just mean summing up its features and functions; it means saying something that will allow outsiders to care.

People should care about the Oculus Rift because it is bringing a new level of immersion to gaming. Oculus' tagline "step into the game" tells us very little about how the headset actually works but it shows us exactly why we should care.

The entrepreneur should boil down their story until they have a "minimum viable identity". What is the least they can say about their product while still transmitting the essence of it to a buyer? Think iPod's tagline "puts 1000 songs in your pocket". It is a value proposition, showing off all the iPod's important features at once. Mobile, light, convenient and if the product name is good enough, then no tagline is needed.

2 Find an actual human who'll use it

Many crowdfunders think they have a great product but they do not know a single person who would use it.

Oculus was a success because its creators already knew they had a great product – it had already caused a buzz on VR forum Meant to be Seen, and had received recognition from popular programmer John Carmack.

It does not need celebrity endorsement to validate the product. The most effective way to find out if people will use the product is to ask them.

Netflix's founders Reed Hastings and Marc Randolph started by manually mailing DVDs to friends who wanted to see movies. They asked real humans and delivered straight away. The trick is not just to ask but to give. "Would you like one of these new cupcakes?" – "How much would you like to pay for it?" – "Okay, give me those two bucks in your pocket and here it is. What do you think?"

It is important to make sure people actually like the product before launching the campaign; if nobody wants to use it when they are offered directly, it is not funding that is needed.

3 Ask for the right amount of money

Many Kickstarters fail because their founders simply do not understand how to ask for money. Ask for too much and however amazing the product is, it will not get funded. Ask for too little and the project seems like a joke.

How much money does the entrepreneur actually need (for materials, for marketing, for research) to mobilize the next steps of their plan? This should be their campaign goal. Oculus' $250,000 goal was practical, considering the mammoth task of turning an "early developer kit" into a consumer-ready VR product. Consequently, Oculus received 100% of that goal in less than four hours.

The entrepreneur should bolster their chances of succeeding by playing to human psychology. Studies show that people are more likely to donate if the request either appeals to their sense of egoism or altruism. But not both. Requests with mixed messages alert the recipient to the act of persuasion.

It is important to remember that it is better to actually get funded by a crowd rather than one impressed donor, so allow people to donate small.

4 Make rewards that do not suck

Campaign rewards are entrepreneurs' opportunity to turn ideas into a list of objects and experiences that they can, and will, deliver to their future customer.

Therefore, entrepreneurs should use rewards to turn backers into early brand ambassadors. This Andean farm offered backers the chance to name a chicken. Filmmaker Matt Porterfield rewarded top backers by tattooing their names on his arm. For backers of Potato Salad by Zack Danger Brown, the experience of donating far surpassed the value of the product itself (a bowl of potato salad), with crazy stretch rewards like "I will rent out a party hall and invite the whole internet to the potato salad party".

Entrepreneurs should go further and turn backers into team members; evolve their product with their help. Oculus launched a developer kit so that developers would be enticed to adapt their games for the Oculus headset; Oculus got funding while at the same time evolving their product. And to encourage whole teams to get involved, the penultimate reward was a "studio kit", a set of ten developer kits along with support from the creators.

5 Get over your fear and tell people

Many entrepreneurs do not even tell their families about their idea. They are scared of being "one of the bad ones". This becomes a self-fulfilling prophecy; the less entrepreneurs talk about their campaign, the fewer people will see it, and their chances of getting funded shrink to nothing.

If entrepreneurs are scared of failing, they will be able to judge how good their idea is. There is a reason why FailCon is so popular. Uber CEO Travis Kalanick is a regular there; he used to fail so much it was as if he was doing it deliberately. Now there is a direct correlation between his failure and his success. Sharing his ideas, and finding out they were failures, taught him how to make better products.

Entrepreneurs can create positive buzz about their product just by talking about it. According to the Mere Exposure Effect, developed by Robert Zajonc, the more someone sees something, the friendlier they feel towards it. This is the power of social media marketing: crowds of people learn to like a product simply because it becomes familiar to them.

Entrepreneurs should leverage their personal networks and find their toughest crowd and tell them, too. Andrew Jiang posted about his Kickstarter, the Superbook, on discussion threads like the r/Android subreddit. He used this tough crowd of hardcore Android fans to generate microlevel discussion that helped him adapt the Superbook to precisely suit their needs.

6 Get ready for more money

The worst mistake an entrepreneur can make is to prepare for a successful Kickstarter and then leave it at that. They should prepare for the next funding step now or their idea will struggle to be more than a crowdfunding campaign.

From an impressive early prototype, Oculus carefully rode their momentum into a Kickstarter backed by 9,522 people, and then into a seed round that gathered $2.55 million (interestingly a very similar figure to the one they earned on Kickstarter), and so on, until they were bought by Facebook for $2 billion.

Other successful products choose to forgo traditional venture capital. Organic chocolate brand sweetriot started with a $50,000 campaign on Indiegogo. Then, as a more experienced and established idea, they joined CircleUp, a selective fundraising platform that connects emerging consumer brands with experienced investors. Here, entrepreneurs have to apply and investors have to be accredited, eliminating the slush pile effect.

What if you succeed?

If the campaign succeeds, the entrepreneur will not just have money – they will have the first iteration of their business, including a group of customers who are already rooting for them. The entrepreneur should prepare themselves because once those customers are watching, there is no going back.

Source: Adapted from Chen (2016).

Summary

Crowdfunding is perhaps the most effective method for those who have time and ideas but lack the financial means to implement them. The majority of people with ideas lack the financial resources to implement their ideas and either borrow from family and friends or seek investment from conventional financial institutions such as banks and venture capitalists. Crowdfunding has evolved into a credible alternative for innovators and creators.

Crowdfunding campaigns should be well-planned and prepared; the success of a campaign depends more on how well-prepared it is than on when it was launched or concluded. A successful pre-launch will most likely result in adequate backing for the initiative. Efforts should consequently be concentrated on developing a fan base for the initiative prior to its introduction.

The pitch is an essential element of every crowdfunding campaign. The effectiveness of a campaign depends on the pitch. Campaign pitches should be straightforward, addressing and responding to the questions "who", "why", "where" and "when" and ending with a "call to action". A successful crowdfunding campaign has a good gauge of the three elements of success: recruiting investors, reaching the financial goal and gathering feedback.

Discussion questions

1 "A good crowdfunding campaign should have a good measure of the three dimensions of success." Discuss the three dimensions of crowdfunding success.
2 A significant part of the success of a crowdfunding campaign lies in the pitch. Discuss the components of a "winning" crowdfunding pitch.
3 Discuss the role of effective communication in the crowdfunding campaign timeline.
4 Enumerate and discuss the "Ten Commandments" of crowdfunding.
5 You are asked to offer tips for a successful crowdfunding campaign. What might these be?

Test questions

1 "The depth of the project description can positively impact on the success of funding." Discuss.
2 To what extent does the provision of video material have a positive impact on the success of funding?
3 What part does experience in project creating play on the success of a crowdfunding campaign?

Glossary of key terminologies

Call to action An appeal for contribution made by a founder at the conclusion of a crowdfunding pitch.
Campaign An organized series of actions geared towards raising funds for a project.
Communication The exchange of information through a medium or channel.

Pitch   A persuasive speech by a founder aimed at causing a reaction by investors to contribute towards the realization of a project.

Plea   Same as a "call to action".

Reward   A token gift given to the contributor to a project.

Ten commandments   A list of "dos" and "don'ts" that is executed to achieve crowdfunding success.

Recommended reading

Forbes, H., and Schaefer, D., 2017. Guidelines for successful crowdfunding. *Procedia CIRP*, 60, 398–403.

Marelli, A., and Ordanini, A., 2016. What makes crowdfunding projects successful 'before' and 'during' the campaign? In: *Crowdfunding in Europe*. Cham: Springer, 175–192.

Risterucci, F., 2016. The ten commandments of crowdfunding. In: *Crowdfunding in Europe*. Cham: Springer, 241–248.

References

Ahlers, G.K., Cumming, D., Günther, C., and Schweizer, D., 2015. Signalling in equity crowdfunding. *Entrepreneurship Theory and Practice*, 39 (4), 955–980.

Allison, T.H., Davis, B.C., Short, J.C., and Webb, J.W., 2015. Crowdfunding in a prosocial microlending environment: Examining the role of intrinsic versus extrinsic cues. *Entrepreneurship Theory and Practice*, 39 (1), 53–73.

Antonenko, P.D., Lee, B.R., and Kleinheksel, A.J., 2014. Trends in the crowdfunding of educational technology startups. *TechTrends*, 58 (6), 36–41.

Barbi, M., and Bigelli, M., 2017. Crowdfunding practices in and outside the US. *Research in International Business and Finance*, 42, 208–223.

Belleflamme, P., Lambert, T., and Schwienbacher, A., 2013. Individual crowdfunding practices. *Venture Capital*, 15 (4), 313–333.

Belleflamme, P., Lambert, T., and Schwienbacher, A., 2014. Crowdfunding: Tapping the right crowd. *Journal of Business Venturing*, 29 (5), 585–609.

Boeuf, B., Darveau, J., and Legoux, R., 2014. *Financing creativity: Crowdfunding as a new approach for theatre projects. International Journal of Arts Management*, 16 (3), 33–48.

Burtch, G., Ghose, A., and Wattal, S., 2013. An empirical examination of the antecedents and consequences of contribution patterns in crowd-funded markets. *Information Systems Research*, 24 (3), 499–519.

Burtch, G., Ghose, A., and Wattal, S., 2014. Cultural differences and geography as determinants of online prosocial lending. *Mis Quarterly*, 38 (3), 773–794.

Chen, W., 2016. *How oculus VR crowdfunded their way to a $2 billion business* (A 6-Step Checklist). Available from: www.inc.com/walter-chen/how-oculus-vr-crowdfunded-their-way-to-a-2-billion-business-a-6-step-checklist.html [Accessed 24 November 2022].

Cholakova, M., and Clarysse, B., 2015. Does the possibility to make equity investments in crowdfunding projects crowd out reward – based investments? *Entrepreneurship Theory and Practice*, 39 (1), 145–172.

Cohen, M., 2017. *Crowdfunding as a financing resource for small businesses.* (Walden dissertations and Doctoral Studies Collection). Available from: https://scholarworks.waldenu.edu/dissanddoc?utm_source=scholarworks.waldenu.edu%2Fdissertations%2F3757&utm_medium=PDF&utm_campaign=PDFCoverPages

Coleman, C., 2015. Crowdfunding and online identity: Cashing in on authenticity? *Journal of Music Research Online*, 6. Available from: http://www.jmro.org.au/index.php/mca2/article/view/115/41 [Accessed 12 January 2022].

Colombo, M.G., Franzoni, C., and Rossi-Lamastra, C., 2015. Internal social capital and the attraction of early contributions in crowdfunding. *Entrepreneurship Theory and Practice*, 39, 75–100.

Cordova, A., Dolci, J., and Gianfrate, G., 2015. The determinants of crowdfunding success: Evidence from technology projects. *Procedia-Social and Behavioral Sciences*, 181, 115–124.

Eversheds Southerland, 2013. *The ten commandments of crowdfunding*. Available from: www.eversheds-sutherland.com/global/en/what/articles/index.page?ArticleID=en/global/netherlands/en/the-10-commandments-of-crowdfunding [Accessed 15 December 2022].

Gerber, E.M., and Hui, J., 2013. Crowdfunding: Motivations and deterrents for participation. *ACM Transactions on Computer-Human Interaction*, 20 (6), 1–32. Available from: https://doi.org/10.1145/2530540

Gerber, E.M., Hui, J.S., and Kuo, P.Y., 2012. Crowdfunding: Why people are motivated to post and fund projects on crowdfunding platforms. *In: Proceedings of the international workshop on design, influence, and social technologies: techniques, impacts and ethics*, Northwestern University, Evanston, IL 60208 USA, 11 February, 10–25.

Gura, S.T., 2018. *The 10 Commandments to crowdfunding, thrive Global*. Available from: https://medium.com/thrive-global/the-10-commandments-to-crowdfunding-d2e82aa8b26f [Accessed 23 March 2023].

Hui, J.S., Greenberg, M.D., and Gerber, E.M., 2014. Understanding the role of community in crowdfunding work. *In: Proceedings of the 17th ACM conference on Computer supported cooperative work & social computing*, New York: ACM, 62–74.

Koch, J.A., and Siering, M., 2015. Crowdfunding success factors: The characteristics of successfully funded projects on crowdfunding platforms. In: *Proceedings of the 23rd European conference on information systems (ECIS 2015)*, Muenster: SSRN, 1–15.

Kuppuswamy, V., and Bayus, B.L., 2018. Crowdfunding creative ideas: The dynamics of project backers. In: Hornuf, L. and Cumming, D. (eds.), *The economics of crowdfunding*. Cham: Palgrave Macmillan, 151–182.

Lehner, O.M., 2013. Crowdfunding social ventures: A model and research agenda. *Venture Capital*, 15 (4), 289–311.

Ley, A., and Weaven, S., 2011. Exploring agency dynamics of crowdfunding in start-up capital financing. *Academy of Entrepreneurship Journal*, 17 (1), 85.

Mancuso, J., and Stuth, K., 2014. *Seven deadly mistakes to avoid on social media*. Available from: www.cnki.com.cn/Article/CJFDTotal-CGZN201411026.htm

Marelli, A., and Ordanini, A., 2016. What makes crowdfunding projects successful 'before' and 'during' the campaign? *In: Crowdfunding in Europe*. Cham: Springer, 175–192.

McSweeney, J.J., McSweeney, K.T., Webb, J.W., and Devers, C.E., 2022. The right touch of pitch assertiveness: Examining entrepreneurs' gender and project category fit in crowdfunding. *Journal of Business Venturing*, 37 (4), 106223.

Mollick, E., 2014. The dynamics of crowdfunding: An exploratory study. *Journal of Business Venturing*, 05679.

Mollick, E.R., and Kuppuswamy, V., 2014. After the campaign: Outcomes of crowdfunding. *UNC Kenan-Flagler Research Paper*, 2376997.

Moss, T.W., Neubaum, D.O., and Meyskens, M., 2015. The effect of virtuous and entrepreneurial orientations on microfinance lending and repayment: A signaling theory perspective. *Entrepreneurship Theory and Practice*, 39 (1), 27–52.

Ordanini, A., Miceli, L., Pizzetti, M., and Parasuraman, A., 2011. Crowd-funding: Transforming customers into investors through innovative service platforms. *J. Serv. Manag,* 22, 443–470.

Profatilov, D.A., Bykova, O.N., and Olkhovskaya, M.O., 2015. Crowdfunding: Online charity or a modern tool for innovative projects implementation? *Asian Social Science,* 11 (3), 146.

Riedl, C., Blohm, I., Leimeister, J.M., and Krcmar, H., 2013. The effect of rating scales on decision quality and user attitudes in online innovation communities. *International Journal of Electronic Commerce,* 17 (3), 7–36.

Schwienbacher, A., and Larralde, B., 2010. Crowdfunding of small entrepreneurial ventures. In: D. Cumming (ed.), *Handbook of entrepreneurial finance.* Oxford, UK: Oxford University Press. Available from: https://ssrn.com/abstract=1699183

Song, Y., and van Boeschoten, R., 2015. Success factors for Crowdfunding founders and funders. *arXiv preprint arXiv:1503.00288.*

Stanislovatis, V., 2019. Your first Kickstarter campaign. *Amazon.* Available from: https://www.amazon.com/Your-First-Kickstarter-Campaign-Crowdfunding/dp/169008412X/ref=sr_1_1?crid=2P9BB54RII3OO&keywords=Stanislovatis%2C+V.%2C+2019.+Your+first+Kickstarter+campaign&qid=1692366897&sprefix=stanislovatis%2C+v.%2C+2019.+your+first+kickstarter+campaign%2Caps%2C307&sr=8-1

Urban, G., Sultan, F., and Qualls, W., 2000. Placing trust at the center of your Internet strategy. *MIT Sloan Management Review,* 42 (1), 39–48.

Valančienė, L., and Jegelevičiūtė, S., 2014. Crowdfunding for creating value: Stakeholder approach. *Procedia-Social and Behavioral Sciences,* 156, 599–604.

Xiao, S., Tan, X., Dong, M., and Qi, J., 2014. *How to design your project in the online crowdfunding market? Evidence from Kickstarter.* New York: Kickstarter.

Xu, A., Yang, X., Rao, H., Fu, W.T., Huang, S.W., and Bailey, B.P., 2014. Show me the money! An analysis of project updates during crowdfunding campaigns. *In: Proceedings of the SIGCHI conference on human factors in computing systems.* Toronto, ON, Canada: ACM, 591–600.

Younkin, P., and Kashkooli, K., 2016. What problems does crowdfunding solve? *California Management Review,* 58 (2), 20–43.

Zheng, H., Li, D., Wu, J., and Xu, Y., 2014. The role of multidimensional social capital in crowdfunding: A comparative study in China and US. *Information & Management,* 51 (4), 488–496.

Zvilichovsky, D., Inbar, Y. and Barzilay, O., 2015. *Playing both sides of the market: success and reciprocity on crowdfunding platforms.* Available from: https://ssrn.com/abstract=2304101 or http://dx.doi.org/10.2139/ssrn.2304101

8   The problems encountered
by entrepreneurs in sourcing
crowdfunding

Learning objectives

- Discuss the challenges of crowdfunding
- Discuss the problems of choosing the right crowdfunding platform
- Discuss the problems of building up interest before project launch
- Examine how crowdfunding minefields can be avoided or minimized

Introduction

In recent years, crowdfunding has developed into a viable substitute and alternative to practices that are traditionally associated with financing businesses (Schwienbacher et al. 2012). In most cases, it is an unconventional alternative method of requesting financial support from a large number of individuals through the use of the internet (Ordanini et al. 2011). Due to stringent requirements, limited amounts available and high interest rates, obtaining bank loans became challenging for businesses in the wake of the global financial crisis that began in 2008 (Hendratmi et al. 2019). As a result of this financial crisis, along with the development and globalization of technology and social media, it has become much simpler to use crowdfunding as a source of funding (Schwienbacher et al. 2012), and a great number of countries have adopted this strategy. According to a market report that was published by Massolution (2015), the crowdfunding market in North America is the most significant. In addition to this, this growth has been observed in certain regions of Asia and Europe. In contrast, countries in Africa, South America and the Middle East are still trying to catch up to the rest of the world.

Recent years have seen a rise in the number of online resources that cater to the financial requirements of commercial enterprises located in developing economies. These online communities offer a comprehensive service for a wide range of endeavours, such as charitable giving, farming and the solicitation of financial backing for a new enterprise.

Despite the fact that crowdfunding is widely accepted in developed nations like the United States, France, the Netherlands and the United Kingdom, the rate of uptake of crowdfunding by small business owners and entrepreneurs in developing nations is notably low (Islam and Khan 2019). Numerous studies have been

DOI: 10.4324/9781003193975-8

carried out in a variety of nations, including Australia, China, Germany and others, to investigate the factors that influence the widespread use of crowdfunding (Lee 2016; Ya-Zheng Li 2018; Ley and Weaven 2011; Koch and Siering 2015).

Crowdfunding is often seen as a mechanism with significant potential for expanding entrepreneurs' access to capital in developing economies, despite the fact that its adoption has been relatively slow. This is because of the mechanism's ability to crowdsource small amounts of capital (The World Bank Group 2015). It is common for developing economies to have low penetration levels of traditional financial institutions like banks and funds. As a consequence of this situation, micro and small businesses face systemic discrimination when it comes to gaining access to financing, and they are also required to provide guarantees that are frequently insurmountable for such financing, even when access to such financing is at least formally available. Community organizations and microcredit services have been working hard to find financial solutions to this problem in an effort to address it. However, it is still up for debate as to whether or not these interventions offer a solution that is both effective and sustainable in the long run. In this context, a number of studies compare and contrast microfinance with crowdfunding, and they conclude that the benefits of the former can compensate for the inefficiencies of the latter (Wolf 2017; Oruezabala and Peter 2016).

There are still obstacles impeding the growth and development of the crowdfunding industry, despite its potential. Crowdfunding, like every other source of entrepreneurial financing, has its challenges and disadvantages (Cohen 2017). Lack of regulation, understanding and awareness, as well as fraud and corruption, continue to plague developing economies.

Challenges of crowdfunding

Despite the many strides and benefits of crowdfunding, its challenges must be carefully considered before embarking on its use for raising finance. The challenges of crowdfunding include inadequate knowledge of the phenomenon as well as lack of experience in its use. Others are information asymmetry, risk of fraud, theft of intellectual property and issues of ethics among others. Users must carefully consider these concerns before engaging in crowdfunding to ensure a favourable or successful outcome (Cohen 2017). The following are the major challenges in crowdfunding.

(i) Information asymmetry

As with conventional financing, information asymmetries in crowdfunding occur because investors do not have access to relevant information necessary to make investment decisions. Also, entrepreneurs fail to perform adequate research on the platforms employed in crowdfunding (Sannajust *et al.* 2014). A lack of transparency, credit ratings and a general lack of information on small businesses all compound the issues of information asymmetries in developing economies (Kshetri 2015). As a result of these, businesses without adequate plans and models can turn to crowdfunding and successfully raise capital. However, they will eventually fail with resultant loss of investment to contributors. Increased access to information in the public domain would, however, prevent or reduce losses (Sigar 2012).

One of the distinguishing features of crowdfunding is that it requires the business owner to make a significant amount of information available in the open forum (the internet) in order to encourage people to make financial contributions. Disclosure of pertinent information is required in order to reduce information asymmetry or fraud; however, doing so exposes the entrepreneur to the possibility that his idea will be stolen or copied by another party. Chapter 5 deals with information asymmetry in greater detail.

(ii) Issues of trust

The degree to which start-up entrepreneurs have an impression that various crowdfunding platforms are dependable, trustworthy and technologically competent is referred to as perceived trust (Lee *et al.* 2016). On a global scale, the success of crowdfunding campaigns is directly impacted by a variety of factors, one of the most important of which is trust. This is as a result of the fact that the platform entails the channelling of uncollateralized resources from small owners to finance a particular project or business endeavour via the internet without the need for an intermediary such as a bank. Users of crowdfunding platforms need to be able to have faith in the reliability and safety of platforms; this factor has been shown in a number of studies to have a beneficial influence on the amount of participation those users have in crowdfunding projects (Moon and Hwang 2018; Ya-Zheng *et al.* 2018).

Trust is an essential component for a successful business venture because it is highly improbable that the entrepreneur and the funder will ever meet. The issue of trust is further compounded by the phenomenon of crowdfunding given the investors' deeply ingrained belief in traditional sources of funding such as banks. People's intentions to support incentive-based initiatives and the actual quantity given were directly tied to trust in the project owner as well as the benefits that were on offer (Cholakova and Clarysse 2015; Moon and Hwang 2018; Islam and Khan 2019).

The level of trust and openness of crowdfunding platforms, in terms of post administration, are important variables driving the success of crowdfunding, while a lack of trust is viewed as an obstacle. It is possible to increase consumers' trust in crowdfunding by implementing security measures such as firewalls, allowing encrypted financial transactions, maintaining privacy seals and utilizing authentication methods (Gerber and Hui 2013). Tradition, religion and personal relationship between project owner and investor are also factors that can influence trust (Nor and Hashim 2020).

In light of these considerations, every platform and crowdfunding process must demonstrate to potential backers that it is trustworthy and reliable. This can be done by ensuring website security and prominently displaying the site's security features, as well as by providing full disclosures regarding the platform's terms and conditions and its past successes.

(iii) Theft of proprietary interests

Although all investments come with the risk of loss, crowdfunding investments may be riskier than traditional investments. This is because crowdfunding investments are often made in early-stage companies with little history or track record. Creating a crowdfunding site means advertising the business at its earliest stages. If the business has not copyrighted or patented its idea, it could risk having it stolen and if an imitator beats the business creator to the market, the business can be stolen.

Therefore, the risk of theft of business ideas and intellectual property becomes high as business information is displayed online during crowdfunding (Valanciene and Jegeleviciute 2013; Manchanda and Muralidharan 2014; Mancuso and Stuth 2014). Appropriate steps should therefore be put in place to secure copyrights, trademarks, patents and intellectual property when seeking funding through crowdfunding (Mancuso and Stuth 2014).

(iv) High cost of crowdfunding

The cost of crowdfunding is often in the form of a platform fee which is the charge when a crowdfunding site takes a percentage of all the money the entrepreneur raises through the fundraising. Therefore, it is important for the entrepreneur to also look out for punitive fee structures as some platforms increase fees if the project creator does not meet his/her goal.

Many entrepreneurs and potential crowdfunding users are unaware of the cost of crowdfunding and may rush into the process only to count their losses afterwards. According to Thomas (2014), the initial cost for a $50,000 offer is 23% plus 8% on-going annual costs. The initial and ongoing annual costs for a $750,000 offer are 15% and 4.4%, respectively. SEC filings and accountant fees, as well as administrative and internet platform fees, are additional transaction costs for equity issues (Mashburn 2013).

These additional costs raise the overall issue of transaction costs and therefore an impediment to the use and growth of crowdfunding (Thomas 2013). A streamlined process, on the other hand, could lower overall issue costs (Kitchens and Torrence 2012) and increase crowdfunding use. Potential users should also ensure they have taken due account of all relevant costs in order to have a successful outcome.

(v) Fraud and mal-practices

The possibility of fraud, on the other hand, grows as transactions are conducted over the internet. According to Gobble (2012) and Sigar (2012), the potential for fraud is increased as a result of relaxed restrictions and information asymmetry. The use of personal social networks in fundraising, on the other hand, reduces the impact of fraud. Internet platforms make no guarantees that founders will keep their promises. However, there is no evidence that entrepreneurs have been deceptive although the example of financial institutions such as Lehman Brothers and Bear Sterns stand in the way (Turan 2015).

While there is concern about fraud, the securities market is highly regulated. Mollick (2014) discovered that less than 5% of founders failed to deliver a product on time. The SEC has imposed restrictions that preclude those who do not qualify for funding from crowdfunding through the Exchange (Aronson 2013). Furthermore, internet platforms are not permitted to receive sales commissions (Levine and Feigin, 2014).

Due to the small investment amounts, legal action is unlikely, which means supporters have no legal recourse for fraudulent acts on the part of the founders (Mashburn 2013). Funders are urged to treat their investments as donations if founders fail to deliver. Padgett and Rolston (2014) illustrate the issue of ethics by using the case study of Amanda Palmer, an aspiring artist who raised $1.19 million on Kickstarter after asking for $100,000. The artist later admitted to spending the remaining funds on personal items after receiving the promised rewards, much to the chagrin of the associations. This exemplifies the ethical concerns around how entrepreneurs use raised capital, as well as the investors' right to refunds.

The proliferation of crowdfunding across the world is confronted with a significant obstacle in the form of fraud (Gabison 2015; Achsien and Purnamasari 2016). Renwick and Mossialos (2017), on the other hand, stated that despite the fact that fraud and money laundering represent a considerable risk, the acts are uncommon and do not significantly deter people from participating in crowdfunding. In developing economies however, the problem is made worse by the high number of people who use the internet and by legislation that is either non-existent or ineffective. According to Ibrahim (2019), the proliferation of the internet and the rise in the number of users have undoubtedly brought about their own set of unintended consequences, with cybercrime being responsible for as much as 43% of the total monetary loss in 2016.

A careful approach to investment of any type should be taken as a result of the accumulation of all of these factors, especially one that incorporates the use of the internet like crowdfunding does. Because of fraud the development and growth of crowdfunding as a source of finance for businesses is hindered. It is necessary to have the collaboration of individuals, corporate organizations and the government in order to cut down on fraud and any other sort of illegal abuse of the system (Aderemi *et al.* 2021). The trust of investors would increase, and their investments would be protected from potential losses, if appropriate rules were in place. It is also the responsibility of the owners of crowdfunding platforms to ensure compliance with all rules and ethics, as well as to implement necessary risk management in order to mitigate any and all risks that have been identified or discovered, in order to inspire confidence in additional investors.

The accumulation of fraud cases could damage the reputation of a platform and threaten the entire crowdfunding system and industry. As a result, it is absolutely necessary that platforms be managed in order to reduce the risk posed by the crowd. Crowdfunding for equity has garnered a lot of attention from regulators in recent years due to the fact that it involves the public offering of financial securities, which are an activity that is already heavily regulated. The expansion of crowdfunding is dependent on the existence of a regulatory climate that is favourable to the practice (Yeoh 2014). Regulations that are unique to equity crowdfunding have been enacted in a number of countries both to encourage the practice and to reduce the amount of risk that investors face (Hornuf and Schwienbacher 2017). A handful of countries, including France and the United Kingdom, have even proposed regulations for crowdfunding platforms that are based on loan offerings. Developing countries, especially those in Africa and the Middle East, are still in the process of developing enabling regulatory frameworks.

(vi) Lack of regulation

While crowdfunding regulations exist for the prosecution of crowdfunding activities in most developed nations such as the United States, the United Kingdom, Germany, France and the Netherlands, developing countries in the Middle East, Asia and Africa lack an adequate legal framework for its operation. In Asia and Africa, where laws have been enacted, the laws have been found to be deficient in numerous ways. Several laws, for instance, have imposed stringent requirements, necessitating the closure of numerous platforms unable to satisfy them. Others have imposed limits on the amounts that can be contributed by investors and raised by project owners, and this restriction has inadvertently excluded segments of the entrepreneurial market that would require greater funding otherwise. Although these regulations are intended to "protect the investor", they hinder the growth of crowdfunding as a credible alternative source of capital for entrepreneurs (Bolu 2016; Hornuf and Schwienbacher 2017; Kazaure and Abdullah 2018).

The maintenance and growth of the small and medium-sized business sector is generally recognized as an important policy priority in developing economies. As a result of this, the governments of these countries might think about regulating crowdfunding as a way to encourage innovation and entrepreneurship on their home environment. It is possible that one way to get to this level of development is to model it after the successes and failures of other nations in different parts of the world. In this regard, earlier research carried out in Europe demonstrated that the volume of overall crowdfunding activity per capita in a given market increased in direct proportion to the degree to which platforms operating within the same national market had the perception that the national regulation was adequate (Ziegler *et al*. 2019). To this day, no custom-tailored alternative finance regulation regime has been implemented in these markets, as has been the case in other, more established markets (Ziegler *et al*. 2018). Since there are no regulations that are specific to crowdfunding, businesses that want to provide services that fall within the scope of activities that are already covered by laws are subject to regulations that are general to the financial services industry. In spite of this, a number of regulatory initiatives that support innovation in the financial sector in general have been adopted by a variety of government agencies (Ziegler *et al*. 2018).

Notably, the majority of regulations are for the operation of equity-based crowd-funding, while donation- and reward-based crowdfunding, in which backers do not have a return to share or financial profits from the projects, do not have a significant impact. Nevertheless, Oguama (2020) proposed that donation-based crowdfunding should be regulated so that companies are restricted in particular instances, such as donations for political purposes, similar to what already exists in the developed economies of Europe and the United States of America.

(vii) High Taxation

The high tax rate presents business owners in developing economies with one of the most significant obstacles they must overcome (World Bank 2013; Okoyeuzu *et al.* 2019). In economies like these, the tax structure needs to be flexible enough to accommodate new projects if crowdfunding is going to take off (Amuna *et al.* 2017). It has been suggested that special tax exemptions and incentives be made available for securities that are issued through crowdfunding platforms, as this may encourage qualifying issuers to engage in crowdfunding transactions even more (Numa 2019).

(viii) Complex reporting/disclosure requirements

Apart from the lack of adequate regulation witnessed in many parts of the world regarding the phenomenon, crowdfunding faces additional challenges such as complex disclosure and reporting requirements (Gelfond and Foti 2012; Sannajust *et al.* 2014; Aronson 2013). This topic is dealt with in greater detail in Chapter 11.

(ix) Lack of time/resources

Entrepreneurs expend considerable time on projects which they could manage more effectively if they had the resources. Managing other crowdfunding-related matters such as securities, pricing, promotion and communication with investors can therefore be overwhelming. This thus constitutes a challenge to the crowdfund-ing process (Stemler 2013; Valanciene and Jegeleviciute 2013; Manchanda and Muralidharan 2014). Song and van Boeschoten (2015) observe that founders are unable to devote two days in a week to a campaign despite the fact that they test products in their social community. Williamson (2013) proposes that setting invest-ment minimums could simplify the administration of equity issues. Project owners must therefore weigh the benefits and drawbacks of crowdfunding in comparison to other funding alternatives.

(x) Lack of knowledge and experience

Crowdfunding is a novel idea using numerous platforms; creators may lack the knowledge or experience to use these platforms. The combination of lack of awareness, understanding and knowledge of the process results in a very low rate of success for project owners who use it to raise capital for their ventures. Consequently, those who attempted to use crowdfunding are unlikely to use it again due to the time and effort "waisted" in addition to the "beggar" feeling elicited (Song and van Boeschoten 2015).

(xi) Projects "lost at sea"

It is extremely challenging for the owners of smaller projects to garner serious attention on crowdfunding platforms because of the sheer volume of projects that are listed on these platforms. As a direct consequence of this, a great number of business owners have reported that their projects have been "lost at sea". This is especially true for small businesses that are beginning operations in traditional industries, as the majority of successful crowdfunding projects are in the fields of hardware, software, games and product design (Belleflamme *et al*. 2015). Even in today's day and age, there are still some business owners who believe that if they did not list their projects on crowdfunding platforms, others would take them more seriously (Gregory 2013). As a consequence of this, it is debatable whether or not crowdfunding can truly be considered a "game-changer" or an alternative source of financing for start-up businesses.

(xii) Small social networks

The great majority of initiatives rely on restricted social networks despite the fact that in theory these platforms allow everyone to access anyone, anywhere, at any time (Agrawal *et al*. 2015, Kazaure and Abdullah 2018)). This is not a novel occurrence; in fact, it is well-documented that close social networks are often the first source of funding for businesses (Lee and Persson 2016; Riding 2008; Shane and Cable 2002).

Project success depends on social networks, yet most creators know very little about this emerging trend. Because they are unable to predict the size of their social networks, many innovators fall short of fundraising goals (Hui *et al*. 2014). This is compounded by the social and professional stigma they face (Sangani 2014). Understanding network capabilities, activating network connections and extending network reach have been identified as the three primary problems faced by the creators (Hui *et al*. 2014). Creators must comprehend the capabilities offered by social networks and be able to use this potential to improve the success rate in their fundraising efforts.

(xiii) Lack of industry standard

There are no industry standards because the industry is still in its infant stage. A code of conduct has been published on the website of the United Kingdom Crowdfunding Association (www.ukcfa.org.uk/codeofpractice2), which was established in 2012 by 14 businesses that engage in crowdfunding. However, it has only provided basic guidelines on what crowdfunding platforms should do to ensure that project information is accessible to funders, particularly in the event that a platform fails. This is particularly important because of the potential for fraud associated with crowdfunding. There is not a single requirement that must be met in order to guarantee the uniqueness or quality of the projects. On the other hand, a number of nations are in the process of passing laws and regulations that will make the practice of crowdfunding more secure.

(xiv) Quality of new products

In an exploratory study, Mollick (2014) suggests that the level of quality of the projects being crowdfunded is a significant indicator of the level of success those projects will have. However, the projects that are funded through crowdfunding are extremely diverse, and there is neither a standard nor a tool that can be used to evaluate the quality of the projects. Funders can therefore only rely on virtual information such as the quality of the project video, the speed at which project updates are released, the size of the founders' online network (for example, the number of Facebook friends), and even the spelling errors in the project text in order to evaluate (and essentially second-guess) the quality of the projects, and then base their investment decisions on this information.

(xv) Information technology infrastructure

Access to the internet is crucial to the spread and uptake of online crowdfunding because it relies so heavily on social media and networking sites as well as web-based platforms. One of the biggest obstacles to the sector's growth is the poor state of internet connectivity in many parts of the world's developing economies. In comparison to the global average of 60.8% in May 2019, Africa's internet penetration rate was only 37.3% (Miniwatts Marketing Group 2019). Still, there are regional and national variations in penetration. Such conditions limit the crowdfunding ability of innovators and thus the growth of the phenomenon. The development of infrastructure is sine-qua-non to the growth of crowdfunding, particularly in developing economies of this world.

The problems of choosing the right platform

Choosing the right platform is crucial in crowdfunding and there are several things to consider when choosing the right platform. These include the number of visitors they attract, the type of visitors they attract, costs for running the campaign and their terms and conditions. Pong (2016) posits that entrepreneurs should understand that the choice of platform can impact on their chances of success. He suggests that to determine the "best" crowdfunding platform the following questions should be critically evaluated:

(i) What is the product offered?

The type of product or service offered by the entrepreneur is important in choosing the platform for crowdfunding as very few platforms take on all product or service categories.

For example, while Kickstarter can be used to raise money for creative projects, they do not accept campaigns that are raising funds for charities. Another factor is to determine the stage of the project (for example, if the project is still at a prototype stage or whether any of the products have been sold at all, and only needs funds for mass production). Pong (2016) argues that taking a half-finished concept or an idea to many crowdfunding platforms would simply not work.

(ii) Have similar projects been funded?

It is important to evaluate if the idea or genre is interesting to individuals outside your network. It is equally important to ensure that the platform caters to the audience targeted by the entrepreneur before starting the campaign. In other words, have similar projects been featured before on the chosen platform?

(iii) Which funding model and rewards available?

Crowdfunding sites run either rewards, donation, equity, lending or hybrid-based funding models. Therefore, it is important to understand how each one works, and the impact it will have on the business is also important.

(iv) How much exposure?

In choosing the right platform, the exposure the idea or the innovation has already had is crucial. However, if no one else has heard of the idea, it means choosing a platform that is willing to be the first stage in the marketing process.

(v) A cost-benefit analysis

A cost-benefit analysis is a process that helps one to determine the economic benefit of a decision. It is a useful tool when one wants to avoid bias in deciding the right platform to pitch a crowdfunding campaign. It provides a quantitative view of an issue, so one can make decisions based on evidence rather than opinion or bias. With the data gathered, it is necessary to carry out a cost-benefit analysis of each platform to see which platform suits the project best. It is important to note that the crowdfunding platform chosen can have a significant impact on the result.

The problems of building up interest

Building interest before a project launch is also another type of challenge in the crowdfunding experience. Pong (2016) argues that it is the biggest mistake for businesses to create their campaign first and then try to generate interest. Instead, Pong 2016 suggests that there is need to build interest in the campaign at least three to four months before launching the campaign. This will help in getting an initial large boost to the campaign. The following are ways to build up interest for a successful crowdfunding campaign:

(i) Marketing the crowdfunding campaign

Marketing the crowdfunding campaign is central to its success. The crowdfunding platform only hosts the project but promoting the campaign is the responsibility of the entrepreneurs before it starts. Before the launching of the campaign the entrepreneurs should use social media, press, networking, exhibitions, local radio and promotional materials to create a buzz around the project. It might be ideal for the project creator to have a number of interested investors ready to back the project right from the first day of the campaign. It is also very important to plan promotion of the crowdfunding campaign during the campaign as it may go quiet after the initial launch.

(ii) Gaining social proof for the project

In order to build interest for the campaign it is advisable to talk to friends and family about the project to see whether they are willing to invest in the project. If friends and family are unwilling to invest, it is unlikely that investors with competitive projects would be interested in the project. Therefore, a feedback from friends and family is important to learn from it.

However, if friends and family are interested in investing, then that can be a great sign that the idea is a good one. It is also advisable to ensure that the friends and family are ready to start funding the project on the first day of the crowdfunding campaign. This will help to create interest around the project and can encourage other potential backers to invest.

(iii) Researching similar projects for inspiration and tips

It is essential to research similar past project campaigns whether successful or unsuccessful in order to see what worked and what did not work. Most crowdfunding platforms do not usually take down campaigns once they have finished, thus providing a great opportunity to carry out research and learn from them.

(iv) Creating a video that captures the target audience and promotes the project clearly

Creating a video that captures the audience and promotes the project is a good way of building interest in the campaign. The video should be interesting and clearly present the benefits of the project to the target audience. The content of the video can also be used for future marketing opportunities.

(v) Communicating effectively and honestly with backers and potential backers

To build interest around the campaign and the project, it is important to communicate clearly about what the project is about, what it is trying to achieve, how much money is needed to make it a reality and what will be delivered and when. Communication includes keeping backers up to date with the product and whether or not previous deadlines can be met. It is being honest with the backers.

(vi) Being creative with rewards

It is important to be clear about any rewards for potential backers. It is essential to let them know what is in it for them and to make it as interesting as possible. It is advisable to offer different rewards for different levels of investment. This can encourage a potential backer to add more to their investment.

Avoiding/minimizing crowdfunding minefields

In order to preserve the dependability and good intentions underlying crowdfunding in the developing economies, Aderemi *et al.* (2021) propose a framework consisting of three pillars:

(i) Regulation

Regulation is the foundation of crowdfunding, and as such, crowdfunding intermediaries have a responsibility to ensure the safety of their customers as new laws come into effect. Standards for financial and operational transparency, the protection of data and payments, financial control, the performance of the platform and operational procedures to prevent and identify fraudulent activity are some of the things that fall under this category.

(ii) Education

It is generally accepted that in order to strengthen the dependability of crowdfunding, backers, creators and all stakeholders need to be educated on the advantages of the institution as a whole and the various forms it can take. This is a fundamental tenet. These parameters will be responsible for establishing a fair and suitable guide to protect the financial interests, diversification and exposure of investors and investees across a variety of crowdfunding strategies. This will be accomplished by ensuring that the guide is fair and suitable. In addition to this, it is helpful to provide management with information on fraud, clarifications of risk and possibly testing of investor comprehension.

(iii) Research

Considered a source of inspiration for educational and intermediary research, the third pillar focuses on making data and information accessible in order to facilitate the industry's open and transparent development requirements. This, it is argued, will further increase the competitiveness of the crowdfunding industry.

A case study of Bubble and Balm: when equity crowdfunding goes wrong

Bubble and Balm was a fair-trade soap company. In 2011 it became the first company to raise funding for its start-up through the equity crowdfunding platform Crowdcube, based in the UK. It raised £75,000 from 82 investors, who each contributed between £10 and £7,500 in return for 15% of the company's equity. In July 2013 the business closed overnight, leaving investors with no way of contacting the company or to recover losses. The investors lost 100% of their investment.

What does this mean for the crowdfunding industry, the fastest growing investment sector in the country? The collapse serves as a timely reminder of the inherent risks associated with investing in start-ups, but should not reflect negatively on the equity crowdfunding market generally.

Start-ups will fail regardless of their fundraising. The important issue here is that small investors are treated appropriately and have their rights adequately safeguarded. There should be openness and transparency, and structures and post-transaction services that protect the interests of investors should be implemented to the fullest extent possible. This means the implementation of robust measures to ensure that investors are aware of the risks involved with investing in start-ups, and place restrictions on the amount individuals can invest to ensure that they will never lose more than they can afford.

Failure is a fact of life and investors should crowdfund with full knowledge of the risks involved and ensure that they stick to the golden rule of investing which is diversification.

Source: Kirby and Worner (2014).

Summary

With the advent of the internet, crowdfunding has emerged as a viable alternative fundraising method that has gained traction globally over time. It has contributed to the expansion of businesses and provides business owners with a great deal of freedom when seeking to raise capital. It is interesting to note that the expansion of crowdfunding as a source of financing faces a number of obstacles in many countries, particularly in the developing economies of South America, the Middle East and Africa, which have a large population and significant economic growth opportunities. These include issues with regulation, insufficient levels of awareness and comprehension and rampant fraud and corruption. Significant efforts to regulate the crowdfunding industry are widely acknowledged and praised. However, the sector should not be subject to an excessive amount of regulation in order to avoid discouraging participation and stifling development. In a similar vein, there is an urgent need for increased public understanding of crowdfunding and an environment that facilitates the system's operation.

In these developing markets, the ability of crowdfunding to deliver on its promises of improved access to finance and growth enablement is still something that needs to be proven. Despite this, crowdfunding may become more widespread due to the growing popularity of digital and mobile finance, the low penetration of traditional financial institutions and a long cultural tradition of communal mutual aid. On the other hand, a lack of regulation or regulation that is inadequate, a lack of technological infrastructure such as access to the internet, and societies with low levels of social trust may all be factors that prevent the widespread use of crowdfunding. As a result, in order for there to be a larger-scale adoption of crowdfunding by the general public, the various stakeholders may need to participate in the formulation of pertinent regulations and policies, the implementation of technological solutions, the raising of public awareness and ongoing research. Crowdfunding will experience enhanced growth as a result of these, allowing it to play an even more significant role as an alternative source of financing for businesses.

Discussion questions

1 List the different problems/challenges encountered by entrepreneurs seeking crowdfunding.
2 Discuss the problems associated with choosing the right crowdfunding platform and how these can be overcome.
3 In order to preserve the dependability and good intentions underlying crowdfunding in developing economies, Aderemi *et al.* (2021) propose a framework consisting of three pillars. Identify and discuss these pillars.

Test questions

1 If you fail at your first crowdfunding trial, how might it affect your reputation?
2 How can you protect your idea from being stolen on a platform?
3 Building trust among investors is one of the key challenges of crowdfunding. How can you overcome this problem?

Glossary of key terminologies

Adoption   The acceptance, integration and use of crowdfunding technology.
Discrimination   The recognition and understanding of the difference between one thing and another.
Diversification   A growth strategy that involves entering into a new market or industry.
Financial crisis   Any of a broad variety of situations in which some financial assets suddenly lose a large part of their nominal value.
Firewalls   A system designed to block unauthorized access.
Globalization   The process by which businesses or organizations develop international influence.

Infrastructure The basic physical and organizational structures and facilities needed for the operation of society or enterprise.

Intellectual property Refers to creations of the mind, such as inventions; literary and artistic works.

Intermediary One who acts as a link between people in order to try and bring about an agreement.

Penetration The extent to which a phenomenon is recognized and accepted.

SEC Security and Exchange Commission.

Stakeholders A person with an interest or concern in something.

Tenet A principle, doctrine or belief generally believed to be true.

Transparency The quality of being easy to perceive or detect.

Recommended reading

Aderemi, A.M., Maulida, S., and Maikabara, A.A., 2021. Prospects and challenges of crowdfunding as an alternative funding option in Nigeria. *Muqtasid: Jurnal Ekonomi dan Perbankan Syariah*, 12 (1), 17–31.

Gerber, E.M., and Hui, J., 2013. Crowdfunding: Motivations and deterrents for participation. *ACM Transactions on Computer-Human Interaction*, 20 (6), 1–32. Available from: https://doi.org/10.1145/2530540

Sigar, K., 2012. Fret no more: inapplicability of crowdfunding concerns in the internet age and the JOBS Act's safeguards. *Administrative Law Review*, 473–506.

Valanciene, L., and Jegeleviciute, S., 2013. Valuation of crowdfunding: Benefits and drawbacks. *Economics and Management*, 18 (1), 39–48.

References

Achsien, I.H., and Purnamasari, D.L., 2016. Islamic crowd-funding as the next financial innovation in Islamic finance: Potential and anticipated regulation in Indonesia. *European Journal of Islamic Finance*, 5.

Aderemi, A.M., Maulida, S., and Maikabara, A.A., 2021. Prospects and challenges of crowdfunding as an alternative funding option in Nigeria. *Muqtasid: Jurnal Ekonomi dan Perbankan Syariah*, 12 (1), 17–31.

Agrawal, A., Catalini, C., and Goldfarb, A., 2015. Crowdfunding: Geography, social networks, and the timing of investment decisions. *Journal of Economics & Management Strategy*, 24 (2), 253–274.

Amuna, Y.M.A., Al Shobaki, M.J., Naser, S.S.A., and El Talla, S.A., 2017. Crowdfunding as one of the recent trends in financing emerging and small projects in the Arab World. *International Journal of Business Engineering and Management Systems*, 1, 1–16.

Aronson, D.H., 2013. SEC rule changes signal new regulatory environment for private securities offerings. *Corporate Finance Review*, (September/October), 13–24.

Belleflamme, P., Omrani, N., and Peitz, M., 2015. The economics of crowdfunding platforms. *Information Economics and Policy*, 33, 11–28.

Bolu, I., November 2016. Crowdfunding in Nigeria. *SPA Ajibade and Co*. Available from: www.spaajibade.com/resources/crowd-funding-in-nigeria/

Boum, E., 2016. *Crowdfunding in Africa: Fundraising goes digital in Africa – The emergence of Africa-based crowdfunding platforms*. Available from: http://afrikstart.com/report/wp-content/uploads/2016/09/Afrikstart-Crowdfunding-In-Africa-Report.pdf [Accessed 27 April 2019].

Chao, E.J., Serwaah, P., Baah-Peprah, P., and Shneor, R., 2020. Crowdfunding in Africa: opportunities and challenges. *Advances in Crowdfunding*, 319–339.

Cholakova, M., and Clarysse, B., 2015. Does the possibility to make equity investments in crowdfunding projects crowd out reward – Based investments? *Entrepreneurship theory and Practice*, 39 (1), 145–172.

Cohen, M., 2017. *Crowdfunding as a financing resource for small businesses* (Walden dissertations and Doctoral Studies Collection). Available from: https://scholarworks. waldenu.edu/dissanddoc?utm_source=scholarworks.waldenu.edu%2Fdissertations% 2F3757&utm_medium=PDF&utm_campaign=PDFCoverPages

Gabison, G., 2015. *Venture capital principles in the European ICT ecosystem: How can they help ICT innovation?* (No. JRC98783). Joint Research Centre (Seville site). UR 27651 EN; doi:10.2791/6709

Gelfond, S.H., and Foti, A.D., 2012. US $500 and a click: Investing the "crowdfunding" way. *Journal of Investment Compliance*, 13 (4), 9–13.

Gerber, E.M., and Hui, J., 2013. Crowdfunding: Motivations and deterrents for participation. *ACM Transactions on Computer-Human Interaction*, 20 (6), 1–32. Available from: https://doi.org/10.1145/2530540

Gobble, M.A.M., 2012. Everyone is a venture capitalist: The new age of crowdfunding. *Research Technology Management*, 55 (4), 4–7.

Gregory, M., 2013. *The start-ups struggling to make a name through crowdfunding*. Available from: http://www.bbc.co.uk/news/business- 25403081 [Accessed 12 January 2023].

Hendratmi, A., Sukmaningrum, P.S., Hadi, M.N., and Ratnasari, R.T., 2019. The role of Islamic crowdfunding mechanisms in business and business development. *Global Journal for Business & Social Science Review*, 7 (1), 1–7.

Hornuf, L., and Schwienbacher, A., 2017. Should securities regulation promote equity crowdfunding? *Small Business Economics*, 49 (3), 579–593.

Hui, J.S., Gerber, E.M., and Gergle, D., 2014. Understanding and leveraging social networks for crowdfunding: Opportunities and challenges. *In: Proceedings of the 2014 conference on designing interactive systems*. DIS 2014, 21–25 June. Vancouver, BC, Canada, 677–680. Available from: http://dx.doi.org/10.1145/2598510.2598539

Ibrahim, U., 2019. The impact of cybercrime on the Nigerian economy and banking system. *NDIC Quarterly*, 34 (12). 1–20.

Islam, T.M., and Khan, T.A., 2019. Factors influencing the adoption of crowdfunding in Bangladesh: A study of start-up entrepreneurs. *Information Development*, 37 (1), 72–89. Available from: https://doi.org/10.1177/0266666919895554

Kazaure, M.A., and Abdullah, A.R., 2018. Crowdfunding as financial option for small and medium enterprises (SMEs) in Nigeria. *Pertanika Journal of Scholarly Research Reviews*, 4 (3), 89–96.

Kirby, E., and Worner, S., 2014. *Crowd-funding: An infant industry growing fast* [Staff Working Paper: [SWP3/2014]]. Madrid: IOSCO.

Kitchens, R., and Torrence, P.D., 2012. The JOBS Act-crowdfunding and beyond. *Economic Development Journal*, 11 (4), 42–47.

Koch, J.A., and Siering, M., 2015. Crowdfunding success factors: The characteristics of successfully funded projects on crowdfunding platforms. *In: Proceedings of the 23rd European conference on information systems (ECIS 2015)*, Muenster: SSRN, 1–15.

Kshetri, N., 2015. Success of crowd-based online technology in fundraising: An institutional perspective. *Journal of International Management*, 21 (2), 100–116.

Lee, H.S., 2016. Effect of perceived risk, perceived benefit, and Korea wave to crowdfunding participation in China. *The Journal of the Korea Contents Association*, 16, 204–213.

Lee, S., and Persson, P., 2016. Financing from family and friends. *The Review of Financial Studies*, 29 (9), 2341–2386.

Levine, M.L., and Feigin, P.A., 2014. Crowdfunding provisions under the new rule 506 (c). *The CPA Journal*, 84 (6), 46–51.

Ley, A., and Weaven, S., 2011. Exploring agency dynamics of crowdfunding in start-up capital financing. *Academy of Entrepreneurship Journal*, 17 (1), 85.

Manchanda, K., and Muralidharan, P., 2014. Crowdfunding: A new paradigm in start-up financing. *In*: *Global conference on business & finance proceedings* (Vol. 9, No. 1). Pilani, Dubai Campus: Institute for Business & Finance Research, Birla Institute of Technology & Science, 369.

Mancuso, J., and Stuth, K., 2014. Storytelling and marketing: The perfect pairing? Sharing your 'brand selfie' on social media. *Marketing Insights*, 26 (3), 18–19.

Mashburn, D., 2013. The anti-crowd pleaser: Fixing the crowdfund act's hidden risks and inadequate remedies. *Emory Law Journal*, 63, 127.

Massolution, 2012. *Crowdfunding industry report*, 1–30. Available from: http://ncfacanada. org/wp-content/uploads/2012/10/Massolution-Full-Industry-Report.pdf

Massolution, C.L., 2015. *Crowdfunding industry report*. Available from: http://reports.crowd-sourcing.org/index.php?route=product/product&product_id=54 [Accessed 12 January 2023].

Miniwatts Marketing Group, 2019. Internet World stats [Online]. *Miniwatts Marketing Group*. Available from: www.internetworldstats.com/stats1.htm [Accessed 5 June 2019].

Mollick, E., 2014. The dynamics of crowdfunding: An exploratory study. *Journal of Business Venturing*, 29 (1), 1–16.

Moon, Y., and Hwang, J., 2018. Crowdfunding as an alternative means for funding sustainable appropriate technology: Acceptance determinants of backers. *Sustainability*, 10 (5), 1456.

Nor, S.M., and Hashim, N.A., 2020. Trust motivates funders to participate in Shari'ah crowdfunding. *Geografia*, 16 (2).

Numa, T., 2019. *Modern technology meets capital raising – Cool cash for small businesses*. Available from: www.acedemia.edu

Oguama, L., 2020. *FinTech credit market – Crowdfunding: An evaluation of market models*. *SSRN Electronic Journal*, 3696044, 1–13.

Okoyeuzu, C., Nwakoby, I., and Onwujekwe, O., 2019. Crowdfunding: An alternative to funding women entrepreneurs. *South Asian Journal of Social Studies and Economics*, 5 (2), 1–10. Available from: https://doi.org/10.9734/sajsse/2019/v5i230140

Ordanini, A., Miceli, L., Pizzetti, M., and Parasuraman, A., 2011. Crowd-funding: Transforming customers into investors through innovative service platforms. *Journal of Service Science and Management*, 22, 443–470.

Oruezabala, G., and Peter, S.G., 2016. Equity crowdfunding in Africa: How can investment micro-behaviors make the crowdfunding macro-system work? *In*: J. Méric, I. Maque and J. Brabet, eds. *International perspectives on crowdfunding*. Bingley: Emerald Group Publishing Limited.

Padgett, B.L., and Rolston, C., 2014. Crowd funding: A case study at the intersection of social media and business ethics. *Journal of the International Academy for Case Studies*, 20 (3), 61–66.

Pong, E., 2016. *How to find the best crowd funding source*. Available from: www.floship. com/blog/_find-best-crowd-funding-source/ [Accessed 12 January 2023].

Renwick, M.J., and Mossialos, E., 2017. Crowdfunding our health: Economic risks and benefits. *Social Science & Medicine*, 191, 48–56.

Riding, A.L., 2008. Business angels and love money investors: Segments of the informal market for risk capital. *Venture Capital*, 10, 355–369. https://doi.org/10.1080/13691060802351222

Sangani, K., 2014. Wisdom of crowds [crowdfunding]. *Engineering & Technology*, 9 (3), 82–83.

Sannajust, A., Roux, F., and Chaibi, A., 2014. Crowdfunding in France: A new revolution? *Journal of Applied Business Research (JABR)*, 30 (6), 1919–1928.

Schwienbacher, A., Larralde, B., and Cumming, D., 2012. *The Oxford Handbook of Entrepreneurial Finance*. Baskı. Londra: Oxford.

Shane, S., and Cable, D., 2002. Network ties, reputation, and the financing of new ventures. *Management Science*, 48 (3), 364–381.

Sigar, K., 2012. Fret no more: Inapplicability of crowdfunding concerns in the internet age and the JOBS Act's safeguards. *Administrative Law Review*, 473–506.

Song, Y., and van Boeschoten, R., 2015. Success factors for Crowdfunding founders and funders. *arXiv preprint arXiv:1503.00288*.

Stemler, A.R., 2013. The JOBS Act and crowdfunding: Harnessing the power – And money – Of the masses. *Business Horizons*, 56 (3), 271–275.

Thomas, J., 2013. Making equity crowdfunding work for the unaccredited crowd. *Harvard Business Law Review, Online*, 4 (2014), 62–75.

Turan, S., 2015. Financial Innovation – Crowdfunding: Friend or Foe? *Procedia – Social and Behavioral Sciences*, 195 (2015), 353–362.

Valanciene, L., and Jegeleviciute, S., 2013. Valuation of crowdfunding: Benefits and drawbacks. *Economics and Management*, 18 (1), 39–48.

Williamson, J.J., 2013. The JOBS act and middle-income investors: Why it doesn't go far enough. *Yale Law Journal*, 122, 2069–2080.

Wolf, C., 2017. From harambee to modern crowdfunding: The opportunities and challenges in sub-saharan Africa. *In*: D.T. Redford, ed. *Developing Africa's financial services: The importance of high-impact entrepreneurship*. Bingley: Emerald Publishing Ltd.

World Bank., 2013. *Crowdfunding's potential for the developing world*. Washington, DC: InfoDev. Finance and Private Sector Development Department.

The World Bank Group, 2015. *Crowdfunding in emerging markets: Lessons from East African start-ups*. Washington, DC: The World Bank Group.

Ya-Zheng, L., Tong-Liang, H., Yi-Ran, S., Zheng, Y., and Rong-Ting, Z., 2018. Factors impacting donors' intention to donate to charitable crowd-funding projects in China: A UTAUT-based model. *Information, Communication & Society*, 21 (3), 404–415.

Yeoh, P., 2014. Implications of online funding regulations for small businesses. *Journal of Financial Regulation and Compliance*, 22 (4), 349–364.

Ziegler, T., Shneor, R., Wenzlaff, K., *et al.*, 2019. *Shifting paradigms – The 4th European alternative finance benchmarking report*. Cambridge: Cambridge Centre for Alternative Finance.

Ziegler, T., Suresh, K., Garvey, K., *et al.*, 2018. *The 2nd annual Middle East & Africa alternative finance industry report*. Cambridge: Cambridge Center for Alternative Finance.

9 The role of social relationships and networking in sourcing crowdfunding

Learning objectives

- Examine the role of social relationships and networks in crowdfunding
- Distinguish between social network and business network
- Explore the role of networking in equity crowdfunding
- Discuss the theoretical perspectives of networks in crowdfunding
- Discuss network dynamics in crowdfunding

Introduction

Crowdfunding involves raising small amounts of money from a large number of people, typically via the internet and social networks, to fund a project. In crowdfunding, projects are mainly funded by the project creator's relatively small network of family and friends (Borst *et al.* 2018). Borst *et al.* (2018) argue that mobilizing funders outside this close network positively contributes to the success of crowdfunding.

This chapter analyzes entrepreneurial networks by examining both personal and business networks involved in the crowdfunding process. The chapter explores how networks and social capital play a critical role in the crowdfunding process. Business start-ups leverage, build and draw upon a complex array of network actors and "ties" as they move through the different stages of their crowdfunding journey (Brown *et al* 2019). Brown *et al.* (2019, p. 1) suggest that this form of funding confers important relational benefits to recipients which amount to "more than money". They argue that equity crowdfunding is a highly "relational" form of entrepreneurial finance, requiring holistic forms of empirical investigation.

Social relationship and networking in crowdfunding

The network theory suggests that entrepreneurial growth depends on the set of network relationships (comprising customers, suppliers, competitors, support agencies, family and friends). The theory suggests that firms do not exist in isolation but are part of networks that are industry, market, location or customer related as well as a kind of give-and-take process that occurs in networks (Ekanem 2018). There

DOI: 10.4324/9781003193975-9

are two main theoretical perspectives in the study of entrepreneurial networks: social network and business network.

(i) Social (or personal) network

The social network theory is rooted in sociological literature and is often linked to the seminal work of Granovetter (1973). Social network comprises family members, friends and close acquaintances. The social network approach attempts to measure the impact of an individual's network ties (Brown *et al*. 2019). Granovetter (1973, p. 1361) postulates that "the strength of a tie is a (probably linear) combination of the amount of time, the emotional intensity, the intimacy (mutual confiding), and the reciprocal services which characterize the tie". In his earlier work, Granovetter focused on the role of informal ties in individuals' employment prospects, observing that weak ties with acquaintances such as an "old college friend or a former workmate" play an instrumental role in facilitating information to the "job changer" (Granovetter 1973, p. 1371). Generally, the social network literature places a special importance on the identification and measurement of such ties and network characteristics (Brown *et al*. (2019).

The social network perspective has been empirically examined in the wider entrepreneurial literature and widely accepted theoretically (Leyden *et al*. 2014; Street and Cameron 2007). Hence there is a continued interest in the role of network and social capital in entrepreneurship (Gedajlovic *et al*. 2013). For instance, Kontinen and Ojala (2011) studied the internationalization of family-owned SMEs and found that new weak network ties, often formed at international trade fairs, were very important, whereas family ties were less important. Similarly, empirical work in this regard indicate that different types of ties promote different types of knowledge transfer and learning between bank relationship managers and customers (Brown *et al*. 2019; Uzzi and Lancaster 2003).

However, social network theory has been critiqued with regard to its static nature and lack of its transitive dimension to network analysis (Slotte-Kock and Coviello 2010). Granovetter (1973, p. 1378) point out that focusing only on ties' strength ignores important issues concerning "content" and "network structure over time". This means that other important aspects such as the types of network ties, the relational nature of ties and the role of network ties can be overlooked. Brown *et al*. (2019) add that the temporality of network formation and engagement has also been ignored.

(ii) Business network

Business networks consist of customers, suppliers, competitors, support agencies. The business network perspective is a much more dynamic approach than the social network to studying networks and it focuses on how relationships change and why such change occurs (Brown *et al*. 2019). In researching business networks, Slotte-Kock and Coviello (2010, p. 44) suggest that network development is cumulative because relationships are "continually established, maintained and developed". Similarly, various researchers such as Freytag and Ritter (2005), Hakansson and Snehota (1989), Mattsson (1997), and Ritter *et al.* (2004) have considered interaction between parties to be crucial. Hakansson *et al.* (1999) argue that the connectedness of a business relationship suggests that the boundary of a single such relationship can become blurred. Therefore, firms are embedded in networks "of ongoing business and non-business relationships, which both enable and constrain" performance (Ritter *et al.* 2004 p. 175). In this regard, business networks have been shown to be fundamental in terms of efficiency and development goals of many businesses (Baraldi 2008; Brown *et al.* 2019).

The differences between social network theory and business network theory

As discussed earlier, there are clearly differences between social networks and business networks. Brown *et al.* (2019) suggest that while most researchers have typically examined networks from one or the other of these perspectives, there seems to be merit in a combinative approach towards network analysis, especially given the limitations in both approaches (Slotte-Kock and Coviello 2010). Consequently, Brown *et al.* (2019) argue that while the social network approach views networks as having distinctive boundaries which are mediated by the varying strength of ties, the business network viewpoint is more holistic and views the broader context within which inter-organizational networks exist and the external influences shaping them. Another point of difference is that the business network literature often focuses on established organizations; thereby overlooking the initial nature of ties addressed by the social network literature, which are critical in alleviating resource scarcity as firms commence trading (Brown *et al.* 2019).

The differences between social network (SN) and business network (BN) are illustrated in Table 9.1 with regards to their attributes.

Brown *et al.* (2019) suggest that the distinction is important when examining entrepreneurship, where change is often endogenous as firms grow and networks evolve. They argue that as new ventures grow, the entrepreneur's external orientation increases to obtain external resources such as finance, sources of innovation, human capital, new customers, etc. Consequently, as firms expand, personal networks also expand, transforming into wider overlapping webs of multi-layered exchange relationships. In the longer run, the success of the new business will depend more on the networking activities of the whole organization than that of an individual entrepreneur (Brown *et al* 2019).

Research studies (for example, Gluckler 2007, p. 624) have found an "accumulative advantage" for well networked actors and a corresponding "liability of un-connectedness" for peripheral actors. In other words, inter-personal networks can become inter-organizational networks, which requires an integrated focus combining both personal and business networks to properly ascertain how new ventures grow and evolve (Brown *et al.* 2019).

Table 9.1 Differences between social network and business network

Attributes	Social network theory	Business network theory
Antecedents	Rooted in early sociological literature by Granovetter (1973).	Derived from the industrial marketing literature on buyer–supplier relationships (Hakansson and Snehota 1989).
Nature of theory	The SN perspective focuses on personal networks and the qualitative differences between different types of ties (e.g. strong and weak).	The BN perspective is a more dynamic systemic approach, focusing on how networks change and why change occurs.
Relevance to entrepreneurship	Extant literature within the field of entrepreneurship reveals that personal networks are crucial to the launch of new ventures, especially for alleviating informational barriers. In other words, the SN perspective helps us to better understand the creation of start-ups.	The BN viewpoint tends to be applied to growing firms. Growing firms seek greater tangible resources such as finance, premises and customer access. To obtain these resources, entrepreneurs need to tap into wider and less relationally bounded networks. In other words, the BN perspective helps shed light on how start-ups grow.
Limitations of the literature	A core limitation of the SN perspective is a lack of recognition of how social network ties change over time. The relational nature and role of ties is often overlooked.	The BN literature often focuses on established organizations and thereby overlooks the initial nature of ties, which help to alleviate resource scarcity as firms commence trading.

Source: Brown *et al.* 2019.

Networking and equity crowdfunding

Finance is a critical resource for start-ups and networking can be helpful in this regard. Brown *et al.* (2019) argue that while most empirical work in the network literature has examined access to intangible resources such as advice and information, much less work has been devoted to harder resources such as finance, which is arguably one of the most critical resources for early stage businesses. However, the importance of networking in accessing funding cannot be over-emphasized. This is borne out by evidence from the majority of research studies which suggests that networks heavily mediate access to both debt and equity finance in smaller firms (Hellmann *et al.* 2008; Seghers *et al.* 2012; Uzzi and Gillespie 2002) and play a vital role in coordinating and facilitating interactions between new ventures and funders (Shane and Cable 2002).

Networks are particularly important within equity finance, as it often involves close interpersonal relationships between entrepreneurs and the general investors (Brown *et al.* 2019). Equity funding is often regarded as a disintermediated process where relational connections are more important than anything else because funding oftentimes comes from funders who are within the network of those seeking funding (Drover *et al.* 2017).

In this vein, Borst *et al.* (2018, p. 1397) differentiate between "friendfunding" and "greater distance funding" and suggest that the background of the funders matters for two reasons: First, "friendfunding" consists of funding by family members, friends and close acquaintances. Second, funding is often derived from people at a greater distance (Agrawal *et al.* 2015) since "friendfunding" networks cannot provide all the required funding (Mollick 2014). Mollick (2014) suggests that in those circumstances project creators will benefit when their call for funding also reaches people beyond their existing social network of family and friends. Davidson and Poor (2016) argue that reaching unknown, distant funders becomes more significant for crowdfunding projects with higher target amounts or when the project creator wants to start another crowdfunding project and does not want to approach previous backers.

The network dynamics in crowdfunding

There is little knowledge about the dynamics of successful crowdfunding despite the growing popularity of crowdfunding (Ahlers *et al.* 2015; Mollick 2014). Therefore, in order to fully understand the dynamics of networks in crowdfunding, especially equity crowdfunding, it is necessary to examine the differences in phases of the crowdfunding process. Brown *et al.* (2019) posit that networks undergo substantial changes during the crowdfunding process, which suggests an integrative approach when examining how different network ties form, adapt and reconfigure over time. Network dynamics are very important in the crowdfunding process as each phase of the process focusses on different aspects of the interaction and network development. Brown *et al.* (2019) distinguish three phases of the crowdfunding process, namely, pre-crowdfunding, active crowdfunding and post-crowdfunding.

(i) Pre-crowdfunding phase

At this phase of the crowdfunding process, personal networks dominate which constitute "powerful network enablers" which strongly influence and encourage "entrepreneurs to pursue equity crowdfunding" (Brown *et al.* 2019, p. 27). The personal networks at this stage consist of mostly families, friends, current investors, business advisors and peers that exhibit strong ties. Brown *et al.* (2019) indicate that the referral process at this phase is through "word of mouth" which is the key aspect of the crowdfunding process. The interactions and strong ties within the personal and professional networks help to diminish any concerns (Brown *et al.* 2019) and also help entrepreneurs manage any ambiguity (Ciabuschi *et al.* 2012).

According to Brown *et al.* (2019), the pre-crowdfunding phase is the most crucial aspect of the equity crowdfunding process, because failure to engage with the right kind of networks can undermine the success of the whole campaign. Also, at this phase of the process, close ties can be formed between the platforms and the entrepreneurs because of repeated interactions during the due diligence processes undertaken. As a result of "this recursive process the entrepreneurs become passionate supporters of the platforms. Indeed, through this self-confirming and prosocial behaviour amongst crowdfunded entrepreneurs, many become advocates of the process who then proceed to help other firms with their campaigns" (Brown *et al.* 2019, p. 27).

The shaping of pre-crowdfunding network interactions has been attributed to spatial proximity which tends to take place either with personal networks or other start-ups. Brown *et al.* (2019) suggest that close proximity and repeated exposure to crowdfunding platforms also seemed to foster network ties which are leveraged by entrepreneurs (for example, through their established connections with business angels) to help them to raise finance via crowdfunding.

(ii) Active crowdfunding phase

At this phase of the crowdfunding process, business networks become more important than the social/personal networks. Brown *et al.* (2019) found that at this phase in the process, entrepreneurs focus less on their existing ties and engage more with new ties on the crowdfunding platform mainly because of the nature and volume of information received at this stage of the crowdfunding campaign. This is not to say that strong ties are no longer important. They still remain important but only for moral support rather than for strategic guidance.

It is important to emphasize that at this phase of the crowdfunding process, business network ties are predominantly weak, such as customers and suppliers, but are considered crucial to enable entrepreneurs to successfully achieve their target funding (Brown *et al.* 2019).

(iii) Post-crowdfunding phase

At this phase of the crowdfunding process, the dynamic changes again with the relational mix of ties (Lechner *et al.* 2006) indicating that the role of networks is flexible and transient as against inherent long-lasting relationships (Andersen and Medlin 2016). Brown *et al.* (2019) suggest that during this phase, the focus of entrepreneurs shifts to harnessing weak business network ties, particularly connections with new investors. At this phase,

> previously weak ties, such as links to new investors (both large and small), begin to change and solidify . . . due to increased interactions between the firm and their new investors, drawing on new shareholders as sources of advice, co-creators of new knowledge, brand ambassadors and new customers.
> (Brown *et al.* 2019 p. 29)

In this phase of the crowdfunding process, strong ties become a channel through which weak ties develop.

Relational benefits of networks in crowdfunding

There are numerous relational and network benefits arising from networks in the crowdfunding process. The main benefit of the entrepreneurial networks in crowdfunding is the organizational legitimacy it confers on a new venture, which mitigates the liability of newness (Brown *et al.* 2019; Frydrych *et al.* 2014; Colombo *et al.* 2015). Since platforms conduct due diligence in advance of launching a campaign, a listing on a crowdfunding platform sends out a positive signal of legitimacy to potential investors such as "reputational networks" (Lechner and Dowling 2003), "trust facilitation" (Hite 2005) or "more than money" (Brown *et al.* 2019). Welter and Smallbone (2006) argue that the signal legitimacy increases the level of trust for potential investors especially for new ventures with information opacity. The positive signalling connects ventures with a wide range of other potential investors, especially business angels (Ahlers *et al.* 2015; Brown *et al.* 2019; Hsu 2004), which can also provide future investment opportunities.

Other forms of benefits of the entrepreneurial networks in crowdfunding include media exposure, interaction with new shareholders, end-user engagement and feedback. Brown *et al.* (2019) suggest that entrepreneurs use these new networks to gain media exposure for their venture and to receive customer feedback on product development. Consequently, the feedback loops between entrepreneurs and investors provide important entrepreneurial learning opportunity (Belleflamme *et al.* 2014; Ordanini *et al.* 2011).

Social media usage in crowdfunding

Since crowdfunding gathers funding from large numbers of people (Belleflamme *et al.* 2013; Lu *et al.* 2014), project founders often pitch their projects on various social media channels in order to reach large numbers of people and attract sufficient support (Borst *et al.* 2018). Typical social media channels often used are Facebook and Twitter which help project founders to establish new contacts (Beier and Wagner 2015), who in turn might become funders and contribute to enhance project performance (Borst *et al.* 2018). Lu *et al.* (2014) suggest that Twitter usage contributes to the success of crowdfunding. By the same token, Borst *et al.* (2018) argue that a higher intensity of social media usage will stimulate future donations and, thus, positively affect project performance.

(i) Facebook usage

With 2.4 billion people from across the world using the platform, Facebook is powerful (Patel 2020). Patel (2020) argues that if a business is running a crowdfunding campaign, it has to start from Facebook and establish its reputation on the platform. The power of Facebook should not be underestimated when it comes to marketing crowdfunding campaign as it is a powerful and fast tool to bring leads, fans, loyal backers and fresh data for potential new markets (BackerLand 2019).

Four variables should be focussed on when planning a Facebook campaign. These include image/videos, copywriting, audience and offer. BackerLand (2019) explains why the four variables are important: First, the visual elements should be creative enough to capture your target's attention because people are, for the most part, visual learners, thus making images and video the best way to appeal to the core target. Second, copywriting is just as important as the visual elements, as the words are the primary way to persuade the potential backer to act and begin thinking about helping fund the project. Third, the audience is going to be the people most likely to click on the campaign advertisement. Finally, the offer is the main reason potential backers will click on the campaign advertisement and invest in the project.

Research studies, such as Mollick (2014) and Zheng *et al.* (2014), have established that the size of the number of Facebook friends positively correlates with the success of crowdfunding projects. However, Borst *et al.* (2018) argue that not all project funders are necessarily friends or existing relations. For instance, Hui *et al.* (2014) found that project creators were sometimes disappointed that many friends did not provide support, but at the same time were surprised by the number of previously unknown funders (Hui *et al.* 2014). Similarly, Davidson and Poor (2014) found that the perceived proportion of known funders negatively predicts project success.

Apart from the benefit of reaching weak ties, Borst *et al.* (2019) argue that Facebook helps in reaching latent ties, that is, people as yet unknown to the project creator. By simply liking and commenting on Facebook, messages can appear on the timeline of as yet unconnected people who can also gain access to Facebook pages through use of internet search engines.

(ii) Use of Twitter

Twitter is another form of social media platform, called a micro-blogging site (Lynn *et al* 2020). Microblogging services allow users to send and read short posts instantaneously (Jansen *et al.* 2009; Lynn *et al.* 2020). Although Twitter was originally limited to text, it is now possible to support images, audio, live and recorded video, URLs, and other resources (Lynn *et al.* 2020). The short nature of posts combined with the instantaneous nature of microblogging differentiates it from blogging and other social media resulting in higher update frequencies and more real-time updates (Java *et al.* 2020).

Lynn *et al.* (2020) suggest that Twitter has a number of additional noteworthy characteristics and functionality. First, it is largely an open network, thus interactions are largely in the public domain. Users can follow other users, view their posts and send messages to other users publicly without permission (as is typically the case with Facebook or LinkedIn); it is largely a social network that connects strangers. Second, tweets can feature hashtags which connect a post to a particular theme and acts as coordinating mechanism for users to organize all of the tweets on that theme and identify users with similar or opposing views, thereby facilitating the formation of ad hoc and calculated publics (Bruns and Burgess 2015; Lynn *et al.* 2020). Third, a retweet is a way to forward the message of another user to the followers of the user who retweets. This last characteristic represents a powerful mechanism for information sharing (Lynn *et al.* 2020; Stieglitz and Dang-Xuan 2013).

There are many benefits of Twitter for entrepreneurs and crowdfunding in particular. Extant literature (e.g. Fischer and Reuber 2011; Fischer and Reuber 2014; Lynn *et al.* 2020; Obschonka *et al.* 2017) has identified these benefits. For example, Obschonka *et al.* (2017) suggest that there is a relationship between social media activity of entrepreneurs, start-up engagement and venture financing. These studies have also identified the role of Twitter and online communication in crowdfunding in particular and the relationship between followers and crowdfunding success.

Lynn *et al.* (2020) suggest that participants in the crowdfunding discourse on Twitter tend to interact more with other participants in their sub-community than with users in other sub-communities. Using network theory and the concept of homophily to explain the increased interaction, McPherson *et al.* (2001) suggest that there is the tendency for people to be attracted to others similar to themselves. Lynn *et al.* (2020) also suggest that the use of Twitter reduces the geographic barriers between crowdfunding stakeholders, increases knowledge sharing and facilitates the identification of both projects and investors. Furthermore, participation in the crowdfunding discourse on Twitter may signal support for a project and, thus, attract further interest (Lynn *et al.* 2020).

The interplay of social media messages and social ties

There is a positive correlation between the size of online social networks of project founders (such as the number of Facebook friends and followers) with the success of crowdfunding projects (Mollick 2014; Zheng *et al.* 2014). However, as already discussed earlier, not all project funders are necessarily friends or existing relations of the project creators (Borst *et al.* 2019).

Previous literature on networks has distinguished a variety of relationships (e.g. Borgatti *et al.* 2014). This include kindship relations such as the relationship between family members (Agrawal *et al.* 2015) and perceptual relations such as those existing between known and unknown people (Davidson and Poor 2014). In her study of the characteristics of media activities associated with different strengths, Haythornthwaite (2002) suggests that weak ties result from limited means of communication, while strong ties are created by numerous communication means. She also suggests that people who connect through weak ties mainly communicate via group-wide media, whereas strongly tied persons combine group-wide media with person-to-person communication in private meetings or personal emails. This is because weakly tied people are less likely to communicate and their interaction is more passive such as simply "liking" a Facebook post. On the contrary, people with strong ties have a greater need to communicate with one another using a variety of ways and are more likely to proactively seek out other means of communication (Haythornthwaite 2005).

By the same token, in order to properly understand the different relationships between project founders and funders, Borst *et al.* (2018) analyze a combination of kinship and perceptual relations, distinguishing between known persons with closer (strong) ties or less close (weak) ties and unknown persons who have the potential to form a relationship (latent ties). Borst *et al.* (2018) argue that since strong ties use multiple and more private means of communication, crowdfunding campaigns on social media may not be very effective at reaching this type of relation. "After all, it is likely that strongly tied people have already received news of the crowdfunding project via other means" (Borst *et al.* 2018, p. 1401). They posit that crowdfunding campaigns, using social media, would be more effective in reaching weakly tied people who mainly use group-wide communication. They comment that it is unlikely that weak ties would have received the funding request via other channels.

Apart from the benefit of reaching weak ties, Borst *et al.* (2018) argue that social media also helps in reaching latent ties, that is, people as yet unknown to the project creator. They remark that messages can appear on the timelines of people who are yet unconnected by retweeting or commenting on Twitter, or by liking and commenting on Facebook. Besides, unconnected people can also gain access to Twitter messages and public Facebook pages when they use regular internet search engines. As latent ties are defined as unknown persons who can be reached through digital communication means, Borst *et al.* (2018) suggest that social media will particularly mobilize latent ties to become funders in a crowdfunding project.

Aldrich *et al.* (1997) characterize unknown persons with latent ties as "strangers". These are persons: (i) with whom the entrepreneur has no prior ties, (ii) about whom very little is known, and (iii) where the relationships are entered into for pragmatic reasons, are fleeting and require little or no emotional involvement (Lynn *et al.* 2020). Apart from the strong and weak ties, the strangers are the third group which has not been explored in great depth in the literature (Lynn *et al.* 2020). Therefore, their nature poses obvious challenges in both identifying such actors and mapping relationships and impact and which makes our understanding of their value and importance limited (Aldrich *et al.* 1997).

Social network dynamics in charitable crowdfunding

The social network dynamics in charitable crowdfunding has been largely unexplored (Jiao *et al.* 2021). Charitable crowdfunding aims to obtain funds through the internet for charitable or social purposes (Choy and Schlagwein 2016). This is largely through donations. As in other types of crowdfunding, charitable crowdfunding projects involve three parties: the project initiator, supporters and platforms. The project initiators are those who launch a project to be funded; the supporters are those whose donations and sharing support the project; and platforms facilitate to bring project initiators and supporters together (Liu *et al.* 2018).

A large and increasing number of people are becoming interested in charitable crowdfunding because of the wide reach of social networking (Jiao *et al.* 2021). Similarly, researchers have demonstrated an increased interest in the expanding charitable crowdfunding phenomenon and especially in the reasons that motivate people to support it (Choy and Schlagwein 2016). The motivations are categorized into extrinsic and intrinsic (Deci and Ryan 2000; Jiao *et al.* 2021).

Extrinsic motivations

Extrinsic motivations can be defined as gains individuals expect to make from performing the activity (these are usually external rewards) (Ryan and Deci 2000). There are two types of extrinsic motivations namely, reputation and reciprocity, which are considered to motivate prosocial behaviour in charity (Jiao *et al*. 2021). The dynamics of these motivations are discussed in the following paragraphs.

(i) Reputation

Reputation is defined as "the general judgment or opinions about a person" and can help individuals achieve and maintain their status within a community (Jiao *et al*. 2021, p. 4). Reputation motivation refers to individuals' expectation on reputation feedback from contribution to charitable crowdfunding project (Jiao *et al*. 2021). For example, people are motivated to donate to gain social recognition (Bekkers and Wiepking 2011).

Giving to charitable courses is regarded as a positive and prosocial behaviour. Therefore, people who donate to charitable campaigns are highly regarded by their peers in a community, and they receive recognition and approval from others (Bekkers and Wiepking 2011). Andreoni and Petrie (2004) argue that people often prefer to make visible donations to signal their prosocial behaviour. More specifically, individuals tend to donate if they perceive that doing so will enhance their reputation (Jiao *et al* 2021). When individuals feel that donating money to a project can elevate their reputation, they will be more inclined to do so.

(ii) Reciprocity

Reciprocity can be defined as the gains that people expect to make in the form of future benefits from their present actions (Hung *et al*. 2011). This means that people are motivated to donate by the expectation that they will benefit from these gains in the future (Konrath and Handy 2018). It is a social norm that demands that people help those who have helped them and regulates interpersonal interactions (Hung *et al*. 2011). In this context, reciprocity motivation refers to individuals' expectation on future return for their present contribution to a charitable crowdfunding project (Jiao *et al*. 2021).

In a reciprocal society, there is a belief that everyone should try to repay that which other people have provided for them (Edlund *et al*. 2007; Jiao *et al*. 2021). Feng and Ye (2016) argue that in online communities, reciprocity tends to be generalized, and people may expect future benefits not from the direct beneficiaries of their contributions but from other people who are implicated with the beneficiaries in a social exchange. By the same token, Zhang *et al*. (2017) maintain that reciprocity helps build a sustainable feedback loop in online communities. At the same time, Hung *et al*. (2011) indicate that reciprocity significantly affects how much an individual contributes as individuals share their donation experiences with others to help build reciprocal relationships. Therefore, people who expect reciprocity will participate in more charitable crowdfunding projects of which they approve, and will have a higher intention to donate, to support charitable crowdfunding (Jiao *et al.* 2021).

Intrinsic motivation

Intrinsic motivations refer to the engagement of an individual in an activity for personal interest, as well as for fun and enjoyment (Ryan and Deci 2000). Intrinsic motivations include sense of belonging, joy of giving, altruism, financial constraint.

(i) Sense of belonging

A sense of belonging is defined as the experience of personal involvement in a community that makes people feel they are an integral part of that community (Jiao *et al.* 2021). In other words, it is the feeling of belonging to an integral part of a positive community.

Kim and Drumwright (2016) argue that a sense of belonging is a fundamental motivation for people to form and maintain lasting, positive and significant interpersonal relationships. At the same time, Zhao *et al.* (2012) indicate that this motivation encourages people to voluntarily participate in a virtual community. Aitamurto (2011) submits that people who value a sense of belonging to a community are more likely to participate in crowdfunding campaigns. In charitable crowdfunding, people are motivated to donate because they enjoy the feeling of belonging to a team or community (Jiao *et al.* 2021). These people also perceive the charitable crowdfunding crowd to be positive and wish to be involved in a project with likeminded people (Choy and Schlagwein 2016).

(ii) Joy of giving

The joy of giving is the positive psychological experience of the giver, arising from helping others (Bekkers and Wiepking 2011). It is the anticipated positive emotions or warm glow experienced by helping others (Jiao *et al.* 2021). Bekkers and Wiepking (2011) suggest that the reasons why people gain pleasurable experiences and positive emotional sensations from giving may be that such giving alleviates feelings of guilt, and the "feel good" factor of performing in line with a prosocial self-image and a social norm. Previous studies such as Dolinski *et al.* (2005) and Ugur (2018) have shown that a positive mood generally motivates giving. The positive relationship between donating behaviour and the joy of giving has been proven by psychology literature, which suggests that donating promotes happiness and that, as the level of happiness increases, the likelihood of donating also increases (Ugur 2018). A key motivation for people participating in charitable crowdfunding and making donations is that doing so gives them pleasure and good feelings from helping others (Cecere *et al.* 2017).

(iii) Altruism

Altruism is defined as a personal trait that embodies personal social responsibility and a sense of mission (Rodriguez-Ricardo *et al.* 2019). It is an unconditional kindness towards others without expectation of a return (Fehr and Gachter 2000; Ferguson *et al.* 2012). Jiao *et al.* (2021) defines it as an intrinsic desire to help others without expecting something in return. Jiao *et al.* (2021) argue that people whose giving is motivated by pure altruism are driven by their intrinsic desire to help others, regardless of personal costs and benefits. Altruistic people care about others' well-being and have prosocial attitudes, and enjoy helping others with, in many cases, no expectation of any return (Jiao *et al.* 2021).

In traditional charity, it has long been recognized that altruistic impulses motivate charitable giving behaviours (Echazu and Nocetti 2015; Ribar and Wilhelm 2002). In the context of crowdfunding, projects in need of help are favoured by supporters, which implies that supporters are motivated by altruistic reasons (Burtch *et al.* 2013). Other studies on crowdfunding such as Gleasure and Feller (2016) also suggest altruism to be an important motivation for supporting projects, whilst Jiao *et al.* (2021) indicate that altruism constitutes a significant driver for investors in projects with charitable characteristics.

(iv) Financial constraints

Constraints can be factors that inhibit individuals' ability to participate in events, which include lack of money, time, skill, or interest (Filo *et al.* 2020). Financial constraints are therefore defined as individuals' personally felt financial stresses induced by donating money to charity (Konrath and Handy 2018). Jiao *et al.* (2021) suggest that financial constraints fall within donors' personal sphere and are classified as intrinsic motivations that are negatively related to giving behaviour.

Jiao *et al.* (2021 also posit that the most common reason given for not donating is not having enough money to spare. In the charitable crowdfunding context, people who are financially constrained have little intention to donate money, but are more willing to share a project on their own social network, because that is an important, yet costless, way to support a project (Li *et al.* 2017).

Social interaction in charitable crowdfunding

Social interactions in charitable crowdfunding differ from traditional charity. Liu *et al.* (2018) suggest that charitable crowdfunding behaviour can also be framed as prosocial behaviour in online virtual communities. Jiao *et al.* (2021) argue that the motivations for charitable crowdfunding behaviours differ from traditional charity because of the nature of the IT platforms on which they occur. In this context, Zhang *et al.* (2017) indicate that the supporters in charitable crowdfunding primarily desire to gain non-monetary rather than monetary benefits, whereas in traditional charity people can benefit by gaining monetary rewards (Bekkers and

Wiepking 2011). Therefore, some extrinsic motivations identified in traditional charity (e.g. monetary reward and tax credits) may not be the main drivers of charitable crowdfunding behaviour.

The increase in charitable crowdfunding projects mainly depends on personal social networks by which people share the project with their contacts and ask their friends to support the project. Those friends may also share this project with their contacts and solicit donations. Thus, social interactions between the donor, third parties (the donor's social neighbours) and the project initiator are stronger than with traditional charity (Jiao *et al*. 2021). Jiao *et al*. (2021) suggest that the stronger social interaction is due to peer pressure from seeing that social neighbours have donated and the social influence motivates them also to donate. Stronger social ties with the initiator also motivate people to donate. Therefore, a comprehensive understanding of the motivations that support charitable crowdfunding is essential as such an understanding would enable platforms to attract more people to help each other and create mutually supportive and like-minded communities (Jiao *et al*. 2021). We now discuss the concepts of social influence and social ties under charitable crowdfunding.

(i) Social influence

Social influence has been defined as people's perception of how their friends or close acquaintances believe they should consider a behaviour (Li *et al*. 2017). Individuals' behaviour is influenced by the preferences of their friends or reference group and the social pressure they experience (Jiao *et al*. 2021). Jiao *et al*. (2021) describe this phenomenon as social influence. Barry and Wentzel (2006) suggest that friends' support of a project and peer pressure can drive prosocial behaviour. Jiao *et al*. (2021) argue that such behaviour is carried out to conform to social norms and to improve one's image in the community. Since one is a part of a social network whose approval is valued, this invariably increases the perceived desirability of giving (Schervish and Havens 1997).

In relation to charitable crowdfunding, Sura *et al*. (2017) suggest that projects spread through social network sites because people extend their networks and maintain their social relationships through social network sites. Social pressure and social norms mean that they are more likely to be motivated to support charitable crowdfunding projects when being solicited by friends in their own social network (Jiao *et al*. 2021). Therefore, social influence plays a specific role in shaping donors' behaviours in charitable crowdfunding.

(ii) Social ties

Social ties can be defined as the social interaction between two or more individuals (Dong and Wang 2018). In an online community, Zhang *et al*. (2018) argue that social ties between individuals are strengthened by familiarity and frequency of communication with each other. Liu *et al*. (2018) indicate that social ties depend on the strength of the relationships, the amount of time spent and communication frequency among members of the same community. By the same token, Zhang *et al.* (2017) posit that strong social ties develop over time, and provide the basis of cooperation, trust and collective actions in the online community. Sura *et al.* (2017) argue that online platforms allow users to build social ties through communicating and sharing information, as in physical connections. Jiao *et al.* (2021) suggest that charitable crowdfunding members can communicate with each other through personal messages and comments.

Social network sites create familiarity with the initiator of a project through having dialogues which in turn increase the possibility of contributions, liking and trust (Agrawal *et al.* 2015). People who are closer and more familiar with a project initiator are more inclined to support the project (Borst *et al.* 2018; Jiao *et al.* 2021).

Case study of charitable crowdfunding

FundRazr success stories: Ride to Give

What is Ride to Give?

Ride to Give is a charitable non-profit organization based in Nyack NY, just outside of NYC. Every summer they ride across America from Nyack to Jefferson to raise awareness and money for kids in need. It was founded by Kaete Nazaroff and her husband, eight-time Ironman Dave Nazaroff.

What did they do?

On August 25, 2013, Dave Nazaroff competed at Ironman Canada in Whistler, BC. He completed 2.4 miles of swimming, 112 miles of riding, and then another full marathon. The race was dedicated to Hawk Harrison, a sweet little boy that suffered from a massive spontaneous brain hemorrhage. Since that day, he has had six brain surgeries, four shunt revisions, infection in his Cerebral Spinal Fluid (CSF), multiple blood clots, and has spent over 100 days in the hospital. Fortunately, Hawk is now home and getting better. However, the multiple surgeries and hospital bills have started to become a financial burden on the family and Hawk still needed a wheelchair accessible bathroom and a therapy room for him to thrive in.

Through FundRazr and Ride to Give's efforts, Hawk was able to quickly raise **$24,038**; 20% more than the initial asking amount of $20,000. Building upon the success of Hawk's campaign, Ride to Give decided to start FundRazr campaigns for other children in need as well.

One such campaign was for Jesse. When Jesse was born, nobody wanted him. Luckily, Terri was able to find him and bring him into their loving family of seven. Unfortunately, Jesse suffered a near fatal Acute Respiratory Distress Syndrome (ARDS) attack and became Trach, Ventilator, oxygen and wheelchair dependent. To help him get around, the family needed a rear entry manual lift van.

Ride to Give took notice of their situation and decided to take their story to FundRazr. The crowd was moved by Jesse's story and the campaign reached its goal of **$30,000 in less than a month**. In fact, Jesse's story inspired a little girl, Gertie, who dedicated her race in the ToughKid triathlon to Jesse in a FundRazr sub-campaign. The sub-campaign was equally successful as it raised **$12,400 in two weeks**; 24% higher than their initial goal of $10,000.

Reasons for success

Perks

Despite being cause focused campaigns, Ride to Give was able to creatively manufacture perks to thank all its contributors. Perks included specially designed Ride to Give posters, Ride to Give mugs, Ride to Give desk-top plagues and Ride to Give Blankets. The perks were all memorabilia that served as a thank you and reminder for all contributors who gave to this very special cause. The perks were very successful and many perks were claimed out of stock.

Sharing over social media

Ride to Give did a great job of sharing their campaigns over social media. They were constantly tweeting and posting to create social visibility for their campaigns. Hawk's campaign alone was able to aggregate over 27,000 Facebook likes; now, that's socially visible.

Live updates

Ride to Give also constantly updated their contributors and followers on the campaigns. The updates included campaign milestones as well as conditions of the campaign benefactor and were supported with pictures and other media items. Of course, the updates were shared and because they had pictures, they had more visibility.

Friends and family

Ride to Give's campaigns did not just jump from 0 to $30,000. You can be sure that their first couple of hundred dollars came from family members and close friends. It is important to ask those closest to you to get your campaign off the ground.

Source: https://fundrazr.com/posts/fundrazr-success-story-ride-to-give

Summary

Since crowdfunding is the process of raising funds from a large group of people through small contributions for a project via an open call on the internet, this chapter has explored the role of social relationships between the three actors: the creator who proposes an idea and launches it on a crowdfunding platform asking for a fixed amount or target amount; backers who are basically internet users who provide the funds in exchange for tangible or intangible rewards; and the platform which brings the creator and backers together and makes them exchange ideas, contents and funds. This chapter has demonstrated that the role of these three actors is important in making a campaign successful. The success of a campaign largely depends on the networking skills and efforts of the creator as they need to employ their network to mobilize people to donate and mobilize themselves on social media and persuade people to donate (Kaur and Gera 2017).

The chapter has also demonstrated that it is important for crowdfunding platforms to organize the platform in a manner that enables entrepreneurs to communicate well with the backers or potential investors as doing so will increase the chances of the crowdfunding campaign succeeding. It also allows entrepreneurs to get more insights on the importance of their social network and social interactions on the success of their project, which they can use to increase their ability to receive funds. As demonstrated in this chapter, entrepreneurs can increase the success of their crowdfunding campaign by interacting well with their backers and potential investors.

Discussion questions

1 What are the differences between a social network and business network?
2 Discuss the network dynamics in the context of crowdfunding.
3 What are the relational benefits of networks in crowdfunding?
4 How useful are the different social media platforms in crowdfunding?
5 Discuss the differences between the social network dynamics in charitable crowdfunding and traditional crowdfunding.

Test questions

1 Assess the effect of interpersonal connectivity on the crowdfunding community.
2 Assess the effect of attitudes towards helping others in the crowdfunding community.
3 "The effect of online social networks in crowdfunding markets is substantially greater than that of traditional networks in existing markets." Discuss.

Glossary of key terminologies

Altruism Unconditional kindness towards others without expecting something back in return.
Business network Business networks consist of customers, suppliers, competitors, support agencies.

Extrinsic motivation   Extrinsic motivations can be defined as the gains which individuals expect to make from performing the activity.

Facebook   Facebook is an online social networking website where people create profiles, share information such as photos and quotes about themselves, and respond or link to the information posted by others.

Friendfunding   "Friendfunding" consists of funding by family members, friends and close acquaintances.

Intrinsic motivation   Intrinsic motivations refer to the engagement of an individual in an activity for personal interest, as well as for fun and enjoyment.

Reciprocity   Gains people expect to make in the form of future benefits from their present actions.

Reputation   The general judgement or opinion about a person.

Social influence   People's perception of how their friends or close acquaintances believe they should consider their behaviour.

Social network   Social network consists of family members, friends and close acquaintances.

Social ties   Social interaction between two or more individuals.

Twitter   Twitter is a microblogging and social networking service on which users post and interact with messages known as "tweets".

Recommended reading

Batson, C.D., 2011. *Altruism in humans*. New York: Oxford University Press.

Glowik, M., and Bruhs, S.M., 2015. *Business-to-business a global network perspective*. London: Routledge.

Hakansson, H., Ford, D.I., Gadde, L.E., Snehota, I., and Waluszewski, A., 2010. *Business in Networks*. Hoboken: Wiley.

Hoffman, D.L., and Novak, T.P., 2012. Social media strategy. *In*: S. Venkatesh and G.S. Carpenter, eds. *Handbook of marketing strategy*. Cheltenham: Edward Elgar, 198–216.

Lawton, K., and Marom, D., 2010. *The crowdfunding revolution: Social networking meets venture financing*. Scotts Valley, CA: CreateSpace Independent Publishing Platform.

Na, N., 2000. *The economics of reciprocity, Giving and altruism*. London: Palgrave Macmillan.

Rouze, V., 2019. *Cultural crowdfunding: Platform capitalism, labour and globalization*. London: University of Westminster Press.

Scott, J., and Carrington, P.J., 2011. *The Sage handbook of social network analysis*. London: Sage.

References

Aldrich, H.E., Elam, A.B., and Reese, P.R., 1997. Strong ties, weak ties, and strangers. *In*: S. Birley and I.C. MacMillan, eds. *Entrepreneurship in a global context*. London: Routledge, 1–25.

Agrawal, A.K, Catalini, C., and Goldfarb, A., 2015. Crowdfunding: Geography, social networks, and the timing of investment decisions. *Journal of Economics & Management Strategy* 24 (2), 253–274.

Ahlers, G.K., Cumming, D., Günther, C., and Schweizer, D., 2015. Signalling in equity crowdfunding. *Entrepreneurship Theory and Practice*, 39, 955–980.

Aitamurto, T., 2011. The impact of crowdfunding on journalism: Case study of Spot.Us, a platform for community-funded reporting. *Journalism Practice*, 5 (4), 429–445.

Andersen, P.H., and Medlin, C.J., 2016. Transient commitments and dynamic business Networking. *Industrial Marketing Management*, 58, 11–19.

Andreoni, J., and Petrie, R., 2004. Public goods experiments without confidentiality: A glimpse into fund-raising. *Journal of Public Economics*, 88, 1605–1623.

BackerLand, 2019. *How to use Facebook Ads to get your crowdfunding project fully funded?* Available from: https://medium.com/@team_33864/how-to-use-facebook-ads-to-get-your-crowdfunding-project-fully-funded-dc9926ffd23b [Accessed 13 April 2021].

Baraldi, E., 2008. Strategy in industrial networks: Experiences from IKEA. *California Management Review*, 50 (4), 99–126.

Barry, C.M., and Wentzel, K.R., 2006. Friend influence on prosocial behaviour: The role of motivational factors and friendship characteristics. *Developmental Psychology*, 42 (1), 153–163.

Beier, M., and Wagner, K., 2015. *Crowdfunding success: A perspective from social media and e-commerce.* Available from: http://aisel.aisnet.org/icis2015/proceedings/eBize-Gov/11/ [Accessed 10 April 2021].

Bekkers, R., and Wiepking, P., 2011. A literature review of empirical studies of philanthropy: Eight mechanisms that drive charitable giving. *Nonprofit Voluntary Sector Quarterly*, 40 (5), 924–973.

Belleflamme, P., Lambert, T., and Schwienbacher, A., 2013. Individual crowdfunding practices, *Venture Capital*, 15 (4), 313–333.

Belleflamme, P., Lambert, T., and Schwienbacher, A., 2014. Crowdfunding: Tapping the right crowd. *Journal of Business Venturing*, 29 (5), 585–609.

Borgatti, S.P., Brass, D.J, and Halgin, D.S., 2014. Social network research: confusions, criticisms, and controversies. *Research in the Sociology of Organizations*, 40, 1–29.

Borst, I., and Christine, M., and Ferguson, J., 2018. From friendfunding to crowdfunding: Relevance of relationships, social media, and platform activities to crowdfunding performance. *New Media & Society*, 20 (4), 1396–1414.

Brown, R., Mawson, S., and Rowe, A., 2019. Start-Ups, entrepreneurial networks and equity crowdfunding: A processual perspective. *Industrial Marketing Management*, 80, 115–125.

Bruns, A., and Burgess, J., 2015. Twitter hashtags from ad hoc to calculated publics. *In*: N. Rambukkana, ed. *Hashtag publics: The power and politics of discursive networks*. New York: Peter Lang Publishing Inc, 13–28.

Burtch, G., Ghose, A., and Wattal, S., 2013. An empirical examination of the antecedents and consequences of contribution patterns in crowd-funded markets. *Information Systems Research*, 24 (3), 499–519.

Cecere, G., Le Guel, F., and Rochelandet, F., 2017. Crowdfunding and social influence: An empirical investigation. *Applied Economics*, 49, 5802–5813.

Choy, K., and Schlagwein, D., 2016. Crowdsourcing for a better world on the relation between IT affordances and donor motivations in charitable crowdfunding. *Information Technology & People*, 29 (1), 221–247.

Ciabuschi, F., Perna, A., and Snehota, I., 2012. Assembling resources when forming a new business. *Journal of Business Research*, 65 (2), 220–229.

Colombo, M.G., Franzoni, C., and Rossi-Lamastra, C., 2015. Internal social capital and the attraction of early contributions in crowdfunding. *Entrepreneurship Theory and Practice*, 39 (1), 75–100.

Davidson, R., and Poor, N., 2014. The barriers facing artists' use of crowdfunding platforms: Personality, emotional labor, and going to the well one too many times. *New Media & Society*, 17, 289–307.

Davidson, R., and Poor, N., 2016. Factors for success in repeat crowdfunding: Why sugar daddies are only good for Bar-Mitzvahs. *Information, Communication & Society*, 19 (1), 127–139.

Deci, E.L., and Ryan, R.M., 2000. The "what" and "why" of goal pursuits: Human needs and the self-determination of behaviour. *Psychological Inquiry*, 11 (4), 227–268.

Dolinski, D., Grzyb, T., Olejnik, J., Prusakowski, S., and Urban, K., 2005. Let's dialogue about penny: Effectiveness of dialogue involvement and legitimizing paltry contribution techniques. *Journal of Applied Social Psychology*, 35, 1150–1170.

Dong, X., and Wang, T., 2018. Social tie formation in Chinese online social commerce: The role of IT affordances. *International Journal of Information Management*, 42, 49–64.

Drover, W., Busenitz, L., Matusik, S., Townsend, D., Anglin, A., and Dushnitsky, G., 2017. A review and road map of entrepreneurial equity financing research: Venture capital, corporate venture capital, angel investment, crowdfunding, and accelerators. *Journal of Management*. Available from: https://doi.org/10.1177/0149206317690584.

Echazu, L., and Nocetti, D., 2015. Charitable giving: Altruism has no limits. *Journal of Public Economics*, 125, 46–53.

Edlund, J.E., Sagarin, B.J., and Johnson, B.S., 2007. Reciprocity and the belief in a just world. *Personality and Individual Differences*, 43 (3), 589–596.

Ekanem, I., 2018. Understanding internationalisation approaches and mechanisms of diaspora entrepreneurs in emerging economies as a learning process. *International Journal of Entrepreneurial Behavior & Research*. Available from: https://doi.org/10.1108/IJEBR-02-2018-0068.

Fehr, E., and Gachter, S., 2000. Fairness and retaliation: The economics of reciprocity. *Journal of Economic Perspectives*, 14 (3), 159–181.

Feng, Y., and Ye, H.J., 2016. Why do you return the favor in online knowledge communities? A study of the motivations of reciprocity. *Computers in Human Behavior*, 63, 342–349.

Ferguson, E., Taylor, M., Keatley, D., Flynn, N., and Lawrence, C., 2012. Blood donors' helping behavior is driven by warm glow: More evidence for the blood donor benevolence hypothesis. *Transfusion*, 52 (10), 2189–2200.

Filo, K., Fechner, D., and Inoue, Y., 2020. The donors supporting charity sport event participants: An exploration of the factors driving donations. *Journal of Sport Management*, 34 (5), 488–499.

Fischer, E., and Reuber, A.R., 2011. Social interaction via new social media: (How) can interactions on Twitter affect effectual thinking and behaviour? *Journal of Business Venture*, 26, 1–18.

Fischer, E., and Reuber, A.R., 2014. Online entrepreneurial communication: Mitigating uncertainty and increasing differentiation via Twitter. *Journal of Business Venture*, 29, 565–583.

Freytag, P.V., and Ritter, T., 2005. Dynamics of relationships and networks—creation, maintenance and destruction as managerial challenges. *Industrial Marketing Management*, 34 (7), 644–647.

Frydrych, D., Bock, A.J., Kinder, T., and Koeck, B., 2014. Exploring entrepreneurial legitimacy in reward-based crowdfunding. *Venture Capital*, 16 (3), 247–269.

Gedajlovic, E., Honig, B., Moore, C.B., Payne, G.T., and Wright, M., 2013. Social capital and entrepreneurship: A schema and research agenda. *Entrepreneurship Theory and Practice*, 37 (3), 455–478.

Gleasure, R., and Feller, J., 2016. Does heart or head rule donor behaviours in charitable crowdfunding markets? *International Journal of Electronic Commerce*, 20 (4), 499–524.

Gluckler, J., 2007. Economic geography and the evolution of networks. *Journal of Economic Geography*, 7 (5), 619–634.

Granovetter, M.S., 1973. The strength of weak ties. *American Journal of Sociology*, 1360–1380.

Hakansson, H., Havila, V., and Pedersen, A.C., 1999. Learning in networks. *Industrial Marketing Management*, 28 (5), 443–452.

Håkansson, H., and Snehota, I., 1989. No business is an island: The network concept of business strategy. *Scandinavian Journal of Management*, 5 (3), 187–200.

Haythornthwaite, C., 2002. Strong, weak, and latent ties and the impact of new media. *The Information Society*, 18 (5), 385–401.

Haythornthwaite, C., 2005. Social networks and internet connectivity effects. *Information, Community & Society*, 8 (2), 125–147.

Hellmann, T., Lindsey, L., and Puri, M., 2008. Building relationships early: Banks in venture capital. *Review of Financial Studies*, 21 (2), 513–541.

Hite, J.M., 2005. Evolutionary processes and paths of relationally embedded network ties in emerging entrepreneurial firms. *Entrepreneurship Theory and Practice*, 29 (1), 113–144.

Hsu, D.H., 2004. What do entrepreneurs pay for venture capital affiliation? *The Journal of Finance*, 59 (4), 1805–1844.

Hui, J.S., Gerber, E.M., and Gergle, D., 2014. Understanding and leveraging social networks for crowdfunding: Opportunities and challenges. *In: Proceedings of the 2014 conference on Designing interactive systems*. 677–680. Available from: https://doi.org/10.1145/2598510.2598539

Hung, S.Y., Durcikova, A., Lai, H.M., and Lin, W.M., 2011. The influence of intrinsic and extrinsic motivation on individuals' knowledge sharing behaviour. *International Journal of Human-Computer Studies*, 69 (6), 415–427.

Jansen, B.J., Zhang, M., Sobel, K., and Chowdury, A., 2009. Twitter power: Tweets as electronic word of mouth. *Journal of the American Society for Information Science and Technology*, 60, 2169–2188.

Jiao, H., Qian, L., Liu, T., and Ma, L., 2021. Why do people support online crowdfunding charities? A case study from China. *Frontiers in Psychology*. Available from: https://doi.org/10.3389/fpsyg.2021.582508

Kaur, H., and Gera, J., 2017. Effect of social media connectivity on success of crowdfunding campaigns. *Procedia Computer Science*, 122, 767–774.

Kim, E., and Drumwright, M., 2016. Engaging consumers and building relationships in social media: How social relatedness influences intrinsic vs. Extrinsic consumer motivation. *Computer Human Behavior*, 63, 970–979.

Konrath, S., and Handy, F., 2018. The development and validation of the motives to donate scale. *Nonprofit Voluntary Sector Quarterly*, 47, 347–375.

Kontinen, T., and Ojala, A., 2011. Network ties in the international opportunity recognition of family SMEs. *International Business Review*, 20 (4), 440–453.

Lechner, C., and Dowling, M., 2003. Firm networks: External relationships as sources for the growth and competitiveness of entrepreneurial firms. *Entrepreneurship & Regional Development*, 15 (1), 1–26.

Lechner, C., Dowling, M., and Welpe, I., 2006. Firm networks and firm development: The role of the relational mix. *Journal of Business Venturing*, 21 (4), 514–540.

Leyden, D.P., Link, A.N., and Siegel, D.S., 2014. A theoretical analysis of the role of social networks in entrepreneurship. *Research Policy*, 43 (7), 1157–1163.

Li, J.J., Chen, X.P., Kotha, S., and Fisher, G., 2017. Catching fire and spreading it: A glimpse into displayed entrepreneurial passion in crowdfunding campaigns. *Journal of Applied Psychology*, 102 (7), 1075–1091.

Liu, L., Suh, A., and Wagner, C., 2018. Empathy or perceived credibility? An empirical study on individual donation behavior in charitable crowdfunding. *Internet Research*, 28 (3), 623–651.

Lu, C.T., Xie, S., Kong, X., and Yu, P.S., 2014. Inferring the impacts of social media on crowdfunding. *In: Proceedings of the 7th ACM international conference on Web search and data mining.* Chicago, IL, USA: University of Illinois at Chicago, 573–582.

Lynn, T., Rosati, P., Nair, B., and Mac an Bhaird, C., 2020. An exploratory data analysis of the #crowdfunding network on Twitter. *Journal of Open Innovation: Technology, Market, and Complexity*, 6 (80), 1–22.

Mattsson, L.G., 1997. Relationship marketing" and the "markets-as-networks approach" – A comparative analysis of two evolving streams of research. *Journal of Marketing Management*, 13 (5), 447–461.

McPherson, M., Smith-Lovin, L., and Cook, J.M., 2001. Birds of a feather: Homophily in social networks. *Annual Review of Sociology*, 27, 415–444.

Mollick, E., 2014. The dynamics of crowdfunding: An exploratory study. *Journal of Business Venturing*, 29 (1), 1–16.

Obschonka, M., Fisch, C., and Boyd, R., 2017. Using digital footprints in entrepreneurship research: A Twitter-based personality analysis of superstar entrepreneurs and managers. *Journal of Business Venture Insights*, 8, 13–23.

Ordanini, A., Miceli, L., Pizzetti, M., and Parasuraman, A., 2011. Crowd-funding: Transforming customers into investors through innovative service platforms. *Journal of Service Management*, 22 (4), 443–470.

Patel, S., 2020. *How to use facebook marketing to boost your crowdfunding campaign.* Available from: www.samitpatel.net/use-facebook-marketing-boost-crowdfunding-campaign-beginners-guide-part-1/ [Accessed 13 April 2021].

Ribar, D.C., and Wilhelm, M.O., 2002. Altruistic and joy-of-giving motivations in charitable behaviour. *Journal of Political Economics*, 110 (2), 425–457.

Ritter, T., Wilkinson, I.F., and Johnston, W.J., 2004. Managing in complex business networks. *Industrial Marketing Management*, 33 (3), 175–183.

Rodriguez-Ricardo, Y., Sicilia, M., and Lopez, M., 2019. Altruism and internal locus of control as determinants of the intention to participate in crowdfunding: the mediating role of trust. *Journal of Theoretical and Applied Electronic Commerce Research*, 14 (3), 1–16.

Ryan, R.M., and Deci, E.L., 2000. Intrinsic and extrinsic motivations: Classic definitions and new directions. *Contemporary Educational Psychology*, 25, 54–67.

Schervish, P.G., and Havens, J.J., 1997. Social participation and charitable giving: A multivariate analysis. *Voluntas*, 8 (3), 235–260.

Seghers, A., Manigart, S., and Vanacker, T., 2012. The impact of human and social capital on entrepreneurs' knowledge of finance alternatives. *Journal of Small Business Management*, 50 (1), 63–86.

Shane, S., and Cable, D., 2002. Network ties, reputation, and the financing of new ventures. *Management Science*, 48 (3), 364–381.

Slotte-Kock, S., and Coviello, N., 2010. Entrepreneurship research on network processes: A review and ways forward. *Entrepreneurship Theory and Practice*, 34 (1), 31–57.

Stieglitz, S., and Dang-Xuan, L., 2013. Emotions and information diffusion in social media – Sentiment of microblogs and sharing behaviour. *Journal of Management Information System*, 29, 217–248.

Street, C.T., and Cameron, A.F., 2007. External relationships and the small business: A review of small business alliance and network research. *Journal of Small Business Management*, 45 (2), 239–266.

Sura, S., Ahn, J., and Lee, O., 2017. Factors influencing intention to donate via social network site (SNS): From Asian's perspective. *Telematics and Informatics*, 34 (1), 164–176.

Ugur, Z.B., 2018. Donate more, be happier! evidence from the Netherlands. *Applied Research in Quality of Life*, 13, 157–177.

Uzzi, B., and Gillespie, J.J., 2002. Knowledge spillover in corporate financing networks: Embeddedness and the firm's debt performance. *Strategic Management Journal*, 23 (7), 595–618.

Uzzi, B., and Lancaster, R., 2003. Relational embeddedness and learning: The case of bank loan managers and their clients. *Management Science*, 49, 383–399.

Welter, F., and Smallbone, D., 2006. Exploring the role of trust in entrepreneurial activity. *Entrepreneurship Theory and Practice*, 30 (4), 465–475.

Zhang, C.B., Li, Y.N., Wu, B., and Li, D.J., 2017. How WeChat can retain users: Roles of network externalities, social interaction ties, and perceived values in building continuance intention. *Computer Human Behavior*, 69, 284–293.

Zhang, S., De La Haye, K., Ji, M., and An, R., 2018. Applications of social network analysis to obesity: A systematic review. *Obesity Reviews*, 19 (7), 976–988.

Zhang, X., Liu, S., Deng, Z., and Chen, X., 2017. Knowledge sharing motivations in online health communities: A comparative study of health professionals and normal users. *Computer Human Behavior*, 75, 797–810.

Zhao, L., Lu, Y., Wang, B., Chau, P.Y.K., and Zhang, L., 2012. Cultivating the sense of belonging and motivating user participation in virtual communities: A social capital perspective. *International Journal of Information Management*, 32 (6), 574–588.

Zheng, H., Li, D., Wu, J., and Xu, Y., 2014. The role of multidimensional social capital in crowdfunding: A comparative study in China and US. *Information & Management*, 51 (4), 488–496.

10 The scope of crowdfunding as a niche market

Learning objectives

- Examine the dynamic state of crowdfunding as a niche market
- Discuss the catalysts for crowdfunding
- Explore the popularity of crowdfunding as an alternative source of finance in entrepreneurship
- Discuss whether crowdfunding can close the financing gap for small firms
- Examine the correlation between crowdfunding and small firms' performance

Introduction

The rise of social media and rapid technological development has had a significant impact on the market for entrepreneurial finance. There has been an increase in the financing opportunities for new ventures through the emergence of new players and new financial intermediaries (Block *et al.* 2018). Crowdfunding in its various forms has developed into a veritable source of seed capital in many industries (Block *et al.* 2020). This chapter intends to increase our understanding of this new segment of entrepreneurial finance as a niche market.

According to Block *et al.* (2020), crowdfunding has attracted much attention in the academic literature. Crowdfunding is the topic of the majority of the most frequently cited papers published over the last five years in top entrepreneurship journals (Block *et al.* 2020). The most cited paper published in *Small Business Economics* from 2015 is on crowdfunding (Vismara 2016). Block *et al.* (2020) further claims that of the ten most frequently downloaded papers in 2019 that were published in *Small Business Economics* in 2017–2019, five are about crowdfunding and FinTech. These papers received approximately 30,000 downloads (Block *et al.* 2020).

There is a long-term and continuous funding gap in the entrepreneurial finance market. Eldridge *et al.* (2021) suggest that there is an estimated potential finance gap, which is not currently covered by mainstream finance. Similarly, Close Brothers (2016) suggest that 540,000 businesses in the UK are unsure about being able to access the finance they may need to grow or even survive. Therefore, since entrepreneurship and particularly SMEs typically represent a major business segment

DOI: 10.4324/9781003193975-10

and form the backbone of an economy and represent an essential source of economic growth, it is necessary to provide alternative financing options for this business sector (Robu 2013; Gros 2016).

What is a niche market?

A niche market is a segment of a larger market with its own particular needs or preferences, which may be different from the larger market. An entrepreneur who wants to go on a crowdfunding platform to appeal for funding needs to create a product that appeals to a small specialized section of the entire market. There are certain characteristics of crowdfunding which make it a niche market which include less competition, brand loyalty, marketing insight, direct targeting, customer relationships, increased visibility, word of mouth marketing, honed expertise, less resources and greater fun. These characteristics are discussed in detail in the following pages in the context of crowdfunding.

(i) Less competition

Crowdfunding enables greater interactions with backers who help entrepreneurs to develop a highly specific product or service. This results in fewer products in the market with the exact same offering. The more specific the product or service, the less companies to compete with for customers.

(ii) Brand loyalty

Niche marketing makes it possible for projects to build their brand loyalty. Finding a niche and playing to that strength makes it possible for backers to be provided with products and services they need and desire. This creates a competitive advantage because products or services in a niche market are difficult to replicate.

(iii) Marketing insight

Crowdfunding allows the entrepreneur to market to a niche segment of the market; thus, allowing greater knowledge of the customers, who they are and what their needs are. This insight knowledge of customers can help in creating products and services that best serve them. The entrepreneur is then able to best tailor his or her landing page, video, rewards, campaign page, social content, etc. to the niche market. The marketing insight takes the entrepreneur beyond raising funds into learning about new products, innovations and ideas to better serve that market.

(iv) Target audience

Crowdfunding allows the entrepreneur to focus on their niche, which makes the strategies to keep people/backers more engaged in the campaign become even clearer. This enables entrepreneurs to target their promotions to those most likely to pre-order their products. These are the people who meet the requirements for the niche. With this approach, the entrepreneur is able to reach a larger percentage of people who are more likely to back their campaign.

(v) Customer relationships

Crowdfunding enables entrepreneurs to focus on the quality of their relationships with customers and to nurture these relationships. A small customer base has its benefits which can include more personalized emails, more diligent follow ups and more frequent appreciations. It can also enable the accommodation of special requests when it comes to stretching goals, offer better add-ons and get to know the customers on a more individual level or basis. Each of these practices enables the entrepreneur to better serve their backers, thus further enhancing the relationship with them and solidifying their loyalty.

(vi) Increased visibility

Crowdfunding creates uniqueness and businesses with a unique product or service tend to stand out. With crowdfunding, getting in front of the right people is more important than getting in front of a lot of people.

(vii) Word of mouth marketing

Word of mouth marketing is one of the benefits of crowdfunding. People truly trust what their friends and family recommend and it is a great tactic to use with crowdfunding. In crowdfunding, people tend to be in frequent contact with others within their social circle, which translates to more opportunities to get the word out about the products or services. The better the niche is served, the more likely they are to recommend the products or services to others.

(viii) Honed expertise

Marketing to a niche market means becoming an expert or leader within that niche. For most crowdfunding backers, a well-made and hyper-targeted product is more important than size or brand name. An expert at something does not only mean obtaining more customer trust, it also means gaining more brand recognition. Crowdfunding enables a product that is hyper-targeted which undoubtedly stands out.

(ix) Less resources

Effective digital marketing requires a deep understanding of the audience. Crowdfunding as a niche market directs attention to a specific group with a specific need, which makes it that much easier to understand their needs. Moreover, any successful marketing hits the audience in the right place at the right time with the right content. This means using less resources with less work to get the message across that resonates with the group.

(x) Greater fun

Most projects for crowdfunding arise from interests, passions, or special abilities. This means that the entrepreneur is doing more of what he or she loves. The entrepreneur is more likely to enjoy talking to their backers because they are passionate about the same thing. The entrepreneur is more likely to enjoy responding to questions because those answers come from the heart and they are also likely to enjoy updating their campaign page because it is just writing more about what they love.

The catalysts for crowdfunding

The development of the internet and the Web 2.0 technologies are the catalysts in propelling the crowdfunding movement as entrepreneurs have access to a global investment pool, and information can be disseminated without geographical boundary hindrances (Belleflamme *et al.* 2014; Harrison 2013). Harrison (2013) describes crowdfunding as the use of the internet to make fundraising accessible to everyone, whether individuals or businesses.

While other research studies have supported the arguments that technological developments have surpassed barriers-to-entry and made access to finance easier for small businesses, the global financial crisis of 2008 has been suggested as another catalyst. These researchers argue that the global financial crises paved the way for significant changes, primarily on the supply side (Ahlstrom *et al.* 2018; Block *et al.* 2018). Estrin *et al.* (2018) posit that in the aftermath of the financial crisis, there was a distinct lack of funds for early stage financing. In fact, potential investment funds were being held back with the banks complaining of the cost being too high to contemplate smaller transactions. Furthermore, though some seed money was available through angel investors in the UK, further capital for growth and funds for day-to-day liquidity were hard to obtain (Estrin *et al.* 2018). It is therefore not surprising that finance literature has emphasized crowdfunding as becoming a spectacle within the financial ecosphere with an estimated market size of $34 billion in 2015 (Eldridge *et al.* 2021).

The global financial crisis of 2008 gave banks the impetus to retrench from riskier financing such as loans to new businesses. By doing so, it provided traction towards crowdfunding as an alternative to traditional bank-financing (Ahlstrom *et al.* 2018; Dunkley 2016). The financial crisis has helped raise the status of crowdfunding platforms such as Kickstarter in the US and Seedrs in the UK. A large volume of literature has been written about crowdfunding and how it is closing the financing gap (Belleflamme *et al.* 2014; Cichy and Gradon 2015).

Research studies have also reported that social networks have allowed entrepreneurs to reach a large number of backers because network participants can watch the investment decisions of other investors which potentially spreads the information about the project (Vismara 2018). Moreover, social capital has been argued to be a key factor in how entrepreneurs succeed in their crowdfunding campaigns (Agrawal *et al.* 2015; Dorfleitner *et al.* 2018; Eldridge *et al.* 2021; Vismara 2016).

Other catalysts include pricing and regulation (Hornuf and Schwienbacher 2017). Hornuf and Schmitt (2016) and Block *et al.* (2018) argue that the state of a country's regulatory system is a contributing factor in driving crowdfunding growth. Eldridge *et al.* (2021) emphasize that a stronger regulation enables entrepreneurial finance by lowering entry cost and ensuring contractual certainty.

The features of crowdfunding as a niche market

The uniqueness of crowdfunding as a niche market is demonstrated in its impact on firms' growth, ability to retain control over the company, and lack of geographical barriers for investors. Other factors which make crowdfunding a niche market include lower or no investment threshold, lower cost of capital, opportunity to invest like accredited investors and greater degree of satisfaction.

1 Impact on firm growth

The various ways in which crowdfunding impacts a firm's growth are discussed in the following points.

(i) Incremental innovation

There are different perspectives on how crowdfunding can impact opportunities for firm growth and development, with a general consensus that crowdfunding has the potential to provide support for small businesses in some particular areas (Eldridge *et al.* 2021). Apart from increased access to funding, there can be a number of non-financial benefits to small businesses utilizing crowdfunding, with the contribution towards incremental/radical innovation viewed as the greatest benefit, as it promotes firms' growth (Eldridge 2021; Paschen 2017; Stanko and Henard 2016).

In demonstrating how crowdfunding is a niche market, Stanko and Henard (2016) suggest that crowdfunding is changing how entrepreneurs bring new products to the market. It has allowed thousands of innovating entrepreneurs to raise money, build brand awareness and join a broader conversation with large numbers of potential backers, while still in the product development process. Stanko and Henard (2017, p. 2) stress that "crowdfunding has quickly evolved into a commonly used vehicle to help innovating entrepreneurs get products developed and is one of the ways that innovative, small organizations have been able to access capital since the financial crisis".

However, some studies suggest different levels of impact, which are dependent on other factors (Eldridge *et al.* 2021). For example, Eldridge *et al.* (2021) argue that equity crowdfunding should increase the level of innovation in small firms due to idea generation and external feedback from backers. By the same taken, Herve and Schwienbacher (2018) posit that these influence mechanisms play an important role in establishing the link between innovation and entrepreneurial firms. Herve and Schwienbacher (2018) have also argued that equity crowdfunding can reduce the funding gap for innovative start-ups by offering new sources of capital to innovation-driven firms. This is significant if crowdfunding acts as a source of finance to projects that would not be funded otherwise (Eldridge *et al.* 2021).

In a study conducted by Stanko and Henard (2016) to assess the contribution of crowdfunding to product development, the findings suggest that the number of updates provided to backers and openness to external ideas are significant contributors towards increased innovation and subsequent growth. Similarly, Paschen (2017) suggests that, apart from access to finance, when small firms exploit crowdfunding platforms, they obtain external support to grow their businesses. Thus, small firms use the concept of an environment of openness to provide constant updates to backers while receiving feedback to improve their products and enhance their understanding of customer preferences (Eldridge *et al.* 2021).

Eldridge *et al.* (2021) posit that crowdfunding can also generate money in a more efficient way than traditional investors such as banks and professional equity investors like business angels and venture capital funds, thus, potentially contributing to innovation activities. Eldridge *et al.* (2021) also indicates that crowdfunding can influence the innovation process in start-ups through a subtler way by acting as a conduit for the crowd to provide feedback to the entrepreneur. For example, crowds can provide ideas on the development of the product during and after the campaign, and extend valuable information on the future demand for the new product. In this way, crowdfunding enables the participation of the crowd in the innovation process itself (Eldridge *et al.* 2021). Schwienbacher and Larralde (2012) argue that this is the reason that crowdfunding is often associated with crowdsourcing, which also clarifies the mechanism through which the wisdom-of-crowd effect is observed.

(ii) The "wisdom-of-crowd" argument

The principle of the wisdom-of-crowd states that the crowd displays more wisdom than an individual (even an expert) when solving problems or making decisions (Eldridge *et al.* 2021; Polzin *et al.* 2017; Schwienbacher and Larralde 2012). Eldridge *et al.* (2021) argue that as the crowd can offer direct feedback on the product, it can potentially be more valuable to the firm than professional investors' guidance on business development. Eldridge *et al.* remark: "Not only can crowds provide a new source of financing to innovation-driven projects, they can also offer new ideas and feedback" (Eldridge *et al.* 2021, p. 109). At the same time, Stanko and Henard (2017) argue that while it might be intuitive to look at crowdfunding as a primarily financial exercise, the true value of crowdfunding is the ability to learn from backers and to use them as ambassadors for the crowdfunded product.

Furthermore, Stanko and Henard (2017) suggest that backers are central to understanding crowdfunding's potential innovation effects. Principally, crowdfunding allows early stage entrepreneurs access to capital, but it also allows them to potentially engage with a large number of individuals in ways that were previously unavailable. In support of Eldridge *et al.* (2021), Stanko and Henard (2017) posit that crowdfunding backers not only offer their money, but also their opinions. Backers often want to become engaged in product development alongside the innovating entrepreneur, as that experience is typically considered by backers to be a rewarding part of the process (Agrawal *et al.* 2014). This injection of large numbers of external voices into the product development process has the potential to dramatically impact innovation efforts and might lead to a heightened focus on radical innovation (Stanko and Henard 2017).

The argument of "the wisdom of the crowd" explains that the backers can be more effective in solving problems in a company than individuals or teams, and this eventually means that crowdfunders are more effective than several individual investors (Golic 2014). Against this background, the risk overtaken by backers can be much lower, and not just because of the smaller amount of money they invest individually, but due to the fact that they can become consumers. The moment the product is launched in the market they have the drive to promote the product, especially if they participate in the distribution of income. By contrast, when the project/venture is financed by large investors, the product promotion would require a significant advertising campaign (Golic 2014).

(iii) Cost reduction

One of the reasons why companies use crowds is cost reduction (Schwienbacher and Larralde 2012). Golic (2014) posits that by participating in the creation of a product and improving its design, crowdfunders contribute to creating value for the entrepreneur. Moreover, it allows the company to reduce the length of the development of new products, as well as their costs, and to have a better accepted product in the market. Golic (2014) concludes that, without additional costs, no other form of investment but crowdfunding can facilitate the sale of the product in advance. As a niche market, it can be said that crowdfunding is now one of the most promising tools to facilitate innovation, facilitate the generation of jobs and ensure economic growth.

De Buyser *et al.* (2012) indicate that crowdfunding is one of the most attractive ways to fund new ideas, small business and job generation. De Buysere *et al.* (2012) also describes crowdfunding as a very democratic tool that enables the creation of value on many levels, not only in the domain of finance. By enabling easier access to investor capital for businesses that would otherwise have had a hard time obtaining it, equity crowdfunding should stimulate the local and national economies through new business formation and more job creation (Picardo 2020).

Similarly, Eldridge *et al.* (2021) and Paschen (2017) suggest the scope of crowdfunding as a niche market by arguing that crowdfunding supports small business growth through the reduction of the cost of financing and the provision of knowledge from eternal backers. However, Cumming *et al.* (2021) suggest that the degree of growth may depend on the crowdfunding model employed since backers may be more interested in equity crowdfunding models because of the ownership stake in the investment and therefore more likely to contribute to ideas and provide feedback.

Nonetheless, Eldridge *et al.* (2021) argue that crowdfunding reduces the requirement for long-term debt (which has a negative correlation with firm growth) by value creation, increasing the level of reserves within a firm, which allows for financing expansion. Consequently, there is a positive relationship between crowdfunding and growth opportunity, as the provision of additional funding allows for the financing of growth. In addition to this argument, crowdfunding enables the entrepreneur to test the waters to see whether the idea has merit without taking on too much financial risk. With crowdfunding it is possible to test the market and get some reactions before spending money on inventories, materials or development which beats funding an unproven project/idea with the more expensive traditional sources of finance.

(iv) Customer loyalty

In support of the assertion of crowdfunding as a niche market, Estrin *et al.* (2018) found that entrepreneurs use their communication with investors via the crowdfunding platforms to further develop their products and create a loyal customer base. Although Estrin *et al.* (2018) acknowledged that equity crowdfunding cannot be a substitute for expert guidance provided by traditional early-stage financiers, it does hold promise for building a marketplace for the budding entrepreneurs in the sense that equity crowdfunding platforms can be used to create new growth opportunities. This is possible as participants on the equity crowdfunding platforms can engage with each other through posts, comments and followers, creating a wisdom-of-crowd effect (Eldridge *et al.* 2021). In addition, information cascades potentially and becomes a channel for the speedy and costless transfer of knowledge from customers to the entrepreneurs (Schwienbacher and Larralde 2012; Vismara 2018). Eldridge *et al.* (2021) therefore conclude that equity crowdfunding is a niche market which enhances customer loyalty, small firm growth opportunity, increased innovation and financial performance.

(v) A valuable form of marketing

Crowdfunding enables entrepreneurs to pitch their businesses through online platforms which can be a valuable form of marketing and result in media attention. It can provide the entrepreneur valuable signals about the market potential of the product/project that they want to run (Schwienbacher and Larralde 2012). It is a good way to test the public reaction to a product/idea. Golic (2014) argues that specifically, it indicates that demand for the product will be good if it is demonstrated that there is great interest in investing in the presented venture, and if it is assumed that investors are at the same time the potential consumers/customers.

Crowdfunding is also used for marketing purposes since it provokes interest in new projects in the early stages of their development and it helps to achieve competitive advantage even before the projects see the light of day (Golic 2014; Mollick 2014). According to Gajda and Walton (2013), the concept of crowdfunding as a niche market is reflected in the fact that the investors are also potential customers and ambassadors of the project and assist in its promotion through their own networks. The investors are usually identified with the project, being open to change and willing to help to ensure the social confirmation of the concept (Golic 2014).

It is also a valuable form of marketing since it is possible for the campaign to go viral or spread quickly across social media, exposing the product or service to a large number of potential customers which could have been impossible to reach otherwise. The distinctiveness of crowdfunding as a valuable form of marketing is that a successful campaign validates the business idea. This is because reaching or exceeding the fundraising goal removes every doubt and proves that there is a demand for the product or service.

2 Retaining management control over company

Unlike the traditional sources of funding such as business angels and venture capital which allow investors significant control over company decision, crowdfunding does not give investors such rights. Therefore, when a company has raised capital through crowdfunding, the entrepreneurs do not lose control of their companies or their right to make their own business decisions except it is equity crowdfunding which allows investors to have some degree of control (Valanciene and Jegeleviciute 2013). Depending on the type of crowdfunding, a successful campaign can mean that the entrepreneur only delivers rewards to backers without having to give up any equity or lose any control of the company. This makes crowdfunding a niche financial market.

3 No geographical barriers to investors

Compared to other forms of financing, a big advantage of crowdfunding as a niche market is the removal of geographic barriers to investment, which means that the geographical distance between the entrepreneur and the investor is not a problem (Belleflamme *et al*. 2014; Golic 2014). For example, when Sellaband offered royalty sharing to investors, more than 86% of the funds were from people who were more than 60 miles away from the entrepreneur, and the average distance between creators and investors was approximately 3,000 miles (Agrawal *et al*. 2014).

Although crowdfunding encourages people to invest in their communities and thus contribute to sustainable economic development, it also allows most businesses to raise funds globally (Valanciene and Jegeleviciute 2013). This means that the concept of crowdfunding as a niche market is reflected in the fact that it enables local projects to attract global investors (Golic 2014).

4 Lower/no investment threshold

The amount of money required by entrepreneurs is another factor which makes crowdfunding a niche market. Bhide (1992) argues that financiers all have different pre-defined amounts they are willing to invest. For example, initial public offerings (IPOs) have a legal minimal threshold to be placed on the stock market which prevents small companies to use it (Botazzi and Da Rin 2001; Schwienbacher and Larralde 2012). In addition, the cost of implementation of IPOs is rather high and places a condition that companies should reach a certain threshold and have reduced the risk factor (Berger and Udell 1998). Furthermore, venture capitals (VCs) usually have high minimum investments that make them unsuited to the needs of small ventures (Bhide 1992). Schwienbacher (2007) and Schwienbacher and Larralde (2012) argue that this may lead to a crucial trade-off as to when to start entrepreneurial activities, since smaller amounts need to be financed by other investor types like business angels.

Besides, small business finance is highly and disproportionally affected by macroeconomic conditions (Berger and Udell 1998). Other factors include market forecasts, stock market health; overall economy health, and monetary policy all have effects on small business finance (Schwienbacher and Larralde 2012). Black and Gilson (1998) also argue that VC financing is also affected by market conditions because their entry is conditioned by their exit strategy based on the stock market health.

5 Lower cost of capital

Lower cost of capital also makes crowdfunding a niche marker. Agrawal *et al.* (2014) opine that creators typically access capital for early-stage ventures from sources such as personal savings, home-equity loans, personal credit cards, friends and family members, angel investors and venture capitalists. Under certain conditions, crowdfunding may enable creators to access capital at a lower cost than traditional sources for three reasons:

(i) Better matches

Creators match with those individuals who have the highest willingness to pay for equity in their venture (or for early access to their new product, etc.) where the search for such matches occurs across a global rather than local pool of potential funders. Thus, as opposed to traditional online mechanisms for financing early-stage creative ventures, access to capital is not so strongly influenced by the creator's location as discussed earlier.

(ii) Bundling

Non-equity-based crowdfunding demonstrates that under certain conditions funders value early access to products, recognition for discovering innovations, participating in a new venture's community of supporters, and other non-pecuniary rewards in return for financial backing. To the extent that platforms facilitate a hybrid approach and allow creators to bundle the sale of equity with other rewards they wish to offer (e.g. early access to products, limited-edition products, recognition), creators may be able to lower their cost of capital by "selling" goods that are otherwise difficult to trade in traditional markets for early-stage capital.

(iii) Information

To the extent that crowdfunding generates more information than traditional sources of early-stage capital (e.g. interest from other investors, ideas for product modifications and extensions from potential users), this information may increase funders' willingness to pay, thus lowering the cost of capital. For example, according to Agrawal *et al.* (2014), despite the negative reaction Pebble creator Eric Migicovsky received from traditional early-stage investors, the information conveyed via the crowdfunding community's strong response to his product validated his hypothesis that a wearable device with that particular design and set of features would have broad appeal. This information helped in lowering his cost of capital.

6 Opportunity to invest like accredited investors

Prior to crowdfunding, only accredited investors, who are usually high net-worth individuals who have certain defined levels of income or assets, could participate in early-stage, speculative ventures that held the promise of high reward and equally high risk (Picardo 2020).

The minimum amount of threshold for such investments was usually quite high. However, equity crowdfunding makes it possible for the average investor to invest a much smaller amount in such ventures. Thus, it provides a level playing field between accredited and non-accredited investors (Picardo 2020).

7 Greater degree of satisfaction

Investing through equity crowdfunding can give the investor a greater degree of personal satisfaction than investing in a blue-chip or large-cap company (Picardo 2020). This is because the investor can choose to focus on businesses or ideas that resonate with them, or that are involved with causes in which the investor has a deep belief. For example, an environmentally conscious investor may choose to invest in a company that is developing a more effective method of measuring air pollution. Equity crowdfunding may offer more avenues for such targeted investments than publicly traded companies.

Crowdfunding: closing the financing gap for small firms as a niche market

It is generally known both in developed and developing countries that start-ups and SMEs face immense difficulties securing finance from conventional sources such as bank financing, as well as bearing the burden of debt repayment during the initial stages of their development. This is one of the main reasons why small businesses fail during the consolidation stage. It is also well known that start-ups and small businesses have even fewer sources of financing with most being dependent on personal resources, family and friends.

In their report, "Banking on Growth: Closing the SME funding gap", Close Brothers (2016) point out the following as the evolving financial requirements of an SME:

- SMEs are not using the right types of finance: micro SMEs are reliant on personal savings; overdrafts are overused by SMEs of all sizes to fund growth; personal credit cards are regularly used to meet cash flow needs
- Despite the myriad of options available, 540,000 businesses in the UK are now unsure about being able to access the finance they may need to grow or even survive
- A lack of longer-term planning, especially among small firms, is exacerbating the problem
- Weak support from banks is failing to resolve these issues with just 19% of SMEs saying bank advice always meets their needs

The question then is: Can crowdfunding close the financing gap for small firms? Is crowdfunding the answer to small firms' funding gap? Research studies such as that by Perkins (2014) suggest that SMEs face challenges in gaining access to finance which leads to the conclusion that crowdfunding can close the funding gap for small firms.

Perkins (2014) reveals that there is a £4.3 billion gap between loan applications by SMEs and loans actually obtained by such businesses. The average finance gap for small businesses with 10–49 employees is £11,752 per business, while for medium-sized businesses (i.e. firms with 50–249 employees) the average funding gap is £69,961 (Perkins 2014). Three hundred and one (301) senior financial decision-makers from UK SMEs took part in the Perkins (2014) study and two-thirds expressed dissatisfaction with the traditional sources of funding for small firms. They stressed that bank bureaucracy, for example, would put them off from applying for bank loans.

Although there has been a significant improvement from the banking sector with regards to small business loans, various studies (such as Agrawal *et al.* 2014; Borello and Veronica 2015) have warned that small businesses may still struggle to secure loans because of the stringent criteria applied to such loans. Perkins (2014) argues that crowdfunding may be the answer to the finance gap within the small firm sector. In support of this argument, Perkins (2014) presents some examples of crowdfunding ventures in the hospitality sector such as Pizza Rossa which successfully raised £440,000 in just 17 days through a crowdfunding campaign. Another example is The Clove Club, which raised money through crowdfunding to become the first crowdfunded restaurant to make it onto the World's 50 Best Restaurant 2014 top list.

Various studies have demonstrated that the banks are not providing small businesses with the funding they need. It is argued that crowdfunding can help in addressing the banking shortfall and offer a good opportunity to credit-worthy businesses to access the much-needed finance which is not easily available from the traditional sources. Therefore, we can argue that crowdfunding provides a veritable alternative finance to small businesses, thus filling the finance gap. We also argue that crowdfunding opens up banking sector competition through the provision of alternative finance.

Impact of crowdfunding as a niche market

An international survey was undertaken by Crowdfunding Capital Advisors in 2014 to investigate crowdfunding marketing benefits, job creation, follow-on investment and return on investment. The survey was directed at companies that had successfully raised capital via rewards, equity and debt-based crowdfunding (the survey specifically excluded philanthropic causes). The findings point to crowdfunding as a niche market. The details are as follows:

- Crowdfunded companies increased quarterly revenues by 24% on average, post crowdfunding (not including amounts raised by crowdfunding).
- Equity-based crowdfunded companies increased revenues by 351% (after the crowdfunding campaign). None of the companies had received money from capital markets before.
- 39% of companies hired on average two new employees per company after crowdfunding.
- Within three months of a crowdfunding campaign, 28% of the companies had closed an angel investor or venture capital round. However, crowdfunding might discourage business angels or venture capitalists from participating, due to the hassle of having to deal with many small investors.
- Every hour invested in a successful crowdfunding campaign returned US$813. On average, a company invested 135 hours of staff time during 45 days, estimated at about US$2,100.
- The minimum and maximum amounts raised via crowdfunding ranged from US$15,600 to US$936,000.

Source: Robano (2015).

Crowdfunding: a niche market for the creative industries

Crowdfunding is a growing and increasingly mature industry. It has become a significant way for people to fund their ideas and projects across a number of industries. In particular, it has become significantly popular in the creative industries.

In recent years there has been a growing recognition of the significance of the creative industries in knowledge-based economies. Not only are they regarded as a vehicle to foster growth and employment, but they also contribute to promoting innovation and skills development and maintaining cultural identity, and play an important role in enhancing cultural diversity.

As a result, many countries, regions and cities are attracted by their potential as an engine for development (OECD 2014). The importance of the creative industries in Europe has been steadily increasing in recent years. The employment volume of the creative industries of 6.4 million is high above that of the automobile and chemical industries (2.2 and 1.9 million respectively) (EENC 2011). In Europe around 80% of enterprises in the creative industries consist of SMEs (HKU 2010).

However, one of the greatest obstacles faced by entrepreneurs and enterprises in the creative sector is how to access funds to finance their endeavours. Considering that creative industries' main asset is intangible, financial institutions such as banks often fail to sufficiently recognize their economic value (HKU 2010). For this reason, many entrepreneurs and SMEs are now turning to crowdfunding as an alternative source of access to capital. In the creative sector, crowdfunding also has a unique dual function of providing both private financing and generating publicity and attention for a project.

For example, in 2013, 3 million people pledged US$480 million to Kickstarter, the most successful creative crowdfunding platform in the United States, and funded over 19,900 creative projects (Kickstarter 2013).

Furthermore, it can be stated that crowdfunding is already an established financing instrument in the creative industries, with a large space for growth. Policies should be oriented to the potential role of creative crowdfunding as a driver of innovation and competition in the creative sector is likely to keep growing, thus creative SMEs and entrepreneurs' access to information and knowledge about which project characteristics and crowdfunding practices are feasible to success are key for achieving growth and sustainability.

Source: Robano (2015).

Crowdfunding: a niche market for gender entrepreneurship

Female borrowers seek and receive less start-up capital than male entrepreneurs. One reason for this disparity is a lack of female representation among investors of start-ups, and a potential solution is to increase the proportion of women in decision-making roles. Both the problem and the solution implicitly rely on homophily – that women will support other women given a chance. However, a lack of clarity over when and how homophily influences individual choices makes it uncertain when better representation is actually advantageous.

Using data from crowdfunding, Greenberg and Mollick (2014) empirically examine whether a higher proportion of female investors leads to a higher success rate in capital-raising for women. They find that women outperform men, and are more likely to succeed at a crowdfunding campaign, all other things being equal. This effect primarily holds for female borrowers proposing technological projects, a category that is largely dominated by male borrowers and investors.

Source: Greenberg and Mollick (2014).

Summary

In this chapter, crowdfunding is not only seen as an alternative way to fill the gap in the absence of capital for small businesses which have been marginalized by traditional funding sources, it is also seen as a niche market. The chapter has also examined the correlation between crowdfunding and small firms' performance and has clarified the various aspects of crowdfunding as a niche market and the benefits of its use for small businesses and thus gaining more knowledge on this fast-growing phenomenon. Although the various alternative forms of funding have their advantages and disadvantages, it is highly likely that crowdfunding is the cheapest source of funding for most projects (Belleflamme *et al.* 2014). According to Belleflamme *et al.* (2014), crowdfunding can be seen as a broader concept whose sole aim is not only to raise funds, but it is also a way to develop corporate activities through the process of raising funds.

Crowdfunding is still at its infancy, but has the ability to transform businesses in an unprecedented way. With the rapid changes and evolution of technology, the uniqueness of crowdfunding as a niche market is probably a tip of the iceberg with regards to how it can transform business models. It changes the game by enabling more people to have a stake in the product/service, which can also redefine ownership in the new digital age.

Discussion questions

1 How would you define a niche market in the context of crowdfunding?
2 Discuss the features of crowdfunding as a new market niche.
3 What are the catalysts for the development of crowdfunding as a niche market?
4 Is crowdfunding the answer to the finance gap for small firms?

Test questions

1 Students should debate the extent of the impact of crowdfunding on:

  (i) SME innovation
  (ii) SME growth

2 Students should critically discuss the sustainability of crowdfunding as a niche market.
3 What do you understand by the term "finance gap"? Do you think a "finance gap" still exists for small businesses?

Glossary of key terminologies

Accredited investor   Accredited investor is a high net-worth individual or a business entity that is allowed to trade securities that may not be registered with financial authorities. They are entitled to this privileged access by satisfying at least one requirement regarding their income, net worth, asset size, governance status, or professional experience.

Bundling Bundling is a marketing strategy where companies sell several products or services together as a single combined unit.

Financing gap A finance gap arises when the demand for finance is greater than the willingness of financial institutions to supply it at current market conditions.

FinTech A new financial technology which connects modern and, mainly, internet-related technologies with established business activities of the financial services industry.

Incremental innovation Incremental innovation is a series of small improvements or upgrades made to a company's existing products, services, processes or methods.

Wisdom-of-crowds The idea that large groups of people are collectively smarter than individual experts.

Recommended reading

The Art of Service, 2020. *Finding niche markets a complete guide.* Brendale: The Art of Service – Finding Niche Markets Publishing.

Cumming, D., and Hornuf, L., eds., 2018. *The economics of crowdfunding: Start-ups, portals and investor behavior.* Cham, CH: Palgrave Macmillan.

Dresner, S., 2014. *Crowdfunding: A guide to raising capital on the internet.* Hoboken: Wiley.

Evans, D.S., and Schmalensee, R., 2016. *Matchmakers: The new economics of multisided platforms.* Cambridge: Harvard Business Review Press.

Gompers, P., and Lerner, J., 2011. *The money of invention.* Boston: Harvard Business School Press.

References

Agrawal, A., Catalini, C., and Goldfarb, A., 2014. Some simple economics of crowdfunding. *Innovation Policy and the Economy*, 14, 63–97.

Agrawal, A., Catalini, C., and Goldfarb, A., 2015. Crowdfunding: Geography, social networks, and the timing of investment decisions. *Journal of Economics and Management Strategy*, 24 (2), 253–274.

Ahlstrom, D., Cumming, D., and Vismara, S., 2018. New methods of entrepreneurial firm financing: FinTech, crowdfunding and corporate governance implications. *Corporate Governance: An International Review*, 310–313.

Belleflamme, P., Lambert, T., and Schwienbacher, A., 2014. Crowdfunding: Tapping the right crowd. *Journal of Business Venturing*, 29 (5), 585–609.

Berger, A.N., and Udell, G.F., 1998. The economics of small business finance the roles of private equity and debt markets in the financial growth cycle. *Journal of Banking and Finance*, 22 (6–8), 613–673.

Bhide, A., 1992. Bootstrap finance: The art of start-ups. *Harvard Business Review*, 70 (66), 109–117.

Black, B., and Gilson, R., 1998. Venture capital and the structure of capital markets: banks versus stock markets. *Journal of Financial Economics*, 47, 243–277.

Block, J.H., Colombo, M.G., Cumming, D.J., and Vismara, S., 2018. New players in entrepreneurial finance and why they are there. *Small Business Economics*, 50 (2), 239–250.

Block, J.H., Groh, A., Hornuf, L., Vanacker, T., and Vismara, S., 2020. The entrepreneurial finance markets of the future: A comparison of crowdfunding and initial coin offerings. *Small Business Economics*. Available from: https://doi.org/10.1007/s11187-020-00330-2.

Borello, G., and Veronica, D.C., 2015. The funding gap and the role of financial return crowdfunding: Some evidence from european platforms. *Journal of Internet Banking and Commerce*, 20 (1), 1–20.

Botazzi, L., and Da Rin, M., 2001. Venture Capital in Europe and the Financing of Innovative Companies. *Economic Policy*, 34, 231–269.

Cichy, J., and Gradon, W., 2015. Crowdfunding as a mechanism for financing small and medium-sized enterprises. *eFinance-Financial Internet Quarterly*, 12 (3), 38–48.

Close Brothers, 2016. *Banking on growth: Closing The SME funding gap* (London). Available from: www.closebrothers.com/system/files/press/Banking-on-Growth-Closing-the-SME-funding-gap.pdf [Accessed 3 June 2021].

Cumming, D., Vanacker, T., and Zahra, S., 2021. Equity crowdfunding and governance: toward an integrative model and research agenda. *Academy of Management Perspectives*, 35 (1). Available from: https://doi.org/10.5465/amp.2017.0208

De Buysere, K., Gajda, O., Kleverlaan, R., and Marom, D., 2012. *A framework for European crowdfunding*. Available from: www.crowdfundingframework.eu/index.html [Accessed 6 June 2021].

Dorfleitner, G., Hornuf, L., and Weber, M., 2018. Dynamics of investor communication in equity crowdfunding. *Electronic Markets*, 28, 523–540.

Dunkley, E., 2016. Crowdfunding rides to the rescue of many SMEs. *Financial Times*. Available from: www.ft.com/content/a1b69b96-475b-11e5-af2f-4d6e0e5eda22 [Accessed 3 June 2021].

EENC., 2011. Crowdfunding Schemes in Europe, cited in Robano, V., 2015. Case study on crowdfunding working party on SMEs and entrepreneurship (WPSMEE). *ResearchGate*. Available from: www.researchgate.net/publication/312889188

Eldridge, D., Nisar, T., and Torchia, M., 2021. What impact does equity crowdfunding have on SME innovation and growth? An empirical study. *Small Business Economics*, 56, 105–120.

Estrin, S., Gozman, D., and Khavul, S., 2018. The evolution and adoption of equity crowdfunding: Entrepreneur and investor entry into a new market. *Small Business Economics*, 51, 425–439.

Gajda, O., and Walton, J., 2013. *Review of crowdfunding for development initiatives: Evidence on demand*. Available from: http://dx.doi.org/10.12774/eod_hd061.jul2013.gadja;walton [Accessed 12 June 2022].

Golic, Z., 2014. Advantages of crowdfunding as an alternative source of financing of small and medium-sized enterprises. *Proceedings of the Faculty of Economics in East Sarajevo*, 8, 39–48. Available from: https://doi.org/10.7251/ZREFIS1408039G.

Greenberg, J., and Mollick, E.R., 2014. *Leaning in or leaning on? Gender, homophily, and activism in crowdfunding*. Available from: http://ssrn.com/abstract=2462254

Gros, D., 2016. How would brexit affect finance for SMEs? *The Guardian*. Available from: www.theguardian.com/smallbusiness-network/2016/apr/05/how-would-brexit-affectfinance-for-smes [Accessed 3 June 2021].

Harrison, R., 2013. Crowdfunding and the revitalization of the early stage risk capital market: catalyst or chimera? *Venture Capital*, 15 (4), 283–287.

Herve, F., and Schwienbacher, A., 2018. Crowdfunding and innovation. *Journal of Economic Surveys*, 32(5), 1514–1530.

Hornuf, L., and Schmitt, M., 2016. Success and failure in equity crowdfunding. *CESifo DICE Report*, 14 (2), 16–22.

Hornuf, L., and Schwienbacher, A., 2017. Should securities regulation promote equity crowdfunding? *Small Business Economics*, 49(3), 579–593.

Kickstarter, 2013. The year in Kickstarter, cited in Robano, V., 2015. Case Study on Crowdfunding Working Party on SMEs and Entrepreneurship (WPSMEE), ResearchGate. Available from: www.researchgate.net/publication/312889188

Mollick, E., 2014. The dynamics of crowdfunding: An exploratory study. *Journal of Business Venturing*, 29(1), 1–16.

OECD, 2014. *Tourism and the creative economy. An OECD Scoreboard – Highlights*. Austria: OECD Publishing.

Paschen, J., 2017. Choose wisely: Crowdfunding through the stages of the start-up life cycle. Business Horizons, 60 (2), 179–188.

Perkins, C., 2014. *With a Little help from my friends: Is Crowdfunding the answer to the SME finance gap?* Available from: www.bighospitality.co.uk/Article/2014/05/12/Crowdfunding-SME-finance-gap [Accessed 6 July 2021].

Picardo, E., 2020. Invest through equity crowdfunding: Risks and rewards. *Investopedia*. Available from: www.investopedia.com/articles/investing/102015/invest-through-equity-crowdfunding-risks-and-rewards.asp [Accessed 3 July 2021].

Polzin, F., Toxopeus, H., and Stam, E., 2017. The wisdom of the crowd in funding: information heterogeneity and social networks of crowdfunders. *Small Business Economics*. https://doi.org/10.1007/s11187-016-9829-3

Robano, V., 2015. Case study on crowdfunding working party on SMEs and entrepreneurship (WPSMEE). *ResearchGate*. Available from: www.researchgate.net/publication/312889188

Robu, M., 2013. The dynamic and importance of SMEs in economy. *The USV Annals of Economics and Public Administration*, 13 (1), 84–89.

Schwienbacher, A., 2007. A theoretical analysis of optimal financing strategies for different types of capital-constrained entrepreneurs. *Journal of Business Venturing*, 22 (6), 753–781.

Schwienbacher, A., and Larralde, B., 2012. Crowdfunding of small entrepreneurial ventures. *In*: D. Cumming, ed. *The Oxford handbook of entrepreneurial finance*. Oxford: Oxford University Press, 369–391.

Stanko, M., and Henard, D., 2016. How crowdfunding influences innovation. *MIT Sloan Review*, 57 (3), 15–17.

Stanko, M., and Henard, D., 2017. Toward a better understanding of crowdfunding, openness and the consequences for innovation. *Research Policy*. Available from: https://doi.org/10.1016/j.respol.2017.02.003

Valanciene, L., and Jegeleviciute, S., 2013. Valuation of crowdfunding: Benefits and drawbacks. *Economics and Management*, 18 (1), 39–48.

Vismara, S., 2016. Equity retention and social network theory in equity crowdfunding. *Small Business Economics*, 46 (4), 579–590.

Vismara, S., 2018. Information cascades among investors in equity crowdfunding. *Entrepreneurship Theory and Practice*, 42(3), 467–497.

11 Areas for government assistance

Learning objectives

- Review the regulatory framework for crowdfunding
- Explore the role of blockchain technology in regulatory compliance and security
- Examine government's efforts towards the development of crowdfunding

Introduction

The global markets for crowdfunding ventures have expanded at a rapid rate during the last few years. Crowdfunding has garnered increasing global attention in the fields of economics, politics and regulation due to the almost €50 billion raised globally between 2010 and 2017 (Chervyakov and Rocholl 2019). The market is dominated by United States-based platforms that have raised a total of €25.8 billion. The European Union comes in second with a total of €16.9 billion while Asia raised €5.5 billion (Chervyakov and Rocholl 2019). With limited cross-border trade, the proportion of European Union markets (excluding the United Kingdom) remains low. Collectively, these three regions are accountable for 99% of the world's crowdfunding activity.

The average annual growth rate of funds raised between 2011 and 2017 was 80% in the US, 85% in Europe, and 557% in Asia (Chervyakov and Rocholl 2019). In other word, the crowdfunding business in Europe and the rest of the world has proven amazing growth rates and a large amount of untapped potential over the past several years. A policy framework that allows for continuing expansion would facilitate the realization of this potential (Ziegler *et al.* 2017, 2018; Chervyakov and Rocholl 2019).

As a result of the quick and consistent expansion of crowdfunding, governments are becoming increasingly aware of the opportunities and hazards involved with it (Chervyakov and Rocholl 2019). One of the most significant obstacles to the growth of these companies is Europe's inability to establish a clear and consistent legislative framework. There may be trade-offs between investor protection and the encouragement of financial innovation and economic progress in the regulation of crowdfunding. Financial Conduct Authority (FCA) regulates the operations of both peer-to-peer lending and equity-based crowdfunding. In contrast, neither the

DOI: 10.4324/9781003193975-11

United Kingdom nor the United States have yet to govern reward-based crowd-funding (RBC) and donation-based crowdfunding (DBC). In the latter two models, the absence of norms and regulations raises serious concerns, such as the likelihood of fraudulent behaviour and malpractice.

In March of 2018, the European Commission presented a set of measures with the purpose of resolving the key deficiencies of the existing regulatory framework and replacing it with an EU-wide regime (European Commission 2018). The JOBS Act was not put into law until 2012, and there has been a delayed rollout of relevant legislation in the United States till date.

Regulatory support of government

By the year 2010, peer-to-peer lending companies in the financial technology industry had started springing up in every region of the world. The financing needs of small and medium-sized enterprises (SMEs) were the subject of some of the earliest examples of peer-to-peer lending. Funding Circle was one of the first companies in the financial technology (FinTech) industry to apply the peer-to-peer (P2P) lending model exclusively to business loans not long after the company was established in 2010 (Milne and Parboteeah 2016). Although consumer loans still make up the majority of peer-to-peer lending model iterations, the asset class has greatly grown to include a wide range of other types of loans.

The "Peer-to-Peer Finance Organisation" of the United Kingdom was the first business association to concentrate solely on peer-to-peer lending when it was established in 2011. Despite the fact that this business association discontinued activities in recent years, it was established at a critical juncture in the course of the development of the environment in the United Kingdom. This association formed a code of conduct, which led to the formation of "self-regulation" rules. These guidelines were developed well in advance of any official regulations that the industry was required to comply with. In 2013, the Financial Conduct Authority in the United Kingdom held its first consultation on crowdfunding, which encompassed several different forms of online lending that are together referred to as "loan-based crowdfunding". The Financial Conduct Authority (FCA) has had oversight of the peer-to-peer lending industry in the UK since it was established in 2014. By the year 2016, there were several instances all across the world of P2P and marketplace activities being regulated, either in their planned or existent forms.

By the end of the decade, crowdfunding had developed into a phenomenon that was seen all around the world and was becoming increasingly frequent. Nearly every country in the world has at least one platform offering crowdfunding. The crowdfunding market in China is projected to be the largest in the world in 2017, with an estimated value of US$356 billion (Ziegler *et al.* 2018). Specifically, China offers an intriguing evolution path in a context that is characterized by a regulatory environment that is relatively underdeveloped, where loans are riskier than they are in the United States or the United Kingdom, where the credit referencing system is not fully developed, and where loans are primarily financed by households. China offers an intriguing evolution path in this context because it is characterized by these factors. Because of these factors, China makes for an interesting case study about the possible future course of action (Milne and Parboteeah 2016).

However, during the past few years, there has been an increase in worry surrounding the possibility of fraud in the crowdfunding market, particularly in China. This is especially the case in the wake of the demise of a number of platforms, after having been uncovered that some of them had been operating as a "Ponzi scheme" (Albrecht *et al.* 2017). At the end of 2016, the China Banking Regulatory Commission issued a series of interim rules for the peer-to-peer lending market in an effort to lessen the likelihood of credit risk occurring in the industry (Chorzempa 2018). Retail investors, thanks to the establishment of a "capital pool", were able to lend directly to the platform, as opposed to the case in other jurisdictions, providing funds for particular loans or loan sections that were mediated by the platforms.

To solve the problems caused by Chinese platforms behaving more like deposit takers, the establishment of a "capital pool" was required as a solution. A course correction has been necessary as a consequence of this crackdown, which has led to a 34% decrease in market volume for the Chinese crowdfunding business between 2017 and 2018 (Milne and Parboteeah 2016; Albrecht *et al.* 2017). Due to regulatory crackdowns and the exit of platforms accused of problematic behaviour, the market is expected to recover gradually, although how quickly and to what extent is unknown.

Review of the regulatory framework for crowdfunding

(i) Recent developments in crowdfunding

In the past few years, there has been a substantial increase in the use of crowdfunding all over the world. Crowdfunding was used to raise around €48.5 billion across the world between the years 2010 and 2017 (Chervyakov and Rocholl 2019). The market is dominated by platforms located in the United States, which have raised a total of €25.8 billion, followed by platforms located in the European Union, which have raised €16.9 billion, and platforms located in Asia, which have raised €5.5 billion (Chervyakov and Rocholl 2019).

The tremendous rise of the business is best illustrated by the average annual growth rate of funds raised between 2011 and 2017: in the United States, the average annual growth rate was about 80%, in Europe 85%, and in Asia 557% (Chervyakov and Rocholl 2019). In a nutshell, the crowdfunding industry in Europe and the rest of the world has demonstrated extraordinary growth rates over the course of the past few years. Even if these remarkable growth rates come to an end, there is still a large amount of potential (Ziegler *et al.* 2017, 2018; Chervyakov and Rocholl 2019). The realization of this promise would be aided by the establishment of a policy framework that enables continued expansion.

Crowdfunding is a technique that is growing at a rapid and continuous rate, and as a direct result, governments are becoming more aware of the vast number of issues and opportunities that it brings. As a direct consequence of this fact, a number

of national authorities have given good responses to proposals for the establishment of a legal framework that offers protection not just to investors but also to
issuers or project owners. Continued efforts are being made by governments to find
ways to improve and expand the amount of money that may be raised by new and
small businesses.

Crowdfunding regulation began with the US Jumpstart Our Business Start-ups
Act (JOBS Act). Its 2012 adoption aimed to simplify capital market access for
early-stage companies. The Act provided eligible companies with the ability to
raise capital through equity-based platforms while also exempting certain crowdfunding transactions from the requirement to register. However, the regulation also
included a number of restrictions on the maximum amount that could be invested
each year, in addition to tailored disclosure procedures and disqualification criteria
for those who the Act refers to as "bad actors" (i.e. issuers with certain criminal
convictions).

As a result, the JOBS Act has undergone several revisions to make the process
of raising capital potentially simpler and less expensive, and it now permits small
companies to sell their shares to the general public, making it possible for virtually
anyone to invest in a business through crowdfunding, while also allowing companies seeking equity funding to publicly advertise their offerings. Also, the JOBS
Act has been amended to let small businesses sell their shares to the general public.
There are a few regulations on investment and lending instruments that have been
enacted at the European level in Europe. These regulations do exist, but they are
not particularly geared towards crowdfunding-related activities. As a result, a number of countries in the EU have implemented their own regulatory frameworks, the
majority of which are geared towards regulating investment-based crowdfunding.

European crowdfunding platforms that offer investment instruments must comply with either their home countries' financial authorities or the European Commission's stricter standards. This is the case regardless of whether the platform is based
in the European Union or outside of it. This need is subject to change depending on
the various kinds of instruments that are made available by the platform. Because
of this, there may be various regulations covering capital requirements, disclosure
provisions and other forms of limitations that apply to issuers and investors correspondingly. These regulations may alter depending on the type of constraint.

Platforms that offer crowdfunding for investments can get authorized in one of
the following three ways, depending on their particular circumstances:

1 If the Markets in Financial Instruments Directive (2014/65/EU, generally
  known as MiFID), applies to the instruments that are being offered by the
  platform, then it is necessary to obtain something that is referred to as a
  MiFID passport. Now that this is in place, platforms that have been granted
  authorization can comply with the so-called single authorization principle
  by offering regulated investment services not only in their home countries
  but also in other EU countries. This can be done by providing the services in
  their home countries as well as in other EU countries. On the other hand, the
  accompanying stiffer constraints on capital needs and additional disclosure

standards are generally considered as being excessively costly and onerous to comply with. This is due to the fact that they place more requirements on disclosure.

2 Article 3 of the MiFID allows EU member states to apply the legislation to home-state enterprises. Such platforms can only receive and send orders and provide financial advice. This is the only permitted use of the authorization. In addition, their sphere of activity is restricted to the member state in which they have their headquarters, and they are governed by a domestic framework that is better suited to support crowdfunding. This limits the scope of their activities.

3 A platform is required to obtain authorization under the applicable domestic regime in order to operate. If the platform is of the opinion that it will not offer any instruments that are governed by the MiFID, such as non-readily realizable securities, then the platform is exempt from this requirement.

(ii) Looking ahead to the future

The standards and regulations that are in place to govern crowdfunding are undergoing constant revision and improvement. In the United States, crowdfunding regulation is handled at the federal level, so it is highly standardized. On the other hand, regulation in the European Union is primarily carried out at the level of individual member states. This results in a wide variety of regulatory frameworks and, consequently, business models.

In spite of the fact that the absence of a uniform legislative framework at the EU level is not anticipated to hamper the regional development of crowdfunding in the member states, there are hurdles for the further development of crowdfunding markets in Europe. These problems include restrictions placed on behaviour that occurs across borders and regulations that are frequently burdensome.

A low level of international crowdfunding activity is comparable to the concentration of bank lending and investment within the domestic market. This is despite the fact that there is abundant evidence to suggest that crowdfunding continues to be a predominantly local source of financing, indicating the existence of a home bias. For this reason, making it easier for individuals to participate in activities that span international borders should go hand in hand with making it easier for crowdfunding to thrive throughout Europe. Authors such as Véron and Wolff (2015) and Demertzis et al. (2017) have argued that increased international financial integration is necessary for the development of capital markets. This is because increased international financial integration can contribute to an increase in the size and liquidity of the market, as well as improve the transparency, reliability and comparability of the information that is currently available. In addition, increased international financial integration can contribute to an increase in the size and liquidity of the market.

In addition, Chervyakov and Rocholl 2019 argue that it is reasonable to anticipate that the overall volume of the crowdfunding market in the EU will significantly decrease as a result of Brexit. This prediction is based on the fact that it is reasonable to anticipate that the overall volume of the crowdfunding market in the EU will significantly decrease. Even though it is not entirely clear how this would affect the development of crowdfunding within the EU in countries other than the UK, the effect will most likely be negligible as long as the legal framework is not changed.

To provide a concise overview, there are not a great deal of exemplary policies that have yet to coagulate across the different national regimes in Europe. This is true across the continent. In spite of the fact that certain pillars of the legal frameworks, such as the maximum amounts that can be invested and the requirements for prospectuses, appear to be the same, there are significant differences between the lower and upper limits of these parameters. For example, the maximum amount that can be invested is the same in all of the legal frameworks, but the minimum amount that can be invested varies significantly. For instance, the maximum sums that can be invested remain the same, despite the fact that different standards for prospectuses have been imposed. It is important to note that the range of activities that are permitted to be sponsored by legitimate types of crowdfunding varies greatly from one member state of the EU to the next, and this is something that should be taken into consideration. Although it may not be ideal to have a legislative framework that is applicable to all EU states, the lack of a consistent legislation on the level of the EU presents hurdles for crowdfunding activities that take place beyond national borders. This puts the idea of a Capital Markets Union (CMU) in peril and has the potential to result in the market being more fragmented rather than the hoped-for convergence of best practices.

The need for harmonized EU regulation

Although there are extensive and varied financial regulations in each of the member states of the EU, and several of those member states have built regulatory frameworks for crowdfunding, there has been no attempt to unify these set of laws. As a result of these non-harmonized rules, there is a significant amount of variation in the manner in which crowdfunding platforms function, the scope of activities that are permitted, as well as the procedures for obtaining a license. The existing state of the law has resulted in a certain amount of misunderstanding as well as problems that are not helpful to practitioners operating in the crowdfunding space. It was very difficult for Crowdfunding Service Providers (CSPs) to conduct business on a global scale because there was a wide variety of regulations and regulatory obligations to comply with, in addition to the fact that they were not granted passporting privileges. Following the acknowledgement of the issue by legislative bodies, these bodies have moved to enact legislation regarding crowdfunding platforms.

The new EU legislative framework

The European Commission issued the European Crowdfunding Service Provider Regulation (ECSPR) in October 2020 as its law to regulate the crowdfunding business within the EU. The goal of the new legislative framework is to create one of the world's largest harmonized regulated environments for crowdfunding. This will be accomplished by ensuring a harmonized EU crowdfunding regime and assuring legal certainty of the rules regulating crowdfunding activities across all EU member states. The ECSPR is now directly applicable in all countries that are members of the EU effective March of 2022.

Scope

EU Crowdfunding Service Providers (CSPs) must follow the European Crowdfunding Service Provider Regulation (ECSPR). A CSP is a legal entity that runs a business that provides an online platform for the public (crowd) to connect enterprises seeking funding for their projects. The "project owner", "borrower" and/or "offeror" is the business seeking finance for a project using a CSP's online platform. A "crowdinvestor" is a natural or legal person who funds a project. Since investment and lending-based crowdfunding services can be organized as funding alternatives to regular financial services, the ECSPR applies to CSPs delivering such services. Thus, the ECSPR does not apply to CSPs offering donation, reward, or peer-to-peer-lending-based crowdfunding or consumer loans. ECSPR excludes offers over EUR €5 million. Such offers are dealt under the MiFID II, the EU Prospectus Regulation.

JOBS vs. ECSPR

It is essential for the ECSPR to be competitive when viewed from a global perspective if it is to contribute to the development of a more innovative financial sector in Europe. United States of America has been a leader in the adoption of legislation and a regulatory framework for the practice of crowdfunding and given the sizeable volume of the industry, it is an important jurisdiction to use as a point of comparison with the European Crowdfunding Regulation (Härkönen 2022). The ECSPR incorporates a significant number of the authorizing and investor protection provisions that are relevant to the legal system in the United States. However, there are also differences, such as the maximum monetary amount that can be invested and the ongoing disclosure requirements that must be met. The ECSPR has only become operational in March 2022 and it may be necessary to have further reviews in the future.

Other areas of government support

(i) Information

It is generally acknowledged that in order to strengthen the dependability of crowdfunding, backers, creators and all stakeholders need to be educated on the advantages of the institution as a whole and the various forms it can take. Additionally, it is necessary to provide clarifications on the risks, as well as information on fraud. Awareness on the part of the stakeholders is necessary for the continuation and expansion of the phenomena. When it comes to protecting the financial interests, diversification and exposure of investors and investees across a number of crowd-funding strategies, the government can lend a hand in the establishment of clear guidelines, advice and training of stakeholders.

(ii) Research

Data and information must be available and accessible to facilitate open and transparent development and to increase the competitiveness of the crowdfund-ing industry. Government assistance in terms of research funding will make this possible.

(iii) Taxation

One of the biggest challenges facing business owners today, especially in de-veloping markets, is the high tax rate. If crowdfunding is to succeed in economies like these, the tax system must be adaptable enough to accommodate new ventures. In order to promote the expansion of crowdfunding transactions, it is the respon-sibility of the government to implement special tax laws and other incentives for securities issued through crowdfunding platforms.

(iv) Infrastructure development

Because it relies so heavily on social media and networking sites as well as web-based platforms, crowdfunding absolutely requires users to have access to the internet. The poor status of internet access in many regions of the world's emerging economies, where internet penetration is as low as 37%, is one of the most sig-nificant challenges facing the industry's expansion. This constraint makes it more difficult for innovators to raise funds through crowdfunding, which in turn slows the expansion of the phenomenon. The growth of crowdfunding is contingent upon the development of infrastructure, and this is especially true in developing econo-mies. Infrastructure development is therefore an area where government support is required.

Blockchain technology in crowdfunding

Crowdfunding relies on the relationship of trust between investors and project backers. Fraud and other anomalies present a formidable hurdle to the global spread of crowdfunding (Gabison *et al.* 2016; Achsien and Purnamasari 2016). Gabison *et al.* (2016) claim that contributors to online crowdfunding campaigns are vulnerable to fraud since standard legal and reputation protection safeguards may not be effective. This is supported by Ahmad *et al.* (2021), who emphasized the absence of a certification criteria to post a project and the absence of a legal obligation to deliver what was promised. Other concerns with crowdfunding iden-tified by other academics include the major delay or non-delivery of rewards and/or products, the cessation of communication with backers after missed delivery dates, the non-refund of backers' funds and information asymmetry. As is the case with conventional finance, information asymmetries exist in crowdfunding because investors lack access to the pertinent information required to make investment decisions. In emerging economies, information asymmetries are exacerbated by a lack of openness, a general dearth of data on small enterprises and the absence or ineffectiveness of legislation (Kshetri 2015). According to Ibrahim (2019), the growth of the internet and the increase in the number of users have surely had unforeseen repercussions, with cybercrime accounting for 43% of the overall monetary loss in 2016. This has severely damaged confidence in the system.

As in many fields of endeavour, the advent of new technology has immense potential for crowdfunding groups. Blockchain is a unique, independent and transparent technology that maintains the transparency of transactions between parties. The implementation of blockchain technology is causing significant upheaval in a wide variety of industries throughout the world because it has a number of advantages over more conventional methods.

Blockchain may be thought of as a distributed database that contains records of all executed and shared transactions between participants. Blockchain possesses the qualities of data decentralization, persistence, anonymity and auditability (Zheng *et al.* 2017).

This innovative technology was first put to use as the foundation for cryptocurrency, but it is already finding application in an increasing number of industries and sectors. It is expected that the bulk of global technology would adopt blockchain as an efficient way to carry out online transactions in the near future. Platforms that facilitate crowdfunding are one area in which blockchain technologies can find use in the future.

By applying Ethereum smart contracts to the crowdfunding website, Blockchain solves issues of trust and transparency. This enables the contracts to be fully completed automatically, which eliminates the possibility of fraud and ensures the timely delivery of projects.

Transactions and blocks are the two fundamental components that make up the technology behind the blockchain. The block is a collection of data describing the transaction as well as other associated properties such as the correct sequence, timestamp of creation and so on. The transaction is the activity that is initiated by the participant. The transaction records, also known as blocks, in a blockchain cannot be altered because they are cryptographically connected to one another. This signifies that once a block has been entered, it cannot be changed or deleted and cannot be removed from the list. Blockchain technology utilizes consensus procedures as a means of establishing its reliability. As a result, there will be less of a need for trust to exist between the various nodes of the network because this will ensure that all system nodes have an identical copy.

The process of building consensus across a blockchain network is referred to as mining. Mining is necessary since it assures that any data that are uploaded to the ledger are secure and cannot be altered by unauthorized parties.

The blockchain's attractive selling point is its ability to support smart contracts. A smart contract is a piece of code that may be executed and that is stored on a blockchain. Its purpose is to enable, execute and enforce the conditions of an agreement. When the predetermined circumstances are satisfied, it is activated so that the agreements are automatically carried out. There are a number of platforms, including Bitcoin, NXT and Ethereum, that are capable of implementing smart contracts. The software code, a storage file and the current balance of the account are all included. Users are able to build contracts by publishing transactions on the blockchain network, and by putting smart contracts into a crowdfunding system, it is possible to establish a contract that holds a contributor's funds until a particular date or aim is accomplished. Depending on the results of the vote, the funds will either be given to the people who initiated the project or given back to the people who contributed them in a safe manner.

The technology known as blockchain has the potential to tackle issues that arise in crowdfunding, such as fraud, money laundering and information asymmetry. Because the data stored in a blockchain is viewable by anybody, potential investors can review the data stored on a block to determine whether or not the project is legitimate. The use of blockchain technology in a crowdfunding system promotes transparency, which can help eliminate information asymmetry and boost stakeholder confidence in contributing to and raising cash via a crowdfunding platform. Blockchain technology was developed by Bitcoin creator Satoshi Nakamoto (Sadat *et al.* 2019).

The ability to operate with high efficiency and low costs, as well as the integrity of blockchain data that cannot be altered and, as a result, can be trusted once entered into the ledger, are some of the advantages of blockchain technology. On the other hand, concerns relate to the distributed system's high consumption of power and computing resources, which is a potential drawback.

How blockchain technology helps crowdfunding

1 Decentralization

Blockchain technology makes it easy for small businesses and start-ups not to rely on any particular platform or a combination of them in order to be able to raise funds. Small firms are no longer bound by the whims and caprices of the most popular crowdfunding platforms. This means that any project or venture has a chance of getting funding.

Blockchain also eliminates the problem of transaction costs in the form of fees, thus making crowdfunding less expensive for both creators and investors. It also eliminates the problems associated with information asymmetry.

2 Provision of equity

Blockchain provides investors with equity or similar forms of ownership such as Initial Coin Offering (ICO). This enables new ventures to save money on hiring employees by compensating them with partial ownership of the business. This enables the venture to concentrate on hiring professionals such as marketers and advertisers.

3 Security

Blockchain provides security to crowdfunders from possible internet fraud surrounding crowdfunding. This is possible because in most blockchains the data is structured into blocks and each block contains a transaction or bundle of transactions. Each new block connects to all the blocks before it in a cryptographic chain in such a way that it is almost impossible to tamper with.

Blockchains also provide participants with enhanced transparency, which makes it difficult to corrupt blockchains through manipulation. Moreover, blockchains may contain multiple layers of security at both the network and installation levels.

4 Accountability

Blockchain can provide greater accountability in crowdfunding by providing built-in checks or milestones which will prevent funds from being released without provenance or legitimacy. By so doing, it prevents huge sums of money from being squandered by those who have malicious intensions and prevents illegal businesses from raising funds through crowdfunding contracts. It also prevents those who are not qualified to carry out crowdfunding campaigns.

Case studies of blockchain in equity management

NASDAQ Linq: private equity market based on blockchain

Nasdaq launched its blockchain platform, Nasdaq Linq, in 2015, and conducted experiments using blockchain technology for transactions of securities. The purpose of the experiments was to demonstrate that equity transactions can be digitally managed on a blockchain platform. Linq is a private corporate equity management tool. Its system supports digitized confirmation of equity rights, significantly saving time and paper. Some start-up companies have tried Linq, and completed share registration and transactions. NASDAQ Global Software Development Director Zinder said that the use of blockchain technology was of great significance in improving private corporate equity distribution.

Antshares technology: digital asset management platform based on blockchain

According to the Antshares whitepaper, Antshares is based on blockchain technology; it digitizes physical assets and property rights, and uses a peer-to-peer (P2P) network to realize decentralized network protocols for financial services such as shareholder registration, issuance of stocks, equity transfer and transactions and clearing and settlement of equity transactions. The services can be used in equity crowdfunding, P2P lending, digital asset management and smart contracts.

To explore the practical applications of blockchain, Antshares carried out trials on compliance with regulations. User authentication and anti-money laundering protocols are embedded in the Antshares Application Programming Interfaces (APIs). It legitimizes the relevant activities. Third-party payment, banking and other financial institutions may use Antshares protocols to achieve compliance.

Although the current application of blockchain in digital asset management is still in the exploratory stage, results based on the literature review, analysis of features of blockchain and cases of blockchain applications suggest that blockchain technology has high value and good prospects in resolving the problems of equity crowdfunding and optimizing its process.

Source: Zhu and Zhou (2016)

Peer-to-peer crowdfunding for local governments

Peer-to-peer lending is a technique of financing which circumvents banks by linking a borrower directly with an individual or organization that has money to lend. By eliminating the middle man, the lender can earn higher returns on their money compared with putting it in a regular bank account, and the borrower can benefit from a faster, more flexible process.

Crowdfunding has made a significant impact in the business community and the creative sector because of its ability to raise money quickly and flexibly, avoiding traditional sources of finance. But it has yet to become as widely adopted among local authorities (Muirhead 2017).

Muirhead (2017) argues that the limited take up of crowdfunding so far may be in part due to the fact that local governments are rightly cautious about a new phenomenon and the associated intense enthusiasm when it comes to handling public money. However, some of this caution can come from the confusion about what exactly crowdfunding is, how it can be used in a local government context and how to weigh its risks and benefits.

LGiU (2017) suggests that a number of local authorities now use peer-to-peer lending platforms. Some use their economic development funds as a means of lending to local small businesses, whilst others use treasury funds to lend as a way of earning attractive returns. When using economic development funding, local authorities use platforms to directly target small businesses in their region. The platform sources the borrower and carries out a credit assessment of each one. Funds are then allocated from the local authority based on their lending criteria. Platforms take care of all payments, thus reducing the administrative burden on the government body while helping them to meet their economic growth aims.

LGiU (2017) further suggests that the central government can also use platforms to inject finance into small businesses. For example, the government-owned British Business Bank (BBB) in the UK has lent millions through platforms like Funding Circle, MarketInvoice and Ratesetter. This enables the government to lend to thousands of businesses across the UK, whilst also earning reliable returns.

Similar to equity crowdfunding, local governments in various countries/jurisdictions can use P2P lending platforms to invest into local businesses, social enterprises and charities which they have identified as needing support (Muirhead 2017). Muirhead (2017) also suggests that they can also invest their reserves through P2P lending platforms, if the investment options available suit their risk appetite. These demonstrate that local governments can, with sufficient education, use P2P crowdfunding as an efficient means of investing in local firms and social enterprises to boost economic growth and fund their programmes, especially in light of tightening budgets.

To this end, LGiU (2017) provides some guidance on how the government can invest into local businesses, social enterprises and charities through peer-to-peer (P2P) lending platforms:

- Local governments can use P2P lending platforms as a way of managing their investments into local businesses they have identified as needing support. This is already being done by many councils including Camden and Lambeth in the UK.
- Equally, local governments could in theory invest in social enterprises, local charities or other organizations in a similar manner, but not through the more established platforms.
- As part of their Treasury management, local authorities could invest their reserves through P2P lending platforms, if the investment options available suit their risk appetite. Equally, they could apply to borrow money for bigger projects themselves. For instance, Warrington Council in the UK has set up its own P2P lending platform which facilitates lending between public sector organizations.
- Local governments could get involved with P2P lending as a facilitator rather than an investor, by brokering relationships between local organizations needing finance and the platforms themselves.

However, LGiU (2017) suggests that the first step for an investor is to assess their own local government's strategic priorities and work out if crowdfunding can help to achieve any of these because there is no sense in adopting crowdfunding for the sake of it. It is suggested that it is important for those working in local governments to educate themselves about their options with regards to crowdfunding to be able to make informed decisions and construct persuasive business cases when necessary.

As funding cuts continue to put a strain on both statutory and discretionary services alike, increasing public engagement with community services will become even more essential (LGiU 2017). Asking the community to prioritize and fund their own projects could have the threefold benefit of involving residents, continuing important services and reducing the financial burden on the council. Equally, in the context of 100% business rate retention being implemented in the next few years, LGiU (2017) argues that local governments may increasingly be looking for ways to attract and retain businesses in their region, and crowdfunding may be a way of achieving this.

Examples of local governments using P2P funding

There are not yet many case studies of many local authorities utilizing crowdfunding mechanisms but there are examples of councils in some countries embracing crowdfunding.

In the United States, local authorities have been crowdfunding to promote the uptake of vacant properties and to regenerate local areas. For example, the Mayor's Office of Civic Innovation in San Francisco launched their Living Innovation Zones, which designate public areas that businesses or groups can bid on to temporarily showcase innovative projects, using crowdfunding as a key part of the finance toolkit.

In the UK, Warrington Council has set up its own P2P lending platform which facilitates lending between public sector organizations. Also, in the UK, in response to a City Council's proposal to remove an abandoned flyover, the local community crowdfunded over £40,000 to pay for a feasibility study looking at creating an elevated park instead.

Other successfully crowdfunded projects in the United Kingdom include the roll-out of free WiFi in Nottinghamshire, the construction of a community centre in South Wales, and the opening of an entrepreneur hub in High Wycombe in a former empty building.

While many other countries may not currently be at the forefront of local authority crowdfunding, these examples are becoming an effective means of coping with increasing budgetary restraints, and are definitely ideas that can be replicated in local authorities in other countries to deal with similar restraints.

Source: Adapted from Muirhead 2017

Tips for using P2P funding in local governments

- Peer-to-peer lending is still a relatively young industry (roughly ten years old), but the industry's largest platforms set up a self-regulatory body in 2011 called the Peer-to-Peer Finance Association (P2PFA), which promotes high standards of conduct and consumer protection on top of the full set of regulations set by the Financial Conduct Authority – so these are a good place to start.
- Whilst some platforms have had some issues recently, debt crowdfunding is a more developed market than equity crowdfunding and lending is usually less risky than equity investing in general. Therefore, it necessary to make sure research is done of the platform that is to be used.

- Whilst platforms carry out thorough credit assessment checks on all borrowers before they are listed on the platform, the best way to mitigate risk as an investor is to diversify investment across as many borrowers as possible. Investors should expect borrowers to default as this is a very normal part of lending, but by spreading investment across as many borrowers as possible, the investor reduces the impact of bad debt on their portfolio.
- Platforms provide credit checking of borrowers but investment is not covered by the Financial Services Compensation Scheme. Some platforms offer a "bad debt guarantee", where losses are offset by a "provision fund" that is funded by investors when they first start lending. A stated priority in the FCA's regulation of the sector is that platforms have full wind down plans in place so that investors still receive loan repayments in the event of a platform ceasing to trade. Even so, it is worth checking what might happen to investors' money if the platform itself shuts down.
- Remember that lending through these platforms is an investment, so any capital invested is at risk and returns are never guaranteed – regardless of any bad debt provision funds. Therefore, investors must be prepared to lose the whole amount of their investment.
- A large majority of lending through platforms is unsecured with a personal guarantee, therefore platforms' historical loss rates should be used as a good indication of a platform's credit assessment capabilities. These can all be found on the P2PFA's website.
- Most platforms offer a secondary market so an investor can sell their loans if they choose to leave the platform before the loan matures. Therefore, this should be borne in mind when choosing a platform.
- Independent financial advice should always be sought, although they will not provide advice on each and every investment made through a platform. However, they will be able to guide towards a suitable platform based on the type of lending being made on a portfolio, i.e. business, consumer or property lending.
- A lawyer should always be consulted; asking them to check the investment terms, whether borrowing or lending. It is worth knowing what will happen if the borrower cannot repay the loan. Is there any a preferential agreement for some investors? What happens to the loan agreement if the platform should close down?
- Research should be carried out about any P2P lending platform through which investment is intended, starting with members of the P2PFA, who adhere to rigorous self-imposed standards to ensure consumer protection. Some questions should be asked, such as: Have they been in any sort of trouble before over their methods? How long have they been operating? What is the default rate of businesses listed on their platform? Of course, this information might take a few years before it appears. How do they conduct their due diligence?

Source: Adapted from LGiU (2017)

Summary

In the midst of a pervasive threat of employment crisis and insecurity, crowdfunding is a critical utility, particularly for small and new businesses. The persistent expansion of the industry is further evidence that crowdfunding is an absolute requirement for business owners to raise funds for their ventures. Despite a favourable environment, traditional crowdfunding in the EU has been impeded by problems of malpractices such as fraud, information asymmetry and money laundering, which had prompted various legislative curbs on the activities of fundraising by member EU states. This is in contrast to the United States, where traditional crowdfunding has been very successful. The lack of a clear and uniform regulatory framework in Europe is a key hindrance to the expansion of these businesses. It is therefore essential for governments to make it easier for small businesses to gain access to funds by cultivating an enabling environment and enacting laws that serve such specific purpose. The European Crowdfunding Service Providers Regulation (ECSPR) is a significant step forward for the European crowdfunding industry, and the unification of regulatory frameworks across the European Union is one factor that should contribute to economic growth through the launch of new businesses and job creation. It is pertinent to note that neither the EU nor the US have yet to regulate reward-based crowdfunding (RBC) and donation-based crowdfunding (DBC). The absence of laws and regulations of these models raise serious concerns as has been highlighted.

Government support is required in the enactment of new legislations and continued review of existing regulations to assure the growth of crowdfunding. Government assistance is also required in the area of enlightenment and creation of societal awareness for the phenomenon, provision of necessary infrastructure, favourable tax regimes, training, advice and funding for research in order to ensure the continued development and growth of the industry.

The distributed ledger technology, also known as blockchain, is a tool that offers tremendous hope for the crowdfunding industry all over the world. The technology is a revolutionary and disruptive innovation that aims to reduce bureaucracy and regulation without compromising existing legislation on business conduct. Because the blockchain technology offers a distributed public ledger, it increases the level of transparency and as a result, participants can conduct business without worrying about imposition. Most importantly, blockchain technology gets rid of information asymmetry in its entirety, which satisfies the needs of every stakeholder for authentic proof and complete transparency. Government's continued investment in the development of this and other emerging technologies as well as regulatory framework and environment would assist in mitigating problems of regulatory compliance and security.

Discussion questions

1 Give a synopsis of crowdfunding regulation in the United States and the European Union.
2 What would you consider as the efforts of governments in the development of crowdfunding?
3 Crowdfunding relies on the relationship of trust between stakeholders. What are the main issues of concern and how does blockchain technology solve the problems?

Test questions

1 To what extent can blockchain technology help in solving the problems of regulatory compliance and security?
2 How does blockchain support crowdfunding?

Glossary of key terminologies

Bad actors   Person or organization responsible for actions that are harmful or illegal or that have criminal convictions.

Blockchain technology   A unique, independent and transparent technology that maintains the transparency and integrity of transactions between parties.

CMU   Capital Markets Union – an economic policy to create a single market for capital in the EU.

CSP   Crowdfunding Service Provider – a legal person established within the EU to provide crowdfunding services as defined under the ECSPR.

DBC   Donation-based crowdfunding – a way to raise funds for a business or project without any promise of reward or repayment.

EC   European Commission – a part of the executive of the EU.

ECSPR   European Crowdfunding Service Provider Regulation – A regulation harmonizing CF among EU member states.

FCA   Financial Conduct Authority – the conduct regulator for financial services firms and financial markets in the UK.

Financial integration   A phenomenon in which financial markets in neighbouring, regional and/or global economies are closely linked together.

FinTech   A catch-all term of technologies that automate and improve traditional forms of finance for businesses and customers alike.

Information asymmetry   An imbalance in knowledge between two parties that conveys competitive advantage of one of the parties over the other.

JOBS Act   Jumpstart Our Business Startups Act – A law passed to encourage funding of small businesses in the United States.

Legislative framework   A particular set of rules aimed to improve the internal market for goods and services in the EU market.

MiFID   Markets in Financial Instruments Directive – an EU law that standardizes regulations for investment services across all member states.

P2P   Peer-to-Peer lending – a form of financial arrangement which allows people to lend or borrow money from one another without going through the bank.

Passporting   A system that enables products and services to be traded without barrier within the EU.

Policy framework   A document that sets out a set of procedures or goals used for decision-making.

RBC   Reward-based crowdfunding – a form of crowdfunding where money is raised from people in exchange for the promise of a reward.

Smart contract   A piece of code that can be automatically executed on a blockchain to enforce the conditions of an agreement.

Recommended reading

Chervyakov, D., and Rocholl, J., 2019. *How to make crowdfunding work in Europe* (No. 2019/6). Bruegel Policy Contribution Issue 6/2019. Berlin.
European Commission, 2018. Proposal for a regulation on european crowdfunding service providers (ECSP) for business. *COM*, 113. Available from: https://eur-lex.europa.eu/legal-content/EN/TXT/?uri=CELEX:52018PC0113
Gebert, M., 2017. Application of blockchain technology in crowdfunding. *New European*, 18.
Härkönen, E., 2022. ECSPR versus the United States crowdfunding regime. *In: Regulation on European crowdfunding service providers for business*. Cheltenham: Edward Elgar Publishing, 796–807.
Massolution, 2015. *2015CF crowdfunding industry report*. Available from: http://reports.crowdsourcing.org/index.php?route=product/product&product_id=54
Sadat, N., *et al.*, 2019. Blockchain based crowdfunding systems. *Indonesian Journal of Electrical Engineering and Computer Science*, 15 (1), 409–413.

References

Achsien, I.H., and Purnamasari, D.L., 2016. Islamic crowd-funding as the next financial innovation in Islamic finance: Potential and anticipated regulation in Indonesia. *European Journal of Islamic Finance*, 5.
Ahmad, N.A., and Syed Abdul Rahman, S.A.H., July 2021. Applying ethereum smart contracts to blockchain-based crowdfunding system to increase trust and information symmetry. *In: 2021 7th International conference on computer technology applications*, 13–15 July. Vienna, Austria: Association for Computing Machinery, 53–59. https://doi.org/10.1145/3477911.3477920.
Albrecht, C., Morales, V., Baldwin, J.K., and Scott, S.D., 2017. Ezubao: A Chinese Ponzi scheme with a twist. *Journal of Financial Crime*, 24 (2), 256–259.
Chervyakov, D., and Rocholl, J., 2019. *How to make crowdfunding work in Europe* (No. 2019/6). Bruegel Policy Contribution Issue 6/2019. Berlin.
Chorzempa, M., 2018. *China needs better credit data to help consumers* (No. PB18–1). China: Peterson Institute for International Economics.
Demertzis, M., Merler, S., and Wolff, G., 2018. Capital Markets Union and the fintech opportunity. *Journal of Financial Regulation*, 4 (1), 157–165.
European Commission, 2018. Proposal for a regulation on European Crowdfunding Service Providers (ECSP) for business. *COM*, 113. Available from: https://eur-lex.europa.eu/legal-content/EN/TXT/?uri=CELEX:52018PC0113
Gabison, G., 2016. Policy considerations for the blockchain technology public and private applications. *SMU Science and Technology Law Review*, 19, 327.
Ibrahim, U., 2019. The impact of cybercrime on the nigerian economy and banking system. *NDIC Quarterly*, 34 (12), 1–20.
Kshetri, N., 2015. Success of crowd-based online technology in fundraising: An institutional perspective. *Journal of International Management*, 21 (2), 100–116.
LGiU, 2017. *Crowdfunding for local authorities*. Available from: https://lgiu.org/briefing/guide-to-crowdfunding-for-local-authorities/
Milne, A., and Parboteeah, P., 2016. *The business models and economics of peer-to-peer lending*. Brussels: European Credit Research Institute. Available from: https://ssrn.com/abstract=2763682 or http://dx.doi.org/10.2139/ssrn.2763682

Muirhead, H., 2017. *Crowdfunding: Opportunities for local government, LGiU.* Available from: https://lgiu.org/crowdfunding-opportunities-for-local-government/

Véron, N., and Wolff, G., 2015. *Capital markets union.* Netherlands: Bruegel Institute.

Zheng, Z., Xie, S., Dai, H., Chen, X., and Wang, H., 2017. An overview of blockchain technology: Architecture, consensus, and future trends. *In: 2017 IEEE international congress on big data (BigData congress) .* New York: IEEE, 557–564.

Zhu, H., and Zhou, Z., 2016. Analysis and outlook of applications of blockchain technology to equity crowdfunding in China. *Financial Innovation*, 2 (29). Available from: https://doi.org/10.1186/s40854-016-0044-7

Ziegler, T., Johanson, D., King, M., Zhang, B., Mammadova, L., Ferri, F., *et al.*, 2018. *Reaching new heights: The 3rd Americas alternative finance industry report.* Cambridge: Cambridge Centre for Alternative Finance.

Ziegler, T., Reedy, E.Y., Le, A., Zhang, B., Kroszner, R.S., and Garvey, K., 2017. *The Americas alternative finance industry report: Hitting stride.* Cambridge: Cambridge Centre for Alternative Finance.

12 Case studies of successful crowdfunding campaigns

Learning objectives

- Discuss successful and unsuccessful crowdfunding campaigns
- Learn the strategies adopted by companies which make them successful in their crowdfunding campaigns.
- Learn the strategies which make companies unsuccessful in their crowdfunding campaigns
- Understand how to put theory into practice

Introduction

It is undeniable that entrepreneurship is becoming increasingly popular with a reported 72% increase in the number of businesses since 2000 (Ward 2021). However, starting a business is not easy and requires a substantial amount of initial outlay. Therefore, the question is, how are these start-ups being funded? With 57% of start-ups being self-funded via personal savings and credit (Entis 2013) due to the difficulty faced when applying for bank loans, small firms are turning to alternative funding methods such as crowdfunding to fund their ventures.

Crowdfunding (CF) has become an extremely popular source of finance for start-ups in recent years. As a result, there have been many questions surrounding this method, including the actual strength of the companies that are seeking funding and those of the investors themselves and the reliability of crowdfunding platforms.

This chapter discusses four cases with three successful crowdfunding campaigns and one unsuccessful. These case studies are intended to help the student to put theory into practice, and to learn the strategies adopted by these companies which make some successful and the others unsuccessful.

The case studies are selected to demonstrate international diversity. Case 1 is a British company using a local platform, "Crowdfunder". Case 2 is an American company using an American platform, "Kickstarter". Case 3 is a French start-up which uses a community platform, "Hellotipi" while Case 4 is a start-up in Boston, USA, which also uses "Kickstarter".

DOI: 10.4324/9781003193975-12

Case study 1

Craft beer micro brewery case: Wildcraft Brewery (Norfolk)

This case consists of a 30 minute interview with the Founding Partner of Wildcraft Brewery, Mike Deal, in 2016. The interview was followed up with an on-site visit to the brewery near Buxton, Norfolk, for 1.5 hours.

Founder's background

Mike is a teacher and around 2010 when his marriage broke up he began to get interested in picking wild berries and fruits and using them in home brewing for wines and beers. Mike has previous industry experience, having been a top salesman for Bulmers cider in the East of England, so has a large network of industry connections. A few years ago he seriously began thinking of turning this interest into a viable business. A year ago, he met his business partner Mark Goodman whose parents have an old barn that is the right size to house the brewery. The business is therefore in a rural farm location near Buxton, around 10 miles North of Norwich (Norfolk).

The business

Wildcraft Brewery aims to produce fruit beers, drawing on continental influences (notably from Belgium). They use locally sourced and foraged products with the aim of producing a *"Born in Norfolk"* product. All products are vegan and cater to coeliacs and the business aims to be green and eventually carbon neutral.

Initially Mike tested the market with local tastings in his home village of Old Costessy and has consulted with a small number of local pubs to find out what beers they prefer. By holding "brew day" experiences it has been possible to develop interest and the local market for the beer, but as yet the brewing has been on a small localized scale and it was realized about a year later that external financing would be required to create a larger sustainable business.

The current product range includes seven beers (ranging from 6% to 3.8% gravity and including stout and pale ale), of which two are fruit based, and five are fruit liqueurs (for which the base spirit is bought in). Four (4) beers will operate as all year-round standards – not seasonally foraged, and additionally there will be a monthly foraged fruit beer speciality.

The beers will have a seasonal nature, reflecting the available fruit and will offer variety and differences between batches. No two brews will be quite the same, but they are certain that they will offer a high-quality distinctive product which will keep the private and commercial pub/bar customers happy. Furthermore, they hope to have a benchmark of production developed over time which will lead to specialist collector interest for specific period brews. They want to be an experimental brewery and are currently exploring coffee beer with a local supplier. All products which are not foraged locally by themselves and customers (from the local community) aim to be supplied by local producers and suppliers. The aim is to be totally different, meeting the requirement of the Reindeer pub in Norwich where the owner has stated that the demand is high for new beers; "*the wackier the better!*"

The new process just installed will substantially increase production and they plan to initially run at around 30% of ideal capacity initially in the first year (from October 2016), brewing at least once a week, potentially increasing to a maximum of three times per week. Mike feels they are at that level of demand now and can slowly expand. The time off from brewing will be spent marketing and time will be spent getting feedback from pub customers via social media, letting the customers drive the brewery to some extent (this is a novel idea). Mike likes the idea of developing social media (direct) marketing approaches.

Marketing sales strategy

They will sell in the following ways:

 (i) Pubs, shops, hotels based in Norfolk at first to keep travel distribution distances down. They will probably use recyclable kegs which are non-returnable, but these are going up in price since Brexit so may look at E-kegs rental which may prove more cost effective.
 (ii) Bottle market through beer club and delivery to door with returnable glass.
(iii) Brewery direct sales through brew day events and also external events. They have three sizes of marquees they can set up and local (farm) land to hold small events.

Unit cost of products

500ml bottle cost 28p plus 17p for the bottle itself.
 72-pint kegs cost £80 to £110 (a little more than £1 per pint)
 They sell a pint at £3.20 and bottles at £2.50.
 Delivery is free around Norfolk and for the private members market it is a big plus, but can be linked to their commercial market supplies.

Expansion plans

Current expansion plans fall into two distinct phases: (i) initial establishment of the brewery involving the purchase of brewing equipment and getting the barn serviceable with electricity. This initial cost is in the region of £35k (including £20k CF). The business timetable is running about one month behind schedule. (ii) the second phase will involve greening and expanding the business and will take up to five years.

The main greening requirements will be installation of renewable energy sources such as solar PV panels for electricity (on barn roof which is East and West facing) and water filtration which will enable the water by-product to be cleaned and used for local crop irrigation. They also plan to build composters and to use by-product CO_2 in plant nurseries and sales.

They are already considering how further external finance will be raised and whether crowdfunding will be required. The brewery currently only employs Mike full-time on £1,000 per month, with Mark putting in some free labour after work, until year two. It is expected that in year two both founders will work full-time in the business.

Financing strategy and use of CF

Once Mike had a partner on board and expanding the home brewing activity could become a reality, it was quickly realized that around £35k would be required for initial equipment purchase and refurbishment of the barn to enable the business to operate. A business plan was drawn up along with financing requirements and sales forecasts. The owners provided around £15k of their own capital alongside around £20k of CF (slightly less as around £2,500 of CF raised was their own capital).

Mike was certain he did not want to use bank finance and looked into options for CF. He did not consider bank finance as he knew that they would not receive any finance without a trading record or collateral. As he had neither he was discouraged from contacting banks. He mentioned that it was problematic setting up a commercial bank account, as this took three months. He also looked at debt CF, but found that these type of UK funds like Funding Circle and Zopa were only suitable for businesses with at least 18 months trading track record.

Although he noted that there were US CF platforms that would support his business he was drawn to using a local platform that offered reward based financing. His plan was to sell reward offers such as three bottles of beer for £10 up to 250 at one pound per bottle. He hoped to attract some pubs and they did secure three local pubs through their CF offer. A problem for the pubs however, is the uncertainty of delivery, whilst the domestic customer investors appear less concerned about delivery timetables.

Experience of using the CF platform

The platform chosen was "Crowdfunder". They required 5% of the funds raised as their fee and provided a basic web platform offering an HTML proforma webpage set-up which Mike found awkward to work with and present pictures on. The site works on a 60 day promotional period, with options to extend by a week.

In the event the promotion was successful, but followed a number of key phases:

(i)   First, there was a need to develop other associated social media networking and Mike established a Twitter platform with 2,500 followers, along with a FB website. This took a couple of months to put in place. They also gained mainstream media publicity through local EDP (Eastern Daily Press) articles and local radio.

(ii) Second, once the offer went live there was a rapid uptake of interest in the first couple of weeks, during which £9k was raised. A lengthy lull in investment followed and it was then that Mike realized that if he put some of his own money into the offer, others would follow. This proceeded on a circa 4x ratio following £500 investment and £2000 investment of his to get the final push. It was somewhere through this process that they discovered that local "brew day" tasting events were also excellent fundraisers. The main free tasting event they held had 400 people attending and probably led to £8–9k in investment overall.

(iii) Towards the end they were still £3k short of target and the CF platform extended the offer by a week. Then an investor came in with £1k and it was noticeable that this was followed by a final investment rush, leading to a small amount of oversubscription. This was welcome as after expenses in paying CF platform fees, credit card fees and paypal, the net sum raised was £17k. Around £2k of pledged funding never materialized, presumably because investors did not have sufficient funds to meet their pledged bills.

In summary the CF platform received 331 backers, raising £21,998 in 63 days.

Future funding

Whilst they have now secured initial funding to see the business through the phase one expansion from a 100 litre to 818 litre brewing system there is still plenty more external financing required to meet their expansion plans over the next two to five years. They are unclear just how much funding will be required (probably initially £40k to get the site completed with green energy elements and then a further phase in excess of £100k to set up distillery for fruit liqueurs). They have already embarked on a plan to secure four–five main investors to supply £40k for a combined 25% share of the business. Initially there were seven–eight potential investors after the CF campaign, but this whittled down to around four, with one person providing a loan of £10k at 3% annual interest. They have already secured a couple of investors and they are selecting people who also have hands on expertise that can be useful to the development of the business, such as a local electrician and an inventor of a green energy turbine.

In the medium term the shareholder funds will enable the development of a distillery in about two years' time to produce the fruit liqueurs fully themselves. They currently buy in the liqueur, but would need to get licensing and create a bonded secure room. They are definitely considering a second round of CF funding to develop the distillery and further greening options for the business. This includes examining bio-fuel options. They would consider further reward funding, possibly CF lending or equity, but are not fully aware yet of the various funding options that could be available. The owner had not considered angel network funding as such, but would consider equity share investment. With the scale of funding required at £100k plus they may look to a different platform. (*It was intimated that a different platform might have wider national coverage and investor base, but Crowdfunder is the largest rewards-based UK platform in the UK – it is just that they focused on raising funds from Norfolk area so that they could keep reward delivery costs down*).

The water filtration system using reed beds will cost around £50k and they expect this to be funded through reinvestment of the first year's surplus (after Mike's income). HP will be considered as an option for a potential company vehicle purchase, but this has yet to be fully considered. This would lead them to a different scale of operation and there is wide interest already in their distillery products, as the initial round of CF demonstrated popularity for their fruit liqueurs.

Summary of current capital structure

The business is located in a converted farm barn and surrounding ground, currently provided rent free by the founding partner's parents. Initial investment to refurbish the barn to health and hygiene regulatory compliance, install utilities and install cold room and brewing equipment was completed in early October 2016. Total cost was circa £35k including £15k founder investment and £20k CF reward-based investment which has yet to be repaid.

MANAGEMENT DEFICIENCIES

The founders recognize that they are currently weak on financial management and rely on an accountant friend to help out. They are looking to their key investors to add value to the business and may seek further investors in the future to help expand the business in terms of markets and green technologies.

Regulatory requirements

The main regulatory requirements are around health and hygiene and involve a special floor for the barn with waterproofing and anti-bacterial content, along with wall spray to seal brick dust. The bottling areas are the only stage of the process where air can get in.

Postcript

An aspect of the CF donation process that the business found difficult to gauge was the level of investor repayment. Mike is still considering whether this was a bit too generous and they did not take into account the postage costs for delivery to small domestic clients. However, they plan to hold an open day for the investors in which they come to them and can collect their reward repayments.

Follow-up interview work

The interview was for 30 minutes by telephone and digitally recorded. A second onsite interview of around 1.5 hours was undertaken and photographs were taken. The follow up site-based interview took place with Mike on Monday 10 a.m., 12/09/2016.

About Crowdfunder (www.crowdfunder.co.uk)

Crowdfunder is an established UK-wide site offering reward, community shares and equity based finance, which has raised over £27m for business start-ups and development and community and charitable activities. It is the UK's largest rewards based CF platform, working with support from EU, national and local governments, banks and large corporate companies.

*The case material is extracted from a case study written by Dr Robyn Owen and we are grateful for the permission to use it.

Source: Mac an Bhaird *et al.* (2019)

Case study 2

Think Board case – peel and stick whiteboard films

Think Board is the creation of a Babson student, Hanson Grant. This business venture was born out of one of Hanson's earlier ideas. He had created white board T-shirts but found that the T-shirt idea was not going to work. He was thinking through how to use this to his advantage until his friends connected the dots for him. Think Board is a whiteboard film that can turn any surface into a dry erase board.

In April 2015, a team of undergraduates and graduate students as well as alumni of the Babson College Centre for Entrepreneurship competed for $20,000 grand prizes in the Babson Entrepreneurial Thought and Action (BETA) challenge. A team of three semi-finalists presented in each category their ventures to a panel of ten judges and one from each category was selected for the $20,000 prize. The competition was tough as the team did an excellent job by making use of networks outside the private business school. The closely contested prize made the work of the judges extremely difficult. The competition included ventures producing everything from a hand-hygiene measurement and analytic platform for medical facilities to a provider of clean energy to slums in developing countries to a tea company.

Entrepreneurial background

Although the winners of the undergraduate and graduate categories represented a diversity of ideas in the challenge, they personally come from a lineage of entrepreneurship. Hanson Grant, a junior at Babson, had the beginnings of his winning idea when he started a t-shirt company in high school. He was experimenting with adhesives and dry erase coding, while trying to invent a dry erase t-shirt. When he graduated from high school he left the t-shirt company behind. However, the entrepreneurial spirit remained in him. His two parents are entrepreneurs and self-employed and he wanted to follow his parents' footsteps. Although he applied to a few East Coast schools, he decided to settle with Babson college when the school accepted him.

During Professor Len Green's Ultimate Entrepreneurial Challenge course, students were given the opportunity to come up with original ideas which were out-of-the-box ideas from ordinary objects. It was during the elective course that Hanson Grant put together the second piece of his winning idea. His group was given a mug and told to convert it into something entrepreneurial. They made it into an optimism mug by cutting it off half way so as to remain always half full.

The brainstorm

Grant was brainstorming ideas with regard to a writing surface. Therefore, he took what he had learned from adhesives and dry erase surfaces and created a clear sheet of dry erase surface with an adhesive back. He put it on his dorm room desk and as soon as he did that others in the dormitory started taking notice and asking about the product. His mates absolutely liked it.

Suddenly, Grant had a product which he named Think Board. He did not only have a product, he also had a market. When he realized that college students do not have a lot of money, he started reaching out to businesses. These businesses can put their own logos on the Think Boards they put in their offices. Finally, Grant partnered with a local middle school to put Think Boards on students' desks.

Grant saw opportunity for growth in businesses as a target market. He also had schools as his target market. Therefore, he spent some time developing the product based on recommendations from teachers and students and introduced the product to other schools. His target was to be in five middle schools by the end of the summer of 2016 and 50 schools before the fall's semester and finally reaching the whole nation by the end of that year.

The inspiration

It all started at his dormitory room at Babson College as he needed a space to write down his business ideas and remain organized from week to week. He could not drill holes into the wall to set up a massive whiteboard nor did he want to paint his walls with whiteboard paint. This was the birth of Think Board – a dry erase film which was not only easy to install, but it also looked beautiful, and worked very well.

He stuck the first version of the product to the wall purely so he could write down other business ideas. The real inspiration came after he had written down about 50 ideas on the "board" and were seen by many of his friends. Needless to say, the friends did not only like it, they also thought the idea was great and cool. They started making enquiries as to where they could get one for themselves.

It is important to comment that everything starts with an idea which then needs to be actioned upon and made to flow. It is also important to share the idea with friends and bounce it off each other. By so doing the ideas will grow. It may take some time to realize that the product the entrepreneur wants to create is staring at them in the face the whole time.

The financing strategy

After enough of Grant's friends had demanded the product, he stayed up late to launch a website. As soon as he created a website, he was inundated with orders.

After about a month's sales, he was introduced to the idea of using Kickstarter for crowdfunding by his friends. Think Board launched a campaign on the popular crowdfunding website Kickstarter where Grant's start-up hoped to raise $10,000 to take it to the next level with production and distribution. Within 30 days, Grant was able to raise the $10,000 successfully which he required, but more important than that, his focused marketing paid off as he was contacted by a news station to give an interview. The publicity made the campaign worthwhile for him.

The crowdfunding platform

Kickstarter is an American corporation based in New York which maintains a global crowdfunding platform focused on creativity. It is one of a number of crowdfunding platforms for raising money from the public, which bypasses traditional financial institutions. To raise money using the platform, entrepreneurs or project creators choose a deadline and a minimum funding goal. If the goal is not met by the deadline, no funds are collected and any finance pledged returned.

The Kickstarter platform is open to backers from all over the world and to project creators from many countries, including the US, UK, Canada, Australia, New Zealand, The Netherlands, Denmark, Ireland, Norway, Sweden, Spain, France, Germany, Austria, Italy, Belgium, Luxembourg, Switzerland and Mexico.

Kickstarter applies a 5% fee on the total amount of the funds raised. Their payments processor applies an additional 3–5% fee. Unlike other fundraising platforms, Kickstarter claims no ownership over the projects and the work they produce. The web pages of projects launched on the site are permanently archived and made available or accessible to the public. The websites and uploaded materials are not edited or removed after funding is completed.

Kickstarter does not give guarantees that people who use the platform to post projects will deliver on their projects or use the money to execute their projects. Similarly, there are no guarantees that the completed projects will meet backers' expectations. Kickstarter advises project backers to use their judgement on supporting projects. They also warn project creators about legal damages from project backers if they fail to deliver on their promise. It is also important that creators do not underestimate the total cost required or the technical difficulties involved because the projects might also fail even after a successful fundraising campaign.

Source: Adapted from *http://poetsandquants.com/2015/04/21/75k-given-away-at-babson-challenge/*

Case study 3

Media No Mad case

Description of the company and the crowdfunding round

Media No Mad is a French start-up founded in October 2007 by Benoît Laurent and his wife Emilie Agniel. This company's unique activity is the development of a website called *benoot.com*. The principle of this website is to create a community of travellers that would share their photos, videos, sounds and comments about places they have visited while traveling around the world. It is based on a few items which include the possibility for members to create their own travel diaries accessible to all, an application displaying pictures and videos in a fancy way, and a Google Map pointing where these pictures have been taken. These enable pictures taken to be found in a particular place and also to know where in the world a particular sight can be found.

Finally, this firm expects advertising to be their main, if not unique, source of income as most internet-based businesses. Digital advertisement works in two ways: for most small websites, media agencies (like Google) provide pay-per-click advertisements, but on bigger websites with more traffic, space can also be bought, e.g. for regular advertising boards. Consequently, the success of the business, or in other words the revenues of Media No Mad, are strongly correlated with the number of single-users visiting the website.

Out of necessity?

In order to launch the second version (V2) of the website, Media No Mad needed more money. This V2 was vital to the firm in the sense that the current version (V1) was considered to be only for testing products. Therefore, if they wanted to increase their community, they would need to offer more functionalities and a better navigation experience.

Originally, they collected funds from local partners, such as banks and local incubators, but mostly they had to invest their own savings. After failing to raise a second round of money from regular sources like business angels and other private individuals, they decided to use their networking skills to find investors from the internet.

Communicate to everybody but just select a few

First of all, they needed to communicate their offer to their close network. To that extent, they created a separate operation called BuzzMoney and a separate website where they described their approach and were welcoming candidates. As they were already very involved in networking and blogging, they knew other internet users with very powerful networking skills. These people were very enthusiastic about the project and had strong faith in it. As a result, the communication around the project grew exponentially and attracted more and more people. It first started from blog posts, but then went to other network sites such as Facebook and Twitter. At some point, it also reached regular media on the internet and also on television and newspaper. However, at the moment it reached regular media, investors had already been found and hence this communication was only useful to promote the company by itself, not the funding round anymore.

A survey which was ultimately conducted revealed that 70% of the current investors had read articles on blogs, 20% heard of it from word of mouth, and only 10% knew the website beforehand! This clearly shows how efficient and broad the communication had been.

In order to maintain privacy, confidential information such as their business plan and shareholder contracts were not publicly disclosed on the website but required a private login. The login was given to those who asked for it and seemed to be serious enough about the bid. For instance, they would avoid giving it to potential competitors or children. The main part of the selection process was rather natural. Firstly, it was needed to provide private information, which filtered some users. Secondly, if the candidacy was accepted, the potential shareholder was required to sign a non-disclosure and non-competition agreement, which contributed to the rest of the filtering process. In general, those who were not really motivated in that deal or that had reasons not to sign the agreement (for instance, a competitor would make his job illegal if he did sign the paper) quickly abandoned the project.

Investing more than money

Their original plan was to raise €90,000 in order to pay for a developer's salary, communicate and optimize search engine requests (also referred to as SEO techniques). Obviously, the developer would be in charge of adding functionalities to the current website, and the rest of the money was meant to increase traffic and recruit new users.

The €90,000 were cut into 300 shares of €300 each and were designed to accommodate 80 investors. That would amount to 23% of the overall capital, the two founders possessing 500 shares each, which represents €300,000 in total. Finally, after a month of fundraising, they obtained promises for €55,800 which adds up to 186 shares from 81 investors, and 15% of the capital. It was discovered from a survey conducted that most investors bought only one share (55%), one-third bought two shares and the highest number of shares being five (11% of the cases). This means that on average, 1.7 shares were sold per investor.

As soon as they reached €55,800, they decided it was enough and stopped raising further funds. This was because their investors would not only provide them with money, but will also build on their skills to develop, communicate and reference the website, all of this at no cost for the company. In fact, the selected investors were web experts, marketing experts, professional search engines optimizers, or at least had experience as being customers. From the survey carried out, it was found that crowdfunders were relatively young. They were between 18 and 36 years old, with a median and average of respectively 25 and 26.2. Forty per cent were still students and the rest had jobs related to IT. The founder also added that many entrepreneurs had joined the crowd.

For most of them, the concept of investing in a company in order to make a later profit by reselling the shares was not the most important reason for investing. As a matter of fact, when they were asked if they were expecting to make high profits from the deal, 78% answer that they were not planning to earn from it neither did they want to make a loss. However, what they sought was mostly to participate in the exciting adventure of building a start-up, since 100% partly or fully agreed to the statement that they wanted to be part of an entrepreneurial project. They were therefore captivated by the challenge and the experience they could derive. By the same token, the investors also had faith in the product and the managerial team, as 89% partly or fully agreed that the product had potential and the team was competent in what it does.

Finally, a few members also added another motivation in the open comments. Since it involves more than 80 investors, they also thought it would be a good way for them to extend their network. In fact, since all were gathered around the same project, it was very likely that they will build strong relationships. Ultimately, each member will have access to the competences that belong to this network.

In order to provide incentives for investors to participate, the owners built a community platform on Hellotipi, which is originally a website meant for families to share content. In this manner, they could ask shareholders for their opinion. It was therefore not very surprising that 100% of the sample visited the platform. Moreover, 11% only read its content and did not participate, but everyone else participated actively. However, with regards to the frequency of visit, 56% visited the platform a few times a week, and the rest (4%) about once a week, so all came at least once a week. In conclusion, the sample was very participating as expected, and this cannot be taken as insignificant.

In the end, the founders had no legal obligation to consider the investors' comments on the community platform since they still possessed 85% of the shares, but are likely to do it because they need their participation and would also suffer from negative opinions. Undeniably, the web was a wonderful means to spread awareness about their project, but likewise it would be very efficient in spreading unhappy investors' critics.

On legal matters

The French legal form of Media No Mad is a SARL, which corresponds to a limited company, whereby associates are only responsible for the amount of capital they brought to the company. As a result, they cannot have more than 100 shareholders, as limited by French law. This is the reason why they had to create such big shares (€300), because they needed to limit the number of investors. Furthermore, French law forbids private companies to submit an offer to buy shares to more than 100 qualified participants (i.e. moral persons legally able to be a shareholder). The publicity about the overall crowdfunding round was public, but the final shareholder contract can only be given to sign to 100 people, even if some of them eventually decide not to invest. As a result, if they had needed more money or more shares and were still targeting small shareholders, they would have had to go to the public market, i.e. the stock market.

In order to receive the money and signatures, they finally had to go from virtual to physical and organized some kind of funding tour around France, so they could meet all investors for dinners in different cities. Shareholders, as any others, signed a contract preventing them from collaborating with competitors as long as they possess shares. This way, they reduce competition but above all make sure that strategic information does not leave the company.

Finally, it is important to mention that the founding team did not launch that operation alone out of the blue. They received advice from Add Equatio, a company specializing in financial and legal advice for entrepreneurs seeking to raise funds.

Some lessons from Media No Mad

Overall, the aim of this investment was obviously to raise money. However, they ended up raising something more valuable and sustainable than money, namely skills. Therefore, it looks like angel or venture capital funding, with the difference that this time 81 people put their skills and abilities together in order to provide optimal thinking and services. As mentioned earlier in this book, the crowd can be more intelligent than individuals because everyone can build on each other's skills. In this case, investors had very diverse skills, all more or less related to the project. Therefore, letting investors have their say has to be considered as an asset rather than a liability.

Next, while they targeted people from their network, those were so enthusiastic about the idea that they created a huge buzz about it and it soon became famous. Therefore, the importance of networking and efficient communication can be seen here. In order to eventually reach motivated skilled investors, it is crucial to reach as many people as possible in the first place. To achieve this, using Web 2.0 tools such as social networks or even non-internet media is crucial. Moreover, intelligent filtering also needs to be carried out. In this case, the selection was rather natural given the legal and privacy constraints potential investors were facing. This was a rather time and money-effective process.

Another observation is that investors do not have financial motivations. What they want is to participate in innovative projects, be able to say "I did it", obtain recognition and personal satisfaction. These are intrinsic motivations. To allow these motivations to be satisfied, it was necessary to take more advantage of Web 2.0 and build a participative platform so that shareholders can become knowledge-sharers. In addition, the investors were interested in the project by itself, i.e. the product and the team, which is quite rational since otherwise it would mean that they would be only investing because they have nothing better to do. In this regard, it is hard to say whether help from VCs/business angels is better or not. As a matter of fact, those are professional investors and wish to earn money from the deal. Consequently, they will have a strong incentive to make the business profitable, which does not seem to be the case for crowdfunders. In fact, crowdfunders have very little to lose if the company goes bankrupt. By creating debt, it is likely that people would be expecting returns at a fixed term, therefore feeling less comfortable in the case of a bankruptcy. Nevertheless, equity holders might have more incentives to make the company grow.

Another point that was interesting was the willingness of investors to expand networks. It has long been a fact that good networks are a huge advantage in the business world, and even more in entrepreneurship, as many authors have recently discussed. Networking has also evolved with Web 2.0 and the development of professional network websites like Viadeo or LinkedIn. With crowdfunding, investors benefit from the creation of a network that can be stronger than traditional ones.

Indeed, investors are not on any platform because they have to be, they are there because they want to be. They all share more or less the same passions and interests and do this for fun. Therefore, the relationships they build are not quite like professional ones but rather like personal ones. Later, they will benefit from these when it comes to business opportunities or issues.

About information asymmetry, it can be said that it was rather low. Indeed, once potential investors were (self) selected, they obtained access to business plans and other information as any VC or angel would have. Moreover, since most of them do have a foot in the industry, they already know the potential outcome of the project and need not be convinced by the entrepreneur. About the entrepreneur's own potential, since he had already proven relatively successful on the web (all the information can be found freely on the internet) and reached his own network, that by definition made him known, it was not an issue whether shareholders would have faith in him or not. Clearly, that could not have happened with bankers for these might not be that much aware of the web industry and would not rely on informal sources of information such as those on blogs or *Facebook*. This is what makes the strength of crowdfunding: potential investors are not professional financers and have therefore fewer requirements in terms of the source or quality of the information. What eventually counts is that they can trust the person they have in front of them. There is a more human contact than with other means of finance; entrepreneurs and investors are peers.

Later, on legal issues, only the number of shareholders was capped. They could only have raised more money by increasing the mean amount invested, hardly the number of investors. However, it is highly possible that people willing to invest more money would not have such intrinsic motivations and would rather seek financial rewards. This actually proves to be true, because the business angels and bankers that were first asked to fully finance the second round of funding refused. An IPO would accommodate virtually unlimited shareholders, but they might not be skilled. Assuming that this is not an issue, what about managing them? Although Web 2.0 makes it easier to keep in contact with investors, it is likely that too many of them would decrease their ability of being heard. In fact, the time the entrepreneur devotes to relations with investors is limited and will not increase if the number of investors does. If there are a lot of shareholders, the time devoted per investor will be pretty small. Consequently, investors might actually not feel valued in their help and lose all motivation to invest.

Finally, a note on debt versus equity: in this case, equity was used. They eventually gave away 15% of their capital, which kept them in control of the company. Yet, this is not the only scenario; two alternative scenarios could have happen. The first is the scenario whereby the crowdfunders obtain less than 50% of the shares. In this case, the entrepreneurs retain total control over the firm. Second, if they were to give more than 50%, it would be likely that they would still be main shareholders (possessing the biggest share of capital) because crowdfunders are very fractioned. Nevertheless, in any decision that requires say half or even two-thirds of the capital to agree, the fragmentation might prove harmful since shareholders have different interests.

Source: Schwienbacher and Larralde (2012).

Case study 4

Enerchi bites case

Annie and Marla Feldman knew they wanted to work together. Apparently, they were very close because they are identical twins. They not only looked alike, but they also shared a lot of the same interests. When Marla, a yoga enthusiast, developed a post-workout snack that all the people in her regular yoga class loved, the sisters thought they might have found a product that would give them the opportunity to build their business, Enerchi Bites. After running several test events where they distributed their energy food to rave reviews, the women decided that it was time to do a bigger test and raise some sorely needed funds at the same time.

After months of experimentation, Annie and Marla came up with a healthy bite-size alternative snack. They came up with the name "Enerchi Bites" by combining "energy" with "chia", as in the chia seeds that were one of the main ingredients. Chia seeds are the new super food and the two sisters wanted to differentiate themselves with an organic and natural ingredient, although they have since seen that more companies in the food industry are also adopting the seeds.

From home they started working on the recipe and focused on creating a less sweetened product than regular energy bars, using only natural ingredients. They experimented with 10–12 different flavours but soon realized that simpler was better. So, they narrowed it down to just three: Coconut Oatmeal Raisin, Apple Cinnamon, and Cocoa-date.

Making the treats at home, they came up with the first production line and shared it with friends who shared their fit and healthy lifestyle. As it became popular, more people began to ask where they could buy Enerchi Bites. The twin sisters, using their savings, conducted several grassroots tests and placed their product at events such as yoga conventions and gave out samples at gyms and yoga centres. The initial feedback was generally positive since people liked the "cookie dough-like" texture and also liked the re-sealable packaging. This feedback helped them to come up with the tag line: "Eat what you like, share or save the rest." Consequently, Annie and Marla made their way into retail by using their contacts at organic stores, yoga studios, small natural groceries stores and cafes. Today, consumers can find Enerchi Bites in 15 retail locations.

By February 2013, Annie and Marla began selling Enerchi Bites – all-natural, bite-sized snacks that provided, "enough to hold them over for the bike ride home, but not enough to ruin their dinner". Their new business was a collaborative effort born out of their unique but complementary entrepreneurial desires. It also aligned nicely with their personal health goals and habits. Marla wanted to create healthy snacks that would appeal to a broader range of health and fitness enthusiasts beyond yogis and that would provide a healthy boost of energy. Annie's desire was to channel her entrepreneurial spirit into an endeavour that afforded her the creative freedom to launch, manage and grow her own business. A yoga and fitness enthusiast herself, Annie felt that linking with her sister to take Enerchi Bites into the marketplace was the right move at the right time.

Growing production

Because Enerchi Bites was well received, the sisters wanted to grow the business. The first step was to increase production and in order to do so they had to move out of their home kitchen. Finding a decent industrial kitchen was not easy. They first sublet space in a bakery located 30 minutes outside Boston, but things did not work out. They lost a couple of months and ultimately went to a Kitchen Inc., a shared industry kitchen in nearby Somerville. They were drawn to Kitchen Inc. because they were welcomed into the community of like-minded food entrepreneurs. The downside was the expensive hourly rate and the fact that they were not using much of the kitchen's most expensive equipment as they required only an outlet, a counter, and a sink.

In five months, they grew production from 200 to over 600 pounds and the workload increased accordingly. As the production increased they had to pack each Enerchi Bite into a four-bites bag, which took them around four hours to have a single production run ready for retail. Given that their production runs were still around 260 pounds per month, their distribution was somewhat simple. They became keenly aware that as their production volume grew, scaling distribution would present a far more complex challenge. For example, to enter bigger organic and natural stores like Whole Foods, they would have to obtain kosher and gluten-free certifications, which were costly and would require higher sales volumes to justify the investment. In order to grow their production and therefore their reach, they decided to run a crowdfunding campaign on Kickstarter.

The Kickstarter campaign

In summer 2014, Annie and Marla launched their Kickstarter campaign. Marla thought it was a good opportunity to raise awareness and, at the same time, obtain funds to make some changes in their operation. Although the twin sisters had been warned by experienced people about going on Kickstarter and some potential problems, they did nothing to prevent them. In hindsight, they could have done a much better job.

According to their Kickstarter page, they set a fundraising goal of $10,000 and wanted to use the funding to accomplish four objectives: transition to a new kitchen facility, research and develop new and improved packaging, new flavours, and to apply for specific food certifications, including Gluten Free, Kosher and Non-GMO.

Annie and Marla each had their own ideas about the value of Kickstarter. Marla relished the challenge of creating buzz about their product and viewed a Kickstarter campaign as a public-relations and marketing vehicle to showcase their product to an extended network of people. However, Annie was not as enthusiastic as her sister. She figured that they could more easily raise the money that they needed by going directly to friends and family. Among Annie's other concerns was that she felt, with so many other popular projects on Kickstarter, that their campaign might not reach a wide audience.

One of their friends who worked in video production offered to help with the video. Annie notes that the video is the most important piece of the campaign, as it is the only vehicle to engage with the audience. Therefore, they created a very straightforward video using Kickstarter guidelines. They thought that now they could be more creative and work around the guidelines. The video was the only tool they had to engage with the audience. Therefore, they had to pay attention to every detail. They had to be very structured on how they told their story and spent more time in editing it.

They had a list of rewards according to the donation amount, from special shout-outs on their website to a chef-plated dinner with Enerchi Bites founders. Marla added a buffer to cover fulfilment costs, but delivery fees ate most of their proceeds since they decided to personally deliver some of the rewards in the Boston area. They thought it was not only about the money, but also about having a good experience.

Annie and Marla offered their supporters an assortment of rewards based on each supporter's level of contribution. For example, a $5 pledge was rewarded with a thank you note on a print by Aura Lewis, who helped the sisters design the Enerchi Bites logo. More generous supporters were rewarded with everything from t-shirts and bags of Enerchi Bites to the opportunity to spend the day behind the scenes with Annie and Marla at Kitchen Inc. The complexity of managing rewards and providing timely fulfilment was a costly challenge.

They went live on August 4, 2014, with a goal to raise US$10,000 in 45 days. Soon they were inundated with requests from social media companies who were looking to help the Enerchi Bites twins increase their reach outside their friends and family and to exceed their pledge goal. Believing they could use some extra help getting their message out, they selected one of these companies and hoped for the best. However, the experience they had with the social media agency that they hired was not pleasing as they did not get any more people through the agency's efforts and it cost the sisters a lot of money and time.

With just one week remaining, Annie and Marla were still 20% short of their goal. The sisters had foreseen this situation and developed a backup plan in case they did not make their target. For a Kickstarter campaign to be successful, it has to raise 100% of the pledged funds. Before launching the campaign, they had an emergency plan ready: they reserved some money from their friends and family and themselves to make sure they would be successful.

The campaign reached its funding goal on October 4, 2014, and for Annie the results were not that surprising. Once the campaign was over, they analyzed the data and found that 85% of the total dollars came from friends and family. So, they did not get the external level of validation they were expecting. Considering the costs to create the campaign, fulfil the rewards and pay Kickstarter its commission, Enerchi Bites netted only 45% of the money raised (see Table 12.1).

Was the campaign worth it? They could have aimed for a more ambitious amount, but the sisters felt that US$10,000 was realistic for the food industry, although there are some industries, such as videogames, where entrepreneurs target much more money.

Table 12.1 Enerchi Bites

Details	Amount ($)
Amount raised	**10,183.00**
less amount Marla and Annie contributed	500.00
Net raised	**9,683.00**
Expenses:	
Kickstarter commission	509.15
Amazon Pay (commission for processing contributions)	407.32
Video production (donated)	0.00
Social marketing company	500.00
Rewards	2,500.00
Fulfilment	1,200.00
Total expenses	**5,116.47**
Net proceeds	**4,566.53**

Source: (Adapted from Zacharakis *et al.* (2016)

Results

For Annie and Marla, the Kickstarter campaign did not generate enough funds to really scale their business. However, they did learn quite a bit. With their learning from the campaign as well as from their experiences running the business to date, Annie and Marla now find themselves at the point where they must make a critical decision: go or no-go? While their campaign did, in fact, reach its stated financial goal, they still wonder if they can scale up production, meet their research and development needs, and complete a redesign of Enerchi Bites packaging. They need more money. Should they launch another campaign or are there other sources they should consider?

Source: Zacharakis *et al.* (2016, p. 3–7)

Summary

In recent years crowdfunding platforms have become very popular among entrepreneurs and business start-ups. Statistics of the most popular platforms indicate that every year more projects are created. Although many campaigns have been successful, there have also been some failures. In the case of Case Study 4, the campaign did not move the business forward as much as the creators had hoped. However, for Case Studies 1–3 the campaigns were not only successful in raising funds, but they also helped the creators to better understand the market and take advantage of the opportunity to move their business forward.

We summarize this chapter by repeating Zacharakis *et al.*'s (2016, p. 11) thoughts regarding entrepreneurs considering a crowdfunding campaign:

- *Define the objective of your campaign:* whether it be market validation or raising funds to grow; this will help you create both your video and content.
- *Consider the costs associated:* fulfilment can represent a huge percentage of your raised funds.

- *Tell the story before launching the campaign:* take some time to make sure that a lot of people know about your product and your campaign. Two or three months before you launch, talk to the press and tell them your story. This might create awareness outside of your own network.
- *Create a lot of content:* every video, image, infographic, illustration and even the story of the product are shareable items.
- *Have everything in place before pledging funds:* we have found some entrepreneurs who have a great idea, but don't have a clue how to produce their products. They receive the funds and constantly postpone delivery dates.
- *Talk to people with experience:* there are a lot of stories behind every crowdfunding campaign; take some time to talk to experienced people and learn from their mistakes and good practices.
- *Split work with your partner(s):* when you launch the campaign, be very structured when dividing work so that each partner advocates for specific tasks.
- *Use your network wisely:* ask your friends and family to share the materials created for the campaign.

Discussion questions

1 In the successful cases, should the creators have targeted more funding?
2 In all cases, were the financial results worth their efforts?
3 What should entrepreneurs take into account when considering a crowdfunding campaign?

Test questions

1 What do you think the creators of Case study 4 could have done differently?
2 What lessons have you learned from the case studies?

Glossary of key terminologies

Brexit A term used to represent the withdrawal of the United Kingdom from the European Union.
Crowdfunder A UK crowdfunding platform for fundraising.
Hellotipi A French crowdfunding platform which was originally a website meant for families to share content.
Indiegogo Indiegogo is an American crowdfunding website.
IPO Initial public offering.
Kickstarter Kickstarter is an American crowdfunding platform focused on creativity.
VC Venture capital.

Recommended reading

Dresner, S., 2014. *Crowdfunding: A guide to raising capital on the internet*. Hoboken: Wiley.
Steinberg, D., 2012. *The Kickstarter handbook. Real-life crowdfunding success stories.* Philadelphia: Quirk Books.

References

Entis, L., 2013. Where startup funding really comes from (Infographic). *Entrepreneur Franchise 500* [online]. Available from: www.entrepreneur.com/article/230011 [Accessed 7 April 2021].

Mac an Bhaird, C., Owen, R., Drakopoulou Dodd, S., Wilson, J., and Bisignano, A., 2019. Small beer? Borrowers' perspectives of peer to peer lending in the craft beer sector. *Strategic Change: Briefings in Entrepreneurial Finance*, 28 (1), 59–68.

Schwienbacher, A., and Larralde, B., 2012. Crowdfunding of small entrepreneurial ventures. *In*: D. Cumming, ed. *The Oxford handbook of entrepreneurial finance*. Oxford: Oxford University Press, 369–391.

Ward, M., 2021. *Business statistics* (Briefing Paper, Number 06152) [online]. London: House of Commons Library, 3. Available from: https://researchbriefings.files.parliament.uk/documents/SN06152/SN06152.pdf [Accessed 7 April 2021].

Zacharakis, A., Muller, J.H., Quintana, G., and Ripke, T., 2016. *Crowdfunding: A tale of two campaigns*. Brighton: Babson College, Harvard Business School Publishing.

Appendix

Links to support students

1 Forbes' seven tips for writing a compelling crowdfunding pitch:

www.forbes.com/sites/theyec/2018/08/30/seven-tips-for-writing-a-compelling-crowdfunding-pitch/#5c0b25a31e48

2 Simon Sinek: "Start with Why: People don't buy what you do, they buy why you do it"

www.shortform.com/summary/start-with-why-summary-simon-sinek?gclid=Cj0KCQiA1NebBhDDARIsAANiDD2uozvuBFVP5D9CQSAYpNxAfPdZ3kEd7tHrOwWCFRiV6LrZPiinL6QaApDdEALw_wcB

3 Advantages and disadvantages of crowdfunding:

www.nibusinessinfo.co.uk/content/advantages-and-disadvantages-crowd-funding

4 Bring a creative project to life – On Kickstarter:

www.kickstarter.com/

5 Financial Conduct Authority – Crowdfunding Investment:

www.fca.org.uk/investsmart?gclid=Cj0KCQiA1NebBhDDARIsAANiDD0QebFngKVejwWOmyXaGz1ha8M3tx5SAiD8mkZ_mVgS9mByWdggh-l0aAiqgEALw_wcB&gclsrc=aw.ds

6 Crowdfunding good causes – Nesta:

www.nesta.org.uk/report/crowdfunding-good-causes/?gclid=Cj0KCQiA1NebBhDDARIsAANiDD3LoaggelSsdbnoilezm6tR1TQXlNHkUZ5D-PLg38yHILrEIZSUmcgaAoHHEALw_wcB

7 Crowdfunding toolkit for community investment – Nesta:

www.nesta.org.uk/blog/crowdfunding-toolkit-community-investment/

8 Nine crowdfunding platforms for charities, community groups and social entrepreneurs:

www.nesta.org.uk/blog/9-crowdfunding-platforms-for-charities-community-groups-and-social-entrepreneurs/

9   Matched crowdfunding – new ways for people and institutions to collaborate on funding projects:

www.nesta.org.uk/blog/matched-crowdfunding-new-ways-for-people-and-institutions-to-collaborate-on-funding-projects/

10   Which type of crowdfunding is best for you?

www.entrepreneur.com/starting-a-business/which-type-of-crowdfunding-is-best-for-you/228524

11   14 potential issues with crowdfunding and how to solve them

www.cleverism.com/14-potential-issues-with-crowdfunding-how-solve-them/

12   Key challenges and drawbacks with crowdfunding

www.thebalancemoney.com/key-challenges-and-drawbacks-with-crowdfunding-4116031

13   The five hidden challenges of crowdfunding

www.forbes.com/sites/theyec/2019/11/19/the-five-hidden-challenges-of-crowdfunding/?sh=56cc2bae7d29

14   The 8 challenges facing crowdfunding platforms in 2021

www.lemonway.com/en/business-insight-en/8-challenges-facing-crowdfunding-platforms-2021/

15   Crowdfunding legal issues and tips to prevent mistakes

www.upcounsel.com/crowdfunding-legal-issues-and-tips

16   Crowdfunding legal issues for small businesses

www.liveabout.com/crowdfunding-legal-issues-for-small-businesses-398020

17   How crowdfunding works

www.crowdfunder.co.uk/how-crowdfunding-works?msclkid=3d7c22a99bbd15e3983341d7b1044d07&utm_source=bing&utm_medium=cpc&utm_campaign=EX%20%7C%20CF%20%7C%20UK%20%7C%20Search%20%7C%20Crowdfunding&utm_term=how%20to%20crowdfund&utm_content=How%20To%20Crowdfund

18   Crowdfunding for charities – GoFundMe official site

www.gofundme.com/

19   Guide to crowdfunding for students

www.thescholarshiphub.org.uk/guide-crowdfunding-students/

20   How to crowdfund your degree

www.savethestudent.org/student-finance/how-to-crowdfund-your-degree.html

Index

Note: Page numbers in *italics* indicate figures and those in **bold** indicate tables.

272   *Index*

Printed in the United States
by Baker & Taylor Publisher Services